THE

ILIAD OF HOMER.

TRANSLATED INTO ENGLISH VERSE.

BY

W. G. CALDCLEUGH,

AUTHOR OF "EASTERN TALES" AND "THE BRANCH AND OTHER POEMS."

PHILADELPHIA:
J. B. LIPPINCOTT & CO.
1870.

PREFACE.

Homer is the oldest profane writer of whom we have any knowledge. He is believed, according to the best accounts, to have lived about nine hundred years before the Christian era; this would make him coeval with some of the writers of the Old Testament, and give him a very high antiquity. He is reported to have been blind, but if so, his infirmity must have overtaken him at a late period of his life, for there is no author who has given us a more vivid description of the outer world. He describes nature with the greatest fidelity: beasts, birds, fishes, and even insects,—so that his perceptive powers seem to have been proportional to his knowledge of human character, in which, with the exception of Shakspeare, none can compete with him. His birthplace is unknown,—seven cities contended for the honor, and altars were erected and sacrifice offered to his memory.

His poems, the Iliad and Odyssey, have been handed down with the greatest veneration, and are believed to be almost as perfect as when first produced. Of these the Iliad has always held the first rank; the Odyssey is an account of the wanderings of Ulysses, and is compared by Longinus to the setting sun, or an achievement of Homer in his old age; yet his admiration of it was so great that he is careful to remind us that he is speaking of the *old age of Homer*.

But the Iliad he styles the sun in its meridian; for fire and sublimity, and beautiful and melodious versification, it has never been equaled. It is true, there are other writers in whose works passages may be found not inferior to any in Homer, but there is none who has been able to sustain such an elevation of thought and language from beginning to end. He commences in the simplest manner, and, as he proceeds, gradually warms up, resembling, as it has been well said, the wheel of a chariot taking fire by its own rapidity.

The subject of the poem is wrath—wrath, the most terrible of the passions; the passion which almost transforms man into a demon, which is productive of so much evil, and which in the end so surely entails upon its possessor retribution and remorse. This moral the poet teaches in the most striking manner, showing how Achilles, in indulging his wrath, brought upon his countrymen a "myriad of woes," and upon himself the most bitter anguish. The story is very short: the Greeks are encamped before Troy, upon which they make war for the sake of Menelaus, whose wife the Trojan Paris has stolen away. Agamemnon, the general of the Greek forces, upon an unwarrantable pretext, robs Achilles of a beautiful captive maid; the chief in anger withdraws from his companions, praying to Jove that he would send destruction upon them. By the withdrawal of this distinguished warrior, the Greeks suffer great slaughter, and, with an offer of costly gifts, beg their champion to return. For a long time he refuses; but finally allows his friend Patroclus, clad in his armor, and accompanied by his Myrmidons, to take the field. The scale of battle is now turned, and the Trojans are driven back, but Patroclus is slain. The loss of his dear comrade deeply affects Achilles; and regarding the Trojans as the cause of his bereavement, he issues from his retirement, and, after prodigies of valor, succeeds in routing the enemy and slaying Hector.

On this slight basis Homer has reared his magnificent

creation. His hero is of course Achilles, a colossal character, as Mr. Gladstone rightly calls him, and whose superhuman exploits are, with great art, reserved for the latter part of the poem. This extraordinary personage was a study to writers of antiquity much in the same manner as the Hamlet of Shakspeare is to us, though no two beings ever possessed qualities so opposite. Achilles is a type of the perfect warrior, in an age when the softening influences of Christianity were unknown; he is fierce and implacable toward his enemies, yet capable of the warmest friendship, of which no finer instance was ever known than that which existed between himself and Patroclus; his generosity is unbounded, and his thirst for glory almost borders on insanity. Like all endowed with strong passions, he is much given to the melting mood: his interviews with his mother are always accompanied with tears; he weeps for Briseis and for Patroclus; and, after dragging Hector's corpse round Troy, he mingles his tears with those of the venerable Priam, when he comes begging that his son's body may be restored. His noblest trait is his sincerity; this, which is at once the result and cause of his great courage, gives him his ascendency over his fellow-men, and makes him more than a match even for those superior to him in intellect.

> Who dares think one thing, and another tell,
> My soul abhors him as the gates of hell.—POPE.

This is the prelude of his speech to the ambassadors, and through his whole career he fully exemplifies it. His religious sentiments are also strongly developed; he frequently sacrifices to the gods, and has a constant sense of their superintending care; nor, notwithstanding his impetuosity, is he destitute of self-control; he takes the advice of Minerva when about to punish his wrong-doer,

1*

returning his half-drawn sword into its scabbard, and, when the whole army gives itself up to feasting, he alone passes the day fasting. Though his delight is the field of battle, he is not destitute of resources, but amuses himself in his leisure hours with his lyre. To these qualities of mind and heart beauty of person is superadded; he is represented as the handsomest man in the Greek army, and excels all in strength and activity, having the title of swift-footed, which probably refers not so much to fleetness as to that agility and quickness of movement common to mercurial temperaments. A character endowed with such shining features naturally attracted the admiration of mankind and the regard of the gods, hence he is often styled "Jove-nurtured" and the "favorite of Jove." But it is the lot of humanity that what is brightest is often the most evanescent; and, with that profound knowledge of the laws of Providence peculiar to Homer, he takes care to remind us through the poem that this eminent personage is short-lived.

> All more than common menaces an end.—YOUNG.
> So quick, bright things come to confusion.—SHAKSPEARE.

The other characters, though far inferior in power to Achilles, are drawn with equal skill. We have the politic Agamemnon, somewhat selfish and covetous, and once at least feeling power and forgetting right; yet, in the main, a wise and popular ruler. We have Ulysses, famed for wisdom; the aged and prudent Nestor, from whose lips flowed a stream of eloquence sweeter than honey; Ajax, blunt in manners and not remarkable for mental endowments, yet honest and of gigantic stature and indomitable courage. The youthful Diomed is also conspicuous for his chivalrous exploits, and we cannot but admire his tenacity of purpose when others are wavering, and his determination to continue the war to its bitter end. Menelaus, too, the injured husband, acts a prominent part; he is pious, but otherwise without any striking traits,—moderation is his chief characteristic; he seems to have been one who, in private life, would have made an estimable citizen, but he is wanting in self-confidence and unfitted to cope with the fiery spirits among whom fortune has thrown him.

On the Trojan side appears Hector,—the gentle and brave Hector,—the bulwark of Troy, the sincere patriot, and model husband. Homer seems to have taken pains to delineate the character of this noble chief, and we cannot help pitying his misfortunes and tragic fate. In contrast with him stands his brother, the effeminate Paris; handsome, but unprincipled, the violator of hospitality, who stole Helen from her home, and was the author of the war and of his country's calamities. Helen, the partner of his guilt, with all her frailties, excites our compassion; and her continued self-reproach and penitence, together with her surpassing beauty, disarm even her enemies. Her lot is indeed a hard one,—compelled to live among those who have such cause to hate her, far from her native land, and, as she tells us herself, without a friend in the world. In contrast with her we have Andromachè, Hector's beloved wife; she is a model of domestic virtue,—and the celebrated parting of herself and husband presents one of the finest pictures of conjugal affection to be found in the whole range of literature. The aged Priam, King of Troy, is also a marked figure in the poem; his great age, and the miseries which gather so thickly around him, are truly objects of compassion; his large family; his many sons captured or fallen in battle, especially his beloved Hector; the worthless Paris still remaining,—all these make us feel for the venerable patriarch, though possessing no peculiar virtues to challenge our admiration.

The poet has heightened the interest of his work by the introduction of the deities, and the scene is continually shifting from earth to heaven. Jove sits upon the highest peak of Olympus, and, with the golden balances of destiny in his hands, looks down on the plain of Troy, where events of the greatest moment are transpiring. At one time he forbids the divinities to act on either side; and at another grants them permission. They fly swifty from heaven to earth—now skimming across the ocean waves, and now rustling over the topmost branches of the forests. Neptune is introduced to us emerging from the sea, clad in golden robes; seated in his splendid chariot, he rides over the billows, while the monsters of the deep rise from their watery caverns and gambol round their king.

The descriptions of natural scenery in Homer are exquisitely beautiful; like the myriad-minded Shakspeare, nothing escapes him. He describes mountains with the morning mists creeping up their sides, and the big white clouds remaining motionless on their summits during the long summer day; dark, shady dells, with water-falls dashing down, whose loud roar is heard in the distance. He paints thunder-storms and snow-storms; gives us the ever-varying aspects of the sea—its changes of colors, its glassy smoothness, its black tempests, the continual noise of the surf rolling on the extended shore, and the dash of the angry waves on the rocky coast. He is perfectly at home also in the occupations of rural life, such as plowing, sowing, reaping, threshing, the gathering of fruits, and other employments of the husbandman. His similes taken from the chase are very frequent, indeed almost too much so; yet they are finely drawn, and show what an important place hunting held among mankind in the early ages. As for his battle scenes, they have never been equaled by any writer, ancient or modern. The poet knew the taste of his countrymen,—who looked upon war as the noblest field of enterprise, and regarded courage as the highest virtue; hence he has devoted so much of his work to feats of arms, and taken such pains in describing them. Yet, though these scenes occur so frequently, they are depicted in such vivid colors, and with such a variety of incident, that we do not grow tired with their repetition; but, on the contrary, gaze with increased interest as the story progresses and the long procession of martial characters passes before us. The valor of these ancient warriors astonishes us. We see to what a pitch of endurance human nature can be raised; how the mind may triumph over the fear of death; and the most timorous cannot fail to have their spirits aroused and their fortitude strengthened by such heroic examples. It is no wonder that Alexander the Great styled the Iliad the "proper food of a warrior," and when, in his wars with Persia, he captured a costly casket, that he used it as a depository for his favorite poem.

In regard to the moral of the Iliad, as was observed before, it exhibits to us the bitter effects of wrath; and the poet, who seems to have been as familiar with the laws of Providence as with those of nature, shows us how time brings its compensations, and that sure retribution follows every violation of the divine code. Agamemnon, in the pride of his power, robs Achilles of the fair Briseis, but he is compelled, in the sequel, not only to restore her, but seven other beautiful maidens, and a long list of presents besides. Achilles, in his passion, devotes his countrymen to destruction, and begs Heaven, with tears, that his desire may be accomplished; Jove grants his request; but his iniquitous request involves him, in the end, in the deepest tribulation,—it touches him in his tenderest point, bringing about the death of his dear Patroclus, whom he loved as his own soul. His misery now is greater than ever; his lamentations reach the ears of his goddess-mother Thetis, who emerges from the sea and inquires the cause of his trouble, reminding him that Heaven has com plied with his petition and given him the amplest revenge on Agamemnon. What a picture of the vanity of human wishes, and what a depth of agony does the reply of the weeping warrior exhibit, —

> True, mother dear, Jove's promise is fulfilled;
> But what of that—since Patroclus is dead!

The versification of the Iliad is almost faultless, scarcely a feeble line is to be found in it; it commences like some grand strain of music, and so continues, without faltering, to the end, revealing as it proceeds the terrible, the sublime, the pathetic, the beautiful; yet, whatever be the subject, even if commonplace, the ear is always delighted with the melody of the verse. The sound, too, is continually harmonizing with the sense; and we seem to hear the loud peal of the thunder, the roar of the sea, the clash of the mail-clad warriors, the twang of the bow-string, and the whizzing of the spear. Indeed, the language of this antique poem has doubtless contributed much to its preservation; its majestic thoughts and noble imagery receive a double charm crystallized in such beautiful verse, and it now stands before us, like the Parthenon of Athens, an object of wonder and delight; yet, unlike that renowned edifice, it comes to us in an unimpaired state,—not a column shattered, not a sculptured frieze defaced,—thus showing how indestructible are the works of intellect, and the superiority of mind over matter.

The following translation, the desultory occupation of a few years, is submitted to the public with much diffidence. Written principally for the amusement of the translator and his friends, he makes no claim to the qualifications necessary for the success of such an undertaking; yet, perhaps, some of the admirers of Homer may honor the work with a perusal, if only to see in what light any new version may place their favorite author.

CONTENTS.

BOOK XII.

BOOK XIII.

BOOK XIV.

BOOK XV.

BOOK XVI.

BOOK XVII.

BOOK XVIII.

BOOK XIX.

BOOK XX.

BOOK XXI.

BOOK XXII.

BOOK XXIII.

BOOK XXIV.

THE ILIAD OF HOMER.

BOOK I.

THE QUARREL OF THE CHIEFS.

ARGUMENT.

The Greeks are encamped on the shore in front of Troy.—A pestilence breaks out in the army.—Achilles calls a council, at which Chalcas, the prophet, declares the cause of it to be the refusal of Agamemnon to ransom the captive maid whom he had taken in battle, and whose release had been begged by her father Chryses, priest of Apollo.—The king finally restores her, and indemnifies himself by seizing Briseis, another captive female who belonged to Achilles.—Achilles, in great wrath for this insult, withdraws from the war, and prays his mother, the sea-goddess Thetis, to go to Olympus and beg Jupiter to take part with the Trojans, and bring defeat on the Greeks.

SING of Achilles' wrath, oh heavenly muse,
Which brought upon the Greeks unnumbered woes,
And sent so many heroes to their doom;
Whose bodies, strewed unburied o'er the plain,
Became the prey of vultures and of dogs:
So Jove decreed, when first a quarrel rose
Betwixt the godlike warrior Achilles
And Agamemnon, sovereign of men.
Who of the gods the quarrel set afoot?
Apollo 'twas; he, angry with the king,
Sent through the camp a plague; the people died,—

2

For Agamemnon insulted Chryses,
Apollo's priest; he to the Greeks had come
With costly gifts, his daughter to redeem,
And bearing in his hand the golden wand
And flowery garlands of his patron god,
He supplicated all the Greeks, but most
The two commanders, sons of Atreus.*
  Hear me, ye sons of Atreus, and ye Greeks:
May the gods dwelling on the Olympian mount
Grant all you wish; may Priam's city fall,
And ye in safety to your homes return;
But, oh, restore to me my darling child,
Receive my gifts, and reverence my god.
Then shouted all the Greeks their full consent
The priest to honor, and accept his gifts.
But Agamemnon was much displeased,
Roughly dismissed him, and thus harshly spake:
  Let me not find thee in the camp, old man,
Long loitering; nor hither come again,
Lest e'en thy garlands and thy rod divine
Protect thee not; as for thy daughter, I
Will not restore her till her charms decay.
But to my home in Argos shall she go,
Far from her native land, sharing my bed,
And laboring at the loom. Begone, I say,
Whilst safely thou canst go. Thus spake the king.
The old man, trembling, heard him and obeyed.
Silent he went, retiring from the camp,
Along the margin of the roaring sea;
Then to Apollo, all alone he prayed:
  Hear me, Apollo, god of the silver bow,
Ruling o'er Chrysa, Tenedos, and Cilla,
If e'er with garlands I have crowned thy shrine,
Or offered up the fat of bulls and goats,
Grant this my prayer: may thy avenging darts
Upon the Greeks be sent for these my tears.

---

* Menelaus and Agamemnon.

Thus Chryses prayed, nor was his prayer unheard,
For full of wrath, down from the Olympian mount,
Apollo came; upon his shoulders hung
His splendid quiver and his costly bow;
The angry arrows rattled as he trod;
Like night he came, so terrible his frown.
Outside the camp he took his seat, and shot:
His silver bow twanged horribly; first fell
The mules, the dogs died next, then on the men
The deadly arrow of the god descended.
The mournful funeral piles forever smoked,—
Nine days the plague among the people raged,—
Achilles, on the tenth, convened the host,
Moved by fair Juno, for she loved the Greeks,
And was distressed at seeing them destroyed.
The people were accordingly convened,
And swift, Achilles, rising in their midst,
Harangued them thus: Oh, sons of Atreus!
High time it is, I think, that we return,—
We cannot stand both pestilence and war;
But come, some prophet let us seek, or priest,
Or dream interpreter (for Jove sends dreams),
Who may explain to us Apollo's wrath:
Whether 'tis sent for sacrifice unpaid,
So that by fat of bulls and goats appeased,
He may perhaps remove from us this plague.
He said, and took his seat; then Chalcas rose,
Best of the soothsayers, who knew both past,
Present, and future; he, by his skill divine,
The fleet had guided o'er the sea to Troy;
And now, discreetly counseling, he spake:
Thou ask'st me, oh, Achilles! to explain
Apollo's wrath; thy wish shall granted be.
But first thy oath and promise I require
That thou protection will to me afford;
For we may now a great man irritate,
A Grecian chief; and dreadful is a lord
Contending with a man of low degree;

For, though he may his anger smother up,
He'll bear a grudge and have revenge at last.
Speak then and say, wilt thou protection give?
 Him answering, then Achilles thus replied:
Cheer up, and boldly speak thy prophecy,
For by Apollo, who inspires thy thoughts,
No one, whilst I'm alive, shall do thee harm;
Not e'en if Agamemnon thou namest,
Who boasts to be superior to us all.
 Cheered by his words the worthy prophet spake:
'Tis not for prayers neglected we are blamed,
Nor yet for hecatombs,* but for his priest,
Who was by Agamemnon insulted;
Nor would he to him his dear child restore,
Nor take his gifts; for this Apollo sends,
And yet will send further calamities;
Nor will he this dread pestilence remove
Till to her father he restores the maid
Unransomed, with a sacred hecatomb.
Thus first appeased, he may persuaded be.
 He said, and took his seat; then rose the king,
Heroic Agamemnon, full of wrath,
Much agitated. His eyes shot fire,—
On Chalcas sternly looking thus he spake:
Prophet of ills! ungracious e'er to me,
Dearly thou lovest to utter what is bad;
No good thing canst thou speak, no good thing do,
And now thou sayest Apollo sends these woes
Because Chryseis I refuse to ransom,
Wishing to keep the maid and take her home;
For e'en to Clytemnestra, I prefer her,
My lawful wife; to whom she equal is
In mind, in beauty, and accomplishments;
Yet, still, I'll give her up if so 'tis best,
For I would save my people, not destroy.
Prepare me, then, some compensation just,

* A hundred oxen.

That I alone may not unportioned be;
For thus you see another takes my prize.
  Him answering quickly, swift Achilles spake:
Oh, son of Atreus! noblest of men
And yet most greedy, how can the valiant Greeks
A prize assign thee? all divided was
Whene'er we plundered any hostile town;
Nor can a new division now be made.
Restore this woman as the god commands,
And when we sack some other Trojan town
Doubly and trebly we'll indemnify.
  Him answering, then king Agamemnon spake:
Oh, brave Achilles! godlike as thou art,
Be not deceived, nor think to cozen me.
Shalt thou retain thy portion of the spoil
And I have none? Must I restore the maid?
Then if the Greeks some other prize bestow,—
Such as I think a just equivalent,—
'Tis well; if not, I'll come on thee, or Ajax,
Or Ulysses, and seize their prize instead;
Nor care I for his wrath whoe'er he be;
But these things afterward we will arrange.
Now come, a proper vessel let us launch,
And in it let us place a hecatomb
And fair Chryseis; some chief shall have command,—
Ulysses, Idomeneus, or Ajax,
Or thou, Achilles, terriblest of men,
That thus Apollo pacified may be.
  Him sternly answering, thus Achilles spake:
Ah! man most impudent and fond of gain,
How can the Greeks be ruled by one like thee?
'Twas not on Troy's account that I came here,—
No herds or steeds of mine they ever stole,
Nor ravaged fruitful Phthia, my domain;
A distance vast divides our boundaries,
And shady forests and resounding seas,—
But 'twas on thy account, oh, shameless man!
To aid thee in revenging Menelaus;

And for such benefits I'm thus repaid.
Thou threatenest to rob me of my prize
Which the Greeks gave me, and which well I earned ;
My portion never yet has equaled thine
When we have captured any hostile town,
Though by my hand most of the work was done ;
But when division of the spoil was made
Thou got the most, whilst I, worn out with toil,
Took back some little pittance to my ships ;
But now I go to Phthia; so 'tis best,
Nor wilt thou prosper thus dishonoring me.
He said ; and Agamemnon thus replied :
Begone, if 'tis thy wish, I beg thee not
On my account to stay ; enough there are
To honor me ; but chiefly, all-wise Jove,
Of all our chiefs most odious art thou ;
Quarrels and battles are thy sole delight.
If valor's thine, the gods that valor gave.
Home with thee, with thy ships and company,
Rule o'er thy Myrmidons, for I defy thee.
But hearken now, and to my threat take heed :
Since fair Chryseis must be given up,
I willingly obey the god's command ;
But, going to thy tent, I thence shall take
Thy blooming maid, the beautiful Briseis,
That thou and others may hereafter fear
To put themselves upon a par with me.
He said ; and greatly was Achilles moved ;
In dread suspense he paused, what course to take—
Whether his sword to draw and slay the king,
Or to refrain and moderate his wrath.
Whilst thus he was in doubt, and from its sheath
His sword was drawing, wise Minerva came ;
From heaven she came, sent by fair Juno,
Who loved and honored both the chiefs alike ;
She stood behind him, seizing his auburn hair,
To all but him she was invisible.
Achilles was amazed, and turning round

Beheld the goddess, whom he knew at once.
Her eyes fell on him and were terrible;
Then with winged words he spake, and thus began:
Why art thou here, daughter of mighty Jove,
To see the insolence of Agamemnon?
Perhaps thou soon wilt see his punishment.
To him the blue-eyed goddess thus replied:
From heaven I come to moderate thy wrath;
Fair Juno sent me, for she loves you both.
But come, cease from this strife, let go thy sword,
Contend with words if thou must still contend;
Thou, for this insult, shall rewarded be,
And gifts inestimable shall yet be thine.
Her answering then, Achilles thus replied:
Oh, goddess! thy command shall be obeyed,
Though much I am incensed; 'tis for the best,
The gods will honor those who honor them.
He said; and holding still the silver hilt
Thrust back the mighty blade into its sheath;
Nor did he disregard Minerva's words.
But she had vanished, flying to the domes
Of high Olympus, the abode of Jove
And all the deities. Yet still the chief
Continued Agamemnon to upbraid.
Oh, precious wine-bibber! with a dog's face
But with a heart as timid as a deer,
Thou never durst with the courageous Greeks
To go to war or fight the enemy;
This would be death to thee. Thy part it is
To plunder those who dare to contradict.
A king, indeed, devouring his people!
And what a people such a king to bear!
But hear me now—a mighty oath I swear,
For by this scepter on the mountain cut,
By the sharp axe, and stripped of boughs and leaves,
Which ne'er shall come to life or sprout again,—
'Tis by our judges borne, the sacred badge
And emblem of our laws; by it I swear

The time may come when all shall need Achilles—
When mighty Hector's devastating sword
Shall ruin bring. Then shalt thou grieve in vain
For injuring thus the noblest of the Greeks.
  Thus spake the chief; and, casting to the ground
The golden-studded rod, resumed his seat.
The king was much incensed, but naught replied.
  Then Nestor rose, sage orator of Pylos,
From whose lips there flowed a stream of eloquence
Sweeter than honey. Two generations
He had seen, and o'er the third still ruled;
Thus wisely counseling, the old man spake:
  Oh, heavens! a sorry sight is this for Greece!
What joy for Priam, and for Priam's sons,
And all the Trojans too, when they shall hear
That Greece's greatest chiefs are quarreling!
But hearken, as you both my juniors are,
For I with better men than you have lived,
And always from them met with due respect;
For never have I seen, nor ever shall,
Such men as Pirithous and Dryas,
Exadius too, and godlike Polyphemus
And Theseus also,—men like gods were they,
Bravest of mortals that e'er trod on earth.
They with the horrid mountain Centaurs fought,
And slew them dreadfully. These were my friends;
I left my distant home to go with them,
For they invited me. I fought my best—
No mortal now on earth with them could cope,
Yet they respected and obeyed my words;
You too obey—'tis for your own good;
Rob not Achilles of his maid, oh, king,
She was a gift presented by the Greeks;
Nor thou, Achilles, with the king contend,
For never monarch held a nobler throne.
If thou art brave, 'tis owing to thy birth—
Thy mother was a goddess. But in power
He is above thee, ruling such a host.

Then, Agamemnon, lay aside thy wrath ;
I pray thee cease to quarrel with Achilles,
For he our bulwark is in dreadful war.
   Him answered then the noble Agamemnon :
Truly, old man, thou givest good advice;
But this man thinks o'er all to domineer,
And wishes all to yield and bow to him ;
But one he'll find who is not quite so weak ;
Because the gods have made him such a warrior,
Has he a right to swagger and insult ?
   Him answering then, Achilles thus replied :
A wretched creature truly would I be
Were I to do whate'er thou biddest me;
O'er others thou mayest rule, but not o'er me ;
But bear in mind what I shall tell thee now:
As for this maid, I will no longer strive ;
You gave her to me—take her if you please,
But dare lay hands on other goods of mine
And thy black blood shall stain my glittering spear.
   Thus having spoke, the rival chiefs arose,
And the assembly of the Greeks dispersed ;
Then to his ships and tents Achilles went,
With good Patroclus and his Myrmidons.
   But Agamemnon a galley launched,
Equipped with twenty well selected oarsmen ;
In it he placed the sacred hecatomb,
And led aboard himself the fair Chryseis ;
The wise Ulysses acted as commander.
Thus they embarked, and plowed their watery way ;
The people then were ordered by the king
To purify themselves. They all obeyed,
And their ablutions in the ocean cast ;
Next by the sea-side hecatombs they slew
Of goats and oxen to divine Apollo ;
The smoke and smell ascended to the skies.
Thus was the army of the Greeks employed.
   Nor did the king delay his angry threat ;
But Eurybates and Talthybius called

His heralds and his faithful ministers:
Depart, ye heralds, to Achilles' tent,
And, leading fair Briseis by the hand,
Bring her to me. If he resistance makes,
I with a host will come and take by force;
And this to him will more unpleasant be.
Thus with harsh orders he the heralds sent.
They went unwillingly along the shore,
And to the quarters of Achilles came.
They found him sitting by his tent and ship;
Nor was he overpleased beholding them.
Confused they stood, fearing the mighty chief;
Nor spake they to him, nor their errand told.
He knew what brought them there, and thus began:
Hail, heralds! messengers of gods and men!
Draw near; I blame not you, but Agamemnon,
Who sends you here to lead away Briseis.
Go, good Patroclus, bring the maiden forth
And let them take her; but be ye witness,—
Witness before the gods and mortal men,
And in the presence of this ruthless king,—
If ever in the hour of need I'm asked
To save from ruin the unhappy Greeks,—
Oh, he is mad, and knows not what he does;
Forgets the past and braves the dreadful future!
He said; and Patroclus, his friend, obeyed,
Brought forth the fair Briseis from the tent,
And gave her to the men to lead away,
Nor did the maiden willingly depart.
Then, bursting into tears, Achilles left
And sat him down upon the ocean's shore.
On the dark sea he gazed, spread forth his arms,
And, to his mother praying, thus began:
Oh, mother! since I'm doomed to be short lived,
Olympian Jove at least should honor me;
But little is the honor I receive,
For I by Agamemnon am disgraced,
Who robs and keeps from me my lawful prize.
Thus spake the chief, tears streaming from his eyes.

His venerable mother heard his prayer;
In ocean's depths she sat by her old sire.
Quick she ascended, rising like a cloud
Out of the hoary sea, and sat her down
Close to her weeping son, called him by name,
And, with her arms around him, thus began:
What ails thee, child, and wherefore dost thou weep?
Hide not thy grief, but let me know it all.
With many a groan, Achilles thus replied:
Thou knowest already. Why tell to thee,
Who art a goddess and informed of all?
We marched on Thebè, Aëtion's sacred town,
The place we sacked and brought away the spoil;
A just division by the Greeks was made,
And fair Chryseis fell to Agamemnon.
Then Chryses came, Apollo's sacred priest,
Offering a costly ransom for his child,
And, bearing in his arms the golden wand
And flowery garlands of the Archer god,
He supplicated all the Greeks, but most
The two commanders, sons of Atreus.
Then all the people shouted their assent
The priest to honor and his ransom take.
But Agamemnon was much displeased,
And, with insulting language, sent him back.
The old man, very angry, went away,
And when he prayed, Apollo heard his prayer—
For much he loved him. Then a dart he shot—
A deadly dart—into the Grecian camp;
The people died by heaps, so great the plague.
Apollo's will a faithful seer revealed;
I said at once the god should be appeased.
This greatly stirred the wrath of Agamemnon,
Who threatened what has really come to pass;
For in a ship the Greeks the beauteous maid
To Chryses send, with presents for the god.
But from my tent the heralds just have gone,
And the fair maid Briseis carried off—

She whom the Greeks assigned me as my prize.
But if thou canst, I pray thee aid thy son!
Haste to Olmypus, then, and speak to Jove,
If ever gracious thou hast been to him
By word or deed. For often when at home,
I've heard thee in my father's palace boast
That it was thou that saved the Thunderer,
When certain of the deities rebelled—
Juno, his wife, and Neptune, and Minerva—
Who thought to bind the king of gods in chains.
But thou didst loose his chain, calling to heaven
Briareus—hundred-handed giant;
So he is called on high, but on the earth
Egeon is his name; greater in strength
E'en than his sire is he; he helped thee,
And joyfully sat down at Jove's right hand.
Him the gods feared, and from their plot abstained.
Put him in mind of this; embrace his knees;
Beg him assist the Trojans; drive the Greeks
Back to their ships with slaughter and dismay.
Then may they all enjoy their precious king,
And then will Agememnon discover
His cursed folly in insulting thus
The best and noblest warrior of the Greeks.
He said; and Thetis, weeping, thus replied:
Oh, my poor son, would thou hadst ne'er been born!
Oh, that in peace like others thou couldst live
Unharmed, and free from tears; short is thy life,
And yet of all men thou most wretched art;
Under a baneful planet wast thou born.
Yet will I go to snow-capped, high Olympus,
And tell thy message to loud-thundering Jove,
But thou in quiet by thy ships remain,
Nursing thy wrath, nor mingle in the war;
For Jove went yesterday beyond the sea
To attend a feast of the blameless Æthiops;
The gods all follow him. Some twelve days hence
He will return; then to his brazen domes

I will repair, and, falling at his feet,
Will ask his favor, and not ask in vain.
She said, and left him much incensed,
And sadly grieving for the beauteous maid
Who just now from him had been torn away.
Meanwhile Ulysses had to Chrysa come—
Come with his ships, bearing the hecatomb.
The harbor entering, they furled the sails,
Lowered the mast and stowed it in its place,
Then rowed their vessel nearer to the land,
And made her fast with anchors and with ropes.
Then through the surf they leaped upon the shore,
And landed, too, the sacred hecatomb,
And fair Chryseis, whom Ulysses led
Up to the altar where her father stood,
And having placed her in his hands, thus spake:
Oh, Chryses! Agamemnon, king of men,
Hath sent me to return to thee thy child,
And to thy god this hecatomb to give,
That thus we may appease him for the woes
Which now he sends upon the suffering Greeks.
He said, and placed the maiden in his hands.
With joy the father his dear child received,
Then round the shrine the hecatomb they ranged,
Washing their hands, and sprinkling barley meal;
And for them Chryses prayed with lifted hands:
Hear me, Apollo, god of the silver bow,
Ruling fair Cilla, Tenedos, and Chrysa;
Thou heard'st my former prayer and honored me,
Sending destruction on the Grecian host;
Hear now my second prayer, and from the Greeks
Remove forthwith this direful pestilence.
Thus Chryses prayed, nor was his prayer unheard.
Then they all prayed, and sprinkled barley meal;
Then slew and flayed the beasts, cut up the thighs,
Wrapped them in double fat, with meat on top;
Next, with split wood the old men burnt them up
And poured out sparkling wine. The youths stood by,

Each bearing in his hand a five-pronged fork.
The thighs consumed, the entrails next they taste;
Then in small pieces cut the carcass up,
Placed them on spits and roasted skillfully.
Their labors o'er, the banquet they prepared,
And each was feasted to his heart's content.
The boys now came with cups of brimming wine,
Handing them round among the happy guests;
And all day long the youths melodious sang,
And hymned the praises of divine Apollo,
Who listened and with pleasure heard their strains.
When night came on, and darkness closed the scene,
They all lay down upon the beach and slept;
But when the rosy light of morn appeared
They re-embarked, returning to the camp.
Apollo sent them a propitious breeze;
They raised the mast and spread the flowing sail,
The swelling canvas with the wind was filled,
And round the keel the purple billows roared
As the swift vessel plowed her watery way.
But when at length they reached the Grecian camp,
They drew the ship upon the sandy shore,
And propped her up with poles on either side,
Then to their tents and vessels all dispersed.
  Meanwhile Achilles sat, nursing his wrath;
Sat by his ships, nor mingled in the war,
Nor in the councils of the heroic chiefs.
Remaining by himself he pined away,
Yet longing all the while to take the field.
  Twelve days had now elapsed, and Jove returned,
He and the deities, to high Olympus.
Thetis her promise to her son remembered;
Emerging from the sea at early dawn
She swiftly mounted to the heavenly realms,
Where, seated by himself, the god she found
Upon the highest summit of Olympus.
She sat before him, clasped with one hand his knees
And fondly placed the other on his chin,

Then with imploring words she thus began:
Oh, father Jove! if, with the other gods,
I ever have a service done to thee,
Grant my request—honor my short-lived child,
Whom king Agamemnon has insulted
And robbed him of his prize; do thou at least
Crown him with honor; send victory to Troy,
Until the Greeks shall reverence my son,
And give him all the glory he deserves.
She said; but Jove vouchsafed her no reply.
Long he sat silent; yet Thetis to him clung,
And thus again importunately prayed:
Speak out and promise; say but yes or no;
Fear hath no place with thee; tell me at once
How least of all the immortals I'm esteemed.
With deep emotion, Jove at length replied:
A serious matter thou persuadest me to;
Juno will be offended and will scold;
She chides me without ceasing, and still says
I always help the Trojans in this war.
Depart thou, then, lest she observe thee now;—
Yet thy request shall not unanswered be.
I with my head will nod; then be assured;
A greater sign than this I cannot give;
For what I once acknowledge with a nod
Is then established irreversibly.
Thus having said, and his dark brows inclined,
Great Jove his purpose showed, and gave the nod.
As his head moved his locks ambrosial shook,
And all Olympus trembled. Then they parted.
She plunged from heaven down to the briny deep,
And to his palace mighty Jove returned.
The gods all rose upon their sire's approach—
None kept his seat, but all a welcome gave—
Then on his throne he sat. But Juno knew
That silver-footed Thetis—child of the sea—
Had with her husband held a conference,
And with reproachful words addressed him thus:

Who of the gods again has been with thee?
Oh, full of art!—'tis ever thy delight
To have some secret business of thine own,
And of thy plans to keep me in the dark!
To whom replied the king of gods and men:
Think not, oh, Juno! my whole mind to know;
A burden it would be too great for thee—
Wife though thou art; all that's right and fit
I will inform thee of; nor gods nor men
Shall before thee receive intelligence.
But what I wish to hide, seek not to know.
He said; and Juno to him thus replied:
How dost thou talk, great son of mighty Saturn!
Into thy secrets have I ever pried?
Scheme and deliberate to thy heart's content;
But strong suspicion have I in my mind
That silver-footed Thetis—child of the sea—
Has somewhat swayed thee; for at dawn to-day
She sat beside thee and embraced thy knees,
And thou didst promise her, I much suspect,
That thou would'st honor to Achilles grant
And doom to slaughter many of the Greeks.
She said; and much incensed great Jove replied:
Suspicious wretch! whom nothing can escape,
What doth thy cunning gain, except my hate?
Grant thou art right; my pleasure I will do;
Then sit thee down and due obedience show,
Lest some chastisement I inflict on thee;
Nor wilt thou then be rescued from my hands—
No—not by all the deities combined!
He said; but venerable Juno feared—
She feared, and daring no reply, sat down;
The gods indignant murmured at the scene.
Then up rose Vulcan—architect divine—
Who grieved to see his mother mortified,
And thus in soothing words addressed them all:
A shame it is, and not to be endured,
That for the sake of miserable men

Uproar and quarrel should arise in heaven;
No pleasure will our joyous banquets give
If wrath prevails. My mother I advise
To be submissive to dear father Jove,
Lest he again may scold, and spoil our feast.
Great is the power of the Olympian king,
And he could hurl us from our heavenly seats;
Speak to him, then, in soft persuasive words,
And he to us again will pleasant be.
He said, and rising, placed the golden cup
In his dear mother's hands, and thus went on:
Be patient, mother, and restrain thyself,
Lest I be pained at seeing thee chastised.
No help could I impart, so great is Jove;
For once when I to thy assistance came
He seized me by the foot and hurled me o'er
The heavenly threshold; all day I fell,
And dropped in Lemnos at the set of sun.
The people of the island took me up
And kindly treated me. Thus Vulcan spake.
His mother, fair-complexioned Juno, smiled,
And smiling, took the goblet from his hands.
Then to the other deities in turn
He from the vase delicious nectar poured.
Great laughter rose among the happy gods
At seeing Vulcan play the cup-bearer.
Thus did they feast all day till even-tide.
Nothing was wanting; music they had, and song;
Apollo played his lyre, the Muses sang—
Sang with delicious voice, responsively.
But when the sun went down they sought repose,
And to his separate mansion each repaired,
Built by lame Vulcan, architect divine.
Jove, too, retired, and by his side his queen
Upon a splendid golden couch reposed.

BOOK II.

DESCRIPTION OF THE ARMIES.

ARGUMENT.

Jupiter, in order to bring about the slaughter of the Greeks, sends a false dream to Agamemnon, persuading him to commence the fight at once, for Troy will certainly be taken.—The king, overjoyed, resolves to obey the vision, but first tries the temper of the army by artfully proposing an abandonment of the war, and a return to Greece.—The Greeks prepare to return, but are dissuaded from their design by the management of Ulysses, and now in good earnest get ready for the fight.—A catalogue of the ships and leaders is given.

THE gods and warrior knights slept soundly—
All but Jove; he slept not, pondering how
He best might honor and exalt Achilles,
And ruin send on many of the Greeks.
This scheme at length appeared to him the best:
To send an Evil Dream to Agamemnon;
And having called him, thus the Thunderer spake:
  Fly, Evil Dream, swift to the Grecian camp,
And, entering the tent of Agamemnon,
Speak to him just as I commission thee:
Bid him with all his might to arm the Greeks,
For now, perchance, great Troy may captured be.
The Olympian deities are all agreed;
Juno has bent them to her sovereign will,
And o'er the Trojans dreadful woes impend.
  He said; and swiftly the False Vision flew—
Flew to the Grecian camp, and Agamemnon.
He found him in his tent, steeped in sweet sleep,
And, putting on the likeness of old Nestor—

Whom of the elders most the king admired—
Stood by the monarch's couch, and thus began :
Sleep'st thou, oh, son of Atreus renowned !
It ill becomes a counselor and chief
To whom the people's welfare is intrusted
To waste the night in sleep. Then hear me quick :
Jove's messenger I am, who, though unseen,
Yet dearly loves and greatly pities thee.
He bids thee arm with all thy might the Greeks,
For now, perchance, great Troy may captured be.
The Olympian deities are all agreed ;
Juno has bent them to her sovereign will,
And o'er the Trojans dreadful woes impend.
Bear what I say in mind—forget it not
When thou awakest from thy ambrosial sleep.
Thus spoke the Dream, and, melting into air,
Left the king scheming what was not to be ;
Foolish, he thought, that on that very day
Great Troy would fall, nor did he understand
The secret counsel and design of Jove,
Who still was planning miseries and woes
For Greeks and Trojans both, in dreadful war.
The hero starting from his sleep, awoke,
The voice divine still sounding in his ears ;
Upright he rose, put on his beauteous robe,
O'er which a cloak magnificent he threw ;
His splendid sandals to his feet he bound,
And from his shoulders slung his glittering sword ;
His ancient scepter in his hands he bore ;
And, thus arrayed, went to the Grecian camp.
Aurora now climbed the Olympian mount,
Diffusing light to deities and men ;
The heralds then were ordered by the king
To call a meeting of the Grecian host.
They called ; and quickly all the people came ;
But first a council of the elders met
Around the ship of Nestor, king of Pylos,
And thus the prudent Agamemnon spake :

My friends, last night a vision I beheld;
In form and likeness, it resembled Nestor;
And, standing by my bed, addressed me thus:
Sleep'st thou, oh, son of Atreus renowned!
It ill becomes a counselor and chief
To whom the people's welfare is intrusted
To waste the night in sleep; then hear me quick,
Jove's messenger I am, who, though unseen,
Yet dearly loves and greatly pities thee:
He bids thee arm with all thy might the Greeks,
For now, perchance, great Troy may captured be.
The Olympian deities are all agreed;
Juno has bent them to her sovereign will,
And o'er the Trojans fearful woes impend;
Bear what I say in mind. Thus having spoke,
The vision flew away, and I awoke.
Then come, and let us arm the valiant Greeks;
But first their disposition I will sound,
And bid them to their native land return.
You, on your part, do just the contrary,
And mingling with them, bid them to remain.
He said, and took his seat; then Nestor rose—
Nestor, wise sovereign of sandy Pylos,
Who thus discreetly counseled, and began:
My friends and chieftains of the valiant Greeks,
If any other such a dream had told
We should have said he lied, and disbelieved;
But this was witnessed by our king himself;
Come then, and let us arm the Grecian host.
He said; and rising, from the council went,
And with him went the other sceptered chiefs,
Obedient to their sovereign's command.
Meanwhile the people in assembly met.
As swarms of bees in one continuous stream,
Keep issuing from the crevice of a rock;
And spreading here and there, o'er all the field,
Alight in clusters on the vernal flowers.
So, many nations, from the ships and tents

Along the shore, to the assembly trooped;
Rumor, Jove's messenger, among them blazed,
And stirred the passions of the excited throng.
Clamor was there, and, as they took their seats,
The very earth beneath the tumult groaned.
Nine heralds cried aloud; bade them be still
And listen to the voices of their chiefs.
At last the crowd was quiet and composed;
Then, in the midst, king Agamemnon rose,
With Vulcan's curious scepter in his hand--
Vulcan to Jove, at first had given it,
And Jove to Mercury, who gave it next
To Pelops, who could tame unruly steeds;
Pelops again to Atreus handed it;
He, when he died, to rich Thyestes left it;
From him, it then to Agamemnon came,
Ruler of many islands, and of Argos;—
Leaning upon it, thus the monarch spake:
  Hearken, my friends, heroes, and warriors!
Great woes befall me, from the hand of Jove;
Cruel, he once his solemn promise gave
That Troy should be destroyed ere I returned;
But now an evil purpose he reveals,
That, after losing multitudes of men,
I must unhappy, back to Argos go.
Such is the sovereign will of mighty Jove,
Who many famous cities has destroyed,
And will destroy, so boundless is his power.
A shameful thing it will hereafter be
That the brave Greeks were baffled in a war
With a weak nation, as it seems we are.
For should each side a friendly census take,
Reckoning alone the citizens of Troy,
And we the Greeks, divided into tens,
And for the ten, one Trojan pour out wine,
Many a ten would want a cup-bearer;
So much do we the citizens exceed;
But many are the auxiliaries they have,

Who help to check and frustrate my designs.
Already, too, nine years have rolled away;
Our ships and cordage now begin to rot;
Our wives and little ones remain at home
Most anxiously awaiting our return;
And yet the work for which we hither came
Is unaccomplished still, and like to be.
Come, then! and let us in our ships embark
And flee away back to our native land,
For Troy by us will never captured be.
He said; and in each mind a tumult raised,
Of all who were not privy to his scheme.
The throng heaved to and fro, as when the sea
Is lashed to fury by a northeast wind,
And black tempestuous clouds obscure the sky;
As when a breeze blows o'er a field of grain
And the ripe ears keep waving in the wind,
So were the people moved. With shouts they ran
All hastening to their ships; beneath their feet
Rose clouds of dust, as with one voice they cried
To launch their barks into the hoary sea;
They cleared a passage for them through the sand,
Removed the props; the clamor rose to heaven.
Then would the Greeks most surely have returned
If Juno had not to Minerva spake:
Alas! great daughter of almighty Jove,
Shall the Greeks flee over the briny deep,
Returning to their homes and native land?
Shall Priam boast that he has gained his point,
And Argive Helen still be left in Troy,
On whose account such multitudes of men
Have lost their lives upon a foreign shore?
Go, then, restrain the people with fair words,
Nor suffer them to launch their gallant ships.
She said; nor did the goddess disobey.
Down from the Olympian mount in haste she flew,
And quickly lighted in the Grecian camp;
There wise Ulysses by himself she found,

Nor had he gone his vessel to prepare,
For heavy grief oppressed his anxious mind.
Standing by him, Minerva thus began :
Son of Laertes, most renowned Ulysses !
Why flee ye thus, over the briny deep
Returning to your homes and native land ?
Shall Priam boast that he has gained his point,
And Argive Helen still be left in Troy,
On whose account such multitudes of men
Have lost their lives upon a foreign shore ?
Go, then, restrain the people with fair words,
Nor suffer them to launch their gallant ships.
She said ; and he the goddess recognized ;
In haste he ran, throwing away his cloak,
The herald, Eurybates, picked it up ;
Then to king Agamemnon he went,
And from him his paternal scepter took.
With this he walked toward the Grecian ships ;
Whatever chief or man of note he met
He thus in words of gentleness addressed :
It ill becomes thee, friend, to show such fright ;
Rather sit down and help to calm the rest.
You know not yet what 'tis our king intends ;
He is but sounding us, and may chastise.
We heard not all that was in council said ;
He may incensed become, and punish us.
Kings are most terrible in wrath and power,
And rule their people by a right divine ;
But when a common man he chanced to meet,
And found him bawling out officiously,
He struck him with his scepter, and reproved :
Keep quiet, wretch, and let thy betters speak ;
No power hast thou, no strength nor influence,
And art of no account in peace or war.
We must not have so many masters here ;
Nor is it proper that a mob should rule—
One chief we have, one king, to whom great Jove
A scepter gave, and whom we must obey.

Thus through the host he went, commanding all;
Then, with much tumult, from their ships and tents
Back to the assembly, the people rushed
As when a wave of the resounding sea
Dashes upon a rock with deafening roar.
Then all sat down, each in his proper place—
All but Thersites; he a cynic was,
Unmannered and without propriety;
But most he loved to rail at men of note;
The vilest person he that came to Troy,
Humpbacked he was, and lame, and had a squint;
His head, misshapen, to a point arose,
With a few scattered hairs upon the top;
He to Ulysses and Achilles bore
A special grudge, and often would abuse,
But now his wrath was turned on Agamemnon,
And, though the Greeks with much displeasure heard,
Thus loudly bawling, he reviled the king:
What dost thou want? of what dost thou complain,
Oh, son of Atreus? thy tents are full of gold,
And of the fairest maids thou hadst thy choice
Whene'er we captured any Trojan town.
More gold dost thou require?—the ransom price
Of some rich Trojan youth, whom we, the Greeks,
Conquered in war and brought away alive?
Or dost thou still another damsel want
To keep for thine own use? Should'st thou, a chief,
Bring evil on thy men? Oh, what weak men!
Not Greeks, but Grecian dames—oh, what a shame!
Home let us go at once and leave him here,
Enjoying, if he can, his ill got gains.
Achilles, too, he just now has abused,—
A much superior man in all respects,
From whom he took away his lawful prize.
Well was it that the chief restrained his wrath,
Or thou, Atrides, ne'er hadst wronged again.
Thus spake Thersites, railing at the king;
Then hastily arose divine Ulysses,

And, sternly eyeing him, he thus rebuked:
Oh, babbling wretch! fine speaker though thou art,
Yet hold thy tongue, nor with our princes strive,
For this I say, no viler man than thou
Came with the fleet to Troy. No longer, then,
Make free with kings, nor talk of a return;
We know not yet the course that things may take,
Nor whether to return or stay is best.
Thou railest too about the many gifts
The generous Greeks bestowed on Agamemnon.
Now, hear me speak, and what I speak I mean:
If e'er thou ravest in such style again,
Sure as Telemachus is called my son
Thy garments from thy naked loins I'll cut,
And, giving thee a drubbing most severe,
Will drive thee from the camp in woeful plight.
He said, and laid his scepter o'er his back;
He writhed with pain, tears started in his eyes,
And on his flesh a bloody welt arose;
Foolish he looked, but trembled and said naught,
Then sat him down, wiping away his tears.
The Greeks, though in distress, all laughed outright,
And each one to his neighbor thus remarked:
Many good acts Ulysses has performed
In peace and war, but none so good as this,
Stopping the mouth of such a slanderer,
Who will not soon again revile our kings.
Thus spake the Greeks; but wise Ulysses stood
Holding his scepter, and, like a herald,
Near him Minerva was, stilling the throng,
And, bidding all to listen to his words,
He, wisely counseling, addressed them thus:
Oh, Agamemnon! now the Greeks intend
To make thee, as it were, a laughing-stock;
Nor do they keep the promise which they made
When from the shores of Greece they hither came—
That not till Troy was sacked would they return;
Yet now they cry like children to go home.

4

But to be baffled in one's plans is hard ;
'Tis tedious to be one month from home,
Tossed in a ship mid wintry storms and gales,
And absent from one's wife and family ;
And yet to us nine years have rolled away
Since we embarked; nor can I find much fault
That such a life is growing wearisome ;
But to return defeated would be base,
After enduring such a lapse of time.
Bear up, my friends, a little longer, then,
That we may know whether the prophecy
Will turn out true that Chalcas gave to us ;
For well we know, and all were witness
Who yet survive, of what took place at Aulis,
Where our ships mustered on their way to Troy.
We on an altar offered to the gods,
Close to a fountain, perfect hecatombs,
Beneath a lovely plane-tree's shady boughs,
Whence gushed a sparkling stream of crystal water.
There, as we looked, a wondrous sight we saw,
For from beneath the altar glided forth
A horrid serpent, spotted on the back,
Sent by great Jove. He up the plane-tree coiled ;
There, on the topmost branch among the leaves,
Were eight young sparrows lying in their nest ;
The hen that hatched them out made up the ninth.
Them he devoured, twittering piteously,
Whilst the poor mother still kept fluttering round
Her young, lamenting ; her by the wing he caught,
And swallowed too. Then Jove worked wondrously,
Turning the horrid serpent into stone.
We stood amazed, beholding such a sign
Amid the sacrifice. Then Chalcas rose,
And thus in prophecy the thing explained :
Why stand ye silent, oh, ye warrior Greeks ?
Jove sent this sign,—late its accomplishment,
But not its fame,—that will eternal be ;
For as this snake did the nine birds devour,

So with the Trojans we nine years must fight;
But on the tenth proud Troy will surely fall.
Then let us still remain, heroic Greeks,
Until we capture Priam's mighty town.
He said; and with loud shouts the Greeks replied,
Making their vessels echo with the sound,
And praising great Ulysses' noble words.
Then next arose and spake Geranian Nestor:
Oh, gods! ye all, like foolish children, prate,
In utter ignorance of warlike arts;
Whither have fled your promises and oaths?
Into the fire all your vows are cast;
Your weighty cares and solemn sacraments;
Your counsels and right hands of fellowship;
And ye at this late day sit arguing!
Do thou, oh, Agamemnon! still be firm,
And in the coming conflict take command.
The few among us that dissentions sow,
Let them to ruin go; they would return
Before they rightly know the mind of Jove—
Whether his promise he'll fulfill or no;
For Jove, I say, a promise gave to us
Upon the very day that we embarked—
Lightning he flashed, and showed propitious signs.
Let no one, therefore, think of a return
Till he has ravished some fair Trojan dame,
And thus avenge the injuries of Helen.
If any still is bent on going back,
Let him but touch his vessel and he dies.
But thou, oh king! be well advised thyself,
And harken to the counsel that I give:
Divide the army into companies,
That tribe may stand by tribe, and clan by clan.
If this be done, then wilt thou better know
Who of the leaders fails to do his part,
Who of the men, and who the valiant are;
For marshaled thus they all will fight their best.
Then shall we know why Troy is not o'erthrown—
By Heaven's decree or by our cowardice.

Him answering then, king Agamemnon spake:
Truly, old man, thy counsel takes the lead
Of all the Greeks; by Jove, had I but ten
Such counselors as thou, quickly would Troy
Be captured and destroyed. But mighty Jove
Sends trials on me, and afflicts me much,
For I have with Achilles fallen out
About a maid, and it was I began it;
But should we ever become friends again,
Swift ruin will upon the Trojans fall.
Now take your meals, and then prepare for war—
Sharpen your spears, be ready with your shields;
Your horses feed, inspect your chariots;
This day in dreadful battle will be spent
Till night shall intervene and stop the fray.
The sweat shall flow in torrents from our limbs,
And to our spears our weary hands shall cleave;
Our horses, too, will sweat beneath the yoke.
But whom I find retreating from the front,
Trying to hide among the hollow ships,
Him will I slay and cast him to the dogs.
He said; and loudly shouted all the Greeks
As when the waves, driven by tempestuous winds,
Dash on a jutting rock of some high promontory,
Lashing the stones with an incessant roar.
Rising in haste they scattered through the camp,
Lighted their smoking fires and took their meals;
And each one prayed to the immortal gods
To spare his life in the approaching fight.
Then Agamemnon to almighty Jove
Offered a bullock, five years old and fat;
Then called to council all the older chiefs—
Nestor the first, and royal Idomeneus;
Next the two Ajaxes and Tydeus' son;
Ulysses was the sixth, wisest of all.
Brave Menelaus at his own suggestion came,
Knowing the cares that on his brother weighed.
These stood around the ox, and sprinkled meal,
And thus in prayer king Agamemnon spake:

Oh, mighty Jove! dwelling above the clouds,
Let not the sun go down nor darkness come
Before the halls of Priam I destroy
And burn his palace gates with hostile fire;
Let my spear pierce through Hector's coat of mail,
And round him may his comrades bite the dust.
Thus prayed the king; but Jove gave no assent:
He took the offering, but plagued the offerer.
After the prayer, they sprinkled barley-meal;
Slaughtered the victim, flayed, and cut him up;
The thighs and meat they covered o'er with fat,
Then roasted with split wood; the entrails then
They placed on spits and held above the fire.
But when the thighs were burnt and entrails tasted
The bullock they cut up and cooked in style;
When all was ready, they the banquet spread,
And each was feasted to his heart's content.
Then in their midst rose Nestor, and thus spake:
Oh, son of Atreus! royal Agamemnon!
No longer let us sit debating here,
Nor still put off the work the gods command;
But come and bid the Grecian heralds call
The men to congregate around the ships,
And let us leaders through the army go
And stir the people up to bloody war.
He said; nor did the king refuse assent,
But bade the clear-tongued heralds cry aloud
And call the Grecian warriors to the field.
The heralds sounded, and the people met;
The chiefs among them moved, and marshaled them.
Minerva, blue-eyed goddess, too was there,
Holding the immortal ægis* in her hands;
A hundred golden fringes from it hung,
Each of the value of a hundred oxen.
With this she fiercely through the army ran,
Imparting strength and valor to each heart;

---

* The shield of Minerva.

They looked with pleasure now on horrid war,
Nor thought they any more of friends or home.
As when some woody mountain is on fire,
Whose light immense is visible afar,
So flashed the splendid armor of the Greeks
As o'er the field they marched in bright array.
Like flocks innumerable of water-fowl,
Of cackling geese, or cranes, or long-necked swans,
Which on the Asian meadows congregate,
By beautiful Cayester's winding stream;
Round and around they fly on sportive wing,
And with tremendous clamor wheeling down,
Settle at last upon the echoing field.
Thus many nations, from the ships and tents,
Marched o'er Scamander's plain; the earth beneath
Shook with the trampling of the horse and foot
As on Scamander's verdant fields they stood,
Thick as the myriad leaves and flowers of spring.
As in a cow-yard in the summer-time
Innumerable swarms of flies alight
On the sweet milk that fills the brimming pails,
So against Troy marched the devouring Greeks.
As shepherds separate large flocks of sheep
That happen in the pastures to be mixed,
So the chiefs marshaled each his squadron band.
There, too, was Agamemnon, king of men,
With breast like Neptune, loins like fiery Mars,
And with the head and eyes of thundering Jove;
And as amidst the herd the bull excels
The other animals, so on that day
Shone Agamemnon most conspicuous,
Such glory had he from immortal Jove.
Tell me, ye Muses of the Olympian mount—
For ye are deities and all things know,
But we hear rumors only, and know naught—
Who were the chiefs and leaders of the Greeks?
As for the multitude, had I ten mouths,
Ten fluent tongues, a throat and lungs of brass,

I could not of myself attempt to name,
Unless assisted by the heavenly Muse.
However, I will all the leaders give,
And tell the number of the ships they brought.
Leitus and Penelius were the chiefs
Of the Bœotians: Arcesilaus,
And Clonius, and Prothoënor, too,
Ruling o'er those who in Hyrie dwelt,
And rocky Aulis; Schœnus, also,
And Scholos, and Eteon's hilly land,
Wide Mycalessia, Thessia, and Græa.
And of those round Harma, and Ilesion,
And Peteon, and Hylè, and Ocalea,
And of the well-built city of Medeon;
Of Thisbè, famed for doves, and Eutresis;
Of Haliartus, and its verdant plains;
Of Coronè, Glissa, and Platæa,
Also of those who dwelt in lower Thebè,
A well-built town, and of Onchestus too,
Where Neptune's lovely, sacred grove is seen;
And of the people who in Arnè dwelt,
A country full of vines; Medeia also,
Nisa, the fair, and distant Anthedon.
With these were fifty vessels, and in each
Were six score of Bœotia's noblest youths.
Of those of Aspledon and Orchomenus,
Iälmen and Ascalaphus were chiefs;
In Actor's palace born, both sons of Mars.
Their mother was the fair Astyochè,
Who, to her room ascended a pure maid,
And there the god embraced her secretly.
With these two chiefs came thirty gallant ships.
The Phocian forces were by Schedius led,
And Epistrophus, sons of great Iphitus.
Pytho belonged to them, Cyparissus,
Daulis, and Panopè, and lovely Crissa,
Anemoria, and Hyampolis:
They ruled besides o'er those inhabiting

The banks of Cephissus, a sacred stream;
And of Lilæa and its tributaries.
Forty good ships by these two chiefs were led,
Next the Bœotians, on the left they camped.
  Ajax Oileus o'er the Locrians ruled,
Smaller in size than Ajax Telamon,
Quite small he was; but swift upon his feet,
And wore a linen corselet on his breast.
None of the Greeks could cast a spear like him;
He led the people who in Cynos dwelt,
And those of Opus, and Calliarus,
Bessa, and Scarphè, and Augea fair,
Tarphè, and Thronium, by Boägrius' stream.
Forty black ships this chief accompanied,
All Locrians, dwelling on the other side
Of fair Eubea's famous sacred isle.
  Of the Abantes, mighty warriors,
Who in Eubea dwelt, and in the land
Of Isteia, famous for its vines;
In Chalcis, and in Eretria too;
In Dium's lofty city, and Cerinthus,
By the sea-side; and of those of Styra,
And Carystus,—o'er these great warriors,
All famous spearmen, with long, flowing hair,
The chief was Elephenor, a heart of oak,
And he, too, forty gallant vessels brought.
  Of those who in the well-built Athens dwelt,
Town of the demi-god Erectheus,
Sprung from the earth, and whom Minerva nursed,
And settled him at Athens by her shrine,
Where, year by year, the Athenian youths
Offer their sacrifice of bulls and goats;
O'er these was chief, Menestheus, Peteus' son,
Famed for his skill in drilling, horse and foot;
No man on earth could equal him in this
Save Nestor, who had more experience.
Fifty black ships this chief accompanied.
  Twelve ships by Ajax Telamon were led

From Salamis; his forces he arranged
Near where the men of Athens were drawn up.
Of those of Argos, and high-walled Tyrithè,
Of Hermionè, and Asinè too,
Built on a bay; of vine-clad Epidaur;
Of Maseta, Trœzenè, and Eionè,
Of those inhabiting Ægina's isle,
The Achaian youth; these were commanded
By the great hero, dauntless Diomed,
And Sthenelus, son of Capaneus;
Euryalus also, was the third chief,
Son of Mecistheus, a royal man;
But the brave Diomed had chief command.
Eighty black ships these chiefs accompanied.
Of those who in Mycenè's well-built town,
And in rich Corinth dwelt, and Cleonè,
In Ornia, and Aræthyrea the fair:
In Sicyon, where once Adrastus reigned,
Of those of Hyperesia and Gonoëssa,
Of Pellenè and Aegion on the coast,
And the extensive land of Helici,—
O'er these king Agamemnon was chief,
Bringing along a hundred gallant ships;
His forces were most numerous by far,
And the most brave; he, clad in shining brass,
Excelled in glory all the other chiefs,
So great himself and leading such a host.
Of those who dwelt in rocky Lacedæmon,
In Pharè, and in Messa, famed for doves;
Of fair Augia, Brysia, and Sparta,
Of those who in Helos and Amyclæ dwelt;
In Laäs, and the town Aetylos,—
O'er them his brother, Menelaus, ruled;
His sixty vessels were arrayed apart:
With fiery zeal, he to the war had come,
Eager to have revenge for Helen's wrongs.
Of those of Pylos, and Arenè fair,
And Thryon, and the fords of Alpheus;

Of well-built Æpy, and of Cyparissa,
And of the men of Pteleon, and Helos,
And Dorion too, where the sweet muses
Meeting the bard Thamyris, on his way
From Eurytis, ended his songs forever.
For he had madly boasted that he could
Sing better than the heavenly Muses e'en.
They, angry at his folly, struck him blind;
His voice divine was into silence hushed,
And his sweet lyre he never played again.
Chief o'er these people was Geranian Nestor,
And ninety hollow ships accompanied him.
  Of those Arcadia inhabiting,
Under the breezy mountains of Cyllenè,
Hard by the tomb of Æpytus, a race
Of hardy heroes; the men of Pheneus
And Orchomenus, rich in flocks and herds;
Of those of Stratie, Ripè, and Enispè,
Of lovely Mantinea, and Tegea,
Of Stymphelus, and Parrhasia,—the chief
Was Agapenor, brave Ancheus' son,
With sixty ships, filled with Arcadian men.
The ships they came in were presented by
King Agamemnon, for they of Arcady
Unskillful were in maritime affairs.
  Of those Buprasium inhabiting,
And noble Helis, far as Herminè,
Distant Myrsinus, and the Olenian rock,
Alisium also; four chiefs commanded.
Each had ten ships with the Epeians filled;
Amphimacus and Thalpius were their names,
Sons of Teatus and Eurytus.
Next was Diores, son of Amarynceus;
Great Polyxenus was the fourth commander,
Son of Agasthenes, from Augeus sprung.
  Of those who from Dulichium's limits came,
And the Echinades, a sacred group,
Lying in front of Elis, on the sea,

Meges was chief, brave son of Phyleus,
A favorite of Jove, who fled from home
By reason of a quarrel with his sire :
Forty black ships this chief accompanied.
Ulysses led the Cephalenians,
Who in Neritos dwelt, and Ithaca,
In Crocylia, and Ægilipa,
In Samos and Zacynthus, and all those
Who lived upon the mainland opposite,—
O'er these the wise Ulysses was the chief.
Twelve ships he had whose sides were painted red.
Thoas, the son of Andræmon, was chief
Of the Ætolians, who in Pleuron dwelt,
In Chalcis by the sea, and Pylonè,—
In Olenus and rocky Calydon ;
For Æneus was dead ! and all his sons
And fair-haired Meleager was no more !
So the Ætolians were by Thoas ruled.
Forty black ships this chief accompanied.
The Cretans were by Idomeneus led,
The famous lancer. Of those from Lycastus,
And from Gnossus, from Gortyna, well built ;
And from Miletus, from Phestus, Lyctus,
And from Rhytion, all large-sized cities ;
And from the other hundred towns of Crete,—
These the great spearman, Idomeneus led,
And with him Merion, like to Mars.
Eighty black ships these chiefs accompanied.
Tlepolemus, the great and valiant son
Of Hercules, of the proud Rhodians,
Was chief ; the Isle of Rhodes divided was
Into three parts : Lindus and Jalyssus
And white Camirus ; o'er these three sections
The famous spearman, Tlepolemus, ruled,
Son of great Hercules by Astyochè,
Whom from Ephyr he brought by Selle's stream
Destroying many cities in his way.
But when Tlepolemus to manhood grew,

He slew Licymnius, his father's uncle,
A heart of oak; then he equipped a fleet,
And with a host of friends fled o'er the sea,
For Hercules' descendants sought his life.
Wandering about, at last he came to Rhodes.
Into three tribes his followers then split,
And were protected and beloved by Jove,
Who gave them riches and prosperity.
From Syrnè came Nireus with three ships,
Son of king Charops and Agläe—
Handsomest was he of all that came to Troy,
Except Achilles; few were his ships and men,
And he was weak and not cut out for war.
Of those of Nisyrus and Carpathus,
Casus, and Cos, where dwelt Eurypylus,
And of the isles Calydian, the chiefs
Were Phidippus and Antiphus, the sons
Of Thessalus, the son of Hercules.
These chiefs accompanied were by thirty ships.
Now, of Pelasgian Argos speak, oh, Muse!—
Those who in Alos dwelt and Alopè;
Of those of Trachys and rich Phthia too,
And Hellas, famous for its lovely dames;
These were Achaians called, and Hellenes
And Myrmidons. Achilles was their chief,
With fifty ships; but they abstained from war.
No leader had they who might marshal them;
For by his ships divine Achilles lay,
Chafing with anger for his lost Briseis,
The lovely fair-haired maiden whom he took
When he Lyrnessus captured with much toil,
Razing its walls, and those of Thebes besides.
He slew Menitus on the self-same day,
And Epistrophus, skillful with his spear,
Both sons of Evenus of royal race.
For this fair lady did Achilles grieve,
But he was shortly to be roused to war.
Of those who dwelt in flowery Pyrrhasus,—

Sacred to Ceres,—and in Phylacè—
In Iton famed for sheep—in Pteleon green—
In Antron by the sea—chief over these
Was brave Protesilas, while he lived;
But now beneath the sod the warrior lay,
Leaving at home a widow bathed in tears,
And house unfinished. A Trojan slew him
As foremost of the Greeks he leaped ashore;
His men were not without a leader left,
Yet still their old commander they desired.
Podarces led them now, a heart of oak,
Son of rich Iphiclus, Phylace's son;
Own brother was he of Protesilas,
But younger and inferior in renown.
Forty black ships this chief accompanied.
  Of those of Phærè by the lake Bœbis—
Of Bœbè, Glaphyra, and Iolcus—
Eumelus, with eleven ships, was chief,
Admetus' much loved son, whom Alcestis
Bore, a woman she of rare attractions.
  Of those of Methonè and Thaumacia,
Of Melibœa and rough Olizon,
The archer, Philoctetes, was the chief.
Seven ships he had, with fifty men
Well skilled in archery, on board of each;
But he was left in Lemnos' isle in pain,
Suffering from a deadly serpent's bite.
There in much grief he lay; nor would the Greeks
A leader so accomplished soon forget;
Yet still a chief they had who marshaled them,
The bastard Medon, son of Oïleus;
His mother was a woman Rhena called.
  Of those of Tricca and high Ithomè,
And of Æchalia, town of Eurytus,
Two excellent physicians were the chiefs,
Wise Podalirius and Machaon,
Sons of the famous Æsculapius.
Thirty dark ships these chiefs accompanied.

Of those who in Ormenium dwell, and round
Hyperia's fountain and Asterium,
And on the white-topped hill of Titanus,
Chief over these was brave Eurypylus.
Forty dark ships this chief accompanied.
Of those of Gyrtona and Argissa,
Of Orthè, Eleon, and white Oloösson,
Of these brave Polypetes was the chief,
Son of Pirithoüs, the son of Jove.
The famous Hippodamia bore him
On the same day that Pirithoüs prevailed
Over the shaggy Centaurs, driving them
E'en from Mount Pelion, far as Æthricè;
His comrade was the stout Leonteus,
Son of Coroneus, son of Cœneus.
Forty dark ships these heroes brought with them.
Twenty-two ships were by Guneus led
From Cyphus; he ruled the brave Enians,
And Perabians on cold Dodona's heights;
They lived by lovely Titaresius,
Whose fair stream flows into the Peneus;
Nor does it with Peneus intermix,
But o'er its silvery surface flows like oil,
For from the river Styx it has its source,
The infernal stream that men and gods adjure.
Prothous, son of Tenthedron, was chief
O'er the Magnesians, who inhabited
The groves of Pelion, exposed to winds,
And on the banks of fair Peneus dwelt.
Forty dark ships this chief accompanied.
These were the chiefs and leaders of the Greeks.
And now, O Muse! relate who was the best,
And who was owner of the finest steeds:
The finest steeds were those of Eumelus—
Apollo raised them in Pieria—
A pair of mares, as swift as birds in speed,
Of the same age were they, color and height,
And terrible upon the battle-field.

The bravest chief was Ajax Telamon,
Since great Achilles had in wrath withdrawn,
For he in valor far exceeded all,
And his steeds too were most magnificent;
But he, enraged with Agamemnon, lay
By his own ships; his idle men meanwhile,
Scattered along the shore, amused themselves
At pitching quoits, and games of archery;
And by the chariots the horses stood,
Cropping the lotus and wild celery;
The chariots themselves were under tents.
Without a chief, the warriors felt lost,
And sauntered round the camp, but did not fight.
But all the rest marched forward to the war,
Their dazzling armor glittering in the sun,
As if the very earth was all on fire.
The ground beneath them groaned, as when great Jove
Shakes in his wrath the land of Arimè,
Where buried deep the giant Typhœus lies;
So as they trod, the earth beneath them shook,
And speedily they marched across the plain.
Iris, Jove's messenger, the tidings brought—
Brought the dread tidings to the men of Troy,
As young and old in Priam's halls they sat
Holding a council. She among them came,
Polites' voice assuming, who, swift of foot,
Stood as a scout upon the burial mound
Of Æsetes, thence to keep watch
When from their camp the Greeks should sally out;
His voice assuming, thus the goddess spake:
Still dost thou waste thy time in talk, old man,
As formerly thou didst in peaceful days!
Dread war approaches now; I have, indeed,
In many a direful conflict mingled,
But never such an army saw before;
Like sand upon the sea-side, or like leaves
They fill the plain and march upon the town.
But, Hector, 'tis to thee I chiefly speak:

Great is the number of our allied troops,
And many tongues and languages they have;
Do thou o'er each a proper leader place,
But o'er Troy's citizens be thou the chief.
She said; and Hector her command obeyed.
The council he dissolved; the people armed;
The city gates were all thrown open wide.
Out poured the army, cavalry and foot,
And mighty was the clamor that arose.
Before the town there is a lofty mound
That rises by itself above the plain—
Men call it Bateïa, but the gods
Say that it is the swift Myrinnè's tomb—
There mustered all the various troops of Troy.
Hector, the mighty chief of nodding plumes,
Was o'er the Trojans; his force was largest,
And by far the best of the whole army.
Chief of the Dardans was Anchises' son,
The brave Æneas, whom fair Venus bore—
A goddess yielding to a mortal's love,
Upon mount Ida's shady mountain top.
His comrades were the valiant Acamas
And Archilochus, sons of Antenor.
Of those of Zeleia, near mount Ida's base,
Drinking the waters of dark Æsepus,
Pandarus was the chief, Lycaon's son,
Whose famous bow Apollo gave to him.
Amphius and Adrastus were the chiefs
Of those of Apæsus and Adrestia,
O'er Pityea and high Teree;
Of Merops, of Percotè, they were sons,
Who as a prophet held the highest rank.
He from the war had wished to keep his boys,
They, their kind father's wishes disobeyed,
And in the murderous conflict lost their lives.
Of those round Percotè and Practius,
Divine Arisba, Sestos, and Abydos,
Asius, the son of Hyrcatus, was chief—

A prince of heroes, who, with fiery steeds,
Had from Arisba come, on Sellè's stream.
The bold Pelasgians, skillful with the spear,
Hippothous led; they inhabited
Larissa's fertile plains; his comrade chief
And brother, was Pyleus; sons they were
Of noble Lethus, the Pelasgian,
Son of Sentamus, of the race of Mars.
Acamas, and the hero, Pyrous,
Led on the Thracians, whose home was by
The flowing water of the Hellespont.
Euphemus, son of Trœzinus, was chief
Of the Cicones, men renowned in war.
Pyræchmes, the Pæonians led—a tribe
Who fought with darts—their home Amydon was,
A distant country, by the Axius laved—
Axius, the fairest river on the earth.
From the Heneti, Pylæmenes came—
Henetia, famed for mules; he was the chief
Over the Paphlagonians, and those
Who dwelt round Sesamus and Cytorus,
And round the stream Parthenius, and Cromna,
Ægialus, and mount Erythine.
Odius and Epistrophus were chiefs
Over the Halizonians—a tribe
From far Alybè, where are silver mines.
The prophet Ennomus and Chromis led
The Mysians; but little did his skill
The prophet aid, for him Achilles slew,
In the dark stream, and with him many more.
Godlike Ascanius and Phorcys led,
From far Ascania, the Phrygians;
Most eager were they to engage in war.
O'er the Mæonians, Antiphus was chief,
And Mestes, sons of Pylamenes,
Born on the lake Gyges; these were chiefs
Of the Mæonians, near mount Tmolus.
Naustes was o'er the strange-tongued Carians,

Who in Miletus dwelt, and Pthira,
And by Mæander's ever-winding stream,
And on Mycalè's lofty mountain top.
His brother chief was famed Amphimacus,
Who, like a silly girl, to battle went
Bedecked with gold; but all his jewelry
Saved not his life; he by Achilles fell,
Who slew him by the stream and took his gold.
  Over the Lycians was brave Glaucus
And Sarpedon, who led the Lycians
From Lycia and Xanthus' whirling stream.

BOOK III.

THE DUEL.

ARGUMENT.

The armies being ready to engage, a single combat is agreed upon between Menelaus and Paris for the determination of the war.—Iris calls Helen to witness the fight.—Paris is conquered, but Venus comes to his assistance, and conveys him away in a cloud to his chamber, where Helen returns to meet him.

THUS were both armies marshaled for the fight.
As for the Trojans, they tumultuous marched
With battle shouts, like flocks of clamorous birds;
Just as the cranes, escaping from the north,
Over the ocean wing their noisy flight,
Bringing destruction to the Pigmy race.
But with one heart, inflamed with martial fire,
The Greeks, well disciplined, in silence moved,
As when the south wind, on some mountain-top
Brings a thick mist, which shepherds much dislike,
But to the robber oft of service proves—
For one a stone's-throw then can scarcely see—
So rose the clouds of dust beneath their feet,
As they with rapid march traversed the plain.
But when they now each other had approached,
The godlike Paris from the Trojan ranks
Stepped forth. A mantle from his shoulders hung
Of leopard's skin; a bow he bore, and sword;
And, shaking in his hand two glittering darts,
He challenged any of the bravest Greeks
To meet him, and engage in mortal strife.

Him when the noble Menelaus saw
Thus stalking haughtily in sight of all,
As when a hungry lion spies with joy
The carcass of a stag or mountain-goat,
Nor can be driven off by dogs or men,
So greedy is he to devour the prey—
Thus rejoiced Menelaus when he saw
The godlike Paris; for he thought that now
He would have satisfaction for his wrongs;
Down from his chariot with his arms he sprang.
But Paris saw him, and was conscience-struck,
And back again within the ranks withdrew.
As when some traveler on a mountain path
Beholds a serpent unexpectedly,
Backward he starts, his cheeks grow instant pale,
And a chill tremor seizes all his limbs—
So Paris shrunk within the Trojan ranks
At thus encountering noble Menelaus.
His brother Hector saw him, and rebuked:
Oh, cursed Paris!—beautiful in form,
Fond of the fair sex, and seducer, too,
Would thou had'st ne'er been born, or died when young,
Rather than thus to live a sad disgrace,
Not only to thyself, but to thy friends!
How will the long-haired Greeks all laugh at thee,
Seeing thy handsome face and splendid form!
They took thee for some valiant champion;
But strength and valor are no gifts of thine.
How durst thou, such a one, to cross the sea
And with thy comrades visit foreign lands,
And from the Apian country steal a dame—
The beauteous spouse of military men;
A sad misfortune to thy grieving sire,
To thine own city, and thy countrymen—
But to thine enemies a joyful thing,
And to thyself most base and scandalous.
Could'st thou not meet the warlike Menelaus!
Thou then had'st known what kind of man he is

Whose wife thou hast enticed to marry thee.
Ah! little will thy tuneful harp avail,
Thy face, thy hair,—the gifts that Venus gave,—
When mingled in the dust thy form shall lie!
Truly, the Trojans are a patient race,
Or for thy misdeeds they had long ago
Put a stone jacket* on thy dainty limbs!
 Thus Hector spake; and Paris thus replied:
Hector! much reason hast thou for thy words,
Nor should I angry be at thy reproof;
For thy undaunted heart is like an axe
In a ship-builder's hand, that cuts through all;
So is thy heart in thy intrepid breast!
But chide me not for Venus' lovely gifts,
Since heavenly gifts are not to be despised,
And the gods grant them just as they see fit.
Yet if thou would'st that I engage in fight,
Cause all the Greeks and Trojans to sit down;
Then in the midst place me and Menelaus,
And let us fight for Helen and her wealth;
Whoe'er shall conquer, let the dame be his,
And let him take her and her riches home.
You others then shall strike a solemn league,
And thus securely dwell in fruitful Troy,
Whilst they again to Argos shall return—
The land of horses and of lovely dames.
 He said; and Hector greatly was rejoiced;
And going in the midst, he with his spear
Restrained his troops, and made them all sit down.
 The Greeks then aimed at him their bows and darts;
But Agamemnon saw him, and cried out:
Shoot not, ye Greeks!—ye Argive youths, be still!
It seems that Hector has a word to say.
 He said; and all were silent and restrained.
Then in the midst the helm-plumed Hector spake:
Hear me, ye Trojans! and ye well-armed Greeks!—

* Stoned him to death.

Hear now what Paris says, on whose account
This war began. He asks you both to pause,
And lay your glittering arms upon the ground;
Then in the midst place him and Menelaus
To fight alone for Helen and her wealth.
Whoe'er shall conquer, let the dame be his,
And let him take her and her riches home;
We others then will be good friends again.
He said; and all sat quiet, nor replied.
Then in the midst brave Menelaus spake:
Now hear me, too, for sorrowful I am,
Nor wish that Greece nor Troy should longer fight,
Since ye have suffered miseries enough
About this quarrel of myself and Paris,
Whose challenge I accept, and let him fall
Who conquered is, and fate ordains to die;
But all ye others separate in peace.
Then hither bring two lambs, a white and black,
One for the earth the other for the sun,
And we a third will offer up to Jove.
Then Priam fetch, that he may take the oath,
For in his sons we have but little faith;
And oaths to Jove must be inviolate.
Young men, besides, are not of stable mind,
But an old man is prudent, and foresees
What plan 'tis best each party should pursue.
He said; and Greeks and Trojans both rejoiced,
Hoping to rest from miserable war.
They backed their chariots against the ranks,
And leaping from them, laid aside their arms,
Which on the ground they stacked, in order due;
Then Hector sent two heralds to the town
To call king Priam, and to fetch the lambs;
And Agamemnon Talthybius sent
Back to the ships, his sacrifice to bring;
The herald hastened and obeyed his words.
Meanwhile, the swift-winged goddess, Iris, flew
To tell the lovely Helen what transpired.

She took the form of fair Laodicè,
Wife of Helicaon, Antenor's son,
Of Priam's daughters called the handsomest.
She found her in the hall, busy at work,
Weaving a splendid piece of tapestry,
On which were pictured all the battle scenes
That the brave Greeks and Trojans underwent
On her account; close by her side she stood,
And thus the swift-winged messenger began:
Come hither, child, and see the glorious deeds
Of the brave Trojans, and the well-armed Greeks,
Who in sad war have heretofore engaged
And made the plain a scene of misery;
But now their bloody arms are laid aside,
And leaning quietly upon their shields,
They sit upon the ground and fight no more;
But Paris and the godlike Menelaus
In single combat will for thee contend;
And he who conquers shall thy husband be.
  Thus Iris spake; and in fair Helen's breast
Awaked sweet memories of her former spouse,
Her home, her kindred, and her native land,
Over her head throwing a silvery veil,
With tearful eyes she from her chamber went,
Nor went alone; two maids accompanied her:
Æthra was one, the daughter of Pitheus;
The other, Clymenè, a bright-eyed girl.
Crossing the town, they reached the Scæan gate—
There sat old Priam, Clytius, and Lampus,
Panthus too, and bold Hicetäon,
With Thymœtes, and Ucalegon,
And wise Antenor, famous counselor;
All these were seated at the Scæan gate.
Old men they were, whose fighting days were past;
But talk they could like chirping grasshoppers,
That sit on trees and sing incessantly.
  Thus sat Troy's counselors upon the tower;
But when the lovely Helen they espied

They thus to one another made remark :
No wonder 'tis that Greeks and Trojans both
Have for a dame like this such woes endured :
She is a goddess, both in face and form,
Yet would that she were back in her own land,
And not still here, a curse to us and ours.
Thus they spake ; but Priam called to her :
Come hither, my dear child, and sit by me,
That thou mayest see thy former spouse, and friends ;
I blame thee not, for 'tis the gods that brought
These Greeks against us in disastrous war.
Come, tell me, who is yonder noble Greek,
That tall and splendid-looking warrior ?
Truly, there are some taller e'en than he,
But in majestic beauty he excels,
And has the air and bearing of a king.
He said ; and lovely Helen thus replied :
Respected father, loved by me and feared,
Would I had died when on that day I came,
Thy son accompanying, leaving my home,
My marriage-bed, my daughter, and my friends ;
But 'twas not so decreed. Ah, woe is me !
As for thy questions I will speak the truth :
Yon man is Agamemnon, Atreus' son,
A worthy king and valiant warrior ;
By marriage, he was once my brother too,
Wretch that I am ! could it be possible !
She said ; and he admiring, thus replied :
Blest son of Atreus, great and fortunate !
Ruling such numbers of heroic Greeks !
In times gone by, I into Phrygia went,
The land of vines ; I hosts of Phrygians saw ;
Horsemen by Mygdon and by Otreus led ;
I saw vast numbers of them there encamped
Upon the banks of the Sangarius.
I was their ally on the day they went
And fought against the famous Amazons ;
But even they were not so numerous
As these battalions of the black-eyed Greeks.

Again, Ulysses seeing, thus he spake:
Tell me, dear child, who is that other man?
Less, by a head, than Agamemnon he,
But broader shouldered, and of stouter frame;
Upon the ground his glittering arms are laid,
Whilst he goes moving up and down the ranks
Like a huge ram among a flock of sheep.
He said; and beauteous Helen thus replied:
That is Laertes' son, the wise Ulysses,
Born in the barren isle of Ithaca,
Yet famed for wisdom and sagacity.
Antenor interrupting, then began:
Lady, I can avouch thou speak'st the truth;
For once with Menelaus, Ulysses came
Upon an embassy on thy account;
They were my guests, making my house their home:
I scanned their characters, and knew them well.
When in the Trojan council they took part,
And on the floor brave Menelaus stood,
He seemed the greatest; but in their seats,
Ulysses had a more majestic look.
At speaking, too, was Menelaus good;
His style was pure, nor was he too profuse,
Nor did he like young men at random talk;
But when the wise Ulysses rose to speak,
He stood at first with eyes upon the ground,
Nor did he wave his scepter gracefully;
But, like an awkward person, held it still—
You would have almost thought he was a fool;
But when his mouth he opened, and harangued
In tones sonorous, with majestic voice,
His words of eloquence like snow-flakes fell;
Few orators with him could then have vied!
Then we all knew what kind of man he was.
Next, seeing Ajax, Priam spake again:
Who is that other Greek, so tall and great,
A head and shoulders taller than the rest?

Him answering, fair Helen thus replied:
That is great Ajax, bulwark of the Greeks.
And yonder, godlike Idomeneus stands,
Who rules o'er Crete, and round him are his chiefs;
Oft when he came from Crete he was our guest.
And now I see a host of other Greeks
Whom I know well, and could repeat their names;
But two great chiefs I miss—where can they be?
Castor and Pollux—a great horseman one;
The other, famous as a pugilist.
Brothers of mine, of the same mother born.
Did they not here from Lacedæmon come,
Or did they like the others cross the sea?
Yet will not in the bloody war take part,
Ashamed to own a sister so disgraced!
She said, not knowing her poor brothers lay
In distant Lacedæmon in their graves.
But now the heralds to the city came,
Bearing the pledges of the gods, two lambs
And a skin flagon filled with precious wine.
A splendid goblet and two golden cups
Were borne by Idæus, who to Priam came,
And, standing by the old man, thus began:
Son of Laomedon, arise! the chiefs
Of Greece and Troy invite thee to the plain,
There to administer a sacred oath,
For Paris and brave Menelaus will fight
In single combat for this Grecian dame.
Who conquers takes the lady and her wealth,
And all the others will be friends again,
We dwelling still secure in fruitful Troy,
Whilst they again to Argos shall return,
The land of horses and of lovely dames.
He said. The old man, trembling, gave command
To yoke his steeds, and quickly they obeyed:
The chariot mounting, he took up the reins,
And by him in the car Antenor stood.
Thus through the gate they flew and reached the plain;

But when the Trojans and the Greeks they reached,
Alighting in the midst of all, they stood.
Then Agamemnon, king of men, arose,
And with him wise Ulysses. The heralds then
Brought forth the sacrifice, and mingled wine;
On the king's hands pure water next they poured,—
Next his sharp dagger Agamemnon drew,
Which in his girdle by his sword he wore,
And from the lamb's head cut a lock of hair,
Which was distributed among the chiefs.
Then, with uplifted hands, the monarch prayed:
Oh, father Jove! ruling from Ida's mount,
Glorious and mighty! and thou, oh, Sun!
Beholding all below; ye Rivers too,
And Earth, and ye infernal deities,
Who punish perjured mortals after death,
Be witness all, and guard this sacred oath:
Should Paris conquer and slay Menelaus,
Let him fair Helen take, and all her wealth,
Whilst we will re-embark and steer for home.
But should the fair-haired Menelaus win,
The Trojans then the lady must restore,
With all her goods, and give the Greeks besides
A proper compensation for the war,
To be recorded for posterity,—
Which if they fail to do, I here will stay
And see the war out to its bitter end.
He said, and cut the lambs' throats with his knife,
And laid them on the earth expiring.
Then from the goblet they poured out the wine
Into the cups, still praying to the gods;
And thus each Greek and Trojan joined in prayer:
Oh, mighty Jove, and all ye deities!
Whoever first these solemn vows shall break,
Grant that the brains of him and his may be
Poured on the ground as now we pour this wine,
And may his wife be ravished by his foe.
They said; but Jove regarded not their prayer.

Then to the warriors king Priam spake:
Hear me, ye Trojans and ye well-armed Greeks,
Now I return again to lofty Troy,
For never with these eyes could I behold
The combat of my son with Menelaus.
Jove only knows, and all the deities,
Which of the two is destined to be slain.
He said; and in his chariot placed the lambs;—
Then, mounting, he stood up and took the reins—
Antenor too rode in the splendid car—
Soon back to Troy they both with speed returned.
But Hector, Priam's son, and wise Ulysses,
Measured the ground, and then the lots prepared,
Using a brazen helmet as an urn,
To know who first should cast his glittering spear.
The people, gathering round, looked on and prayed:
Oh, father Jove! most great and glorious!
Whoever is the cause of all these woes
Let him be slain, and grant that we, the rest,
May make a league, and live henceforth in peace.
Thus prayed the people as they stood around.
Then Hector, chieftain of the nodding plumes,
With face averted, shook the brazen casque,
And from the helmet Paris' name leaped forth.
The people took their seats upon the ground,
Near their fleet steeds and by their shining arms.
Then Paris in bright armor clad himself:
First on his thighs his splendid greaves he placed,
Fitted with silver clasps; next on his breast
The corselet of Lycaon he put on—
He was his brother—and it fitted well;
His silver-hilted sword hung by his side,
And on his arm his huge and massy shield.
Upon his head his helmet then he placed,
With horse-hair crest, that nodded dreadfully;
Then with his hands he grasped his mighty spear.
In the same style was Menelaus armed.
Both parties thus arrayed, they in the midst

Gazed on each other with ferocious looks ;
The Greeks and Trojans wondering beheld,
Shaking their spears, the combatants approached ;
And Paris first his glittering weapon threw,
Striking the center of his rival's shield,
Which was not pierced, for the spear point was bent
Against the buckler's massy covering.
Then the brave Menelaus his foe attacked,
First offering up a prayer to father Jove :
Grant, mighty Jove ! that Paris may be slain,
Who first inflicted injury on me,
That men hereafter may be careful how
They break the laws of hospitality.
He said; and, aiming, hurled his brazen spear,
Striking the shield of Paris in the midst.
Through his strong shield it went, and breastplate too,
And, his soft tunic cutting grazed his flesh ;
But he stooped low, and thus preserved his life.
Then, his sword drawing, Menelaus rushed
Against his foe and struck him on the crest ;
But the false weapon, shivering with the blow,
Flew into pieces, dropping from his hands.
Towards heaven the warrior looked and groaned aloud :
Oh, Jove ! most disobliging of the gods,
I thought to be revenged for Paris' wrongs,
But now my sword is shivered in my hands,
And I have hurled my brazen spear in vain.
He said ; and, rushing, seized his horse-hair crest ;
Pulling him down, he dragged him towards the Greeks,
And choked him with the band beneath his chin.
And now he would have triumphed o'er his foe
Had not the goddess Venus interposed,
Who cut the beautiful embroidered strap
And left an empty helmet in his hands.
He hurled it with contempt among the Greeks,
And still rushed on to slay his Trojan foe ;
But Venus saved him by her power divine,
Bearing him off, wrapped in a fleecy cloud,

And in his scented chamber sat him down.
Then, flying off, she went to call fair Helen,
Whom on the tower 'mid Trojan dames she found,
And, gently nudging, shook her fragrant veil,—
First an old woman's likeness putting on,
Who used to spin for her in Lacedæmon,
And whom in former days she loved right well.
In such disguise the goddess Venus spake:
  Come hither; Paris calls thee to come home.
On a rich couch he in his chamber sits—
Splendid he looks in beauty and attire:
Nor would you think that he had fighting been,
But rather for a dance was just prepared,
Or just returned from some gay festival.
  She said; and stirred fair Helen's tender heart,
Who, when the deity she recognized,
Seeing her blooming tints, her face divine,
Her lovely bosom, and her sparkling eyes,
Awe-struck she stood, and wondering much, replied:
  Why dost thou, goddess, make me thus thy sport?
Still wilt thou lead me to some distant town
Of fair Mæonia, or Phrygia,
To please another favored man of thine?
Or art thou oome to take unhappy me
Back to my former husband Menelaus
Because o'er Paris he has victor been?—
Take him thyself, renounce the happy gods,
Nor on Olympus set thy foot again.
Be his close confidante, keep him from harm,
Till he his mistress make thee, or his wife.
But I will never to his couch return;
Shame and confusion would my portion be,
And all the Trojan dames would censure me;
Truly I now have miseries enough.
  Then Venus, angry at her words, replied:
Oh, silly wretch! provoke me not, lest I
Become thy foe henceforth, and hate thee now
As I before have wonderfully loved.

I can disgust the Greeks, and Trojans too,
And make them both their vengeance wreak on thee
As the prime cause of their calamities,
And thou, poor soul, wilt perish miserably.
  She said; and Helen, fearing her, obeyed.
Wrapped in a splendid white transparent veil,
The goddess leading, she in silence went,
Unnoticed by the other Trojan dames;
When to her husband's handsome house she came
Her maids retired to their usual tasks.
  But she ascended to the lofty hall,
And in her chamber Venus sat her down
Upon a seat nigh to where Paris was.
With downcast eyes, there beauteous Helen sat,
And thus with chiding words her lord addressed:
So, from the fight I see thou hast returned;
Would thou had'st died, slain by that noble man,
My former spouse! Oft have I heard thee boast
How much superior to him thou wast
In valor and in skill—go call him out,
And have with Menelaus another fight.
But no—take my advice, let him alone,
Nor show such folly to the world again,
Or by his sword thou surely wilt be slain.
  Thus Helen spake; and Paris thus replied:
Chide me not, lady, quite so bitterly;
True—with Minerva's aid the Greek has won;
This is his lucky day, and mine may come,
For I have patron gods as well as he.
But come, to love's sweet pleasures let us yield,
For never such desire I felt before;
Not e'en when first I carried thee away
From pleasant Lacedæmon, o'er the sea,
Indulging in thy love in Cranaë's isle,
As I the tender passion feel just now.
  He said; and led her to the splendid couch,
Their nuptial-bed, and there they lay reclined.
  Meanwhile the baffled Menelaus raved

Like a fierce lion, seeking through the ranks
Paris to find; but none could point him out;
None out of love had hid him, if they could,
For all the Trojans hated him like hell.
And now king Agamemnon rose and spake:
Hear me, ye Trojans, Dardans, and Allies!
It seems that Menelaus the victor is:
The Argive Helen now surrender up,
And all her wealth; and compensation give,
That may recorded be for future times.
He said; and all the Greeks his words approved.

BOOK IV.

THE BREACH OF THE TRUCE.

ARGUMENT.

The gods deliberate about the war, and agree that it shall continue; whereupon Minerva descends, and persuades Pandorus, the archer, to break the truce by shooting an arrow at Menelaus.—Agamemnon goes through the army, exhorting the chiefs, and encouraging them for the battle.

On heaven's golden pavement sat enthroned
Almighty Jove, and all the deities;
From a gold vase fair Hebè nectar poured;
The gods all drank, and drinking looked on Troy.
Then Jove began to tease his lovely spouse,
And thus in words of raillery addressed:
Two heavenly patrons Menelaus has,
The Argive Juno and the wise Minerva;
But they upon the background always keep,
And seem contented merely to look on;
Whilst smiling Venus by her Paris stands,
Forever ready to protect and aid.
But Menelaus now the victor is.
Let us deliberate what next to do,—
Whether this dreadful war shall still go on,
Or peace shall be the order of the day.
If peace your pleasure is, then Troy shall stand,
And conquering Menelaus may return,
He and the Argive Helen, to their homes.
He said; but Juno and Minerva sighed:
They by each other sat, devising ills
Against the Trojans. Minerva spake not;

Indignant at her sire, she boiled with rage;
But Juno made no secret of her wrath,
And thus addressed her venerable spouse:
Oh, son of Saturn! most tormenting thou,
What hast thou said? Is all my toil in vain,
And must my tedious labors go for naught?
My very steeds are tired of their work,
So wearisome the task I have assumed
In gathering such a mighty host of Greeks
To punish Priam's race, and ruin Troy;
Do as thou wilt; but we cannot approve.
Then with a sigh, cloud-mantled Jove replied:
Oh, strange celestial! full of wrath and spite,
What harm have Priam and his sons done thee
That thus thou dost forever persecute,
And seek to ruin the proud town of Troy?
Go on, then, if thou must! enter her gates,
And glut thy vengeance to the uttermost!
Slay Priam and his sons and eat their flesh!
And then perhaps thou wilt be satisfied,
So that no strife hereafter may arise
About this matter, between me and thee.
But this I say, and bear it in thy mind:
Should I with any city become wroth,
Whose people happen to be friends of thine,
And wish to lay it level with the ground,
Seek not to thwart, but let me have my way
E'en as I now allow thee to have thine;
For of all cities underneath the sun
And starry skies, I honor sacred Troy,
And Priam and his sons, and all the Trojans;
For there my altars ever have been piled
With smoking sacrifice of bulls and lambs;
And pure libations too of costliest wines,
I always had; such piety they showed.
He said; and dark-eyed Juno thus replied:
Three cities of the earth my favorites are,
Argos, and Sparta, and the great Mycenè;

If thou with them art wroth, destroy them all:
I would not wish to hinder if I could,
So much superior in power art thou.
Yet 'tis not meet that I should thwarted be,
For I a goddess am, of Saturn born,
Of the same race and lineage as thou,
And, besides that, thy lawful consort too;
But thou art monarch of the earth and skies,
We with each other then should harmonize,
And so the other gods will all agree.
Then quickly to Minerva give command
To go and mingle with the combatants,
And so contrive it that the men of Troy
May break the truce, and thus renew the war.
She said; nor did the Thunderer refuse,
But thus addressed Minerva, with winged words:
Go, quick! and mingle with the combatants,
And so contrive it that the men of Troy
May break the truce and thus renew the war!
So saying, he the goddess started off.
She took her flight down from the Olympian mount,
Descending to the earth like a strange star
Which shoots across the sky, emitting sparks—
A sign to soldiers and to mariners.
Thus in their midst the splendid goddess came;
Both Greeks and Trojans saw, and wondering gazed,
And each bold warrior to his friend remarked,
That such a portent was not sent for naught,
But must an omen be of peace or war.
Through the armed throng the goddess onward moved,
The form assuming of Laödocus,
A warrior brave, son of Antenor.
Pandarus she sought, Lycaön's son,
A godlike chief, for strength and valor famed.
She found him, with his spearmen all around,
Who followed him from far Æsepus' stream.
Approaching near, the goddess him addressed:
Will brave Lycaön's son be ruled by me?

Then let him aim a shaft at Menelaus;
Great honor Troy would show him for the deed,
But most of all prince Paris would applaud,
And would bestow on thee a rich reward
Should he behold his warlike rival slain,
Pierced by an arrow from thy skillful bow.
Then come, take aim at noble Menelaus,—
First to the archer-god, Apollo, vowing
That thou a splendid hecatomb of lambs
Wilt offer as a sacrifice when thou
Safe shalt return to Zelia's sacred town.
  Thus spake the goddess; foolish, he obeyed.
For, from its case his polished bow he drew,
Made from the horns of a wild mountain-goat,
Slain by himself, who struck it on the breast
Lying in ambush; springing from a cleft
Headlong among the rocks the body fell.
The branching horns were sixteen palms in length:
Which being smoothed were made into a bow,
Finished complete, and tipped with burnished gold.
The bow he bent, with one end on the ground;
His comrades stood beside him with their shields,
To guard him from an onset of the Greeks
Before he had accomplished his design.
Then from his quiver he the lid drew off,
And from it took a deadly feathered shaft,
Which hastily he fitted to the string.
Then to Apollo solemnly he vowed
That he a splendid hecatomb of lambs
Would offer up a sacrifice when he
Safe should return to Zelia's sacred town.
The notch and string he next together brought,
And to his breast the deadly weapon pulled,
The iron head drawn to the very bow,
Which now was almost to a circle bent.
Loud twanged the string, the creaking horns flew back,
And swift the impatient arrow winged its way
Into the center of the Grecian host.

Nor did the gods desert thee, Menelaus,
For there Minerva was, protecting thee.
She turned aside the arrow from thy heart,
Just as a mother brushes off a fly
From the soft features of her sleeping babe;
The shaft she turned against the leathern belt,
Near the gold clasps where the brass corselet met;
Through these the arrow went, and passing on,
Grazed the chief's flesh, and blood began to flow.
As when a Carian or Lydian maid
Tinges white ivory with crimson dye
The cheek-piece for the trappings of a steed—
With care she keeps it out of public view,
Though many a warrior would covet it,
For 'tis intended only for a king—
A splendid ornament for man and horse—
So thy fair thighs and ankles, Menelaus,
Were with the trickling purple blood distained.
King Agamemnon shuddered at the sight,
And his brave brother, Menelaus, too;
But when he saw the arrow's-head outside,
And knew the shaft had not so deeply gone,
His spirits he recovered, and felt safe.
But Agamemnon took him by the hand,
And with a groan (his comrades groaning, too)
Thus to his much beloved brother spake:
Oh, brother, 'twas a fatal league we formed,
When thou stood'st forth a champion for Greece,
Since the false Trojans have their contract broke
And wounded thee. Yet not in vain shall be
These solemn covenants, this blood of lambs,
These pure libations, and these right hands joined,
In which we trusted; for, if broken now,
Great Jove will vindicate in time to come,
And send a heavy penalty on them,
And on their wives and helpless little ones;
For well I know the destined day will come,
When sacred Troy shall miserably fall,

And Priam and his people be destroyed;
When Jove himself shall from the clouds look down,
And flash his angry ægis over them,
Enraged at such an act of treachery.
But great my grief, oh, Menelaus! will be,
If thou shalt perish, meeting thus thy doom!
O'erwhelmed with shame to Greece I will return,
And my dear Argos see—my native land!
For then the Greeks will turn their thoughts towards home,
And bid farewell to Helen and to Troy.
But under Trojan soil thy bones will rot,
E'en within sight of our unfinished work:
Then some proud Trojan, leaping on thy tomb,
Will thus exclaim, So perish all the schemes
Of Agamemnon, who hither led a host
In vain; and now he leads them back,
Leaving the valiant Menelaus behind!
Thus will they speak; then hide me, yawning earth!
He said; and fair-haired Menelaus replied:
Be of good cheer, nor thus alarm the Greeks,
The deadly arrow struck no vital part;
The well-forged brass, the girdle and the belt
Weakened its force, and thus protected me.
Him answering, Agamemnon thus replied:
I trust it may be so, oh, Menelaus!
Yet let us for a good physician send,
Who may the pain assuage, and heal the wound.
He said; and thus Talthybius addressed:
Go, call Machaon here, Talthybius,
Son of the famous Æsculapius—
That he may look at wounded Menelaus,
Who by some Trojan archer has been shot—
A joy to him, but a great grief to us.
He said; nor did the herald disobey,
But for Machaon sought among the Greeks.
He found him with his warriors around,
Who followed him from Tricca, land of steeds;
And, standing by him, thus Talthybius spake:

Up, son of Æsculapius—arise!
'Tis the king calls thee, noble Agamemnon,
That thou mayest look on wounded Menelaus,
Who by some Trojan archer has been shot—
A joy to him, but a great grief to us.
He said, and stirred the good physician's heart,
Who, through the ranks, proceeded to the spot
Where the fair Menelaus surrounded stood
By all the best and bravest of the chiefs.
At once the arrow from the belt he drew,
Breaking the barb,—the girdle then he loosed,
And the brass-plated belt; he saw the wound,
And, wiping off the blood, applied some drugs
Which the wise Chiron to his father gave.
Whilst thus they cared for valiant Menelaus
The Trojans took up arms and made advance,
And the brave Greeks again prepared for war.
Then might king Agamemnon have been seen,
Not backward, nor remiss, but full of zeal,
And rather hurrying on the glorious fight.
His splendid chariot and his snorting steeds
He with Eurymedon, his servant, left,
Charging him strictly to keep close at hand,
So that he might resume them when fatigued;
But he, on foot, mingled among the Greeks,
And whom he saw most eager for the fight
He moved still further with inspiring words:
Keep up your martial spirit, oh, ye Greeks!
For Jove will ne'er with perjured men take part;
And these truce-breakers soon will be the prey
Of ravening birds; their city too shall fall,
And in our ships their children and their wives
We will transport triumphant to our homes.
But whom he found downhearted or remiss
He thus addressed in words of stern rebuke:
Shame on ye, Greeks! Why stand you thus aghast,
Like timid hares which, by the dogs run down,
Stand paralyzed with fright? Will ye stay here

Till to our very ships the Trojans come
To see if Jove will to our aid step in?
Thus through the host he went giving command.
  Then to the Cretan warriors he came;
Round Idomeneus, their king, they stood,
Who, like some forest boar, in strength excelled;
Near him his comrade Meriones was.
The king beheld them both with looks of joy,
And kindly Idomeneus thus addressed:
Oh, Idomeneus! much I honor thee
In peace and war, and at our festivals,
When the red wine we quaff in flowing cups.
There all the other Greeks by measure drink;
But thou and I, more honored than the rest,
Drink as we please from goblets ever full;
Be valiant now as thou hast ever been.
  To him the Cretan monarch thus replied:
Oh, Agamemnon! I thy comrade dear
Have ever been, and will continue such;
But quickly put the battle in array,
Since the false Trojans have their promise broke,
And death and woe belong to truce-breakers.
  He said; and joyfully the king passed on.
To the two Ajaxes he next approached:
They were both armed and ready for the fight—
They and their masses of dense infantry—
As when a shepherd, gazing from a hill,
Sees a dark cloud arising from the sea,
Driven by northern winds, and black as pitch,
Over the ocean it advances fast,
Bringing a mighty tempest in its train.
He, at the sight amazed, collects his flock
And drives them underneath a sheltering cave.
So with the Ajaxes, to battle moved,
Like clouds, battalions of dark infantry,
Bristling with shields and spears. The king beheld
And thus with joy the warlike chiefs addressed:
Ye Ajaxes, to you I need not speak,

So nobly ye lead on your men to war.
By Jove! I only wish that such a heart
Was in the breast of all our warriors!
Soon, then, would Priam's sacred city fall,
And by the Greeks be captured and destroyed.
He said; and, passing by, went further on,
Where Nestor stood, sweet orator of Pylos;
He found the old man marshaling his men
Round him—his comrades were great Pelagon,
Bias, and Chromius and Alastor,
And Hæmon, too, a famous warrior.
The chariots and horse he placed in front,
And in the rear his choicest infantry,
To act as outer bulwarks in the war;
His worst of troops he in the center placed,
So that e'en cowards would be forced to fight.
First to his cavalry he gave command,
And bade them keep compact, nor spread themselves,
And let no horseman, trusting to his skill,
Go forth alone to combat with the foe,
Nor lag behind, so will ye stronger be;
And in his chariot let each warrior keep,
And, standing there, thrust with his outstretched spear.
So in old times our fathers used to fight,
And thus secured their splendid victories;
Thus the old warrior, versed so long in war,
His troops exhorted, giving sound advice.
With joy king Agamemnon beheld
And thus addressed his venerable friend:
I wish, old man, thy strength and vigor were
Such as thy heart; but age creeps o'er us all—
Would'st that thou could'st thy years exchange for youth!
Him answering then, Geranian Nestor spoke:
I wish, indeed, oh, king! I was as when
The godlike Ereuthalion I slew;
But all things are not given at one time.
Then I had youth, but now old age creeps on,
Yet with my cavalry I mean to go,

And hope to aid with counsel and advice,
The proper sphere of those advanced in years;
But let the young men, strong and vigorous,
Brandish the sword and hurl the glittering spear.
He said; and joyfully the king passed on,
And found Menestheus, a horseman famed,
With his Athenian warriors around;
And near him also wise Ulysses stood,
He and his Cephellanians, good men;
But they had not the battle shout yet heard,
Since scarcely had the troops begun to move.
So they stood waiting for some other Greeks
To approach the Trojans and begin the fight.
The king beheld them waiting for the rest,
And with reproving words addressed them thus:
Oh, king Menestheus! and Ulysses,
Thou man of wisdom and of crafty arts,
Why stand ye trembling waiting for the rest?
Your part it was to be the first in fight.
When I a banquet for the chiefs prepare,
Ye then are sure to be among the first;
Then ye delight the roasted meats to eat,
And quaff with pleasure the delicious wine;
But now spectators merely ye would be,
And ten battalions of the Greeks might fall
Before ye take up arms and stir yourselves.
But sternly thus Ulysses made reply:
What words, oh, king! have fallen from thy lips!
How canst thou say we stand and hesitate?
When once the battle fairly shall begin,
Then wilt thou see Ulysses, if thou look'st,
Among the foremost of the combatants.
Thy words were rashly spoke and out of place.
Thus spake Ulysses; but the monarch smiled,
Seeing him angry, and continued thus:
Oh, wise Ulysses! I but gently chide
Nor would presume to give advice to thee.
I know what friendship in thy bosom dwells,

And in these matters we both think alike;
Go on, and if aught evil has been said,
With Heaven's help it shall all righted be.
He said; and leaving him proceeded on.
He found Tydeus' son, great Diomed,
Standing amid his chariots and his steeds;
And near him was his comrade Sthenelus.
The monarch on the youthful hero looked,
And with reproving words addressed him thus:
Ah me! why standest thou here, oh, Diomed!
Trembling and gazing on the battle-field?
Thy father, great Tydeus, did not so;
He in the fight the foremost ever was,
So fame reports him, for I knew him not.
He once a stranger to Mycenè went
Unguarded, with his comrade Polyneces;
They went there seeking for auxiliaries
To help them in the war with sacred Thèbes.
Mycenè willing was to grant their suit,
But warned by mighty Jove, she changed her mind.
Then the ambassadors departed home,
And reached Æsepus' grassy rush-fringed shores.
Next was Tydeus sent to sacred Thèbes;
There many Thèbans banqueting he found,
In Eteocles' splendid palace hall;
Nor did he fear although a stranger he,
Alone among so many foreigners,
But challenged any to a wrestling match.
They wrestled, and with ease he conquered all;
Minerva was his friend and aided him.
The Thèbans were enraged, and fifty youths
Went out to waylay him on his return;
Mæon and Lycophontes led the band.
But the conspirators effected naught,
For, except Mæon, Tydeus slew them all.
Him, warned by Jove, he spared and sent him home.
Such was great Tydeus, who a son begat,
Greater in words, in deeds inferior.

He said; but Diomed made no reply.
Abashed he stood before his king's rebuke;
Not so his comrade Sthenelus, who spake:
Why liest thou thus, oh, Agamemnon!
Thou knowest better, and should'st speak the truth?
'Twas we that captured seven-gated Thèbes
With fewer troops; we scaled her sacred wall,
Led on by auguries and helped by Jove,
The wicked Thèbans perished in their sins.
Such were our deeds; then speak not of the past,
Nor put our fathers on a par with us.
He said; but Diomed rebuked him thus:
Be calm, friend Sthenelus, and hold thy peace.
I am by no means angry with our king
For stirring up his people to the war.
Should the Greeks conquer and take sacred Troy,
Great glory will be his; but should they fail,
Shame and confusion will his portion be;
But come, and let us for the fight prepare.
So saying, from his chariot he leaped
Down to the ground; dreadful his armor rang,
And stoutest hearts might then have quailed with fear.
As when upon the loud resounding shore
A mighty wave, impelled by northern winds,
Comes swelling onward; lifting itself, it breaks
With dreadful roar against the jutting rocks,
And spits its white foam over all the sea:
So moved the dense battalions of the Greeks
In one incessant stream against the foe;
Each chief his orders gave, but for the rest,
You would have thought the mighty host was dumb,
So silent and well disciplined they marched,
With dazzling arms of various workmanship.
But the loud Trojans were like flocks of sheep
Penned in their folds, just ready to be milked,
Which hear outside the voices of their lambs,
And with continual bleatings answer them:
So rose the clamor of the Trojan host;

Nor were the voices nor the shouts the same,
For many nations there were intermixed,
And many tongues and many languages.
Mars urged them on, Minerva too was there,
And Fear, and Panic, and mischievous Strife;
Strife! friend and sister of terrific Mars,
Small though at first, she gradually grows,
Till her gigantic head pierces the skies;
She through the tumult stalked, fanning the flame,
And death and misery accompanied her.
And now both armies to the combat rushed;
Then came the shock of arms; then brass-clad men,
Mingling in fight, against each other clashed.
Then spears were crossed, and shields encountered shields;
Loud was the clamor, loud the victor's shout,
Loud were the groans, as the earth flowed with blood.
As when two wintry torrents downwards rush,
From copious springs, upon a mountain-side,
Then intermingle in some deep ravine,
And wondering shepherds hear the distant roar;
So was the mingling of the combatants,
And such the fearful tumult that arose.
First fell the Trojan chief Echepolus,
A warrior brave, who pressed towards the front;
He by the bold Antilochus was slain,
Who on his helmet struck him, near the plume,
And through his forehead sent the glittering spear;
Death closed his eyes, and like a tower he fell.
Him Elephenor, the Abantian chief,
Seized by the feet to strip him of his arms,
And from the weapon's reach was dragging him;
But unsuccessful was the bold attempt:
Agenor saw him drawing off the corpse,
And as he stooped, struck his uncovered side
With his sharp spear and sent him to his doom.
A dreadful conflict over him arose,
Of Greeks and Trojans; like gaunt wolves they fought,
Struggling together fiercely, hand to hand.

Then Ajax Telamon, Simoisius slew,
A stripling warrior in the bloom of youth;
His mother from the top of Ida came,
She and her parents, to inspect their flocks,
And on the banks of Simois brought him forth;
On that account Simoisius he was called.
Nor did he his dear parents live to bless;
Slain by great Ajax's remorseless spear,
Which struck him on the right side in his breast,
And going through, out at the shoulder came,
He in the dust like a tall poplar fell,
Which by the margin of a meadow grows,
And whose smooth branches are by wheelwrights used
As felloes for a handsome chariot-wheel.
By the sharp axe the lovely tree is cut,
And on the riverside lies withering.
Thus young Simoisius fell by Ajax' hand;
At him the son of Priam, Antiphus,
Hurled through the air his spear; it missed its aim,
But Leucus struck, good comrade of Ulysses,
As he the corpse attempted to draw off,
Piercing him in the groin. He dropped the corpse,
And alongside of it himself fell dead.
Enraged Ulysses was to see him fall,
And clad in shining brass rushed to the front;
Then looking round he hurled his glittering spear.
The Trojans in confusion now gave way;
But not in vain his lance the hero threw,
He struck Democoön, the bastard son
Of royal Priam, who from Abydos came,
Famed for swift mares; him wise Ulysses slew,
Piercing his temples; through them went the spear,
And death's dark shades forever closed his eyes;
He fell, and falling, loud his armor rang.

Then Hector and the foremost ranks gave way;
But the Greeks shouted and drew off their dead.
Still they advanced; Apollo was enraged,
And on the Trojans, looking down from Troy,

Thus loudly shouted, and encouraged them:
Onward, ye Trojan knights! nor to the Greeks
Give way! they are not men of iron or of stone,
So that their bodies are invulnerable;
Nor does the great Achilles, Peleus' son,
Among them fight, but at his ships remains,
Nursing his wrath, and brooding o'er his wrongs.
Thus from the city cried the dreadful god.
But glorious Minerva cheered the Greeks,
Giving her aid to all who needed help.
  Then fell Diores, Amarynceus' son,
On the right ankle struck by a rough stone
Which Pirus, leader of the Thracians, threw—
A chief who came from Ænon; the sharp stone
The bones and tendons crushed; down on his back
The helpless warrior fell, raising both hands
In piteous supplication, to his friends.
Pirus, who struck him, thereupon ran up,
And pierced him in the navel with his spear;
His bowels then upon the ground gushed forth,
And death's dark shades forever closed his eyes.
But Pirus was himself by Thoas slain,
Who ran his spear into the hero's lungs;
Then coming near, the weapon he drew out,
Struck with his sword, and took away his life.
But he could not despoil him of his arms,
For round him gathering, came his Thracian friends,
With their long glittering lances in their hands,
And, valiant though he was, he had to yield—
So he retreated, driven back by force.
Thus Pirus and Diores, side by side
Lay lifeless, stretched upon the dusty ground,
And round them lay a multitude of dead.
  Had some spectator then gone o'er the field,
Led by Minerva, safe from swords and darts,
And able to gaze calmly on the scene,
No fault could he have found with any there,
So well on both sides was the fight maintained.

BOOK V.

EXPLOITS OF DIOMED.

ARGUMENT.

Diomed performs great feats.—He is wounded by Pandarus, but cured by Minerva.—Pandarus is killed, and Æneas is rescued by Venus, who in doing so is wounded in the hand.—Mars rallies the Trojans, but is wounded by Diomed, and returns to heaven in great tribulation.

But on that day none equaled Diomed;
He, above all, shone most conspicuous.
Minerva gave him supernatural power,
And kindled on his helmet and his shield
A dazzling flame, bright as that summer star,*
Which, rising from the sea, so brilliant shines.
Her chief the goddess thus with glory clad,
Then hurled into the middle of the throng.
Among the Trojans was one, Dares named,
A priest of Vulcan, virtuous and rich.
Two sons he had, Phegeus and Idæus,
Well skilled in war; on Diomed they rushed—
One in his car advancing, one on foot.
Approaching, Phegeus hurled his weapon first,
Which only grazed the shoulder of his foe.
Then Diomed aiming, cast his glittering spear,
And struck Phegeus full upon the breast.
He from his chariot fell; his brother fled,
Nor dared to stand his ground and guard the corpse.
Nor would he even thus have saved his life,

* Sirius, or the dog-star.

Had Vulcan not concealed him in a cloud,
That his old father might not childless be.
Then Diomed bade his men to take the steeds,
And lead them off in triumph to the camp.
  But when the Trojans saw good Dares' sons,
One fleeing, and the other lifeless stretched,
A panic seized them; then Minerva took
Mars by the hand, and thus the god addressed:
  Oh, Mars, destroying Mars, spoiler of towns!
Had we not best retire from the field,
And let the Greeks and Trojans fight it out,
Till Jove to one or other victory gives?
So shall we both escape the Thunderer's wrath.
  She said; and brought away ferocious Mars,
And on Scamander's meadows sat him down.
The Greeks then put the Trojan troops to flight,
And every chieftain then dispatched his man.
  And first king Agamemnon Odius slew,—
Chief of the Halizonians was he,—
The mighty warrior from his car he hurled;
He struck him, as he turned, upon the back,
And the spear's point e'en to his breast went through.
He fell, and falling, loud his armor rang.
  Then Phæstus was by Idomeneus slain,
The son of Borus, who from Tarnè came;
Him Idomeneus near the shoulder pierced,
Just as he was about to mount his car;
He met his death, and from his chariot fell,
Then the chief's servants stripped him of his arms.
  Next Menelaus Scamandrius slew—
Good at the chase, a famous hunter he;
Dian herself had taught him how to shoot
All kinds of beasts that through the forest roam.
But little did Diana aid him now,
Nor the good shots he had so often made;
For as he turned, he on the back was struck
By the sharp spear of noble Menelaus,

Which pierced him through, and at his breast came out.
He fell, and falling, loud his armor rang.
  Phereclus was by Merion slain,
Son of Hermonides, the architect,
Who by Minerva had instructed been,
And who in works of curious art excelled.
'Twas he constructed the mischievous ships
That brought such woes on Paris and on Troy,
So little knew he what the gods decreed.
Him Merion struck in his right hip;
The spear went through and to his bladder pierced.
With a loud groan he fell, and met his death.
  Meges next slew Pedæus, bastard son
Of old Antenor, whom his wife, Theano,
Placed on an equal footing with her own,
To please her husband. The sharp spear went through
The back part of his head, cutting his tongue,
And passing through his mouth; lifeless he fell,
Biting the metal with his pearly teeth.
  Eurypylus the brave Hypsenor slew,
Son of Dolopion, Scamander's priest,
Whom all the people honored as a god.
He struck him on the shoulder as he fled,
And with his sword lopped off his brawny arm;
The bloody limb fell on the dusty ground,
And death's dark shades forever closed his eyes.
  Thus in dread fight the combatants engaged;
But as for Diomed, 'twere hard to tell
Which side he fought on; he, 'mid friend and foe,
Rushed like a river with a freshet swollen,
Which bursts all barriers, carries bridges off,
And in a moment sweeps away the toil
And noble structures of laborious men.
So were the Trojan ranks by Diomed broke,
And, though so numerous, they had to yield.
  Him Pandarus saw thus conquering all,
And at him taking aim, a shaft he sent,
Which through his corselet went and shoulder pierced.

His breastplate sprinkling with purple blood
The chieftain saw, and thus with joy exclaimed:
Forward, ye Trojan warriors! ye knights,
The noblest hero of the Greeks is struck;
Nor can he long survive the fatal wound,
Sure as Apollo sent me to this war.
Thus Pandarus spake, nor was his foe subdued;
But, halting by his chariot and steeds,
He thus addressed his comrade Sthenelus:
Haste, Sthenelus, and from thy car descend,
And from my shoulder pluck this bitter shaft.
He said; and from the car his comrade leaped,
And, near him standing, drew the arrow out.
Through his brass mail spouted the purple blood
Then to his patron goddess Diomed prayed:
As to my father thou protectress was,
So now, Minerva, grant thy aid to me;
May this man come within my reach and fall
Who struck me unexpectedly, and boasts
That I shall ne'er again the sun behold.
Thus prayed the chief, nor was his prayer unheard.
The goddess in his limbs new strength infused,
And, drawing near, thus cheered him and addressed:
Courage, good Diomed! and still fight on,
For I thy father's valor will impart—
The very soul that old Tydeus had;
And from thine eyes the mist I have removed,
So that thou mayest distinguish men from gods,
Should any of the gods oppose thee then
Amid the contest; but with Venus fight,
If she comes on, and wound her with thy spear.
So spake Minerva, and then flew away.
But to the front brave Diomed repaired,
And, as before, with martial fire he burned;
Thrice was his courage and his ardor now.
As when a lion in a sheep-fold leaps,
And by the shepherd slightly wounded is,
The feeble wound but rouses him the more,—

The shepherd flies, down springs the savage beast
Among the huddled, unprotected sheep,
And at his leisure slaughters and devours:
So on the Trojans valiant Diomed fell.
Hypenor and Astynoüs then he slew—
One through his bosom piercing with his spear,
The other cleaving with his mighty sword,
And, cutting through his collar-bone and neck,
He let them lie; and then on Abas rushed,
And on Polyïdus, sons of Eurydamus,
An old man and interpreter of dreams,
But he no more his sons' dreams would explain,
For to the war they went, and ne'er returned.
Xanthus and Thoön next the chief attacked,
The darling sons of aged Phænops they;
No other children had he except them
To whom his property he might bequeath:
They both were slain, nor did their father e'er
Set eyes on them again. Mourning he died,
And strangers took possession of his wealth.
Then he slew Echemon and Chromius,
The sons of Priam; in one car they rode.
As when a lion springing on a herd
Slaughters a well-fed heifer or an ox,
Breaking their necks as in a copse they feed,
So from their chariot Diomed dislodged
These Trojan chiefs, and spoiled them of their arms,
The car and horses sending to the camp.
But when Æneas saw his murderous deeds
He searched among the ranks for Pandarus.
At length he found the hero, and thus spake:
Where are thy bow and arrows, Pandarus?
Where the renown thou once in Lycia hadst,
Where none was known superior to thee?
But come, raising thy hands, first pray to Jove
And send an arrow to this mighty one
Who makes such havoc in the Trojan ranks,

Slaughtering so many of our bravest chiefs,—
Some god it may be, who is wroth with Troy
And comes for our misdeeds to punish us.
He said; and to him Pandarus replied:
The one you mean, I think is Diomed;
Such steeds he has, and such a helmet wears,
I know not if he be a god or no;
But if 'tis Diomed, some god assists
And by him always stands invisible,
Turning aside the weapons of his foes,
For I just now an arrow aimed at him,
Which pierced his shoulder through his coat of mail,
And thought I had dispatched him certainly.
But not at all; my arrow flew in vain.
Surely some angry god must baffle us,—
Nor have I here my chariot or steeds.
Yet in my father's house in Lycia
Eleven new handsome chariots I have,
Each safely housed, beneath its covering;
Beside them yoked, in pairs the horses stand,
Eating white barley and the best of corn;
Much did my father, old Lycaön, say,
When I sat out from home to go to war.
He bade me take my car and steeds along
And hold among the Trojans high command;
But I unwisely heeded not his words,
Fearing that in a town besieged like Troy
My steeds might suffer from the want of food.
Thus foolish I my horses left behind,
And, trusting to my bow, came here afoot.
But little does it seem to profit me;
For two great chiefs already have I struck—
Great Diomed and noble Menelaus;
Blood flowed from each, but fruitless were the wounds,
They only seemed to rouse their courage more.
Alas! it was an evil day for me
When I my weapon from the peg took down

And for the sake of Hector came to Troy.
But should I ever to my home return,
And see again my wife and palace hall,
Sure as I live, this worthless bow I'll break
And then consign its fragments to the flames.
He said; and good Æneas answered him:
Say not so, Pandarus; not till we both
In company set out against this man
In full array and try what we can do.
Up, then, and quickly mount my chariot,
That thou may'st see what Trojan horses are,
How swift to scour the plain, or nimbly wheel
And safely bear us back again to Troy,
If 'tis Jove's will that Diomed prevail.
Then take the reins and whip, and I will fight,
Or thou the fighting do, and I will drive.
He said; and thus brave Pandarus replied:
Take thou the reins, Æneas, and the whip,
For better will the horses draw the car
With their accustomed driver than with me.
Should Diomed compel us to retreat,
Missing thy voice, they restive might become,
And we should thus be vanquished by our foe,
Who then would seize the chariot as his prize.
Then drive thy steed thyself, and I will meet
This Grecian warrior with my glittering spear.
Thus speaking, both stepped on the beauteous car
And turned the horses against Diomed.
But Sthenelus beheld them drawing near,
And thus with warning words his friend addressed:
Oh, Diomed, my friend, joy of my heart!
Two men of boundless strength I see approach—
One is the famous archer Pandarus,
The other is Anchises' son, Æneas,
Who boasts that lovely Venus brought him forth.
Come, then, and let us not too hasty be,
But rather mount our chariot and retire,
Lest keeping in the front thou lose thy life.

He said ; and sternly Diomed replied :
Talk not to me of flight, for 'tis in vain,
Nor does it to my family belong
To skulk in battle, or to make retreats.
My strength is fresh, and I on foot will go,
Nor will Minerva suffer me to fear.
Sure one at least within that chariot car
Shall fall and never enter Troy again.
But this I tell thee, and remember it:
Should I be destined both these chiefs to slay,
Stop thou the car, and, rushing on yon steeds,
Seize them, and drive triumphant to the camp,
For they are of the breed that mighty Jove
To Tros presented as a noble price
For his dear son, the handsome Ganymede.
No horses like them were e'er seen on earth;
From them Anchises got his mares with foal
Without the knowledge of Laomedon.
Six colts he had, reserving for himself.
He to Æneas gave the other two:
If we take them, 'twill be a prize indeed.
Thus speaking, to close quarters came the chiefs,
Driving their steeds ; then Pandarus thus spake :
Brave-hearted Diomed, my shaft, 'tis true,
Missed thee at first; but now I'll try the spear.
He said ; and, aiming, cast his glittering lance,
Which through the chieftain's shield entirely went,
And struck against his brazen coat of mail ;
Then loudly boasting, Pandarus cried out:
Surely thou now art wounded in the flank;
Thy doom I sealed and will illustrious be.
But thus the fearless Diomed replied:
You missed, and struck me not, nor will I cease
Till one or other of you bite the dust.
He said; and with Minerva's aid, his lance
Hurling, he drove it through his eyes and nose,
Breaking his pearly teeth; his tongue it cut,
And, passing on clear through his chin, came out,

His shining armor clattering as he fell;
He tumbled from the chariot, a corpse,—
His splendid horses started with affright.
Æneas with his shield and spear sprang down,
Fearing the Greeks might bear away the corpse:
Like a fierce lion guarding it, he kept
Walking around it, with his sword and spear,
And loudly shouting; but Diomed seized
A monstrous stone, so large that e'en two men
Could not together lift, as men are now,
But he alone raised it, and hurled with ease;
It struck Æneas on the thigh and hip,
Breaking the joint, the tendons, and the skin.
The hero fell upon his hands and knees,
And o'er his eyes a veil of darkness spread.
  hen would Æneas surely have been slain
Had not his mother Venus aided him.
Round her dear son her lovely arms she threw
And with her splendid veil protected him
From the sharp spears and arrows of the Greeks.
  Nor did brave Sthenelus forget the words
Of his companion, mighty Diomed,
But stopped his chariot, and his horses tied,
Then rushing up he seized Æneas' steeds
And gave them to his friend Deïpylus,
Whom much he loved, to drive them to the camp.
Then his own car ascending, he advanced,
And after mighty Diomed pursued,
Who with his spear on Venus madly rushed,
Knowing she was a feeble deity,
And not like warlike Pallas or Bellona.
Amid the ranks he found her and attacked,
With his sharp spear striking her tender hand;
Through her ambrosial robe the weapon went,
The splendid robe the Graces made for her:
Her palm he pierced, and from the wound there ran
Ichor, the blood divine that flows from gods
Who eat no bread nor drink the purple wine—

Therefore they bloodless and immortal are.
Screaming aloud, she cast her son away;
Apollo came and hid him in a cloud,
And thus preserved him from his enemies.
But warlike Diomed, loudly shouting, spake:
Daughter of Jove, retire from the field,
Thy part it is poor woman to deceive.
Wilt thou embark in war?—I think henceforth
The very name of war will frighten thee.
He said; and she in misery went off.
Swift Iris led her from the battle-field,
Smarting with pain, her hand turned black and blue.
She found her brother Mars, not far away,
Seated upon the left side of the plain,
His spear and steeds enveloped in a mist.
She fell upon her knees, and asked the god
If he his golden-harnessed team would lend.
Oh, my dear brother, let me have thy steeds
That I to high Olympus may ascend.
Much pain I suffer from a grievous wound
Inflicted by a man called Diomed,
Who I believe would even fight with Jove.
She said; and Mars his splendid horses gave:
The chariot she mounted, sore distressed,
And Iris mounted too, and seized the reins
And lashed the horses, which like lightning flew.
Quickly they reached the high Olympian mount,
The happy habitation of the gods.
There Iris halted the swift-footed steeds,
Unyoked and fed them with ambrosial food.
But lovely Venus fell upon the lap
Of her dear mother Dionè; she her child
Clasped in her arms and tenderly addressed:
Who of the gods has dared to treat thee thus,
As if thou wast some worthless criminal?
The goddess answered: 'Twas proud Diomed,
Because I saved Æneas, my dear son,
And would not let him perish in the fight;

For now the Greeks contend not with their foes,
But are in arms against the deities.
  She said; and thus Dionè made reply:
Be patient, child, and though distressed, bear up.
We gods have often suffered grievous woes
From mortal hands, forever injuring.
Mars suffered at the hands of Ephialtes
And Otus, both sons of Alvœus,
Who bound him with a chain, and thirteen months
Held him as captive in a brazen prison,
Where he had miserably pined away
Had not his step-mother Eribœæ
Told it to Mercury, who got him free.
Juno, too, suffered, when Amphitryon's son
Wounded her bosom with a three-pronged dart;
And fearful was the anguish that she bore.
Dead Pluto also felt the bitter shaft
Of the same mortal, sprung from mighty Jove,
Who struck him in the very gates of hell,
Among the dead, severely paining him.
He, suffering greatly, to Olympus went,
The weapon sticking in his brawny arm.
But Pæon with his ointments healed the wound,—
For he immortal was, and could not die.
Audacious, reckless one, to do such deeds,
And dare to shoot his arrows at the gods!
But against thee, Minerva sent this man,
Foolish and mad; for is he not aware
That he is short lived who with Heaven contends?
Nor will he from the war returning safe
E'er clasp his infant children in his arms.
And let the valiant Diomed reflect,
Brave though he is, a braver he may meet.
Then may his wife, fair Ægialè, start,
And, waking from her sleep, disturb the house
With lamentations for her husband dead.
  She said; and wiped the ichor from the wound:
The pain abated, and her hand was healed.

But Juno and Minerva, looking on,
With words sarcastic spake to mighty Jove.
And first the blue-eyed goddess thus began :
Will father Jove be angry if I speak ?
Venus has just been coaxing some fair Greek
To go astray among the men of Troy,
And as the amorous lady she caressed
The buckle of her girdle scratched her hand.
She said ; and caused the Thunderer to smile.
Then calling to his daughter, thus he spake :
My child, these warlike scenes are not for thee ;
Thy part it is to manage love affairs,
But war to Pallas and to Mars belongs.
Thus on Olympus' top the gods conversed.
But Tydeus' son Æneas still pursued,
Although he knew Apollo aided him.
But little cared he for the mighty god,
So eager was he to destroy his foe
And get possession of his splendid arms.
Thrice he rushed on him furious to slay,
And thrice the god repulsed his dazzling shield ;
But when the fourth attack he madly made,
With voice tremendous, thus Apollo cried :
Rash man, forbear !—reflect, oh, Diomed,
Nor think thyself upon a par with Heaven ;
For widely different is the race of men
From the immortal nature of the gods.
He said ; and Diomed drew somewhat back,
Fearing Apollo's wrath ; who from the field
Æneas took, and sat him down in Troy,
In his own handsome temple placing him.
Diana and Latona there he met,
Who healed the hero's wound and cheered him up.
Meanwhile Apollo formed a phantom shape,
Like to Æneas both in looks and arms :
Around this image Greeks and Trojans fought.
Clashing their bucklers and their ox-hide shields.
Then to his brother Mars the god thus spake :

Oh, Mars, destructive Mars, spoiler of towns,
Canst thou not stay the hand of Diomed,
Who now would even dare to fight with Jove?
Venus at first he wounded on the wrist,
And like a god just now assaulted me.
He said; and took his seat on Troy's high towers,
Whilst Mars descended to the Trojan ranks,
And in the form of Acamas, of Thrace,
The sons of royal Priam thus addressed:
Ye sons of Priam, why so negligent?
Will ye allow the Greeks to slaughter thus
Until the battle reaches e'en your gates?
Æneas too lies prostrate in the dust,
A man with Hector equally esteemed.
But come, and let us rescue our good friend.
So saying, he their drooping spirits cheered.
Then Hector was by Sarpedon rebuked:
Oh, Hector, whither has thy courage fled?
Thou boasted'st once thou couldst the town defend
With thine own brothers and thy relatives,
Without an army or an allied force;
But these thy friends are nowhere to be seen,
They crouch like curs which from a lion run,
And we the allies bear the brunt of war;
But I, a stranger, to thy aid have come
From distant Lycia, where the Xanthus flows.
There a dear wife and infant child I left
And such possessions as might envied be.
I fight myself, and urge my men to fight,
Though I have naught at stake within the town
That the triumphant Greeks may carry off;
But thou standest idle, giv'st no commands,
Nor showest how thy people may be saved.
Take heed thou art not by thy foes entrapped
Who may thy goodly city soon destroy.
Thou shouldst be ever active, night and day
Shouldst stir thy armies up, push on the war,
And reconcile the envies of the chiefs.

Thus spake the warlike Sarpedon; his words
Stung Hector to the quick; who with his arms
Leaped from his beauteous chariot to the ground,
Two lances brandishing: in haste he ran
Among the troops, exhorting them to fight.
The battle was renewed, they stood their ground,
Nor did the Greeks give way nor fear their foes.
As when the wind upon a threshing-floor,
When husbandmen are winnowing the grain,
Raises the yellow chaff and sprinkles them,
So were the Greeks all whitened with the dust
Which by the chariot horses was stirred up
And rose to heaven in clouds from off the field;
For furious o'er the plain the cars were driven.
But Mars, to aid the Trojans, spread a mist
Over the field, and the request fulfilled
Of bright Apollo, who had bid him rouse
The men of Troy, whenever he beheld
Minerva from the Greeks withholding aid.
But he Æneas from his temple brought,
And in his breast fresh energy infused.
His comrades were rejoiced to see their chief
Returned among them, still alive and strong:
None asked him questions, for there was no time,
So fiercely now the bloody battle raged,
Stirred up by Mars, Apollo, and mad Strife.
Then wise Ulysses, and great Diomed,
And the two Ajaxes urged on the Greeks.
They cared not for the Trojans, or their shouts,
But stood like clouds upon a mountain-top
On a calm summer day, immovable,
When winds are lulled, and scarce a breath of air;
Thus the Greeks stood their ground unmoved by fear,
Whilst Agamemnon thus encouraged them:
My friends, stand firm, and quit yourselves like men!
For to the brave a chance of safety lies,—
But to the coward, shame and death belong.
He said, and hurled his spear, striking a chief,

Deïcoon called, friend of Æneas,
Whom as Priam's son the Trojans honored,
Since he was ever foremost in the fight.
Him with a spear the king struck on the shield;
Through it the weapon went, and pierced his groin.
He fell; and falling, loud his armor rang.
Then Æneas slew two famous Greeks,
Crethon and Orsilochus, brothers they;
Their father, Diöcleus, in Pheræ dwelt,
A man of wealth, from wide Alpheus sprung,
A river flowing through the Pylian land.
His son was opulent Orsilochus,
Father of noble-hearted Diöcleus,
Who Crethon and Orsilochus begat.
Brave men, and skilled in every warlike art,
They in the bloom of youth came to the war
In their black ships, accompanying the fleet
For Agamemnon's sake and Menelaus'.
Death met them now and ended their career.
Just as two lions, reared by their tawny dam,
In the dark thickets of a gloomy wood,
Grown to full size, make havoc with the herds
And ravage folds till they themselves are slain,
Surrounded and attacked by well-armed men,
So, conquered by Æneas, these young chiefs
Fell lifeless to the earth, like two tall pines.
Brave Menelaus saw, and pitied them.
Then to the front he went, clad in bright brass,
Shaking his spears; Mars urged the hero on,
That by Æneas he might be subdued.
Antilochus beheld him in the van,
And followed, fearing for his honored chief,
Lest if he fell, the war would be in vain.
And now the warriors were about to fight:
Just as Antilochus drew near his friend,
Æneas then, brave as he was, drew off,
Beholding two such valiant men in front,
Who dragged away the bodies of their friends,

And, to their comrades giving them in charge,
Returned again to recommence the fight.
Next the brave chief, Pylæmenes, they slew,
Who led the bucklered Paphlagonians,—
He by the hand of Menelaus fell,
Struck with a spear upon his collar-bone;
And Mydon, too, his charioteer, was slain.
His arm first broken by a heavy stone
Hurled by Antilochus; down dropped the reins,
And, rushing up, the warrior with his sword
Smote him across the temples; from the car
Lifeless he fell headforemost to the ground,
His head and shoulders buried in the sand,
Which happened to be deep; there long he stuck,
Till trampled down by his own frightened steeds,
Which the Greek seized, and bore them to the camp.
Hector beheld the exploits of these chiefs,
And, shouting loudly, rushed to fight with them.
Troy's strongest phalanxes were at his heels,
Before them went Bellona and fierce Mars;
Wild uproar followed in Bellona's train,
And his huge spear Mars brandished in his hands;
In front of Hector now, and now behind,
Fear fell on Diomed beholding him.
As when a traveler in an unknown land,
Crossing a wide expanse, comes suddenly
Upon the margin of a dangerous stream
Whose roaring waves are white with angry foam,
His course is checked and backward he retreats:
So halted Diomed, and thus cried out:
Well may the noble Hector be admired
As a brave lancer and a daring chief,
For he is ever aided by the gods,
And by him now stands Mars in mortal shape.
Then let us yield, my friends, facing the foe,
Nor with the deities attempt to war.
He said; and onward still the Trojans came.
Then Hector slew two warriors renowned,

The brave Mnenesthes and Anchialus.
They in one chariot rode ; but Ajax
Saw them fall, and pitied them ; near he drew
And with his shining spear struck Amphius,
The son of Selagus, a wealthy man
Who dwelt in Apæsus ; he by fate was led
To join himself with Priam and his sons.
Him Ajax Telamon in the stomach pierced ;
He fell ; whereon the mighty chief ran up
To spoil him of his arms ; a shower of darts
The Trojans hurled, which on his shield he caught,
Then on the prostrate body placed his heel
And from the corpse drew out the glittering spear.
But the bold Greek his armor failed to get,
So thick the shining weapons round him flew,
And fearing lest the Trojans might advance
And he by numbers should be overpowered,
Great as he was, he had at last to yield.
So by main force they drove him from the spot.
Thus Greeks and Trojans labored in the fight.
  Then brave Tlepolemus by fate was led
Against the godlike hero Sarpedon :
The chiefs drew near ; the one the grandson was,
The other was the son of mighty Jove.
And now Tlepolemus spake first and said :
Oh, Sarpedon of Lycia, what means this—
What brings thee here, a man unfit for war ?
They lie who say that thou art sprung from Jove,
Since little art thou like those mighty chiefs
Who in old times were of celestial race ;
Of such as those my honored father was,
The famous lion-hearted Hercules.
He hither came on business, long ago,
About the horses of Laomedon ;
Six ships he only had and a few men,
Yet he took Troy and sacked the sacred town.
But thou art spiritless, and void of power,
And though from distant Lycia thou hast come,

Small is the aid that thou wilt give to Troy;
But wert thou valiant e'en, thy doom is fixed,
For, vanquished by my spear, this day thy soul
Shall surely to the gates of Pluto go.
Thus spake the famous son of Hercules,
And thus the king of Lycia replied:
'Tis true, Tlepolemus, thy sire destroyed
Troy's sacred town; but it was brought about
By the cursed folly of Laomedon,
Who used rough words, returning ill for good;
Nor did he give those valuable steeds
Which he before had promised to thy sire,
And for the sake of which he came so far.
But as for thee, thy mortal end draws near;
Pierced by my spear, the glory shall be mine
To send thy soul to Pluto's gloomy realms.
He said; and now Tlepolemus his spear
Hurled at his foe; both weapons flew at once,
And that of Sarpedon struck the bold Greek
Full in the throat; clear through his neck it went,
And sent him to the dismal shades of death.
But Sarpedon was wounded in the thigh;
The cruel spear passed through, grazing the bone.
But his great father Jove preserved his life.
His comrades from the battle led him off,
With the long weapon trailing on the ground.
Much pain he suffered, none had thought as yet
From the sad wound to draw the glittering spear,
So hurried were they to protect their friend
And place him safely in his chariot car.
The Greeks too carried from the battle-field
The body of their friend Tlepolemus.
Ulysses saw them, and his heart was stirred:
In doubt he hesitated what to do,
Whether to follow noble Sarpedon,
Or to remain and slay the Lycians;
But fate had not decreed that he should be
The one by whom the son of Jove should die,—

Minerva turned him towards the Lycians.
Then Ceramus he slew and Cromius,
Alcander too, Prytanis, and Noëmon,
And Halius also, and Alastor,
And more too would the warrior have slain
Had not the helm-plumed Hector him observed.
Clad in bright brass, he hurried to the front;
The Greeks beheld him, and were terror-struck;
But Sarpedon rejoiced, and moaning spake:
Oh, Hector, let me not lie wounded here
And fall a prey to my triumphant foes,
But in the city let me breathe my last,
Since my dear home I ne'er shall see again,
My wife beloved, nor my sweet infant son.
He said; but Hector made him no reply,
In such a haste he was to meet his foes.
But Sarpedon was carried by his friends,
And underneath a lovely beech-tree placed.
Strong Pelagon, his friend, plucked out the spear:
The hero fainted; darkness veiled his eyes;
Soon he revived, fanned by a cooling breeze
Which from the north sprang up, and saved his life.
But by plumed Hector and by Mars beset,
The Greeks were still not driven to their ships,
Yet neither were they able to advance,
But they retreated somewhat, fearing Mars.
Whom first then and whom last did Hector slay?
Hector, the son of Priam, and dread Mars,
The godlike Teuthras, and the knight Orestes,
Trechus, the lancer, and Enomeus,
And Helenus, the son of Œnops too,
The belted chief Oresbius also,
Who, overfond of wealth, in Hylè dwelt,
Near to the lake Cephissus; near it too
The other rich Bœtians had their homes.
When Juno saw the Greeks thus perishing,
She hastily Minerva thus addressed:
Oh, Heavens! daughter of almighty Jove,

In vain we promised noble Menelaus
That he should capture Troy and safe return,
If dreadful Mars is suffered thus to rage!
Then come, and let us in the conflict share.
  She said; nor did the goddess disobey.
Then Juno, venerable queen, brought forth
Her golden-harnessed steeds; and Hebĕ next
Placed on the chariot's axle-tree the wheels.
Eight-spoked they were, and made of solid gold;
The tires were brazen, silver were the naves;
A wondrous work; the car suspended was
On gold and silver cords, a silver pole
Was to the body fixed; and at the end
A beautiful gold yoke, with golden bands.
Juno, all eager for the coming fight,
Placed the impatient steeds beneath the yoke.
  Minerva then upon the floor let fall
Her beauteous robe, which she herself had made,
And clad in Jove's bright arms, prepared for war.
Her ægis on her shoulders then she hung:
Dreadful it was, with very terror crowned!
In it was Strife, and Strength, and bloody Rout,
And in it too the horrid Gorgon's head,—
That direful monster, portent of great Jove.
Her helmet next upon her head she placed—
Four golden crests it had, immense its size,
A hundred armies might have camped in it.
Into the fiery chariot then she stepped,
And in her hands grasped her tremendous spear,
With which, when wroth, she tames embattled hosts.
Juno lashed on the swiftly-flying steeds;
Heaven's gates flew open of their own accord.
The watchful Hours stood there, on either side,
Ready to lift the purple cloud that hung
Across the entrance of the Olympian domes.
Through it the steeds impetuously rushed;
They found the Thunderer seated by himself
Upon the highest summit of Olympus.

Juno drew up her splendid chariot then,
And thus accosted mighty Jove, and said:
Art thou not angry, father Jove, at Mars
Thus wickedly demolishing the Greeks?
My grief is great, but Venus and Apollo
Look on delighted at this frantic god
Whom they let loose, to act thus lawlessly!
Wilt thou be angry, father Jove, if I
Drive from the battle-field this deity?
She said; and thus cloud-mantled Jove replied
Set bold Minerva at him if thou wilt,
Who well knows how to punish such as him.
He said; nor did the goddess disobey,
But lashed her horses, which like lightning flew
Midway between the earth and starry skies.
As far as one who, sitting on a coast,
Looks o'er the ocean's limitless expanse
And just perceives where sky and water join;
So, at each bound, the heavenly horses sprang:
But when to Troy they came, and on the banks
Of flowing Simois and Scamander stood,
Juno unyoked her steeds, veiled in a cloud,
And Simois furnished them ambrosial food;
But the two goddesses, like timid doves,
Glided along into the battle-field.
But when they reached the thickest of the fray,
Where, around Diomed, the warriors fought
Like flesh-devouring lions, or wild boars,
Then Juno like a brass-clad Stentor stood,
Whose shout is as the shout of fifty men.
Such form assuming, thus she loudly cried:
Shame on ye, Greeks! handsome indeed ye are,
But foul and most disgraceful in your deeds!
Whilst bold Achilles mingled in the war,
Your foes scarce ventured from the gates of Troy,
Such horror had they of his murderous spear;
But now far distant from the town they come,
And fight you, even at your very ships.

Thus saying, she their drooping courage roused.
Then after Diomed Minerva went:
She found him by his chariot and steeds,
Cooling the wound that he had just received.
Profusely he perspired, and raised his belt,
And with his tired hand wiped off the blood.
Near him she drew, and touched the horses' yoke,
And the undaunted hero thus addressed:
Tydeus has a son not like himself,
For Tydeus was a man of stature small,
But he a warrior was; for even when
I bade him to keep quiet, and not fight,
When he as envoy ventured, all alone,
To distant Thebès; I wished him, like a guest,
Surrounded by so many foreigners,
To socially enjoy the feasts they gave.
But he, intrepid as he ever was,
Challenged and conquered all the Theban youths;
Such aid in every contest I bestowed.
And to thee, too, such aid I would impart,
And urge thee with the Trojans still to fight:
But thou art either broken down with toil,
Or some disheartening fear possesses thee;
Henceforth thou must not call thyself the son
Of old Tydeus, the great warrior.
She said; and noble Diomed replied:
I know thee, goddess, daughter of great Jove!
'Tis not that I am overcome with toil,
Nor am I with disheartening fear possessed;
But thy command I study to obey,
Who told me with the immortals not to fight,
Except with Venus; whom, if she appeared,
I with my spear was authorized to wound.
Therefore I keep aloof, I and my men:
For in the battle now great Mars I see.
He said; and blue-eyed Pallas thus replied:
Most valiant Diomed, joy of my heart!

Fear not this Mars, nor any of the gods.
Such mighty aid I mean to render thee :
Drive at him with thy chariot and steeds,
Engage him hand to hand, and dread him not,
This crazy god, this wicked renegade,
Who promised Juno and myself that he
Would fight the Trojans, and assist the Greeks :
But now he does the very contrary.
Thus spake Minerva, and with outstretched hand
Drew Sthenelus, backward, from off the car.
He yielded willingly his place to her.
The chariot mounting, then the goddess stood
Alongside of the noble Diomed.
The iron axle groaned beneath the load ;
A goddess and a mighty chief it bore.
Minerva lashed the steeds, and straightway drove
Against mad Mars, who then had just dispatched
Gigantic Periphas, a warrior brave,
Son of Ochesius, of Ætolia,—
Him had the gory deity just slain.
Upon her head the helmet of black night
Minerva placed, that she might not be known.
When bloody Mars saw noble Diomed,
He let the body lie that he had slain,
And rushed against his foe. When near they were
He o'er his chariot stretched, and thrust his spear,
Eager to take away the warrior's life,
But Pallas seized the weapon in her hand,
And turning it aside, it harmless fell.
Then Diomed attacked, and thrust his spear,
Minerva guiding it, right in the flank
Of fiery Mars, near where his girdle was ;
There in his beauteous skin, she pierced the god,
And straightway drew the weapon from the wound.
Mars roared aloud, as if ten thousand men
Upon the battle-field a war-shout made.
With terror struck, both Greeks and Trojans heard,

So dreadfully the wounded god cried out.
As when a gloomy vapor caused by heat
Arises in the air, so Mars appeared
As, mounting to the clouds, he rose to heaven.
Soon to the mansions of the gods he came,
On high Olympus; then he took his seat
Alongside Jove, and overcome with grief
Showed him the wound, and the immortal blood
That from it flowed, and moaning thus began:
  Art thou not angry at these doings, Jove?
We gods must always into trouble get
Whilst showing favors to the sons of men.
And thou the cause of all the mischief art,
For thou a wicked daughter hast begot,
Whose heart is ever set on evil deeds.
The other gods respect thee, and obey:
But her thou dost indulge, and never chide.
And now she has proud Diomed impelled
To battle even with the deities:
First gentle Venus on the hand he pierced,
And like a god rushed afterwards on me;
But my swift feet withdrew me quick away,
Or I amid dead bodies might have lain,
And been exhausted by repeated blows.
  He said; but looking sternly, Jove replied:
Come not to me with whinings and complaints,
Thou fickle renegade; I hate thee most
Of all the gods who on Olympus dwell!
For naught delightest thee but strife and war.
Thou art thy mother's very counterpart,
Whose temper even I can scarcely tame;
And she I think this trouble brought about.
Yet to thy pain I must relief afford,
For thou my offspring art, of Juno born;
But had thy birth been other than it is,
For these mischievous deeds thou hast performed
Thou had'st long since been banished from the skies.

Thus spake the Thunderer; and Pæon bade
To heal the wound; who did so with good drugs,
Which to the wound he skillfully applied.
As when the juice of figs is mixed with milk,
The milk coagulates, and solid grows;
Thus quickly healed the painful wound of Mars.
Then Hebè washed him, clad him in fair robes,
And sat him down rejoicing at Jove's side.
Thus Juno and Minerva from the field
Drove Mars away, and then returned to heaven.

BOOK VI.

INTERVIEW BETWEEN DIOMED AND GLAUCUS, AND STORY OF BELLEROPHON.

ARGUMENT.

The gods having left the field, the Greeks prevail.—Helenus, a Trojan prophet, commands Hector to persuade his mother and the matrons of Troy to repair to the shrine of Minerva, and beg her to remove Diomed from the fight.—Diomed meets Glaucus; the two heroes are about to engage, but discover that their ancestors had been friends, and exchange gifts.—Glaucus relates the story of Bellerophon.—Hector visits his wife Andromache and takes a tender leave of her.

Thus from the field the deities retired;
Yet o'er the plain the dreadful fight went on
Betwixt Simois and Scamander's stream,
And weapons clashed, and heroes fought and fell.
'Twas Ajax that first broke the Trojan ranks,
And to the flagging Greeks imparted hope.
He slew a Thracian hero great and good,
The valiant Acamas, Eusonis' son;
Him on his helmet by the plume he struck,
And pierced his forehead with the glittering spear,
Crushing the bone; the warrior lifeless fell.
  Next noble Diomed Axylus slew,
A wealthy man, who in Arisbè dwelt,
By all beloved, for he was kind to all.
His friendly mansion by the roadside stood,
And many a visitor he entertained;
But of his guests none came to his relief.

He fell, and with him too Calesius fell,
His faithful servant and charioteer.
  Next Dresus and Opheltius were slain
By brave Euryalus, who then dispatched
The twins Æsepus and Pedasus,
Whom the fair nymph Abarbarea bore
To good Bucolion, a shepherd swain,
Who met the Naiad as his flock he fed.
The beauteous nymph conceived and brought forth twins,
Who both by brave Euryalus were slain
And of their arms despoiled. The next who fell
Fell by the warlike Philopete's hand;
He slew Astyalus; Ulysses next
Killed the Percosian warrior Pydates;
And then the royal Agamemnon slew
Elatus dwelling on Pedasus' heights,
By lovely Satnois' gently-flowing stream.
Phylacus, flying, was by Leitus slain;
And brave Eurypilus slew Melanthius;
Adrastus was by Menelaus seized;
His frightened horses, running o'er the plain,
Caught in the branches of a tamarisk-tree:
The chariot pole broke off, and to the town
Flew the swift steeds, with many more besides.
Hurled from his car, the warrior headlong fell
Upon the dusty ground, beneath the wheels.
With threat'ning spear, brave Menelaus approached,
And, clinging to his knees, the Trojan prayed:
Take me alive, oh, noble Menelaus,
And for my life a precious ransom gain.
My father wealthy is, has gold and brass
And valuable steel laid up in store;
These in abundance he will give to thee
When he shall hear that I have captured been.
  He said; and moved the hero's tender heart,
Who was about to send him to the camp;
But Agamemnon happened to approach,
And, shouting loud, his brother thus reproved:

Soft-hearted Menelaus, why for these men
Art thou concerned? Truly to thee and thine
The Trojans have a great advantage been!
No; slay them all; let none of them escape,
Neither the mother nor her babe unborn;
Let lofty Troy a heap of ruins be,
And let her dead not even find a tomb.
He said; and wisely changed his brother's mind,
Who from his knees his helpless foe repulsed.
The king then thrust his spear into his side.
He turned, and, dying, fell upon his back.
His foot upon his breast the victor put,
And drew the bloody weapon from the wound.
Then venerable Nestor cried aloud:
Oh, friends, heroic Greeks, and sons of Mars!
Let no one for the sake of plunder pause,
But keep on slaying; time enough there is
To strip each corpse, and carry off the spoil.
He said; and roused still more the warlike Greeks.
Then would the Trojans, conquered by their foes,
Have certainly been driven into Troy,
Had not the soothsayer Helenus come up
And spoken thus to Hector and Æneas:
My brothers, since on you the labor falls
To lead our army and to give advice,
Stand here and guard the gates, lest, rushing in,
Our forces may be slaughtered by the foe
Amid their wives, within their very homes;
But when the Trojans to a stand ye bring,
We others will remain, and fight our best.
But to the city, Hector, thou proceed,
And, seeking out our mother Hecuba,
Bid her collect the matrons of the town,
Then straightway to the citadel ascend,
Where great Minerva's sacred temple stands.
There entering, place upon the goddess' knees
The largest, rarest, and most splendid veil
That can be got; and promise her besides

Twelve yearling heifers to be offered up
If she will pity have upon our town
And save from death our wives and little ones,
Driving away this dreadful Diomed,
Whom I pronounce the boldest of the Greeks,—
More to be dreaded than Achilles e'en,
That famous chieftain, of a goddess born,
So fiercely rages this heroic man.
He said; and Hector did as he advised.
Down from his chariot, with his arms, he sprang,
His weapons brandishing; among the ranks
He marched, encouraging the men to fight:
The army rallied; fearful was the strife.
The Greeks desisted from their bloody work,
And, wondering much, began to make retreat;
They thought that from the skies some god had dropped
To aid the Trojans, such a charge they made.
But Hector loudly to his warriors called:
Courageous Trojans, and ye allies too!
Maintain your ground, and quit yourselves like men,
Whilst I to Troy proceed, and bid our wives
And aged counselors to send up prayers
And offer holy sacrifice to Heaven.
Thus having spoke, plumed Hector went away,
His monstrous buckler hanging at his back,
Striking his ankles as he went along.
Now in the middle of the field approached
The noble Glaucus and brave Diomed;
Eager to fight were both; when close they were,
The valiant Diomed thus first began:
Who might'st thou be, bravest of mortal men,
For ne'er in battle have I met thee yet?
Bold must thou be indeed above the rest
To thus step forth, encountering my spear;
Sad is the fate of all that cope with me.
But if thou something more than mortal art,
I will not fight against the heavenly gods.
The brave Lycurgus fought against the gods,

And short-lived was he for his rash attempt.
He through the sacred groves of Nyssa chased
The nurses of young Bacchus. Scared to death,
Each dropped her flowery thyrsus on the ground,
He with a cruel ox-goad smote the nymphs.
Bacchus, affrighted, plunged beneath the waves,
And Thetis in her bosom took the boy,
Trembling with horror at the dreadful scene.
The immortal gods were outraged at the man,
And mighty Jove in anger struck him blind.
Nor did he long survive, so hateful he
To all the heavenly deities became.
Therefore, I say, against no god I fight;
But if a man thou art, eating man's food,
Approach and quickly thou shalt meet thy doom.
Thus Diomed spake; and Glaucus thus replied:
Why dost thou ask my race, oh, Diomed?
As leaves of trees, men flourish and decay:
Scattered by wintry winds, the foliage falls;
But summer comes, and woods again are green:
So leaves bud forth and die; so come and go
The fleeting generations of mankind.
But if my name and lineage thou wouldst know,
I will relate what is to many known.
There is in Argos, famed for steeds, a town,
Ephyrè called, where lived wise Sisyphus.
The son of Æolus was Sisyphus;
He begat Glaucus, who was the father
Of the most excellent Bellerophon,
A man endowed by Heaven with every grace,—
Noble in heart and beautiful in form;
But Prætus, who was king of Argos then,
And to whom Jove despotic power gave,
Devised against the youth mischievous schemes
And from his native country drove him forth.
The wife of Prætus, noble Antæa,
Was smit with love for fair Bellerophon,
And wished her secret passion to indulge.

Her guilty suit the virtuous youth denied,
And to the king the queen thus falsely spake:
Die, Prætus, thou—or slay Bellerophon,
Who sought to violate my chastity.
The king was much enraged at hearing this,
Yet feared to take the young man's life himself,
But sent him into Lycia, carrying
Sealed letters to his relative the king,
In which the youth his own death-warrant bore.
He started off, protected by the gods;
But when to distant Lycia he came,
Where Xanthus' whirling currents swiftly flow,
The king of Lycia gladly welcomed him.
Nine steers he slew, and nine days feasted him;
But on the tenth, when rosy dawn appeared,
His youthful guest he would interrogate,
And asked to see the letters that he brought,
Wherein the deadly message he perused.
Then first he sent Bellerophon to slay
A frightful creature, the Chimæra called:
Of race divine the horrid monster was,
Made up of lion, dragon, and of goat,
And from her jaws emitting dreadful flames.
With Heaven's help the prodigy he slew.
Then with the illustrious Solymi he fought,
And such a battle ne'er was seen on earth;
Then the man-hating Amazons he killed;
Last, as the young man started to return,
The king another wily plot prepared,
Ordering the bravest warriors he had
To lie in wait, and kill him unawares;
But of the ambuscaders none returned,
For excellent Bellerophon slew them all.
The king discovered now his godlike race,
Kept him in Lycia, and his daughter gave
To be his wife; and more than that, he shared
One-half his kingdom with his stranger guest.
The Lycians, too, gave him a fine estate

Of pleasant fields, fruitful in corn and wine.
Three children now Bellerophon begat:
Two sons, Isander and Hippolochus,
And then a daughter Laodamia.
(With Laodamia Jove connection had,
Whence sprang the famous hero Sarpedon.)
At last he hateful to the gods became,
And wandered lonely o'er the Aleian plain,
Distracted and avoiding human kind.
His son Isander was by Mars destroyed
Whilst fiercely battling with the Solymi,
And chaste Diana Laodamia slew.
I by Hippolochus begotten was;
To Troy he sent me, giving much advice.
He told me, in the fight to be most brave,
And above all, to be pre-eminent,
Nor e'er do aught to shame my ancestors,
Who were the noblest people of the land,
Both in Ephyrè and broad Lycia.
Such is my race, and such the blood I boast.
He said; and much brave Diomed rejoiced.
His glittering spear he planted in the ground,
And thus to Glaucus spake, in kindly words:
Why, then, thou art our old paternal guest,
For Œneus, my grandsire, long ago
Was visited by good Bellerophon.
He lodged him in his palace twenty days,
And handsome gifts between them were exchanged:
Œneus gave a splendid purple belt,
Receiving from his guest a golden cup,
Which at my house I left when I came here;
But old Tydeus I remember not:
He left me yet an infant when he went
To Thebès, where he and many others fell.
So I thy host in Argos still will be,
Thou mine, if e'er to Lycia I go,—
And let us, too, each other's spears avoid.
Enough of Trojans I shall find to slay,

And thou enough of Greeks. As friends we will,
In token of our friendship, arms exchange,
That all may know the same affection still
Remains as ever in our families.
  Thus speaking, from their cars the warriors leaped
And grasped each other's hands, and plighted faith.
Then of his senses, Glaucus Jove deprived,
Who changed his splendid golden armor, worth
A hundred oxen, for a brazen one
Valued by Diomed at only nine.
  Meanwhile plumed Hector reached the Scæan gate;
Around him gathered all the Trojan dames,
Inquiring eagerly about their sons,
Their husbands, and their brothers, and their friends.
He bade them all to supplicate the gods,
For fearful ills impended over Troy;
Then to king Priam's splendid dome he went:
Adorned it was with noble porticoes,
In it were fifty rooms of polished stone,
Where with their wives the sons of Priam slept;
Upon the other side, across the hall,
Were the twelve chambers of his sons-in-law,
Where the king's daughters, with their spouses, lay;
There his fond mother met him on her way,
As she a visit was about to make
To her fair daughter Laodicè.
Seizing his hand, her son she thus addressed:
  Why hast thou left the fight and hither come?
The cursed Greeks keep battling round the town
And wear thee out; thou comest here, I think,
To ascend the citadel and pray to Jove.
Then tarry till I bring thee luscious wine
That thou to Heaven libations first may pour;
Then drink thyself; for to the weary man
Wine strength imparts, and weary thou must be,
Thus toiling for thy friends continually.
  Thus her dear son queen Hecuba addressed;
And thus great Hector, the plumed chief, replied:

Nay, venerable mother, bring no wine
Lest it may enervate and weaken me;
And a libation I should fear to make
To mighty Jove with these polluted hands,
For 'tis not right for those defiled with blood
To pray to Heaven, or offer sacrifice.
But go, collect the matrons of the town,
And to Minerva's sacred shrine ascend,
There, entering, place upon the goddess' knees
The largest, rarest, and most splendid veil
That can be got; and promise her besides
Twelve yearling heifers to be offered up
If she will pity have upon our town,
And save from death our wives and little ones,
Driving away this dreadful Diomed.
Then go, good mother; I meanwhile will seek
My brother Paris, try to rouse him up;
Perhaps he may give heed to what I say.
Oh, that the wretched man were in his grave!
For he was born to be a curse to Troy,
To Priam, and to all his family.
The day he dies will be a joyful day,
And I my sorrows then would quite forget.
He said; and to her house the queen returned
And bade her maids the matrons to collect;
But to her perfumed chamber she repaired,
Where her embroidered veils were stored away,
Made by Sidonian women, and brought o'er
By Paris, when from Sidon he set sail
On that same voyage when he crossed the sea,
Bearing away fair Helen from her home:
One of these veils did Hecuba select,
The rarest and most splendid of them all,
To be presented to the deity,—
Bright as a star the brilliant fabric shone.
Then for the sacred shrine the queen set out,
And many noble ladies followed her.
At length they reached the lofty citadel,

And fair Theano, wife of Antenor,
Who was the priestess of the sacred dome,
Opened the doors, and the long train went in.
With wailing tears, they raised their hands in prayer;
Then the queen placed upon Minerva's lap
The splendid veil, and suppliantly prayed:
  Revered Minerva, guardian of our town!
Break Diomed's spear, and cast him to the ground,
And let him lifeless lie before our gates,
And on thy altar I will sacrifice
Twelve heifers that have never borne the yoke
If thou wilt pity have upon our town
And on our Trojan wives and little ones.
Thus prayed queen Hecuba, but prayed in vain.
  Hector meanwhile to Paris' house repaired,
The beauteous palace he himself had built,
Aided by skillful architects of Troy.
Chambers and galleries and halls it had,
And on the summit of the city stood
Near to where Priam and bold Hector lived.
There Hector entered, holding in his hands
His mighty spear, eleven cubits long;
Bright shone its brazen point, and round it ran
A golden ring; he in the chamber found
His brother Paris burnishing his arms—
His splendid shield, his corselet, and his bow.
Near him sat Helen, with her maids around
Engaged in works of elegant design.
Then the bold chief his brother thus addressed:
  Brother, this sullenness is out of place;
Your countrymen are fighting round the town,
Fighting and perishing, and all for thee:
On thy account this bloody war began.
If any other Trojan should hold back,
How would'st thou chide! Up, then, and stir thyself,
Or soon our city may be wrapped in flames.
  Thus spake the chief, and Paris thus replied:
Hector, thy censure I acknowledge just;

Yet let me speak, and hearken to my words :
'Twas not so much in anger I sat here,
But rather to indulge in secret grief;
But now my wife e'en urges me to fight
With winning words; and 'tis perhaps the best,
For this time victory may be my luck.
Then tarry here whilst I my arms put on,
Or go, and I will follow and o'ertake.
Thus Paris spake ; but naught the chief replied.
Fair Helen then in kindly words began :
Dear brother of me, wretched, shameless one!
Would I had died the day that I was born,
Or that some storm or dreadful blast of wind
Had among desert mountains cast me forth,
Or plunged me deep within the roaring sea,
Before these miseries had come to pass ;
But if such ills were by the gods decreed,
My husband should have been a braver man
And sensible to shame and just reproach ;
But he no firmness has, nor e'er will have,
And for his weakness must the sufferer be.
Then come and sit thee down, my brother dear,
Since weary thou must be and overtasked,
For guilty Paris and for shameless me,
Destined by Jove for such a woeful fate
That we hereafter shall remembered be
And our sad story made the theme of song.
She said ; and thus plumed Hector answered her :
Bid me not, courteous Helen, to sit down ;
I cannot do so, for I feel impelled
To hurry back, and aid my countrymen,
Who cannot bear that I should absent be.
But rouse this man that he may overtake
And meet me ere I from the city go,
For I must now to my own home proceed
To see my household, and my infant son
And my dear wife ; for Heaven only knows
If e'er these eyes shall look on them again,
Since by the Greeks this day I may be slain.

Thus having said, plumed Hector went his way.
Soon at his handsome palace he arrived,
Nor did he find Andromache at home.
She, with her maid and infant child, had gone,
And now was standing on Troy's lofty tower,
Lamenting her sad fate, and bathed in tears.
Hector not finding then his wife within,
Stood on the threshold, and the maids addressed:
Tell me, my maidens, where's Andromache—
Does she a visit to her kindred pay,
Or did she with the other ladies go
In supplication to Minerva's shrine?
His faithful stewardess to the chief replied:
Hector, a truthful answer thou shalt have,—
Thy wife no visit to her kindred pays,
Nor did she with the other ladies go
In supplication to Minerva's shrine,
But when she heard that Troy was sorely pressed,
Like one beside herself, she hurried off,
And now is on her way to Troy's high tower,
And with her is her nurse and infant son.
She said; and noble Hector started off:
Through the paved streets he went of the wide town,
And reached the Scæan gate, through which the way
Led to the plain. There running towards him came
His wife, Andromache; daughter she was
Of noble Aëtion, Cilicia's king,
Who 'mid the groves of Hippoplacus dwelt.
She came to meet him, she and her faithful nurse
Bearing his infant son upon her breast;
A lovely child he was, bright as a star;
His father named the boy Scamandrius,
Others Astyanax, or bulwark called,
Since Hector ever had Troy's bulwark been.
Smiling he silently beheld the babe;
But to her spouse Andromache drew near,
Clung to his arms, and weeping, thus began:
Rash man! thy courage will thy ruin be;

No pity hast thou for thy tender child,
Nor thy poor wife, a widow soon to be,
For by the Greeks o'erpowered, thou wilt be slain ;
Nor would I wish to live, bereft of thee.
When thou art dead, no comfort have I left,
But grief and sorrow will be ever mine.
No father nor fond mother have I now ;
My father was by fierce Achilles slain
When he great Thebès destroyed, Cilicia's pride ;
Then Aëtion he slew, but stripped him not,
He reverenced the dead ; but burnt the king,
Him and his arms, upon a funeral pile,
And o'er him raised a monumental mound.
The mountain-nymphs around it planted elms.
Seven brothers too I had, who also fell
On the same day, by fierce Achilles' hand ;
He slew them as they fed their flocks and herds ;
My mother he a captive led away,
But for a precious ransom sent her back,
And she was shortly afterwards destroyed,
By Dian's silvery shafts, in her own halls.
But, Hector, thou to me art mother, sire,
And brother too ; and more than all thou art
My blooming husband ;—oh, have pity then !
Stay where thou art, upon the battlements,
Make not an orphan of thy tender boy,
Nor me a widow ; but draw up thy men
Round yonder fig-tree, where the wall is low,
And where the town is most assailable.
Thrice have the Greeks that very part attacked,
Led on by Diomed and Idomeneus,
By both the Ajaxes and Atreus' sons.
I know not whether 'twas some prophecy
Or their own judgment pointed out the place.
  Thus spake Andromache, and thus replied
Great Hector, chieftain of the nodding plumes :
Surely, my wife, that spot shall be my care,
And every other spot where duty calls ;

But I should blush with shame, and fear to face
The Trojan men, and Trojan ladies too,
If, like a coward, I should shun the field.
Nor could I do it, since I e'er was taught
To be the very foremost in the fight,
Both for my father's glory and mine own;
For well I know the day will surely come
When Troy shall fall, and Priam and his sons,
And Priam's people too, shall be destroyed.
But not for Troy's sad fate so much I grieve,
Nor for king Priam, nor for Hecuba,
Nor for my brothers, nor for the noble chiefs
And many warriors that shall meet their doom,
As I for thee lament; who by some Greek
A weeping captive shall be led away
To distant Argos, where for thy mistress thou
Shalt ply the weary loom, and water draw
From the Hyperian spring unwillingly.
Then as thou weepest, some will pointing say,—
Yonder is Hector's wife, the mighty chief
Who was so famous at the siege of Troy.
Fresh anguish then will wring thy broken heart
At thoughts of such a friend forever lost.
But may this head beneath the sod be laid
Ere I a witness of thy sorrows be.
  He said; and reached his hands to take the boy,
But to its nurse's breast the child shrank back,
Screaming aloud, and frightened at the sight
Of the brass helmet with its nodding plumes.
The parents smiled, and Hector from his head
Lifted his casque, and laid it on the ground;
Then in his arms the lovely babe he took,
Kissed it, and suppliantly prayed to Jove:
Oh, mighty Jove, and all ye deities!
May this my son, as I am, famous be,
And may he wisely govern sacred Troy;
And when from war he comes, may people say
Yon man is braver even than his sire;

His thousands may he slay and take the spoil,
And to his mother be a source of joy.
He said; and to his wife the child returned.
She, smiling 'mid her tears, the babe received,
And clasped it fondly to her fragrant breast.
Her husband looked on her with pitying eyes,
And took her by the hand, and thus addressed:
My dearest wife, lament not overmuch,
For none can slay me ere my time has come;
And no man, whether cowardly or brave,
When once he's born, can shun the stroke of death.
Return then home, thy household cares resume,
Be busy at the distaff and the loom;
But to the men of Troy, and most to me,
The battle-field and warlike deeds belong.
Thus having said, plumed Hector went his way,
And to her home his weeping wife returned,
Oft stopping as she walked, and looking back.
The house she entered, and her many maids
She by her sorrows melted into tears:
They mourned for Hector as already dead,
Thinking that by the Greeks he would be slain,
And from the field would never more return.
Nor did fair Paris in his chamber stay;
Clad in his beauteous arms, he sallied forth
And with quick steps proceeded through the town.
As when some stabled horse his halter breaks,
And, prancing o'er the plain, the river seeks,
His head he throws on high, and his long mane
Streams in the air, upon his shoulders tossed,
Proud of his beauty, galloping he flies
To the green meadows mingling with the mares:
So Paris from his mansion sallied out
Exultant, and in shining armor clad,
Bright as the sun, the handsome youth came forth
And Hector met, just as he left his spouse.
Then Paris first his relative addressed:

Brother, I have detained thee, I perceive,
And though I hastened, am behind my time.
He said ; and thus plumed Hector made reply :
Good soul, no person can with justice blame
Or say thou lackest courage for the fight ;
'Tis only indolence that holds thee back,
Yet still it vexes me, compelled to hear
The Trojans speak of thee reproachfully ;
And they on thy account have suffered much.
But of these things hereafter we will talk,
If a free cup we e'er shall drink to Jove,
Driving these brass-clad Greeks from sacred Troy.

BOOK VII.

THE FIGHT BETWEEN HECTOR AND AJAX.

ARGUMENT.

The contest is renewed with fresh ardor.—It is agreed that it shall be decided by a single combat between Hector and Ajax.—Neither party is victorious.—Priam asks for a truce, for the purpose of burning the dead; and is willing to close the war by paying the Greeks a compensation.—This is not agreed to; but the Greeks strengthen their position by erecting a rampart and digging a ditch.

THEN through the gate Hector and Paris rushed,
Both full of fire, both eager for the fight.
Grateful their presence to the Trojans was,
As is a breeze to tired mariners
Becalmed at sea, long laboring at their oars.
Then handsome Paris slew Menïstheus,
Son of Areïthous, the club-bearer:
Philomedusa was his mother's name,—
They over Arnè ruled; next Hector slew
Euneus; him with his spear he struck
Under the neck, and sent him to his doom.
Then noble Glaucus Iphinous slew,
Piercing him on his shoulder with his spear
As he was vaulting on his splendid mares:
Down from his steeds the warrior fell, and died.
Soon as Minerva thus perceived the Greeks
Falling so fast before their enemies,
She from the summit of Olympus flew
To sacred Troy, where from the citadel

Gazing upon the scene Apollo sat,
Wishing with all his heart for Troy's success.
The deities beneath a beech-tree met,
And to the goddess thus Apollo spake:
  Why art thou here again, daughter of Jove,
To give another victory to the Greeks
And without pity see the Trojans slain?
But if for once thou wilt be ruled by me,
Let us have peace at least for this one day
And afterwards the war may still go on,
Since so 'tis pleasing to ye goddesses,
Who seem determined to destroy this town.
  He said; and thus the blue-eyed maid replied:
So let it be, Apollo; for this cause
I to the earth from high Olympus flew.
But tell me how this truce thou wilt effect.
  Bold Hector I will urge, Apollo said,
To challenge some one of the noble Greeks
To single combat in the open field;
This will provoke the Greeks, and they in turn
Will from their ranks a champion select.
Thus spake Apollo of the silver bow,
And to his scheme the heavenly maid agreed.
  Now Helenus the prophet understood
This secret counsel of the deities,
And, seeking Hector, thus the chief addressed:
Oh, Hector, famed in counsel and in war,
Wilt thou give heed to what thy brother speaks?
Cause then the Greeks and Trojans to sit down,
And challenge to the combat some bold Greek,
For 'tis not yet thy destiny to die.
This revelation from the gods I have.
  He said; and Hector at his words rejoiced,
And by the middle grasping his huge spear,
He pushed the Trojans back. They all sat down;
And Agamemnon too the Greeks restrained.
Apollo and Minerva, on the top
Of a high beech, the shape of vultures took,

And gazed upon their heroes with delight,
Who sat in ranks, close packed, upon the ground,
Bristling with helmets, and with shields and spears.
As when a west wind, rippling o'er the sea,
Heaves up the ocean till it dark becomes,
So the whole plain was darkened o'er with men.
  Then in the midst advancing, Hector spake :
Hear me, ye Trojans, and ye bright-armed Greeks !
Almighty Jove our former truce annulled,
And evil for both parties has devised
Till you victorious have conquered Troy,
Or we shall drive you to your ships again.
The bravest of the Greeks your army claims.
Whoever chooses, let him then step forth
And against Hector be your champion ;
And should I fall beneath his conquering spear,
Let him my armor from my body strip
And bear it off in triumph to the ships,
But to the city let my corpse be sent,
That by the Trojans it may be received
And have the honor of a funeral pile ;
But on the other hand, should I slay him,
His armor will I take and carry back
To sacred Troy, where I will hang it up
As a proud trophy on Apollo's shrine,
But to your ships the body I will send,
So that the Greeks his funeral may make
And raise a tomb by the wide Hellespont :
Then sailing o'er the sea, in future times,
The gazing mariner will point and say.
Beneath yon tomb an ancient hero lies
Who by the hand of mighty Hector fell,—
So shall my glorious name immortal be.
  Thus spake the chief ; but they no answer gave.
Ashamed they were the challenge to refuse,
Yet dreaded to accept. Then quick rose up
With angry look the noble Menelaus,
And groaning in his heart, rebuked them thus :

Oh shame, ye cowards! Grecian dames, not men!
What a disgrace forever it will be
If against Hector we no champion send!
Sit where ye are, till ye to dust return,
Faint-hearted men,—but, as for me, I will
Put on my arms and go against this chief.
The issue of the combat rests with Heaven.
Thus having said, his armor he put on.
Then wouldst thou, Menelaus, have met thy doom,
So much was Hector thy superior,
Had not the chiefs all suddenly rose up
And from thy rash attempt dissuaded thee.
But Agamemnon seized thee by the hand,
And wisely counseling, addressed thee thus:
Art thou beside thyself, oh, Menelaus?
This folly is ill-timed; restrain thyself,
And though thou angry art, no contest have
With one who is far braver than thyself?
For mighty Hector is the dread of all,
E'en great Achilles, that unrivaled man,
Trembles to meet this famous warrior.
Then to thy ranks retire, and sit thee down,
The Greeks some other champion will find,
And this bold Trojan, now so fond of fight,
Will of his challenge soon be sick enough,
And if he falls not, will be glad to rest.
Thus spake the king; and to his prudent words
His brother yielded. Gladly his servants then
Took off his arms. Then sage Nestor rose,
And thus the Greeks addressed: Alas, ye gods!
What sad disgrace, what shame will fall on Greece!
How will good Peleus groan, that aged knight
Who used so frequently to question me
About our chiefs, their names, and families,
When he shall hear our warriors were cowed
By Trojan Hector, whom they feared to fight!
His aged hands to heaven he would raise,
And, sick of life, would pray that he might die.

By Jove !. I only wish I had my youth
As when the Pylians and Arcadians fought
By rapid Celadon, round Phea's walls,
Upon the banks of Jardan's flowing stream :
With them there was great Ereuthalion,
Having the arms of king Areïthous,
Godlike Areïthous, who had the name
Of mace-bearer, for he fought not with bow
Nor glittering spear, but with an iron mace ;
With this the strongest phalanxes he broke.
Him, not by courage, did Lycurgus slay,
But by a stratagem ; he met the chief
Within a narrow path, where his huge club
He could not use ; then with his stealthy spear
He ran the dreadful hero through the waist.
He fell upon his back and lifeless lay ;
Then of his armor he his foe despoiled,
By Mars presented, which he used in war.
But when Lycurgus an old man became,
He to his servant Ereuthalion gave
These very arms, in which he dared his foes.
The chiefs all trembled, and refused to fight ;
Then I stood up, the youngest of them all,
And with Minerva's help, the giant slew.
Down to the earth his monstrous body fell.
Oh, that I still were young, and had my strength,
Soon would plumed Hector then a champion have !
But ye, the bravest chiefs, refuse to fight.
  Thus with reproachful words the old man spake.
Nine chiefs then started up : first, king of men,
The godlike warrior, Agamemnon ;
Bold Diomed next, and the two Ajaxes ;
Then Idomeneus and Meriones ;
With these Eurypilus, Evaneous' son ;
Then Thoas, and Ulysses, godlike man.
These all with Hector now stood up to fight.
Then Nestor, the Geranian knight, thus spake :
By lots, we will decide who it shall be

That from the Greeks shall take away reproach
And for himself besides great glory gain.
He said; and each one marked his several lot,
Then threw it in the helmet of the king.
The people prayed to Jove with upraised hands:
Grant, father Jove, that Ajax be the man,
Or noble Diomed, or Agamemnon.
Then Nestor shook the lots, and first came forth
The lot of Ajax, as they all desired.
The herald passed it to the candidates,
And each disclaimed it as he showed it them;
But when the valiant Ajax took the lot
He knew it by the mark that he had made,
And gazing on it with a look of joy
He cast it to the ground, and thus began:
My friends, the lot is mine, and glad I am,
For I o'er Hector think I shall prevail.
But come, and let me put my armor on,
Whilst ye to Heaven offer up your prayers;
And pray in silence, lest the Trojans hear,—
Or pray aloud, if such your pleasure be.
We have no fear, and all may hear that please:
No one against my will can conquer me
By valor or by skill; nor was I born
And bred in Salamis, I trust, in vain.
He said; and thus to mighty Jove they prayed
Oh, father Jove, ruling from Ida's mount,
Most great, most glorious! to Ajax grant
A splendid triumph o'er this Trojan chief;
Or if thou hast regard for Hector, too,
Grant equal strength and honor to them both.
Then Ajax clad himself in shining brass,
And stood arrayed in all his panoply.
Like mighty Mars, when sent by father Jove
He goes to mingle in the wars of men,
So Ajax moved, the bulwark of the Greeks.
With a grim smile upon his countenance,
With stride majestic, o'er the ground he trod,

His spear tremendous holding in his hand.
The Greeks looked on their champion with joy,
But trembling fell upon the Trojan ranks,
And even Hector's valiant heart was moved;
But he could show no fear, nor make retreat,—
The Trojan champion, and the challenger.
But Ajax now drew near, with his brass shield
Vast as a tower, of seven ox-hides made
By Tychius, an artist most renowned,
Who dwelt in Hylè; he the framework spread
With tough bull-hides, and covered them with brass.
With this before his breast, Ajax advanced,
And thus with threatening words to Hector spake:
Hector, thou now shalt know what chiefs there are
Besides Achilles in the Grecian ranks;
He angry with the king stays at his ships,
Yet many brave enough our army boasts
To cope with thee. Come, then, begin the fight.
He said; and Hector the plumed chief replied:
Oh, godlike Ajax, son of Telamon,
I pray thee, think me not a timid boy
Or a weak woman, to be tampered with.
Battles and slaughters are not new to me,
For I can handle both my shield and spear,
And by the hour fight, if need there be;
I know the art of managing fierce steeds,
And o'er the field can drive the thundering car;
Yet I will no undue advantage take,
But fight thee in a fair and open way.
He said; and, aiming, hurled his glittering spear,
Which pierced the brass of mighty Ajax' shield;
Through six hides went, and in the seventh stuck.
Then Ajax cast his spear, and pierced the shield
Of Hector through and through, his corselet struck
And cut his linen tunic, near the flank.
The hero stooped, and so preserved his life.
Now in close fight, they with their spears engaged
Like hungry lions, or like strong wild boars.

Then Hector struck the buckler of his foe,
And bent his spear against the solid brass;
But Ajax, rushing, pierced the Trojan's shield:
The shock repulsed him, and the glittering spear,
Grazing his neck, caused the black blood to flow.
But the plumed Hector was not conquered yet,
For, stepping back, he with his sinewy hand
Seized a huge stone that lay upon the ground—
With it he struck his rival's mighty shield:
Loud rang the brass beneath the heavy blow.
Then Ajax a much larger rock took up,
Which like a millstone looked; with strength immense
He whirled it at his foe, striking his knees:
Down fell the warrior, leaning on his shield.
But by Apollo's aid he was raised up.
Now hand to hand they with their swords had fought,
Had not the sacred heralds interposed,
Both Greek and Trojan; they their scepters held
Between the chiefs, and thus Idæus spake:
No longer, my dear sons, engage in fight;
Ye both are by cloud-mantled Jove beloved;
Ye both are heroes as the world well knows;—
But night draws near, and night should be obeyed.
He said; and Ajax Telamon replied:
Bid Hector, good Idæus, speak his mind;
He was the challenger, and caused the fight.
To what he says, I cordially agree.
Thus Ajax spake, and Hector, answering, said:
Ajax, some god has gifted thee with strength,
With giant stature, and with wisdom too,
And with the spear no Greek can equal thee;
But let us for the present end the fight,—
Hereafter we the battle may renew,—
'Till Heaven decides who shall the victor be;
For night draws near, and night must be obeyed.
So to your camp return, rejoice the Greeks,
Your comrades, and your friends; whilst I to Troy
Returning will make glad the Trojans too,

And Trojan dames, who for my safety went
In supplication to Minerva's shrine;
And gifts to one another let us make,
So men will say that though we fiercely fought,
We afterwards made up, and parted friends.
  He said; and gave his silver-hilted sword
And scabbard also, with its handsome belt;
Whilst Ajax, on his part, presented him
With a blue girdle most magnificent.
  Then the chiefs parted—one to the Grecian camp,
The other to his throng of Trojan friends,
Who much rejoiced to see their hero safe
And by gigantic Ajax's hands unharmed;
So, scarce expecting he had been alive,
They led him back in triumph to the town.
  The well-armed Greeks led Ajax also back
With joy to royal Agamemnon's tent.
Then the king offered to almighty Jove
A bullock five years old; the beast he slew,
Then skinned and cut it up, roasted on spits,
Then served the viands up in proper style.
They placed in front of Ajax a whole chine,
A mark of honor to their worthy guest.
The feast they all partook of, and were filled.
  Then Nestor rose, judicious counselor,
And wisely speaking, thus addressed his friends:
Oh, Agamemnon, and all ye chiefs,
Many fair Greeks have fallen in the field:
Their red blood moistens all Scamander's plain,
And to dark Pluto's realms their souls have gone.
To-morrow, therefore, let the battle cease,
And let us with our oxen and our mules
The unburied bodies gather up and burn,
A little distance from our tents and ships,
So that each friend his kindred's bones may have
When the war ends, and we shall homeward sail;
And let us raise near to the funeral pile
A lofty tomb, a monument for all;

And let us also build a towering wall,
A bulwark both for us and for our ships,
With gates, that in and out our cars may go;
Outside, for further safety, we will dig
A trench, that we may well protected be,
Should the bold Trojans press too hardly on.
He said; and to his counsel all agreed.
  Meanwhile a panic-struck assembly met
On Troy's high citadel, near Priam's house,
And in the midst Antenor, rising, spake:
Hear me, ye Trojans, Dardans, and Allies!
My honest thoughts I feel impelled to speak.
Come, then, and let us to the Greeks restore
Helen and all her wealth, for now we fight
In violation of our faithful leagues,
And we in such a war can ne'er succeed.
  He said; and took his seat. Then Paris rose,
Fair Helen's spouse, and answering, thus replied:
Thy words, Antenor, most unfriendly are;
Thou knowest better how to speak than this;
But if thou serious art, why then the gods
Have quite bereft thee of thy common sense.
Now my opinion shall the Trojans have:
I say my wife I never will restore,
But all the wealth that she from Argos brought
I will give up, and add still more besides.
  He said; and took his seat. Then Priam rose,
A godlike counselor, and thus harangued:
Hear me, ye Trojans, Dardans, and Allies!
My honest thoughts I feel impelled to speak:
Go, take your usual meals, and keep strict watch,
And let each warrior be upon his guard;
But on the morrow let Idæus go
And carry Paris' message to the Greeks,—
Paris on whose account this war arose,—
And let him make a proposition too:
Whether a truce they will consent to have
Till we shall burn the bodies of the slain.

Then the fierce strife we will again commence,
Till Jove decides who shall victorious be.
He said; and to his counsel all agreed.
Each company prepared, and took their meals:
The next day to the ships Idæus went,
And found the Greeks assembled at the stern
Of Agamemnon's vessel. Drawing near,
He in their midst stood up and thus began:
Ye sons of Atreus, and all ye chiefs!
King Priam bids me Paris' message bring,
If 'tis your pleasure hearken to his words:
Paris, on whose account the war began,
Says that fair Helen's wealth he will restore,
And in addition give some of his own,
But he the lady never will send back,
E'en though requested by the men of Troy.
He bids me also ask the Grecian chiefs
Whether a truce they will consent to have
Till we shall burn the bodies of the slain;
Then the fierce strife we may again commence,
Till Jove decides who shall victorious be.
He said; and silent all the chiefs remained.
At length bold Diomed rose up and spake:
Nor Paris' wealth nor Helen will we take,
For now 'tis plain, and e'en a child might know,
Troy's doom is sealed, and very near at hand.
He said, and with loud cheers the Greeks approved.
Then to Idæus Agamemnon spake:
Idæus, thou the answer of the Greeks
Hast heard thyself; that answer I approve;
But to the truce I no objection make,
For no ill will we bear against the dead,
Nor grudge them funeral rites, if done at once.
Let Jove be witness then of this our league.
He said; and waved his scepter to the gods;
And back to Troy Idæus then returned
And told his message to the citizens,
Who in the assembly still together sat.

Then quickly they prepared to gather wood
And to collect the bodies of the dead.
The Greeks on their part also did the same.
Now from the ocean's heaving billows rose
The morning's sun, and lighted up the fields.
Upon the plain the Greeks and Trojans met:
Hard was it then to recognize the dead.
The bloody bodies they with water washed,
And, weeping, placed them in the chariots,
But Priam bade them not give way to grief;
They raised them silently upon the pile,
And, having burn'd them, back to Troy returned.
The Greeks on their part also did the same:
But at the twilight hour a chosen band
Gathered around the mouldering funeral pile,
And near it raised a monumental tomb;
Close by it then they built a towering wall,
A bulwark both for them and for their ships,
With gates, that in and out their cars might go;
Outside, for further safety, then they dug
A trench, that they might well protected be.
Thus through the night worked the industrious Greeks.
The gods round Jove assembled all looked down,
And saw the mighty structure as it rose.
Then with a groan great Neptune thus began:
Oh, father Jove, will mortal men henceforth
Consult the gods in what they undertake?
See yonder wall, erected by the Greeks,
With its deep ditch, a barrier for their ships.
No splendid hecatombs they offered up
To the immortals, when the work they raised,—
A work whose fame will o'er the earth be spread;
Whilst the great wall I and Apollo built
Round sacred Troy will quite forgotten be.
He said; and angrily great Jove replied:
Oh, Neptune, what a speech is this from thee!
Some second-rate deity might argue thus:
Thy glory shines far as the light extends;

But when the Greeks have to their homes returned,
Destroy this wall, submerge it in the sea,
And cover up the shore with drifting sand,
So will the mighty structure be effaced.
Thus they discoursed. But now the sun went down,
And the Greeks finished their laborious work.
Bullocks they slew, and took their evening meal;
And now from Lemnos' isle a fleet arrived,
Loaded with wine, which king Eunæus sent,
Whom fair Hypsipile to Jason bore.
A thousand measures were for Atreus' sons,
Sent by the monarch as a special gift;
The other Greeks, by barter, got their share—
Some giving brass, some iron, and some hides;
Some oxen traded off, and some gave slaves.
The feast they then prepared, and all partook.
The Trojans in the city did the same.
But for both parties Jove was planning ills,
And thundered all night long most awfully.
The warriors heard, and all turned pale with fear:
They offered up libations to the gods,
Nor dared to drink before they first had prayed.
Then they lay down, and quietly reposed.

BOOK VIII.

THE MEETING OF THE GODS.

ARGUMENT.

Jove assembles the gods, and forbids them to interfere in the war.—He then repairs to Ida, and darts his lightning upon the Greeks.—Nestor and Diomed advance against Hector.—Hector's charioteer is slain.—The Greeks seek refuge within their rampart.—Diomed again sallies forth, and Teucer is wounded by Hector, who takes measures to protect Troy during the night.

Just as the rosy light of morn appeared
Jove on Olympus' top convened the gods,
And thus the assembled deities addressed :
Hear me, ye gods, and all ye goddesses !
My resolution I will signify,
And what I signify must be obeyed :
Whoever of the gods shall in this war
Assistance give to Trojan or to Greek,
Back to his place, chastised, he shall be driven ;
Or shall be hurled to distant Tartarus,
Where a deep gulf there is, with iron gates,—
As far beneath the gloomy bounds of hell
As sky from earth ; then shall ye surely know
How much in power I excel ye all.
But come, make trial of my strength yourselves,
And from the sky let fall the golden chain.
Then pull, ye gods, with all your might and main !
Vain would your efforts be to drag me down ;
But I, with ease, could draw ye up to me,

And lift besides the earth and ocean too,
And round Olympus' summit bind the chain.
There in mid space, the ponderous weight would hang,
Such is the strength, and such the power of Jove.
He said; and struck with wonder, none replied,
So stern his words, so menacing his air.
At length Minerva thus her sire addressed:
Oh, son of Saturn, universal king!
We know thy might is irresistible,
Yet pity have we for the noble Greeks,
Doomed as they are, it seems, to be destroyed.
But in the conflict we will take no part,
As thou commandest; counsel them we will,
So that at least they may not all be slain.
She said; and thus cloud-mantled Jove replied:
Cheer up, dear child! take not too much at heart
The words I spake, for I intend no harm.
So saying, his fleet steeds he harnessed up,—
His steeds with golden manes and brazen hoofs,—
Then he arrayed himself in glittering gold,
And seized his whip, and mounted on the car.
He lashed the horses; willingly they flew
Midway between the earth and starry skies;
Ida he reached, mountain of crystal springs
And savage beasts; to Gargarus he came,
Where he an altar had, and sacred grove:
Then he drew up his car, unyoked his steeds,
And in a misty cloud enveloped them.
But he, exulting in his glory, sat
On Ida's top, and looking down beheld
The town of Troy, the sea, the Grecian fleet.
Meanwhile the Greeks partook of a repast,
A hurried meal, and then prepared for war.
The Trojans also, weaker though they were,
Prepared for battle; they were forced to fight
To save their homes, their wives, and little ones.
The city gates were all thrown open wide;
The forces sallied out, both horse and foot,

And mighty was the tumult that arose.
And now both armies to the combat rushed;
Then came the shock of arms; then brass-clad men,
Mingling in fight, against each other clashed;
Then spears were crossed, and shields encountered shields;
Loud was the clamor, loud the victors' shouts;
Loud were the groans, as the earth flowed with blood.
Thus all the morning raged the dreadful fight
'Mid showers of darts, and heaps of people fell.
  But when the sun had reached the mid-day skies,
Jove took the golden balance in his hands,
In it he placed the heavenly decrees,
The destinies of both the combatants;
The scales he poised; thus were their fortunes shown:
Flight and defeat were destined for the Greeks,
But for the Trojans joyful victory.
Then from the mount he thundered awfully,
And hurled terrific lightning on the Greeks.
Amazement seized them; all grew pale with fear.
Then Idomeneus fled, and Agamemnon,
And the two Ajaxes, heroic chiefs;
Nestor alone remained, unwillingly;
His horse was wounded by an arrow shot
By noble Paris, lovely Helen's spouse;
He struck it by the forelock, in the head,
A fatal spot; the steed in torture writhed,
And the whole team was in confusion thrown.
The aged warrior hastened with his sword
To cut the reins, and free the struggling beast;
Then on him Hector suddenly advanced,
Driving his horses at a furious rate;
And the old man would now have lost his life
Had not the valiant Diomed been near,
Who to Ulysses shouted lustily:
Son of Laertes, whither dost thou fly,
Showing thy heels, as if a coward thou?
Beware lest some one with his weapon now
Come up behind and pierce thee in the back.

Stay and assist this venerable man,
And let us save him from this furious chief.
  Thus spake the hero, but he spake in vain,
His noble comrade heard not what he said.
Onward he fled towards the Grecian fleet;
But Diomed alone maintained his ground,
Stood by the side of aged Nestor's car,
And thus in hasty words, addressed his friend:
Old man, these youthful warriors press thee hard;
The lapse of years has much impaired thy strength;
Thy steeds are slow, thy charioteer fatigued,—
Come hither, then, and mount upon my car,
Then wilt thou see what Trojan horses are,
How swiftly they can wheel, and scour the plain.
I from Æneas just now captured them.
Leave to the servants thy exhausted team,
Then will we both go forth, and Hector then
Will find that I like him can wield a spear.
  He said; nor did old Nestor disobey,
But to Eurymedon and Sthenelus gave
His car and steeds; both mounted then the car
Of noble Diomed. The glittering reins
Were held by Nestor, who lashed on the team,
And soon in front of Hector they appeared.
Then valiant Diomed his weapon hurled,
Yet struck not Hector, but his charioteer,
Whose name was Eniopeus; he fell,
Struck in the breast; his horses reared with fright.
For his slain servant much the Trojan grieved,
And sought another driver in his stead.
Soon Archetolemus the hero found,
And quickly made him mount and drive the car.
Then dreadful deeds had been, then blood had flowed,
And back to Troy the Trojans had been driven
Like frighted sheep, had Jove not interposed.
He loudly thundered, and his fiery bolts
Hurled to the earth, in front of Diomed's steeds;
They, struck with terror at the sulphurous flames,

Trembled and couched beneath the splendid car.
Old Nestor dropped the reins, and in dismay
Addressed his comrade, valiant Diomed:
  Turn back thy steeds, oh, son of Tydeus!
Jove is against us, and 'tis time to fly.
Glory to Hector he to-day decrees;
Good luck some other day may fall on us,—
And vain it is for man to strive with Heaven.
  He said; and thus bold Diomed replied:
Old man, thou givest excellent advice;
But this great trouble wrings my very heart:
Hector, in talking to his friends will say,
I put the warrior Diomed to flight!
Thus will he boast;—oh, may I perish first!
  He said; and aged Nestor thus replied:
Good Heavens! my friend, how strangely dost thou talk!
Should Hector call thee coward—what of that!
The Trojans will not believe his lying words,
Nor will the Trojan dames, whose husbands thou
Hast with thy own good spear so often slain.
Thus having spoke, he wheeled the horses round,
And with the rest fled to the Grecian camp.
  The Trojans and bold Hector followed them,
Crying aloud and hurling showers of darts;
And the plumed chief thus vaunted o'er his foe:
Oh, Diomed! the Greeks once honored thee
With a high seat when they a banquet made
And gave thee brimming cups and choicest food,
But they will never honor thee again,
For thou a timorous woman hast become.
Away, poor girl!—nor think to enter Troy
Or lead her captured people to thy ships—
Hector is here to send thee to thy doom.
  He said; and in suspense the hero paused,
And thought to wheel his steeds and meet the chief:
Thrice he made up his mind to turn and fight,
And thrice from Ida thundered mighty Jove,

A signal to the Trojans of good luck.
Then Hector to his warriors loudly cried:
  Onward, my comrades! quit yourselves like men,
Great Jove assists us, and will glory give;
But the proud Greeks he to destruction dooms.
Foolish!—they built these good-for-nothing walls!
Little will they avail to check my strength,
And o'er the ditch my steeds will swiftly leap.
But when their ships we reach, then think of fire,
That we may wrap their cursed fleet in flames,
And slay our foes, bewildered in the smoke!
  He said; and thus his noble steeds addressed:
Speed on, good Lampus, Æthron, and Podargus,
And Xanthus too! show the good keep you have,
For on the best of barley you have fed,
And often has Andromache, my wife,
Mingled sweet wine and given you to drink,—
Be quick and follow on, that I may seize
Old Nestor's shield, whose fame has reached to Heaven;
Of solid gold it is, handles and all;
And I from Diomed would also strip
That splendid coat of mail, by Vulcan made.
If I get these, I hope this very night
To drive these trembling Greeks aboard their ships.
  Thus boastingly the Trojan warrior cried;
But Juno on her throne trembled with rage,
And made Olympus shake; then she addressed
Neptune, the mighty ruler of the seas:
Hast thou no pity, Neptune, for the Greeks,
Thus sadly perishing before thine eyes?
Yet they in Helicè and Ægæ
Have on thy altars splendid offerings made.
Give them thy countenance and victory,
For should we all combine who love the Greeks,
These Trojans might be easily repulsed,
And haughty Jove, shorn of his ill-used power,
Might sit and grieve on Ida's top alone.
  She said; and Neptune with a sigh replied:

Rash Juno! what a speech is this to make!
I would not join in such a fight with Jove,
Since he by far excels us all in power.
  Thus they discoursed. But all the space between
The ships and walls was filled with men and steeds.
There had the conquering Hector crowded them;
And now he would have set the fleet on fire
Had Juno not bade Agamemnon haste
And rouse the sinking courage of the Greeks.
Among the ships and tents the monarch ran,
With his blue mantle thrown across his arm.
Upon Ulysses' bark he took his stand,
That thence his voice might be the better heard,
For in the center of the fleet it was,
And Ajax and Achilles thence might hear,
Who, trusting to their valor and their strength,
Had drawn their vessels up at either end.—
There took the king his stand, and thus cried out:
Shame on ye, Greeks!—handsome in form ye are,
But in your deeds detestable and foul!
Where are the boasts ye made in Lemnos' isle?
When feasting on the flesh of fatted steers
And drinking goblets of delicious wine,
Each of you said that he could whip with ease
A hundred Trojans at the very least.
Now Hector—only one—puts you to flight,
And threatens to consume our ships with fire!
Oh, Jove! was ever king disgraced like me
Or doomed to suffer such a weight of woe?
Yet in my luckless ship, where'er I sailed,
I never by thy handsome altars passed,
But always stopped, and offered sacrifice,
With prayers, that lofty Troy might be destroyed.
But grant me this at least, almighty Jove!
That we upon our ships may re-embark,
And may not by the Trojans all be slain.
  Thus spake the monarch, shedding many tears.
With pity Jove was moved, and signified

His people should be saved, and all be well.
An eagle then he sent, noblest of birds,
Which in his talons held a little fawn,
And let it on Jove's handsome altar drop.
Then the Greeks offered solemn sacrifice.
But when the heaven-sent bird the warriors saw,
They with fresh vigor on the Trojans turned;
But none such valor showed as Diomed.
He o'er the ditch his flying horses drove,
Assailed his foes, and the dread fight renewed.
He first a crested chieftain overthrew,
The son of Phradmon, Agelaüs called;
Him in the back he pierced, turning his car,
And at his breast the bloody spear came out.
Down from his chariot fell the dying chief,
And as he fell his clattering armor rang.
Next after Diomed rushed Atreus' sons,
King Agamemnon and Menelaus;
Then the Ajaxes and Idomeneus;
Then Meriones and Euryphilus;
Teucer came next, bearing his bended bow,
Behind the shield of Ajax Telamon;
Thence looking round, he would an arrow shoot,
And, having slain his man, would back retreat
Under his valiant comrade's sheltering arm,
Just as an infant to its mother runs.
Whom of his foes slew noble Teucer first?
First fell Orsilochus, and Ormenus next;
Then Ophelestes, and Dætor too,
Chromius and godlike Lycophantis,
And Melanippus, and Homopaön.
These, one by one, he piled upon the earth.
King Agamemnon looked on him with joy,
Destroying thus the Trojan phalanxes,
And, drawing near, addressed the hero thus:
Teucer, dear soul, thou son of Telamon!
Still shoot away, and be a glory thou
Both to the Greeks and to thy aged sire,

Who brought thee up, although a bastard son,
In his own house, and kindly treated thee,—
Honor thy sire, though far away he be.
But this I say, and what I say I mean:
Should Jove decree that I shall capture Troy,
Next to myself, thou shalt rewarded be;
Either a handsome tripod shall be thine,
Or else a chariot and pair of steeds,
Or some fair lady who thy couch shall share.
He said; and noble Teucer thus replied:
Why dost thou urge me, Agamemnon, thus?
I will not flag, but fight my very best,
For from the time the tide of battle turned,
This deadly bow has execution done.
Eight feathered shafts I have already shot,
And eight bold youths lie stretched upon the ground,
But I this raging dog can never hit.
He said; and then at Hector aimed again,
But missed the chief, but good Gorgythio struck,
Struck on the breast; the son of Priam he,
Fair Castianira his mother was;
Equal in beauty to a goddess she;
And as a garden poppy droops its head
When loaded down with fruit and vernal showers,
So the brave chief, bending his heavy head,
Pressed by his ponderous helmet, fell and died.
Teucer again at valiant Hector aimed,
But missed; Apollo warded off the shaft;
But Archetolemus his arrow struck,
The skillful charioteer of Hector,—
Pierced in the breast, he from the chariot fell;
The steeds sprang back; great grief the hero felt
At seeing thus his faithful servant fall;
Yet on the ground he suffered him to lie,
And bade his brother, who was not far off,
To take the reins; nor did he disobey.
Then from his shining car the hero leaped,
And, loudly shouting, seized a monstrous stone;

Then towards Teucer eagerly he ran,
Who from his quiver was just drawing out
A deadly shaft and placed it on the string;
But the plumed Hector struck him with the stone
Upon the shoulder, near the collar-bone,—
A fatal spot. The cord was broke in two,
And from his hand, benumbed, the weapon fell.
Upon his knees he dropped; but Ajax then
Neglected not his wounded relative,
But went, and with his buckler covered him.
Two of his faithful comrades then drew near,—
The brave Alaster and Mecistheus,—
Who bore him groaning to the hollow ships.
  But Jove fresh courage to the Trojans gave,
And to the ditch again they drove the Greeks.
Hector among them foremost ever kept,
With countenance of grim ferocity.
As when a hound a savage boar pursues
Or a fierce lion, close on his steps he hangs,
Clings to his haunches, nor will let him go:
So Hector hung upon the Grecians' rear,
And as they fled, he still the hindmost slew.
But when they crossed the palisades and ditch
In dreadful rout, for multitudes fell there,
They reached the ships, and rallied once again.
Then, cheering one another, they besought
The gods to help them with uplifted hands;
While Hector, with a Gorgon's flashing eyes
And looks as dreadful as ferocious Mars,
In all directions wheeled his splendid car.
  Juno with pity gazed upon the scene,
And straightway to Minerva, thus began:
Good Heavens! daughter of almighty Jove,
We seem to care not for the ruined Greeks,
Who by the hand of one man meet their doom,
For Hector is the author of these ills,
And rages with intolerable pride.
  She said; and thus the blue-eyed maid replied:

Yet surely this great warrior had been slain
By the brave Greeks, e'en on his native soil,
Did not my sire such foolish wrath display,—
Cruel, unjust, and ever against me!
Nor does he bear in mind my services,—
How often I assisted his own son.
Grieved with the labors of Euristheus,
His cries and supplications came to heaven;
Jove sent me down to help the sufferer;
But had I known all that has happened since
When he dispatched me to the gates of hell
To drag away that watch-dog Cerberus,
His son had never from foul Styx returned.
And he for all this kindness hates me now,
And silver-footed Thetis listens to,
Who kissed his knees and stroked his flowing beard,
And begged him with Achilles to take part;
And yet the day will come when he will change,
Call me his daughter dear, and blue-eyed maid.
But harness thou our brazen-footed steeds
Whilst I, Jove's mansions entering, arm myself;
Then will we see if Hector will rejoice
When me upon the field he shall behold;
For many Trojans then shall bite the dust
And be the prey of dogs and ravening birds.
  She said; nor did fair Juno disobey,
But quickly yoked the golden-harnessed steeds.
  Minerva then upon the floor let fall
Her beauteous robe, which she herself had made,
And, clad in Jove's bright arms, prepared for war.
Into the fiery chariot then she stepped,
And in her hands grasped her tremendous spear,
With which, when wroth, she tames embattled hosts.
Juno lashed on the swiftly-flying steeds,
Heaven's gates flew open of their own accord;
The watchful Hours stood there, on either side,
Ready to lift the heavy cloud that hung
Across the entrance of the Olympian domes

Through it the steeds impetuously rushed.
But when Jove saw the deities start off,
Great was his wrath. Swift Iris then he called,
Iris his messenger, with golden wings.
Fly quick, swift Iris ! haste and turn them back,—
A war betwixt these goddesses and me
Would have but one result and shameful be.
Hear what I say, and what I say I mean :
I with my thunder-bolts will lame their steeds,
Hurl these rebellious spirits from their car,
And break their car, and give them, too, such wounds
With my forked lightning as will take ten years
To heal; so that Minerva after this will know
What gain she reaps contending with her sire.
With Juno's folly I can better bear,
For 'tis her nature always to torment.
He said; and Iris, rapid as the storm,
Flew from Mount Ida to Olympus' top,
And met them at the outer gates of heaven.
There she restrained them, and addressed them thus :
What means this madness—whither are ye bound ?
Jove has forbid ye to assist the Greeks,
And threatens if ye do, to lame your steeds,
Hurl you as rebel spirits from your car,
And break your car, and give you, too, such wounds
With his forked lightning as will take ten years
To heal; so that Minerva after this will know
What gain she reaps contending with her sire.
With Juno's folly he can better bear,
For 'tis her nature always to torment.
But thou, most insolent, audacious slut,
How durst thou against Jove to lift thy spear ?
So Iris spake, and swiftly flew away.
Then Juno thus the blue-eyed maid addressed :
Alas, my daughter, born of Saturn's son !
We for the sake of miserable men
Must not attempt to battle with great Jove.
Let each one take his chance, and live or die :

This quarrel of the Trojans and the Greeks
Can only be determined by thy sire.
  She said; and wheeled her brass-hoofed team around.
The Hours unharnessed then the handsome steeds,
And to ambrosial mangers tethered them;
Against the splendid walls they tilted next
The chariot car; and then the goddesses
Upon their golden couches sat them down
Among the deities, disturbed in mind.
Then Jove from Ida drove his beauteous car,
And to his mansion on Olympus came.
Neptune unyoked his steeds, and stood the car
In its own place, with coverlets o'erspread.
Then on his throne the heavenly king sat down,
And all Olympus shook beneath his feet.
But Juno and Minerva sat alone;
No word they spake, no inquiry they made,—
He knew the cause, and thus addressing, spake:
Why, Juno and Minerva, are ye sad?
Your fight against the Trojans ended soon.
Not all the gods combined can master me,
My power and strength are so invincible.
But fear and trembling seized your handsome limbs
Before the battle even had begun;
But this I tell you would have come to pass—
Struck by my bolts, ye never had returned,
Ye nor your chariots, to the Olympian domes.
  He said; but Juno and Minerva sighed:
They by each other sat, devising ills
Against the Trojans. Minerva spake not:
Indignant at her sire, she boiled with rage;
But Juno made no secret of her wrath,
And thus addressed her venerable spouse:
Oh, son of Saturn, what a speech is this!
We of thy mighty power are all aware;
Yet must we pity still the noble Greeks,
Doomed to destruction as they seem to be;
Yet we will cease from war, if such thy wish,

But words of counsel we will still afford,
That through thy wrath they may not all be slain.
She said; and thus cloud mantled Jove replied:
To-morrow greater slaughter shalt thou see,
Nor will fierce Hector from the carnage cease
'Till from his ships Achilles shall rush forth,
Roused to the fight for good Patroclus slain,—
So fate decrees. I care not for thy wrath,
Not if thou wanderest to the farthest realms
Of sea and land, where Japetus dwells,
And ancient Saturn; there no sun is seen,
But deep, dark Tartarus is all around;
I care not for thee, shouldst thou e'en go there,
So impudent and unattractive thou.
He said; but Juno made him no reply.
Now sunk the sun beneath the ocean wave,
And darkness overspread the fruitful earth;
The Trojans grieved to see the day depart,
But grateful to the tired Greeks was night.
A council then the noble Hector called
Some distance from the ships, in a clear space
Upon the margin of the eddying stream,
Where no dead bodies lay; down from their cars
They leaped, to hear their chief beloved of Jove,
Who in his hand held his tremendous spear,
With gold-tipped point, encircled with a ring.
Leaning upon it, godlike Hector spake:
Hear me, ye Trojans, Dardans, and Allies!
I thought by this time we should have destroyed
These cursed Greeks, and set their ships on fire,
And then in triumph have returned to Troy;
But darkness intervened, and saved our foes
And saved their fleet, still beached upon the sand.
To-night then let us yield, and food prepare;
Our steeds we will unyoke, and forage give;
Then from the city fetch fat steers and sheep,
And luscious wine, and bread; then gather wood
And kindle many fires, that all night long

Light we may have, for fear these long-haired Greeks
May steal away across the briny deep.
Let them not easily embark their ships,
But send them, as they climb upon the decks,
Showers of arrows and destructive darts,
That they sad wounds may carry to their homes,
And all henceforth a lesson may receive,
And not again wage war against proud Troy.
Let heralds too throughout the town proclaim
That all the old men and the boys keep watch,
Posting themselves upon the god-built towers,
And let the women kindle blazing fires
In every hall, and let a chosen band
Keep faithful guard, so that no secret foe
May enter while the army is away
This is my word of counsel, men of Troy,
And on the morrow I will speak again,
Praying to Jove and all the deities
To banish from our shores these cursed hounds;
But let us all night long keep careful watch,
And at the early dawn renew the fight.
Then will I see if valiant Diomed
Will drive me from the ships, back to the town,
Or whether I shall bear away his spoils,
First having slain him with my brazen spear;
His spirit on the morrow let him show,
But he, I think, among the first will fall,
And many like him too will meet their doom.
Would that I only felt myself as sure
Of never dying, or could honored be
As wise Minerva, or Apollo are,
As I feel confident that on this day
Death and destruction on the Greeks shall fall.
  Thus Hector spake. The Trojans loudly praised;
Then from the cars the sweating steeds they loosed,
And haltered each to his own chariot.
Fat steers and sheep they from the city brought,
And luscious wine, and bread, and piles of wood;

The odor of the viands rose to heaven.
Thus all night long, upon the battle-field,
Full of high hope the Trojan warriors sat;
Their innumerable fires brightly blazed.
As when in heaven, around the silvery moon,
The twinkling stars conspicuous appear;
The air is calm, and not a breeze is heard;
Bathed in soft moonlight, every object shows,—
The craggy rocks, the woods, the towering hills,—
The joyful shepherd gazes on the scene;
Upward he looks into the starry sky
And tries to pierce the unfathomable blue.
Thus between flowing Xanthus and high Troy
The numerous Trojan watch-fires appeared;
A thousand of them blazed upon the plain,
And around each fifty bold warriors sat.
Their steeds were haltered to the chariot cars,
Eating white barley and nutritious oats,
And waiting patiently for rosy dawn.

BOOK IX.

THE EMBASSY.

ARGUMENT.

By Nestor's advice, Agamemnon sends Ulysses, Phœnix, and Ajax to Achilles, to endeavor to bring about a reconciliation.—The aged Phœnix makes a touching appeal to the incensed warrior, but without effect.

Thus did the Trojans through the night keep watch;
But panic fear possessed the routed Greeks,
And heavy were the hearts of all the chiefs.
As when two mighty winds, the north and south,
Blowing from Thrace, across the fishy sea,
Lift the dark waves, the heaving ocean boils,
Dashing the sea-weed all along the shore:—
So with alarm the sorrowing Greeks were stirred.
But most of all king Agamemnon grieved,
And moving up and down, his heralds sought,
And bade them call, but not to call too loud,
The chiefs to council. Sorrowful they met;
Then in their midst the troubled monarch rose,
And as some fountain from a lofty rock
Pours its dark waters in a copious flood,
So streamed the tears from Agamemnon's eyes;
And deeply groaning, thus the king began:
  Oh, friends, and leaders of the Grecian hosts!
Hard is the lot assigned me by great Jove,
Who promised me that lofty Troy should fall
And I in safety to my home return.
But 'twas a cruel fraud that he devised,

For now he bids me back to Argos go,
After the loss of thousands of my men.
So wills the king of gods, who has destroyed
So many towns, and who will yet destroy;
Then come, and let us launch our gallant ships,
And flee away back to our native land,
For Troy by us will never captured be.
He said, and no one to his words replied;
Silent and sad the whole assembly sat.
At length the valiant Diomed began:
Thy speech, oh, son of Atreus, I oppose,
But be not thou offended at my words.
Thou once didst slight me, telling me I was
Slothful, unwarlike, and of no account:
And this reproach was heard by all the Greeks,
Both young and old. On thee great Jove conferred
A mighty favor when he made thee king,
But valor, choicest gift, was never thine.
And dost thou, as thou sayest, really believe
The Greeks are cowards, and unfit for war?
Why then, depart, if such thy pleasure is;
Thou knowest the way, and yonder are thy ships,
Thy numerous fleet, which from Mycena came.
But we, thy comrades, here will still remain
Till Troy shall yield. But should the rest all flee,
Yet Sthenelus and I alone will stay,
And, with Jove's help, fight till the city falls.
He said; and loudly did the Greeks applaud,
Admiring much the speech of Diomed.
Then rising up Geranian Nestor spake:
Mighty in battle art thou, Diomed,
And equally renowned in council too;
No one can gainsay what thou just hast said;
But still the theme is not exhausted yet.
Youthful thou art, and easily might be
My youngest son, yet wisely hast thou spoke,
And to the chief hast given sound advice;
But since I am thy senior by far,

I now will speak; nor will the king I think
Refuse to hear, or disregard my words:
Cursed be the man who civil discord loves.
But night draws near, and night must be obeyed;
Then come and let us take our evening meal,
And station guards along the trench and wall;
Do thou a banquet then, oh king, prepare,—
Thy tents are full of wine, brought day by day
Across the sea from Thrace's neighboring shore:
Well can a wealthy monarch give a feast.
But when the guests have met, take his advice
Who wisest speaks, for wisdom much we need,
Since by our foes we closely are besieged,
And round our ships their numerous watch-fires burn.
Sad state of things!—enough to make us mourn,
For on this night it will decided be
Whether our army shall be saved or lost.
He said; and to his words they all gave heed:
Then the guards armed, and to their stations went.
Nestor's own son, Thrasymedes, went first,
And bold Iälmen, and Ascalaphus,
Deïpyrus, Merion, and Aphareus,
And Creon's noble son, Lycomedes;
Each of these chiefs a hundred warriors led.
Silent they marched out to the trench and wall,
And sat them down, and took their evening meal.
Meanwhile the chiefs met in the royal tent,
And of the festive viands all partook.
Their thirst assuaged and appetite appeased,
Nestor, whose counsel always was the best,
Rose in their midst, and thus his friends addressed:
Oh, Agamemnon, noble Atreus' son,
With thee I will begin, with thee will end,
For thou our monarch art, to whom Jove gave
Dominion over multitudes of men
To rule them justly, in the fear of Heaven;
And thou should'st counsel give and counsel take,
For the state's welfare all depends on thee.

Now will I speak what seems to me the best,
For good advice I ever seek to give,
E'en from that day when thou Achilles robbed
Of fair Briseis; I protested then
Against the wrong with all my eloquence,
But thou gavest way to haughtiness and rage,
Insulting our best man; a man esteemed
E'en by the gods. The maid thou keepest yet.
But come, and let us try to win him back
With noble presents and with kindly words.
He said; and to his speech the king replied:
Old man, thou well remind'st me of my fault.
That I have erred is not to be denied:
That man alone is worth a mighty host,
And greatly honored and beloved by Jove,
Who has avenged his wrongs and punished us.
But since I erred, and to my wrath gave way,
I willingly his anger will appease
And noble gifts bestow. Now hearken all
Whilst I my presents will enumerate:
Seven tripods that were never used I'll give,
Of gold ten talents, twenty caldrons bright,
Twelve famous steeds, that ever in the race
The prize have gained; no pauper would he be
Who all the gold possessed that they have won:
Seven fair Lesbian dames I too will give,
All skilled in elegant accomplishments,
Selected by myself when Lesbos fell;
No lovelier women e'er were seen on earth.
The maid Briseis, too, I will restore,
And swear a solemn oath that I with her
Ne'er joined in love, approaching to her couch.
These I will give at once; but should Troy fall,
And Priam's noble city e'er be ours,
His vessels I will load with brass and gold
When we divide the spoil; and add beside
A score of ladies, second only to
Helen herself. But when to Argos we

Safely return, Argos, that fruitful land,
My son-in-law I'll make him, and bestow
Such honor on him as I show my son,
The young Orestes, darling of my home.
I have three daughters too, Chrysothemis,
Iphigenia, and Laodicè;
A beauteous bride from these he may select,
And such a splendid dowry receive
As never father to a daughter gave.
Seven fine cities also shall be his,
Cardamylè, green Hira, and Enopè,
The glorious Pheræ, and the fair Æpea,
Antheia, and the vine-clad Pedasus,
All on the sea, the last to Pylos close;
Men rich in flocks and herds inhabit them;
Large tribute will they pay and gifts besides,
And their new ruler honor as a god.
These will I give him, ceasing from his wrath.
Heaven grant that he may be prevailed upon!
Pluto indeed is most implacable,
Therefore most hateful of the gods is he;
But he should yield to me, for I am king,
And boast besides to be his senior too.
   He said; and to him Nestor thus replied:
Oh, royal Agamemnon, noble king,
Thou offer'st to Achilles splendid gifts.
But come, and let us proper men select,
Who quickly to Achilles' tent may go.
These would I name, and let them soon depart:
Let Phœnix, dear to Jove, the leader be,
And wise Ulysses, and great Ajax too,
And with them let the heralds Hodius go,
And Eurybates; but first fetch water,
That with holy hands, and prayers to Jove,
We may his pity gain, and have success.
   He said; and to his counsel all agreed.
Then on their hands the heralds water poured,
And by the boys their cups were filled with wine;

Then their libations made, each took his share,
And from the tent the embassy went forth.
Geranian Nestor gave them much advice,
And earnest counsel to Ulysses most
How best to pacify the angry chief.
  Then on their peaceful errand they set out,
Along the margin of the roaring sea,
Praying to Neptune, as they trod the shore,
That he would melt Achilles' stubborn heart.
They reached the vessels of the Myrmidons,
And found the warrior sitting in his tent;
With song and music he amused himself,
Holding a splendid lyre in his hands,
Mounted with silver curiously wrought:
He found it 'mid the spoils of Eteon's town;
With it he now was soothing his great soul,
And sang of heroes, and their glorious deeds.
By him his friend Patroclus silent sat,
Waiting to speak when he should cease to sing.
Ulysses led the way, and near they drew,
And now the Grecian chiefs before him stood.
  Achilles saw them, and sprang up amazed;
Patroclus too arose, beholding them.
Then by the hand Achilles took his guests,
And thus in courteous language them addressed:
  Hail, warriors, you I recognize as friends!
Surely important business brings you here;
Though greatly wronged, and most incensed I am,
Yet you of all the Greeks are still most dear.
  He said; and brought the strangers in the tent
And sat them down upon a purple couch.
Then to his friend Patroclus thus he spake:
Patroclus, fetch a larger goblet forth,
Mix purer wine, for these are men most dear
Who now are seated underneath my roof.
  He said; nor did his comrade disobey,
But he before the fire placed a block,
And on it sat the carcass of a sheep,

And a fat goat, a loin of pork besides :
Automedon, his servant, held the meat,
Whilst bold Achilles cut the pieces up
And placed on spits ; Patroclus kindled then
A rousing fire, spread out the glowing coals,
And, sprinkling the flesh with sacred salt,
Roasted the meat and placed it on the board;
Then bread he brought, in handsome baskets piled.
Achilles opposite Ulysses sat,
Helping his guests; but bade Patroclus first
To offer to the gods a sacrifice,
Casting a proper portion in the fire.
Then of the savory food they all partook.
But when the chiefs had eat and drank enough
Ajax to aged Phœnix gave a nod;
Ulysses took the hint, and filled a cup,
Which to his host he pledged, and thus began :
  Achilles, health ! well have we feasted here,
Even as when we banquet with a king;
But matters more important than a feast
Concern us now. Disasters threaten us,
And shouldst thou, mighty chief, withhold thy aid,
'Tis doubtful whether we be saved or lost;
For near our ships the foe has pitched his camp,
And all around their numerous watch-fires burn :
Nor will they cease 'till on our fleet they fall!
Jove too has given them propitious signs.
And Hector, glaring with ferocious eyes,
Confides in Jove, and rages terribly!
So mad he is, he fears nor gods nor men.
Impatient, he awaits for rosy dawn ;
He says he then our vessels will attack,
Set them on fire, and consume them all,
And slay us Greeks, bewildered in the smoke!
Greatly I fear his threats will be fulfilled,
Then shall we perish upon Trojan soil,
Far from our Argos, famed for noble steeds!
Rise, then, if 'tis thy purpose, e'en though late,

And from their slaughtering foes protect the Greeks!
Shouldst thou refuse, hereafter thou wilt grieve,
For after ruin comes, 'twill be too late.
Think how thou mayest effectually assist!
Think what advice thy father Peleus gave
When to the Trojan war he sent thee forth!
My son, he said, great strength thou wilt receive
From Juno and Minerva; but take heed
To curb thy haughty soul, and peaceful be,—
Mildness is better far; abstain from wrath,
So thy companions all will love thee more.
Thus spake thy sire, but thou forgot his words;
But even now relent, dismiss thy rage,
For noble gifts our king has promised thee.
Now hearken, whilst his presents I recount:
Seven tripods that were never used he'll give,
Of gold ten talents, twenty caldrons bright,
Twelve famous steeds that ever in the race
The prize have gained; no pauper he would be
Who all the gold possessed that they have won:
Seven fair Lesbian dames he too will give,
All skilled in elegant accomplishments:
Selected by himself when Lesbos fell,
No lovelier women e'er were seen on earth;
The maid Briseis, too, he will restore,
And swear a solemn oath that he with her
Ne'er joined in love, approaching to her couch.
These he will give at once; but should Troy fall,
And Priam's noble city e'er be ours,
Thy vessels he will load with brass and gold
When we divide the spoil; and add besides
A score of ladies, second only to
Helen herself. But when to Argos we
Safely return, Argos, that fruitful land,
His son-in-law he'll make thee, and bestow
Such honor on thee as he shows his son,
The young Orestes, darling of his home.
He has three daughters too, Chrysothemis,

Iphigenia, and Laodicè;
A beauteous bride from these thou mayest select,
And such a splendid dowry receive
As never father to a daughter gave.
Seven fine cities also shall be thine,
Cardamylè, green Hira, and Ænopè,
And glorious Pheræ, and the fair Æpea,
Antheia, and the vine-clad Pedasus,
All on the sea, the last to Pylos close;
Men rich in flocks and herds inhabit them;
Large tribute will they pay, with gifts besides,
And their new ruler honor as a god.
These will he give thee, ceasing from thy wrath.
But if the king is hateful to thee still,
He and his gifts, have pity on the Greeks
Thus sadly perishing, who honor thee
E'en as a god; great wilt thy glory be:
For Hector thou may'st slay, who now comes here
Boasting with furious rage that none with him
Has equal valor or will dare to cope.
He said; and to him thus the chief replied:
Most wise Ulysses, it is meet that thou
Shouldst a direct, explicit answer have,
And not sit whining here and wasting words:
Hateful as hell are hypocrites to me,
Whose thoughts are different from what they speak.
Then hearken while my purpose I reveal;
Nor do I think that Agamemnon will
Persuade me, nor indeed the Greeks combined:
Since he no thanks receives who toils and fights,—
The brave and cowardly all fare alike,—
I nothing gain for all the risk I run;
But like a bird which carries to her young
The food she finds, starving herself meanwhile:
So many bloody days and sleepless nights
I spent in battle to preserve the Greeks.
Twelve cities on the sea I with my ships
Have ravaged; and eleven more on land:

Much valuable spoil I took from them,
All which to Agamemnon I gave.
Whilst he, remaining idle in his tent,
A trifling portion on his friends bestowed,
Whilst he the lion's share retained himself;
Their several prizes all the rest possess;
But I alone have been deprived of mine,
For he has robbed me of my much-loved spouse.
Well, let him have her, and delight himself:
What is this war about? Why did your king
Gather together such a mighty host?
Was it not for the beauteous Helen's sake?
Are Atreus' sons alone fond of their wives?
Their wives, to good men, always are most dear:
So I Briseis loved with all my soul,
Though with my bloody spear I captured her.
Then since he has deprived me of the dame,
And cheated once, let him not try again,
For now I know him, nor can he persuade.
But let him plan with thee, and with the rest,
How best he may protect his fleet from fire
Without my aid; a rampart he has built,
And dug a mighty ditch, and planted stakes;
But Hector is not thus to be restrained.
Whilst I was with you, near the town he kept,
And never further than the beech-tree got;
There once he came, and barely saved himself.
But now no more with Hector will I fight,
But on the morrow, paying vows to Jove
And all the gods, my vessels I will launch,
And then wilt thou behold me setting sail
Upon the waters of the Hellespont;
And if a prosperous voyage Neptune gives,
On the third day rich Phthia I will reach.
There have I great possessions of my own,
And I will carry there my share of spoil,
Iron, and gold, and brass, and lovely dames;
But my chief prize king Agamemnon took.

Of this remind him ; and tell all the Greeks,
Lest he may them deceive, as he did me ;
Nor let the dog e'er look me in the face ;
Ne'er will I act with such a faithless man.
Once he deceived me, but will not again ;
Let him go on, and meet his certain doom,
For Jove has of his senses him deprived.
His gifts are hateful to me, and despised;
Him and his gifts I value not a hair,
Nor would I take them, even if they were
Increased in value more than twenty times ;
Nor should he Orchomenus' riches add,
Nor the vast treasures of Egyptian Thèbes,—
That mighty city of a hundred gates,—
From each of which two hundred chariots rush ;
Nor were his gifts as numerous as the sand
Would I by Agamemnon be moved
Till for this insult I have had revenge.
Nor will I wed his daughter, though she were
Lovely as Venus, as Minerva wise ;
Let him some other son-in-law select,
Some other Greek, of nobler blood than mine.
But when I reach my home Peleus himself
Will find a lady who shall be my bride.
Many fair dames there are in Phthia sure,
And Hellas too; daughters of noble chiefs,
From all of these a wife I may select,
And there in marriage joined with a fit spouse
My father Peleus' wealth I will enjoy.
My life more valuable is to me
Than all the riches ever heaped in Troy
In her best days, when peace and plenty reigned,
Than all the treasures of Apollo's shrine
In rocky Pitho. We by plunder may
Gain sheep and oxen, tripods and fleet steeds,
But life once lost can never be regained.
Thetis, my goddess mother, has declared
That o'er me double destinies impend:

That should I at the siege of Troy remain
Immortal glory will my portion be,
But never shall I see my home again.
But, on the other hand, should I return,
Glory I lose, but length of days is mine.
And this advice to all I now would give:
To launch our fleet and sail away for home,
For lofty Troy will never captured be.
Jove o'er the town has stretched his saving hand,
And with fresh courage now the Trojans fight;
Then carry back my message to the chiefs,
As good ambassadors, and bid them plan
Some other means by which to save themselves,
Since this their present scheme will not succeed.
But Phœnix shall remain with me to-night,
That on the morrow he with me may sail
Back to his native land, if so he will.
Thus spake Achilles, and all silent sat,
With wonder struck, so forcible his words.
At length with tears the aged Phœnix spake,
For much he trembled for the Grecian fleet:
  If thou, Achilles, really dost intend
To re-embark and leave us to our doom,
How can I, my dear child, stay here alone,
For aged Peleus sent me forth with thee
To Agamemnon? when thou wert a boy,
Unskillful both in council and in war,
Me thy preceptor he ordained to be,
To teach thee how to speak and how to act:
So I, dear child, can never thee desert,
Not e'en should Jove divest me of my years,
And promise to restore me to my youth,
Such as I was when I from Hellas fled,
Having at home a quarrel with my sire
Amyntor, who with me was much enraged
About a handsome courtesan he loved,
Inflicting on my mother grievous wrong.
She begged me the strange woman to embrace,

And make her thus her aged lover loathe.
I did so ; but my sire became incensed,
Cursed me, and to the hateful Furies prayed
That on his knees no child of mine might sit.
His prayer was heard, both Proserpine and Jove
Decreeing that no offspring I should have.
My father thus enraged, I could not bear
Within the palace longer to remain ;
But my relations begged me not to leave.
Banquets they made, and slaughtered fatted sheep,
Oxen and swine ; and of the old man's wine
Broached many a cask. Nine nights they watch'd me close;
Nor did the fires go out, one of which blazed
Within the yard, the other in the hall;
But on the tenth dark night I sallied forth,
Bursting the chamber door, and reached the hall.
Eluding thus the watchmen and the maids,
From Hellas then I fled, and Phthia reached—
Rich Phthia, that in flocks and herds abounds;
Thy father Peleus received me there,
And loved me as a father loves his son ;
Much wealth he gave, and made me ruler too
O'er the Dolopians, a numerous tribe.
Thee too, Achilles, from my soul I loved,
And made thee what thou art. With me alone
To table wouldst thou go; I cut thy meat,
And, sitting on my lap, thou sipp'st thy wine,
And often slobbered it upon my clothes:
Such was the care and trouble I endured
On thy account; for since the gods decreed
That I should childless be, I looked to thee,
Determined to consider thee my son.
But oh, Achilles ! curb thy haughty soul,
This merciless behavior is not right:
The gods themselves are not inflexible,
Who tower above thee far in excellence,
So great their fame, their virtue, and their power.
These, when we sin, we often may appease

With prayers, with incense, and with sacrifice;
For Prayers the daughters are of mighty Jove:
Ill-favored, squint-eyed, lame, they follow Sin;
But Sin is strong and lively, and runs fast,
Outstripping far the others, and comes first
To every land, inflicting woes on men,
Which 'tis the office of kind Prayers to cure.
Whoe'er respects these daughters of great Jove
Him they assist, and when he asks, give ear;
But he who treats them ill, and drives them off,
Him they report, and beg their father Jove
That Sin may hold him fast and torture him.
But thou, Achilles, wisely honor them,
As bravest men have honored them before.
If Agamemnon did not presents give
And promise more, but still retained his wrath,
I would not then advise thee to relent
Nor help the Greeks, however great their need;
But now he gives thee much, and will give more
Moreover, he has sent the noblest men,
And dearest to thyself, to gain thee o'er,
Whose words and mission do not thou despise,
Though at thy wrath we found no fault at first.
Thus too of the renown of heroes dead
We all have heard, who oft to rage gave way,
Yet were they pacified by handsome gifts,
And often by soft speeches reconciled.
An ancient case in point I bear in mind,
Long since in olden times the thing occurred,
And to you all the tale I will relate.

The Ætolians and Curetes fiercely fought
Round Calydon, and many perished there;
The former were defenders of the town,
The latter sought to raze it to the ground.
Diana had the contest set afoot,
Indignant that Œneus had not laid
The first fruits of the land upon her shrine:
The other gods enjoyed their hecatombs;

But to Jove's daughter he no offerings made,
Either by oversight or by neglect;
But 'twas a grievous error certainly.
Greatly enraged, the huntress deity
Sent a wild sylvan boar, with huge white tusks,
Upon the fields and orchards of Œneus;
Many great trees the monster rooted up,
And cast them, with their blossoms, to the ground.
This beast the youthful Meleager slew,
Œneus' son, he and a numerous band
Of men, and hounds, he had together got,
For a small force would ne'er have conquered him,
So fierce he was, and had so many slain.
And now a quarrel rose about the spoil,
Between the Ætolians and the Curetes,
Who should possess the monster's head and skin.
As long as noble Meleager fought,
Ill fared the Curetes, nor could they stand,
Though numerous they were, before the town;
But when to wrath the warrior gave way,
As happens sometimes to the wisest men,
Then he withdrew to Cleopatra fair,
His wedded wife, nor mingled in the war.
Althea, his own mother, him incensed;
But Cleopatra was Marpessa's child—
Idas her father was, boldest of men,
Who, for his graceful, handsome-ankled wife,
Dared at Apollo e'en a shaft to send.
But when at home the mother and the sire
Would Cleopatra call Alcyonè,
Because her mother, in halcyon tones,
Lamented when Apollo bore her off.
Thus Meleager would no longer fight,
Wroth with his mother for her curses, which
She uttered for her murdered brother's sake.
Oft with her hands she smote the fruitful earth,
And on her knees, her bosom wet with tears,
Begged hateful Pluto and dread Proserpine
To slay her son. The Furies heard her prayer.

Then round the city rose the cry of war;
The foe drew nearer, battering at the walls;
The elders begged their champion to go forth
And save the town. The holy priest they sent
To urge him too, with promise of a gift,
That he the richest piece of land might choose
Of fifty acres—one-half fit for vines,
The other cleared and ready for the plow.
His venerable sire Œneus too
Besought him, going to his chamber door,
Shaking the latch and bidding him to come;
His sisters and his mother did the same;
But Meleager was inexorable.
The more they begged the more the chief refused;
His young companions, dearer far than all,
Joined their entreaties also, but in vain.
Nor did he yield until the war approached
E'en to his chamber, for the wall was scaled,
And soon the city had been wrapped in flames.
Then his dear weeping wife entreated him,
Painting in vivid colors all the woes
Of a sacked town: the heaps of slaughtered men,
The buildings wrapped in devastating flames,
The women and the children captive led!
Hearing these dreadful things, his heart was moved,
And, starting up, he seized his glittering spear.
Thus from their foes his countrymen he saved;
Yet on the hero they conferred no gift.
But be not thou like him, nor wait till thou
By sad necessity art forced to act,
For not so glorious will be thy aid
When our unhappy fleet is set on fire.
Come, then, and take the gifts, for now the Greeks
Will show thee godlike honor. By and by,
Should'st thou think proper to bestir thyself,
No gifts nor equal honor wilt thou gain.
He said; and thus Achilles made reply:
Phœnix, good soul, their honor I need not—

'Tis Jove who honors me, by whose command
I by my ships will stay while life remains.
But I to thee have somewhat too to say:
Disturb me not with thy complaints and tears.
Pleasing and gratifying Agamemnon,
Thou must not love him and incur my hate;
Thou should'st annoy him, as he me annoys;
Share my command, and share my honor too.
Then let these others take my message back;
But thou shalt here repose on a soft couch,
And on the morrow we will counsel take,
Whether to stay here or home return.
He said; and to Patroclus made a sign
To spread a couch, whilst the two other chiefs
Rose up, and from the tent prepared to go;
But, before leaving, thus great Ajax spake:
Most wise Ulysses, famed Laertes' son,
The object of our interview has failed,
And cannot in this manner be obtained;
But to the Greeks the answer we must bear,
Although ungracious. They expecting, wait;
But in his breast Achilles nourishes
An overbearing spirit. Foolish he,
Unwilling to his dearest friends to yield,
Who honor and revere him above all;
Most cruel man!—e'en for a brother slain
His relatives a compensation take,
And, having paid his fine, the murderer lives,
The other party being satisfied;
But thou art angry merely for a maid;
Whereas we seven maidens offer thee,
And add inestimable gifts besides.
A kindly disposition then assume,
Respect thy house, since we are guests of thine,
And none of all the Greeks regard thee more.
Thus Ajax spake; and thus the chief replied:
Most noble Ajax, son of Telamon,
Thou seemest sincere in all that thou hast said;

Yet still my heart with indignation boils
When I think how your king dishonored me
Before the assembled Greeks, as though I were
Some wretched vagabond of no account.
But go ye now, carry my answer back,
For in the battle I will take no part
Till Hector shall attack the Myrmidons
And slay my men and set my ships on fire.
But when the Trojans shall approach my fleet
I think his heart will fail, and he will pause.
He said; and then libations having made,
Ulysses leading, home the chiefs returned.
The servants then were by Patroclus bid
To spread for aged Phœnix a soft couch;
They did so, and with coverlets and rugs
A bed prepared, on which the old man slept.
Achilles in the inner tent reposed,
And by his side fair Diomedè lay,
The lovely captive he from Lesbos brought.
Within another part Patroclus slept,
And with him graceful Iphis, whom his friend
Achilles gave him, when he Scyros took.
Meanwhile the other chieftains reached their tents;
Their comrades gathered round and poured out wine;
Then first king Agamemnon inquired:
Come tell me, great Ulysses, what he says,—
Will he assist us, and protect our fleet,
Or does he nurse his wrath, and still refuse?
He said; and thus Ulysses answered him:
Great Agamemnon, noble king of men!
His wrath not only does he cherish still
But rages yet more furious than before.
He hates thee still, oh, king! and spurns thy gifts;
You and your Greeks, he says, must save the fleet,
And threatens on the morrow to sail home,
And others will advise to do the same,
Since lofty Troy, he says, will never fall;
Jove o'er the town has stretched his saving hand,

And with fresh courage now the Trojans fight.
Such were his words, as these my comrades know;
But aged Phœnix stays with him to-night,
That on the morn he may accompany him
Back to his fatherland, if so he will.
Thus spake Ulysses, but all silent stood,
With wonder struck, so forcibly he spake.
At length the valiant Diomed began:
Oh, son of Atreus, noble Agamemnon!
Would thou hadst never sent this embassy
Offering this angry chief such splendid gifts;
For he before was always proud enough,
Yet thou hast made him worse than ever now;
But let him go or stay, 'tis naught to us,—
When heaven incites, and 'tis his humor, he
Will fight, and not before. But come, attend!
All go to rest, first having eat and drank,
This will recruit us, and fresh vigor give;
But when the rosy light of morn appears,
Before the fleet our cavalry and foot
We will draw up; and thou, oh king,
Shalt lead them on, and with the foremost fight.
He said, and all the other chiefs approved,
Admiring much the speech of Diomed.
Then their libations made, each to his tent
Repairing, laid him down and took repose.

BOOK X.

THE SPIES.

ARGUMENT.

Diomed and Ulysses, as spies, proceed to the Trojan camp, meeting on their way Dolon, a Trojan spy, coming towards the Greeks.—They put him to death, first having gained from him information in regard to Rhesus, king of the Thracians.—They afterwards fall upon the latter, and slay him whilst asleep.

THE chiefs all soundly slept, all but the king,
No sleep for him there was; his restless mind
Was through the live-long night oppressed with care.
As when Jove's thunders roll 'mid pouring rains,
Or hail, or snow, a sign of dreadful war:
So Agamemnon groaned incessantly,
Groaned from the very bottom of his heart;
An inward trembling seized him; now he looked
In the direction of the Trojan plain
And saw, amazed, thousands of blazing fires;
And heard the distant sound of flutes and pipes,
Mixed with the clamorous voices of the men.
Then on his camp and threatened fleet he gazed,
And tore his hair, and groaned and groaned again.
At length this course appeared to him the best:
To go to aged Nestor, and consult
Whether some means of safety might be found.
  Then from his couch he sprung, put on his robe,
And bound his handsome sandals to his feet;
Round him a tawny lion's skin he threw,

Which to his ankles reached; then grasped his spear.
Like trembling seized brave Menelaus too,
Nor did sweet sleep upon his eyelids fall;
He feared lest evil on the Greeks would come,
Who the wide sea had crossed, on his account,
To wage against the Trojans bitter war.
A spotted leopard's skin he round him threw,
And placed a brazen helmet on his head;
Then with his hands he grasped his glittering spear,
And went to rouse his brother, Greece's king,
Whom all the people honored as a god.
  He found him arming, standing by his ship,
And welcome did his brother's visit prove.
Then first the noble Menelaus began:
Why, my dear brother, art thou arming thus?
Wilt thou among the Trojans send some spy?
I fear it will be hard to find a man
To go on such an errand, all alone,
At dead of night among the enemy.
  He said; and Agamemnon thus replied:
Oh, Menelaus! there's need of counsel now,
Both to protect our army and our fleet;
Jove has against us turned, and more regards
Hector and Hector's offerings than ours,
For never have I seen, nor heard of one,
Who in one day has done such mighty deeds
As this great chief, who boasts no heavenly race;
Long will he be remembered by the Greeks,
Such sad disaster has he brought on them.
But go now quickly to the ships and call
Ajax and Idomeneus; I meanwhile
Will aged Nestor rouse, if to the guards
He will consent to go, and orders give;
His son and Merion their captains are,—
Charge of the watch to them intrusted is.
  He said; and thus bold Menelaus replied:
How am I, friend, thy words to understand?
Shall I remain there, waiting till thou come?

Or shall I, having thy command obeyed,
Return to thee again and make report?
He said; and Agamemnon thus replied:
Wait till I come, lest we each other miss,
For the wide camp is crossed with many paths.
And on thy way the warriors arouse,
Kindly addressing each one by his name,
And show no pride, for we must labor now,
Though high our station be; for heavy woe
Seems destined for us both by mighty Jove.
So saying, he his brother sent away;
But he himself to aged Nestor went.
He found him in his tent, on a soft couch,
Around him lay his handsome arms, his shield,
His glittering helmet, and two brazen spears;
Also his rich embroidered belt, with which
The old man girt himself when e'er he fought,
For still he fought, unwilling to give up.
Leaning upon his elbow, thus he spake:
Who art thou, wandering through the camp alone
In the dark night, whilst other mortals sleep?
Dost thou the guard, or some companion seek?
Approach no nearer, but speak out and say
What dost thou want and what thy business here.
Then answered Agamemnon, king of men:
Oh, Neleian Nestor, glory of the Greeks,
'Tis Agamemnon, Atreus' son, you see,
To whom much toil almighty Jove assigns
To be his portion while his life endures.
I wander thus alone, throughout the camp,
Because sweet sleep has from my eyelids fled,
So heavily I am oppressed with care,
And much I fear for the unhappy Greeks,
And am confounded. Trembling has seized me,
And my once valiant heart leaps to my throat.
But come, since thou like me art too awake,
Let us go forward and inspect the guards,

And see if they, overcome with toil and sleep,
Neglect to watch; for close by are our foes,
Who may perhaps attack us in the night.
He said; and Neleian Nestor thus replied:
Oh, noble Agamemnon, king of men!
Hector will not have all things his own way;
But future trouble is in store for him
When great Achilles ceases from his wrath;
But quickly will I rise and follow thee.
Yet first the other chiefs we must arouse:
The valiant Diomed, and wise Ulysses,
Swift Ajax, and Phyleus' noble son;
But some one also should be sent to call
The other Ajax, and Idomeneus,
Whose tents and vessels lie the farthest off;
But I respected Menelaus must blame,
Who sleeps and throws the labor all on thee;
He ought to work and stir the warriors up,
For great calamities are on us now.
He said; and thus the royal chief replied:
Old man, at other times thou well might'st blame,
For often he is tardy and remiss,—
Not on account of sloth or thoughtlessness,
But always looking up too much to me,
And ever waiting until I begin;—
But he was first to-night, and wakened me,
And I have sent him to arouse the chiefs
Whom thou just named. But come, haste to the gates,
For we among the guards will find them all,
For there it was I bade them to collect.
He said; and thus Geranian Nestor spake:
If so it is, none of the Greeks will blame
Or disobey the orders that he gives.
So saying, he his tunic o'er him threw,
And bound his splendid sandals to his feet;
Round him a shaggy purple cloak he drew,
With a large double clasp; then seized his spear,
And starting out, the wise Ulysses sought.

With a loud voice he roused him from his sleep.
The hero woke, and thus the chiefs addressed:
  Who are ye, wandering through the camp by night?
What business of importance brings you here?
Him the Geranian Nestor answered thus:
Noble Ulysses, wise Laertes' son!
Be not offended, evils are on us now;
But come, and with us rouse the other chiefs,
Counsel to take, whether to fight or fly.
  He said, and wise Ulysses raised his shield
And followed; then to Diomed they went;
They found him with his arms outside the tent,
He and his brave companions fast asleep,
Stretched on the ground, their heads upon their shields,
Their glittering spears were stuck into the earth
And shone like lightning in the distance seen.
The chief himself upon an ox-hide lay,
With a gay carpet underneath his head.
Nestor drew near and touched him with his foot,
And rousing him from slumber thus addressed:
Rise, son of Tydeus! waste not the night in sleep!
Our foes, the Trojans, are encamped close by,
And but a little space divides us now.
  He said; and from the ground the hero sprang,
And to the venerable chief replied:
Thy heart indomitable is, old man,
Thou never wilt give up, nor cease from toil;
Are there no younger men to go around
And rouse the warriors? Truly, old man,
It seems impossible to weary thee.
  He said; and to him Nestor thus replied:
Thou speak'st aright; for I have noble sons
And hosts of men who might arouse the chiefs;
But great calamity is on the Greeks,—
Things now are balanced on a razor's edge,
Whether we shall be saved or all be lost;
But go, since thou art younger, and awake
Swift-footed Ajax, and Phyleus' son;
Haste then, if thou dost pity feel for me.

He said; and Diomed around him threw
A tawny lion's skin, and seized his spear,
And rousing all the others, started off.
But when they reached the guards, they found the chiefs
Each with his arms prepared, and wide awake
As trusty dogs which round a sheepfold watch,
Hearing amid the woods some savage beast,
Which from the mountain comes; loud cries are heard,
And great the clamor is of hounds and men;
For on that night no rest nor sleep they find:
So to the guards sweet sleep was wholly lost,—
Their eyes were ever towards the Trojans turned,
Watching to see whether they might advance.
Nestor beheld them vigilant with joy,
And thus the wakeful, trusty men addressed:
Dear children! thus keep watch, be wide awake,
Lest to your foes you may a mockery be.
He said, and crossed the ditch, and with him went
The other leaders to the council called;
And Nestor's son, and Merion came along,
Who had invited been to join the rest.
Crossing the trench, they on a cleared spot sat,
From corpses free, where Hector made a halt,
And the dread fight had stopped, as night drew on;
There sitting down, their conference they held,
And thus old Nestor his opinion gave:
Can we not find, my friends, some daring man,
Who on the outskirts of the Trojan camp
Could catch some straggler, so that we might learn
What 'tis our foes intend? whether to stay,
Threatening our fleet, or to the town return?
Could he learn this, and safely get him back,
Great glory would he gain, and a rich prize;
For every captain of a ship would give
A coal-black sheep and lamb, which would count up,
And make a vast reward; and at our feasts
He should an honored guest forever be.
He said; but all sat silent, nor replied.

At last bold Diomed rose up and spake :
I, Nestor, to the Trojan camp will go ;
But should some comrade accompany me,
More spirit would I have, and confidence ;
For two can counsel take and better act,
But one is slower and less resolute.
He said; and many wished to join him then,—
The valiant Ajax, and Merion,
And Nestor's son, and noble Menelaus,
And brave Ulysses too, wisest of men,
Who ever foremost was in noble deeds.
But now king Agamemnon spake and said :
Most valiant Diomed, joy of my heart !
Choose as thy comrade whom thou likest best
Of the brave chiefs who will accompany thee ;
Nor take thou with thee an inferior man,
However high his station or his rank.
Thus spake the king, fearing lest he might
His noble brother Menelaus choose.
And to him thus the valiant chief replied :
If thou commandest me to choose my man,
How can I pass the wise Ulysses by ?
Who ever foremost is in warlike deeds,
And whom the goddess Pallas greatly loves.
With one as prudent and as sage as he,
Through fire and water I might safely go.
Then wise Ulysses answered him and said :
Give me nor praise, nor blame, oh Diomed,
The Greeks all know precisely what I am.
But come, the night is slipping fast away,—
Two-thirds have gone already, and the stars
Have on their journey rapidly advanced.
Thus having said, their armor they put on.
Thrasymedes to bold Diomed gave
A two-edged sword and shield, for his own arms
The hero at his vessel left behind ;
Upon his head a bull's-hide casque he placed—
No cone nor crest it had ; 'twas of the kind

Cataitix called, such as is worn by boys.
To wise Ulysses Meriones gave
A quiver, bow, and sword, and on his head
A leather helmet placed, secured with straps;
A woolen lining covered it within,
And outside it was fenced with the white teeth
Of a wild boar, set in close rows around.
Antolycus from Eleon brought it as a prize,
But to Amphidamas the Scandean gave;
Amphidamas on Molus it bestowed,
Who gave it next to Merion, his son,
And now, at last, Ulysses' head it graced.
Thus both equipped, the heroes left their friends,
And on their dangerous journey started off.
On their right hand Pallas a heron sent.
They could not with their eye discern the bird
In the dark night, but heard its rustling wings.
Ulysses at the omen much rejoiced,
And to Minerva supplication made:
Hear me, thou daughter of almighty Jove!
Thy aid to me thou ever hast vouchsafed,
And showest me still that thou art by my side.
Oh, help me now, and grant that with success
And glory to our ships we may return,
Having accomplished great things for the Greeks
And to our foes, the Trojans, done much harm!
Thus spake Ulysses, and thus Diomed prayed:
Hear me, indomitable child of Jove!
Befriend me as thou didst my sire befriend,
The great Tydeus, when to Thèbes he went,
Sent by the Greeks upon an embassy.
Upon Æsopus' banks he left his friends,
And all alone among the strangers went.
Kind was the message that he bore to them;
But on his homeward journey he performed,
With thy assistance, most heroic deeds.
So now thy gracious succor grant to me,
And at thy shrine a heifer I will slay,

A splendid beast, ne'er yoked nor used by man,
And her smooth horns shall be o'erlaid with gold.
Thus prayed they both, and Pallas heard their prayer.
Then, like two prowling lions, on they went
Through the dark night, trampling on broken arms,
Through slaughter, o'er dead bodies, and through blood.
Meanwhile bold Hector kept his men awake,
And to a council all the leaders called,
Whom, when assembled, thus the chief addressed:
Who for me now a service will perform,
And for that service gain a great reward?
For I, besides the glory he will reap,
Will give him a fine chariot and steeds,
The best that can among the Greeks be found,
If to the Grecian camp he will repair,
And find out if our foes their vessels guard
Stoutly as ever, or if, out of heart,
They careless are, and think of naught but flight.
He said; but all were silent, nor replied.
Among the Trojans was one Dolon named,
Son of the rich Eumedes was the youth,
The well-known herald; he ill-favored was,
But swift of foot, and was the only son
Among five daughters that his father had.
He now arose, and thus the chief addressed:
Hector, I feel inclined to sally forth
And boldly penetrate to yonder fleet,
And learn what 'tis the enemy intends.
But come, thy scepter raise, and promise me
That thou the handsome chariot and steeds
In which Achilles rides wilt give to me;
Nor will I prove to be a worthless spy,
For e'en to Agamemnon's ships I'll go,
Where the Greek chiefs, perhaps, are counseling
Whether to flee or to renew the fight.
He said; and Hector raised his staff and swore:
By mighty Jove and by his spouse I swear
Those steeds and all their glory shall be thine.

Thus Hector swore, but fruitless was his oath.
Then o'er his shoulders Dolon slung his bow,
And a gray wolf-skin placed upon his back—
A cap he wore covered with weasel fur,
And a sharp javelin carried in his hand.
Then toward the Grecian fleet he started off,
Nor was he destined ever to return.
His comrades leaving, thus he sped along.
  But wise Ulysses his approach perceived,
And thus the valiant Diomed addressed:
Hark! from the camp some man is drawing near;
Either a spy upon our fleet he comes,
Or else to rob the bodies of the dead.
Let us allow him to advance somewhat,
Then we will seize him, rushing quickly up;
But should he run too fast, our spears we'll hurl
And cut him off, so that he can't return.
  So saying, from the pathway they retired,
And lay concealed behind the heaps of dead:
He, in his folly, hastily ran by.
But when the Trojan had such distance run
As at one pull stout mules are wont to plow,—
For they at plowing oxen much excel,—
Then they ran up. He heard the sound, and stood,
Hoping his friends had come to call him back
By Hector's orders; but as nigh they drew,
And were a spear's-throw distant, or e'en less,
Then he perceived that they were enemies,
And ran with all his might. They followed on,
As when, through wood and thickets, two sharp hounds
Swiftly pursue a hare, or dappled fawn,
Screaming with fear the timid creature flies:
So wise Ulysses and bold Diomed
Cut off the spy's retreat and followed him.
But when he now, flying towards the ships,
The outer guards approached, Minerva then
Conferred fresh strength on noble Diomed,
Lest some one of the outposts might be first

To strike the Trojan and great honor gain.
So rushing forward, with his glittering spear,
The warrior thus the fugitive addressed:
Stop! or my spear will overtake thee soon,
And then most certainly thy doom is sealed.
He said, and hurled his lance, not with intent
To wound the man; the weapon merely grazed,
And, o'er his shoulders flying, struck the earth.
He stopped, and trembled,—stammering with fear,
His teeth began to chatter; pale he grew;
Panting, his foes came up and seized his hands.
But he with tears addressed his captors thus:
  Oh spare my life! and take me prisoner;
With a great gift I will redeem myself,
For I at home have heaps of gold and brass,
And splendid ransoms will my father give
When he shall hear that you have captured me.
  In artful words Ulysses thus replied:
Be of good cheer, nor think at all of death,
But come and tell correctly what I ask.
Why wanderest thou alone, through the dark night,
Whilst other mortals are all wrapped in sleep?
Is it to rob the bodies of the dead?
Or art thou sent by Hector as a spy,
Or hast thou at thy own suggestion come?
  He said; and Dolon, trembling much, replied:
I to this trouble was by Hector brought
Against my wish; he promised that he would
Give me Achilles' chariot and steeds,
And sent me through the dark and dangerous night
Among the enemy, to learn if they
Still guard with care their vessels as before,
Or whether, out of heart by their defeat,
They listless are, and think of naught but flight.
  He said; and, smiling, thus Ulysses spake:
Lofty indeed thy aspirations are,
To be the master of Achilles' steeds,
Which few of mortal men would dare to drive,

Except the owner, of a goddess born.
But come, and let me know where Hector is;
Where are his martial arms, and where his steeds;
Where are the Trojan tents, and where their guards
What are their counsels, what their future plans;—
Do they intend to hang about our fleet,
Or to return in triumph to the town?
He said; and to him Dolon thus replied:
I the whole matter faithfully will tell:
Hector and all his counselors have met
Some distance off, round Ilus' sacred tomb.
As to the guards, no special guards there are,
For all the Trojans wakeful are to-night,
Exhorting one another to keep watch;
But the auxiliaries are fast asleep,
And, since they have no wives nor children here,
They leave it to the Trojans to keep guard.
Him answering, thus the wise Ulysses spake:
And are these allies with the Trojans mixed,
Or sleep they separate? Tell me truly now.
He said; and to him Dolon thus replied:
Hearken, and I will truly tell thee all:
Nearest the sea the Carians are encamped,
And the Pæonians, armed with crooked bows,
The Caucons too, and the Lelegans,
And with them the Pelasgians are joined;
On Thymbras' side the Lycians encamp,
The men of Mysia and the Phrygians,
With the bold horsemen of Mæonia.
But why of these details dost thou inquire?
If ye an inroad on the camp would make,
There are the Thracians, who have just arrived;
Their post is on the outskirts of the field—
Rhesus among them is, their wealthy king.
Such horses as he has I never saw,—
Splendid they are, and of majestic size,
Swift as the winds and white as driven snow;
Of gold and silver is his chariot made;

His armor too is gold, a wondrous sight!
More fit for gods to wear than mortal men.
But take me now a captive to your ships;
Or, having bound me, leave me on the spot
Till you return and have discovery made
Whether what I have told is false or true.
He said; but sternly Diomed replied:
Think not, oh, Dolon, to escape my hands,
Though thy report is grateful to our ears;
For should we let thee go, hereafter thou
Wilt hither come again to spy or fight;
But if thou diest, then we need not fear
That thou wilt ever harm the Greeks again.
He said; and as the suppliant touched his beard,
And with a piteous voice for mercy cried,
Quickly his sharp and glittering sword he drew
And smote him through the middle of the neck.
The bloody head rolled muttering in the dust.
Then from the corpse the wolf-skin robe they stripped,
And the light helmet, made of weasel fur;
His bended bow and spear they also took;
And wise Ulysses, lifting them on high,
Thus to Minerva supplication made:
Hail, goddess! these we dedicate to thee,—
In thee we ever hope and place our trust.
Now guide us to these warriors of Thrace.
So saying, he the bloody spoils hung up
On the thick branches of a tamarisk-tree;
And that they might not chance to miss the spot
On their return in the dark gloomy night,
A bunch of reeds and boughs of trees he piled
To mark the spot. Then on the chieftains went,
O'er broken armor and o'er pools of blood,
And soon upon the Thracian allies came.
O'ercome with toil, the warriors soundly slept;
Round them their handsome armor was arranged
In triple rows—their steeds and chariots too.
Among them, in their midst, king Rhesus slept;

Beside him, fastened to the chariot's rim,
Were his swift steeds. Ulysses saw them first,
And, pointing, thus to noble Diomed spake:
There is the man, and there the horses too
That Dolon spake of; now exert thyself,
No time we have to lose, but must be quick,—
Loose thou the steeds, or else dispatch the men,
And leave the horses and the car to me.
He said; and Pallas Diomed inspired
With strength and valor; right and left he slew;
Sad were the groans—the earth grew red with blood.
As when a lion, bent on mischief, leaps
Into a flock of unprotected sheep,
So Diomed upon the Thracians fell
Till twelve were slain; and, as he slaughtered them,
Ulysses, seizing each man by his heels,
Dragged him away, thus leaving a clear path,
So that the horses, as they brought them off,
Might not take fright when they the corpses saw.
But when king Rhesus Diomed approached,
Him too he slew, making thirteen in all.
An evil dream that night the monarch had,
Sent by Minerva, for he seemed to see
The valiant son of Œneus by his side.
Meanwhile Ulysses loosed the splendid steeds.
He tied them with the reins, and with his bow
Drove them along, not thinking of the whip
Which near him lay upon the chariot seat;
Then to his friend he whistled to come up:
But he stood thinking what he next should do,
Whether to carry off the car, in which
The armor lay, or to go on and kill.
Whilst doubting which was best, Minerva came,
Approached the hero, and addressed him thus:
Think of returning now, oh, Diomed,
Lest by the foe thou mayest be put to flight,—
Some other god the Trojans may arouse.
She said; and he, the goddess recognized,

Mounted the car. Ulysses struck the steeds,
And to the Grecian camp they swiftly flew.
  Nor was Apollo mindless of what passed:
Enraged, he saw what Pallas just had done;
Then to the Trojan army he repaired
And Hippocoön roused, a Thracian chief,
Cousin to Rhesus. Up from his couch he sprang.
But when he saw the steeds and chariot gone,
And his brave comrades slaughtered all around,
He wept aloud, and Rhesus called by name.
The Trojans ran together in dismay;
Great was the tumult; wondering they gazed
On such a dreadful, unexpected scene.
  Meanwhile the others sped across the plain,
And reached the spot where Dolon they had slain.
Ulysses stopped the car, and on the ground
Bold Diomed leaped, and, handing to his friend
The bloody spoils, sprang on the car again;
Then they lashed on the steeds, which swiftly flew
Across the field and bore them to the fleet.
  Nestor first heard their coming, and thus spake:
Oh, friends and valiant leaders of the Greeks!
My mind impels me, and I am forced to speak,—
Whether I am right or wrong I cannot say,
But sure I hear the sound of horses' hoofs.
Oh, that Ulysses and bold Diomed
Might hither fetch some noble Trojan steeds;
But ah! I fear lest some disaster they
May have experienced from our cruel foes.
  Scarce had he spoke when up the heroes came!
And lighting from their chariot, met their friends,
Who joyfully received them, and embraced.
Then spake Geranian Nestor and inquired:
  Come, tell me, glorious Ulysses, whence
Got thou these steeds—out of the Trojan camp?
Or did some god, who met you on your way,
Present them to you? They resemble much
The horses of the sun. Oft have I fought

And mingled with the Trojans much in war,
Yet never saw I horses such as these;
Surely, a gift from Heaven they must be,
For Jove and Pallas dearly loves you both.
He said; and wise Ulysses thus replied:
Oh, Nestor, pride and glory of the Greeks!
Some god, if willing, might have given us
These handsome steeds, and even handsomer;
But they are Thracian steeds, newly arrived:
Their master, Rhesus, Diomed just slew,
And twelve of his companions, noted chiefs;
A spy we also slew, by Hector sent,
Whom we found prowling not far from our fleet.
So saying, joyfully the car he drove
Across the trench; greatly they all rejoiced.
But when to Diomed's roomy tent they came,
The animals they haltered to the stalls,
Where, eating corn, his other horses stood.
Ulysses hung up Dolon's bloody spoils
On his ship's stern, till at Minerva's shrine
He as a sacred gift might offer them.
Then wading in the sea, the sweat they washed
From off their necks, and from their tired limbs:
Next to their polished baths the chiefs repaired,
And having bathed, their bodies they anoint
With fragrant oil. Then a repast they had,
And from a flowing bowl pouring sweet wine,
They to Minerva a libation made.

BOOK XI.

THE EXPLOITS OF AGAMEMNON.

ARGUMENT.

Agamemnon distinguishes himself, but is wounded and forced to retire.—Diomed is wounded by Paris, and Ulysses by Socus.—Eurypylus is shot in the thigh, and Nestor conveys Machaon, the physician, from the field.—Achilles sends his dear friend Patroclus to Nestor's tent, who desires him to assume Achilles' armor, and engage in the fight.

Now morning rose, from Tithon's glorious bed,
Shedding her rosy light o'er gods and men :
When to the Grecian ships, dispatched by Jove,
Came Discord down ; terrific monster she,
Bearing war's dreadful portent in her hands.
Upon Ulysses' ship she took her stand,
Which was the midmost vessel of the fleet,
Whence she might cry aloud ; at either end
Achilles and great Ajax had their tents ;
For they relying on their strength had moored
Their ships upon the confines of the host.
There then the dreadful goddess took her stand,
And loud and terrible her war-song rang.
Courage and strength was in each heart infused,—
All were aroused and eager for the fight ;
Nor wished they now to launch their gallant ships,
Nor thought they longer of their distant homes.
  King Agamemnon shouted to the Greeks
And bade the warriors instantly to arm ;
His glittering armor he himself put on :

First round his thighs his beauteous greaves he bound,
Fitted with silver clasps; his corselet next,
Which Cyniras gave him, on his breast he placed:
A pledge of hospitality it was;
For a great rumor had in Cyprus spread,
That a large Grecian fleet was bound for Troy,
And to secure the favor of the Greek
The Cyprian king a present to him made.
Ten bars this corselet had of dusky bronze,
Twelve were of solid gold, twenty of tin;
Three dragons, too, of bronze on either side
Stretched towards the neck, and bright as rainbows shone,
Which in the clouds Jove sets, a sign to men.
Then from his shoulders he his falchion slung,—
Glittering with gold the sheath of silver was,
And fastened to the belt with golden rings.
Next his good shield of beauteous workmanship
The hero took; ten brazen orbs it had,
And in the midst a boss of bronze there was,
With twenty tin ones circling it around;
There too looked out the horrid Gorgon's head,
And Fear and Terror. Silver was the belt,
With a bronze snake entwined, that had three heads.
Upon his head his helmet then he put,—
Four cones were on it, with bright studs around,
Its crest of horsehair nodded dreadfully;
His two sharp spears the warrior then seized,
Whose glittering points shone to the very sky.
  Juno and Pallas honored the armed chief,
And sent forth peals of thunder from on high;
The chariots were ordered to the rear,
For all on foot rushed forth, equipped for war;
Great was the clamor at the early dawn.
The infantry were marshaled by the trench,
The cavalry a little space behind;
Jove caused a dreadful tumult to arise,
And sprinkled bloody dew, a sign of woe.
  Meanwhile the Trojans on the plain drew up,

Marshaled by Hector, their illustrious chief,
By Polydamas, and Æneas, whom
The people honored as a deity;
By noble Agenor, and Polybus,
And young Acamas, beauteous as a god.
Hector in front was seen, with his vast shield,—
And like a large and fiery star appeared,
Which now shines bright, and now is hid by clouds;
So like Jove's dazzling lightning Hector flashed,
In brazon armor clad; now in the van,
Now moving to the rear to give command.
  As for the men, they fought and mowed the ranks
Like reapers in a rich man's harvest field,
Before whose sickles falls the golden grain:
So Greeks and Trojans kept on slaughtering;
Nor was there there a soul that thought of flight;
Like savage wolves they on each other rushed,
And Discord gazed upon the scene with joy.
She only of the gods was on the ground:
The others in their beauteous mansions were,
Upon Olympus' lofty, cloud-capped mount;
Much blame they cast upon the king of gods
For the assistance that he gave to Troy;
But little for their blame the Thunderer cared.
He all apart from them sat by himself,
Rejoicing in his strength, and thence looked down
Upon the Grecian fleet, the town of Troy,
The flashing arms, the slaying and the slain.
  All through the morn, and as the day advanced,
The bloody fight went on, and many fell;
But at the time when wood-cutters prepare
Their mid-day meal, in shady mountain dells,
When, tired with work, their appetites are keen,
Then did the Greeks break through the Trojan ranks,
And loudly shouting, cheered their comrades on.
  King Agamemnon boldly led the way,
And slew a mighty chief, Bienor named,
And his companion brave Oïleus;

He from the car had leaped to meet the king,
Who pierced him in his forehead, through his casque,
Breaking the bone, so that the brains gushed out;
Then the dead chiefs he left with their breasts bare,
For from their bodies he their tunics stripped.
Then Isus next, and Antiphus he slew,
The bastard son of Priam and the true;
They in one chariot rode, but Isus drove,
And Antiphus, his noble brother, fought.
These youths Achilles once on Ida's top
Had caught, and bound with slender osier withes,
Whilst they were pasturing their flocks of sheep;
But for a ransom he had let them go.
These Agamemnon smote, one on the breast,
The other on his head, close to the ear,
He struck, and hurled him dying from his car.
In haste he stripped them of their beauteous arms,
And recognized them as the young men whom
Achilles from mount Ida once had brought.
As a fierce lion easily destroys
The little tender fawns of a swift hind,
Springing upon their couch, he with his teeth
Tears them to pieces, whilst the timorous dam,
Frightened to death, can no assistance give,
But trembling flies, so fearful of the beast,
Through groves of oaks, and thickets, and dense shades:
So of the Trojans none could help their friends,
But terrified themselves, were forced to flee.
Next bold Pisander did the king attack,
Him and his brother, brave Hippolochus,
Sons of the warrior Antimachus,
Who by the wealthy Paris had been bribed
To advise the Trojans Helen to retain,
And to her husband not to give her up.
These, in their chariot, Agamemnon seized,
For, struck with terror, they the reins had dropped;
But on them like a lion rushed the king,
Whilst they in piteous tones for mercy cried:

Take us alive, oh, son of Atreus!
And gifts magnificent shalt thou receive;
Our sire Antimachus, great treasure has,—
Gold in abundance, brass, and iron too;
These as a splendid ransom he will send,
On hearing we are safe, within your camp.
Thus weeping, they in gentle language spake,
But not a gentle answer did they hear.
If, as ye say, the warrior replied,
Ye of Antimachus the children are,
Who gave advice when Menelaus came,
He and Ulysses, to the town of Troy,
To put the two ambassadors to death,
Now for your father's crimes, the forfeit pay.
He said, and hurled Pisander from the car;
Struck in the bosom with his glittering spear,
Stretched on his back the lifeless warrior lay.
Down leaped Hippolochus; him too he slew,
First cutting off his hands, and then his head,
Which, like a ball, he rolled among the crowd.
Them he now left, and dashing forward, rushed
Into the very thickest of the fray,
His comrades following closely at his heels;
Footman slew footman, horsemen by horsemen fall,
Whilst from the plain vast clouds of dust arose.
On rushed the king, slaying where'er he went.
As when a woody forest is on fire,
The whirling flames excited by the wind,
Make fearful havoc in their rapid course;
The crackling twigs and blazing branches fall,
And loftiest trees come crashing to the ground:
So before Agamemnon's furious course
The Trojans fell; whilst o'er the bloody plain
The frightened steeds rattled the empty cars,
Feeling the want of their good charioteers,
Who, on the earth stretched lifeless, soon would be
More by the vultures loved than by their wives.
Meanwhile great Jove saved Hector from the darts,

From the thick dust, and from the bloody rout;
But Agamemnon shouting, still rushed on.
  At length the flying Trojans reached the tomb
Of Ilus, who from old Dardanus sprung:
Near the wild fig-tree stood the monument.
Past it they hastened, making for the town.
The king pursued them, shouting as he went;
His hands invincible were stained with blood.
But when the fugitives the beech-tree reached,
Close to the Scæan gate, they made a halt,
Waiting until their comrades should come up,
Who now were flying all across the plain.
Like oxen by a savage lion chased,
In a dark night; one he has caught and slays,
With his strong teeth he breaks the poor beast's neck,
And tears its entrails out, and laps its blood:
Thus Agamemnon followed up his foes,
Killing the hindmost as they swiftly fled;
Down from their chariots many of them fell
Beneath the king's indomitable spear.
  But when he now the city wall approached,
Jove from his heavenly abode came down,
And took his seat on Ida's shady top,
Holding terrific lightning in his hands.
  Then Iris, golden-winged, he called and said:
Fly swift to Hector, Iris, and thus say,—
Whilst he shall Agamemnon behold
Fighting in front, and routing all his foes,
So long let him upon the background keep,
Exhorting and encouraging his men;
But when king Agamemnon shall retreat,
And be compelled his chariot to mount,
Struck by a cruel arrow or a spear,
Then will I give him strength to fight and slay;
Chasing his foes e'en to their very fleet,
'Till night comes on, and darkness intervenes.
  He said; nor did swift Iris disobey;
She from mount Ida flew to sacred Troy,

And found the noble Hector, Priam's son,
Who stood beside his chariot and steeds ;
Approaching, thus the rainbow goddess spake :
Sagacious Hector, Priam's noble son !
Jove has dispatched me to thee thus to say :
Whilst thou shalt Agamemnon behold
Fighting in front, and routing all his foes,
So long do thou upon the background keep,
Exhorting and encouraging thy men ;
But when king Agamemnon shall retreat,
And be compelled his chariot to mount,
Struck by a cruel arrow or a spear,
Then will I give thee strength to fight and slay ;
Chasing thy foes e'en to the very fleet,
'Till night comes on, and darkness intervenes.
Thus having spoke, swift Iris flew away.
Then Hector from his car leaped to the ground,
With his sharp spear he through the army went,
His men encouraged and renewed the fight ;
His warriors rallied then and met their foes.
The Greeks on their side, too, closed up their ranks.
Fierce was the contest, foot to foot they fought,
King Agamemnon always foremost was,
And wished to be pre-eminent o'er all.
Tell me, ye muses of the Olympian mount,
Who first rushed forth to battle with the king !
Iphidamas, Antenor's noble son,
Nurtured in fertile Thrace, mother of flocks ;
His grandsire Cisseus, fair Theano's sire,
In his own palace reared the infant boy,
And kept him till to manhood he attained,
When to the youth his daughter he betrothed.
But on a rumor of the Trojan war
The young man left his bride and started off
With twelve good ships ; he to Percotè came,
There left his vessels, and on foot set out,
And reached at length the lofty town of Troy.
He now against king Agamemnon came ;

Then hurled the king his spear, but missed his aim.
Not so Iphidamas, who struck his foe
Under his corselet, just upon the belt.
Strong was the thrust he made, but 'twas in vain,
For his sharp spear pierced not the silvery belt,
But bent like lead. King Agamemnon seized
The useless lance and wrenched it from his foe;
Then, like a lion, rushing on the youth,
He smote him in the neck; the Trojan fell.
There died the hero, in his country's cause,
Far from his virgin bride, her charms unknown;
Though to secure her, splendid gifts he gave:
A hundred oxen, and of sheep and goats
From his vast flocks a thousand more he pledged.
So fell the youth by Agamemnon's hand.
The noble Coön saw his brother fall,
And tears of grief gushed from his darkened eyes.
Unnoticed by the king, he stood aside
And pierced him near the elbow with his spear,
Whose glittering point e'en through the arm went through.
The monarch shuddered as he saw the wound,
But would not from the dreadful fight abstain,
For he on Coön rushed with his huge lance
As he his brother tried to drag away
Through the dense throng. He struck him near his shield
As o'er the bloody corpse the hero stood,
Lopped off his head, and sent him to his doom.
So fell Antenor's sons: to Hades sent
By Agamemnon's resistless hand.
So through the ranks the impetuous monarch rushed,
With spear, with glittering sword, and ponderous stones,
Whilst from his wounded arm the warm blood ran;
But when the wound grew dry and the blood ceased,
Fierce pains he felt, sharp as the bitter pangs
That women have to bear in child-birth's hour.
Quick to his chariot the hero rushed,
And bade his servant drive him to his fleet
For much he suffered; yet he cried aloud

And bade the warlike Greeks to still fight on :
Ye chiefs and leaders of the heroic Greeks,
Drive back the foe and keep them from our ships !
Me from the glorious battle Jove withdraws.
Thus spake the king; the charioteer meanwhile
Lashed on the panting steeds towards the fleet—
Their breasts were white with foam, and clouds of dust
Rose as they bore the wounded king away.
  But Hector, on observing his retreat,
With thundering voice to his companions cried :
Trojans and Lycians, quit ye now like men !
Our greatest enemy has left the field,
And Jove will honor now confer on me !
Drive on your steeds, for glory you awaits.
  So saying, he encouraged all his friends.
As when a hunter sets his eager hounds
On a huge lion, or a sylvan boar,
So Hector set the Trojans on the Greeks.
Hector, great Priam's son, a chief like Mars,
With dauntless courage 'mid the first he rushed,
Like an impetuous blast, which, bearing down,
Stirs up the purple billows of the deep.
  Whom first, whom last did noble Hector slay,
When Jove assisted him, and glory gave ?
Assæus first, and next Autinous,
Opites, and Ophiltius, Dolops' son,
And Clytius and Æsymnus, Agelaus,
And Orus and brave Hipponous,—
These were all chiefs. Then multitudes he slew.
As when the west wind drives the southern clouds,
And with resistless fury lashes them,
The ocean's waves are swollen, and rise high—
Whilst the white spray is scattered far and wide :
Thus by bold Hector were the Greeks subdued.
Then had their cause been lost, and they in flight
Been driven, routed, e'en to their very ships,
Had not Ulysses called to Diomed.

Why are we, Diomed, so out of heart?
Come hither, friend, and take your stand by me,
For should our ships by Hector captured be,
Ruin and foul disgrace will be our lot.
He said; and thus bold Diomed replied:
I will remain, my friend, and do my best;
Yet will our efforts prove in vain, I fear,
Since Jove for Troy now fights, and not for us.
He said; and Thymbæus from his chariot hurled:
On his left breast the warrior he struck;
But Molion, his friend, Ulysses slew.
The bodies then they left, and still rushed on
Like two fierce sylvan boars chasing the hounds.
So 'mid the Trojans they sad havoc made,
And the belabored Greeks a respite gained.
Then in their car two valiant chiefs they slew:
Sons of Percosian Merops were the youths—
Of Merops, who excelled in augury,
And from the battle wished to keep his sons;
But they regarded not their sire's advice.
So fate decreed, and so they met their doom.
These Diomed slew, and of their arms despoiled.
Hippodamus and bold Hyperochus
Were by Ulysses slain. Thus mighty Jove,
Looking from Ida's mount, in equal scales
Kept up the fight; on both sides many fell.
Next Paon's son, Agastrophus, was smit
By Diomed, who pierced him through the hip.
No chariot he had on which to flee;
A great mistake he made leaving his car
In his attendant's charge; but he on foot
Among the foremost rushed, and lost his life.
Hector observed his fall, and still advanced,
Shouting aloud and cheering on his men.
Beholding him approach, bold Diomed feared,
And to Ulysses, who was near, thus spake:
Terrific Hector down upon us comes;
But let us stand our ground and drive him back.

He said; and, aiming, hurled his glittering spear,
And on his helmet struck the Trojan chief;
But brass met brass, nor did it pierce his skin;
His triple-covered casque, Apollo's gift,
Repelled the lance and saved the hero's life.
Back he withdrew and mingled with the crowd;
Then on his knee he dropped, with his big hand
Against the earth, and darkness veiled his eyes.
Onward, among his foes, bold Diomed rushed
After his spear, which in the ground had stuck;
But Hector soon revived, leaped in his car
And drove away, and thus preserved his life.
The Greek pursued him with his threatening spear,
And thus, in bitter words, the chief reviled:
Vile hound! thou this time hast escaped thy doom—
Barely escaped; thy god Apollo saved,
To whom in time of fight thou mak'st thy prayer.
But I will meet thee at a future day,
And with some god's assistance slay thee then;
Now I will seek such foes as chance affords.
He said, and slew the spearman Paon's son.
But Paris now, husband of beauteous Helen,
Leaning upon a column at the tomb
Of the old hero Dardanian Ilus,
Bending his bow, took aim at Diomed,
As of his arms Agastrophus he stripped;
Nor did the Trojan's arrow fly in vain,
But struck the Grecian warrior on the foot
And pinned it to the ground. Up Paris sprang,
And from his covert issuing, loudly laughed,
And thus triumphant gloried o'er his foe:
Wounded thou art, nor sped my shaft in vain!
Oh, had I only struck thee in the groin!
Then hadst thou died, and to the Trojans then
Respite would come, who fear thee now as goats,
Timorous and weak, a furious lion fear.
But little heeding him, the chief replied:
Archer, reviler, lady's-man! decked out

With flowing curls, oh, that within my reach
Thou wouldst but come! little would then thy bow
And thy swift arrows be of use to thee!
Now having grazed my foot thou need'st not boast;
I mind it only as I would a wound
Made by a woman, or a silly boy;
Vain are all weapons in a coward's hand.
Far different is it with my deadly spear:
E'en if it strikes but lightly, death is sure;
A helpless widow is the victim's wife,
And his poor children orphans; on the ground,
Crimsoned with blood, his corpse decaying lies,
And flocks of birds his funeral attend.
He said; but now Ulysses coming up,
Seated himself beside him, on the ground,
And from his foot the cruel arrow drew.
Sharp pain he felt; then in his car he sprang,
And bade his servant drive him to the ships.
Then was Ulysses left alone, for none
Of his affrighted comrades durst remain.
Groaning, the warrior thus his thoughts expressed:
Alas! alas! what will become of me?
Should I retreat it will disgraceful be;
Should I be captured it would still be worse;
Jove all the other Greeks has put to flight.
But why debate on subjects such as these?
I know that cowards from the battle fly;
But warriors must always stand their ground,
Whether they wounds receive or wounds inflict.
Whilst thus he thought, the Trojans hemmed him in
As when young men and hounds a wild boar find,
Which from a woody thicket issues forth,
The band surrounds him; he his white tusks shows,
And gnashes terribly his monstrous teeth,
Keeping his adversaries all at bay:
So round Ulysses many Trojans came.
He on the shoulder Deiopis struck;
Then Thoön and Ennomus he slew;

Next with his spear Chersidamas he struck,
Wounding him in the navel, 'neath his shield;
As from his chariot the warrior leaped,
He fell, and falling, grasped the dusty ground.
These he let lie, and wounded Charops next,
Son of Hippasus, and Socus' brother:
Brave Socus then ran to his brother's aid,
And drawing near Ulysses, him addressed:
Illustrious Ulysses, full of art,
Two sons of Hippasus thou must dispatch,
Or else by my good weapon lose thy life.
He said; and struck him on his burnished shield.
The spear went through it, through his breastplate too;
But Pallas turned the weapon's point aside,
So that it touched not any vital part,
But only grazed the flesh; Ulysses knew
He was not wounded mortally, and said:
Ah, wretch! thy doom is drawing very near;
True, I must now retire from the fight,
But on this day death is most surely thine;
O'er thee I'll glory, for thy soul shall go
Swiftly to Pluto's dark and dreary realms.
He said; and struck him, as he turned to fly,
Between the shoulders, right upon the back;
The spear went through and at his breast came out.
With a loud crash the noble hero fell,
And wise Ulysses gloried o'er him thus:
Oh, Socus! son of Hippasus, the knight,
Thy doom has met thee now, and death has seized.
Poor wretch! no sire nor mother wilt thou have
To carry off and wash thy bloody corpse;
But o'er thee birds of prey will flap their wings,
And tear thy flesh; but when my time shall come,
With funeral honors I shall be interred.
He said; and from his breastplate then drew out
The spear of Socus; spouted then the blood,
And the illustrious hero writhed with pain.
The Trojans, when they saw Ulysses bleed,

All rushed upon him, shouting as they came;
Backwards he drew, and to his comrades called.
Thrice the chief shouted with his loudest voice.
Thrice was he heard by noble Menelaus,
Who now the valiant Ajax thus addressed:
Illustrious Ajax, son of Telamon,
Noble Ulysses' voice I surely hear,
As though he by his foes was hardly pressed.
Come, then, and let us go and give him aid;
I fear if left alone he may fare ill,
Though brave he be, and dearly loved by all.
So saying, on he went; the godlike chief
Close at his heels; Ulysses soon they found.
Round him the warlike Trojans gathered thick,
Like tawny jackals round an antlered stag,
Wounded upon the mountain by a shaft
Sent from an archer's bow. Whilst warm the blood,
And whilst his strength holds out, the poor beast flies;
But when the deadly arrow does its work,
The ravenous pack, within some shady grove,
Devour their prey; but then by chance comes up
A hungry lion; now the jackals fly,
And he the carcass at his leisure eats:
So throngs of Trojans on Ulysses rushed,
But with his spear the hero kept them off.
And now came up great Ajax like a tower,
With his huge shield, and stood beside his friend;
In all directions then the Trojans fled.
Meanwhile Ulysses was by Menelaus led
Out of the crowd, and in his chariot placed.
Then Ajax on the Trojans rushing, slew
Doryclus, noble Priam's bastard son;
Pandocus next he struck, Lysander too,
Pyrasus, and Pylastes. As a stream,
Swollen by heavy rains, comes rushing down
A mountain's side, and deluges the plain,
Many dead oaks and pines it bears along,
Till its mad torrents empty in the sea:

So o'er the plain heroic Ajax rushed,
Sweeping the Trojans, slaying steeds and men,
For Hector had not heard of it as yet.
He on Scamander's banks was now engaged,
Where a fierce contest raged, and many fell;
Nestor and Idomeneus were there.
There Hector fought, performing wondrous deeds.
By strength of arm and noble horsemanship,
Whole phalanxes he routed of young men;
Yet would the Greeks have still maintained their ground,
If Helen's spouse, fair Paris, had not struck
On his right shoulder excellent Machaon,
With a three-pointed shaft; the Greeks then feared
Lest their physician they might lose, and thus
Bold Idomeneus to Nestor spake:
  Oh, Nelian Nestor, glory of the Greeks!
Mount quick thy car, and let Machaon mount;
Then quickly to the ships direct thy steeds,
For a physician is worth many men;
He arrows can cut out, and drugs apply.
  He said; nor did his comrade disobey,
But mounted in his car and with him took
The good Machaon, Æsculapius' son.
The horses then he lashed, and swift they flew
Most willingly towards the Grecian camp.
  Cebriones, who by noble Hector sat,
Perceived the Trojans in confusion thrown,
And thus the valiant champion addressed:
Hector, we two are mingled with the Greeks,
Far distant in the outskirts of the fight;
Meanwhile our comrades, cavalry and foot,
Are in sad plight, all in confusion thrown.
Great Ajax Telamon is routing them;
I know him well by the huge shield he bears.
Come, then, and let us thither drive our car,
For there most fiercely does the battle rage;
Great is the slaughter there of horse and foot,
And dreadful is the tumult and the noise.

So saying, he lashed on the splendid steeds,
Which with the car through Greeks and Trojans flew,
Trampling o'er corpses and o'er brazen shields.
The entire axle and the chariot rim
Were stained with blood, splashed by the horses' hoofs
And crimsoned wheels. But Hector longed to spring
Among the heroes in the thickest throng.
Death and destruction on his foes he dealt,
Nor rested for a moment from his work,
But raged among the Greeks with sword and spear
And monstrous stones. Yet Ajax Telamon
He always shunned, nor wished with him to fight.
Then mighty Jove in Ajax terror struck;
He stood confounded, and behind him threw
His big round shield, of seven ox-hides made.
With panic smit, slowly the chief retired,
Like a wild beast, glaring on all sides round,
Turning about, and moving step by step.
As dogs and rustic swains drive from the stall
A ravening lion that has come to steal
A fatted ox; they watch him all night long.
He, eager for his prey, still rushes on;
But 'tis in vain, for numerous javelins fly,
And blazing torches. Furious, he fears,
And, when the morning comes, with saddened heart
The savage creature slowly stalks away:
So Ajax, sad at heart, against his will
Slowly retired from his Trojan foes.
As when a stubborn ass, on whose poor back
Already many cudgels have been broke,
Enters a field and browses on the crop;
But the boys beat him still with many sticks,
Although their strength is small, and with much toil
Succeed at last in driving him away
When he has browsed enough and had his fill:
So the bold Trojans followed Ajax up,
Hurling their missile weapons on his shield;
But the heroic chief, wheeling about,

Would show his mighty strength, and check the foe,
And then again would turn himself to fly;
Yet still he kept them from advancing towards
The Grecian fleet, so terribly he fought.
From daring hands showers of weapons fell—
Some struck his massy shield—some, flying past,
Stuck in the ground, eager to drink his blood.
But when Eurypylus, Evæmon's son,
Saw the heroic Ajax thus hard pressed,
He near him drew and hurled his glittering spear,
And in the liver struck Apisaon;
The Trojan fell. Eurypylus rushed up,
And from the body stripped the armor off.
The godlike Paris saw him as he stooped,
And at the Greek with bended bow took aim,
And his right thigh pierced with the feathered shaft.
The arrow broke, and painful was the wound;
Suffering much, he to his friends withdrew,
And to the Greeks, thus loudly shouting, cried:
Oh, friends and leaders of the warlike Greeks!
Rally and hold your ground, and Ajax aid,
Who by his foes is now most sorely pressed,
And little chance has he of an escape;
But still stand firm and Ajax ne'er desert.
Thus cried Eurypylus, though wounded sore;
His comrades gathered round with shields and spears,
And Ajax meeting them, they all stood firm.
Thus, like a blazing fire, the warriors fought.
Meanwhile old Nestor's horses bore him off.
Him, and the good physician Machaon,
Achilles saw, and recognized the man,
For on his vessel's prow the hero stood,
Gazing upon the melancholy rout.
His comrade, good Patroclus, then he called
With a loud voice; he from his tent came forth
(The chief's misfortunes from that hour commenced),
And to his friend Patroclus thus replied:

Why, oh, Achilles, dost thou call me thus?
Him answering then, the godlike hero spake:
Most noble Patroclus, joy of my heart!
I think the Greeks will kneel before me now,
To such a sad condition are they brought.
But go, dear friend, and ask old Nestor who
Is yonder wounded chief he leads away:
In figure he resembles Machaon;
But of his face no view could I obtain,
So swift the horses hurried him along.
He said, and Patroclus his wish obeyed,
And to the Grecian camp in haste repaired.
Meanwhile old Nestor and his wounded friend
Came to the tent, and from the car got down;
The steeds were by Eurymedon unyoked.
And the chiefs, standing, cooled their tired limbs
In the fresh breeze that from the ocean blew;
Then in the tent they went and sat them down.
The fair-haired Hecamede, old Nestor's maid,
Prepared a drink to set before the chiefs;
She had from Tenedos been brought away,
When by Achilles it had wasted been;
Daughter of great Arsinoüs was she,
And had to Nestor by the Greeks been given
For the good counsel he afforded them.
She now a fine bronze-footed table set—
On it a burnished brazen tray she placed,
With new clear honey and fresh barley meal,
And onions too, as relish for the drink;
A splendid goblet in the midst she set,
With golden studs the vessel was adorned,
Four handles were attached, and round each stood
Two pigeons feeding; and the cup, too, had
A double bottom. When filled up with wine
Few from the table could have lifted it,
But aged Nestor raised it easily;
In it the woman Pramnian wine had mixed,
And o'er it, grated with a brazen rasp,

Some goats'-milk cheese and sprinkled barley meal;
The draught compounded, she the thirsty chiefs
Asked to partake of the refreshing drink;
They did so, and their parching thirst allayed.
In pleasing converse then the time they spent.
   But now Patroclus at the tent door stood.
Nestor perceived him, and from his seat arose,
Then took him by the hand and led him in,
And bade him sit upon the splendid couch;
But his request the visitor declined,
And to the aged warrior thus replied:
   Ask me not, friend, to stay and take a seat.
Irascible is he who sent me here
To inquire who this wounded warrior is;
But now I know—'tis Machaon I see:
And to Achilles I will bear the news,
For thou thyself knowest as well as I
What a stern man he is—how apt to blame
E'en when he has no proper right to blame.
   He said; and aged Nestor thus replied:
Why does Achilles pity thus the Greeks,
Wounded and suffering? He little knows, as yet,
What sore distress has o'ertaken us.
All our best men lie wounded in their tents;
Wounded is Diomed, Tydeus' son,
Ulysses also, and Agamemnon;
Eurypylus is wounded in the thigh
With a keen shaft; and this man from the rout
I hurried off, struck with an arrow too;
And yet Achilles, once our champion,
Cares not for this, nor pities us the least.
Does he still wait till, wrapped in hostile flames,
Our ships are burned and all of us destroyed?
For now my strength is not what once it was.
Oh that I had my youth and active limbs
As when in olden times a contest rose
About a cattle foray! then I slew
Itymonæus, who in Elis dwelt,

For he his herds defending was struck down,
Slain by my spear, and was the first that fell.
His rustic followers then took to flight;
But we much booty gained, and brought away
Of oxen fifty droves, the same of sheep,
Also of swine, and herds of goats the same.
Of sorrel steeds we thrice the number gained—
All mares were they, and with them many colts.
With this rich booty we to Pylus came,
Reaching the city some time in the night.
My father Neleus was much rejoiced
That I a young man had so lucky been.
At early dawn the heralds notice gave
That all should meet, to whom a debt was due,
In wealthy Elis. Then the leading men
A just division of the plunder made,
For the Epeians owed to us of Pylus
A debt long standing; for in times gone by
Great Hercules had ravaged our domain.
Our bravest chiefs were slain; and of twelve sons
That Neleus begat I only live,
So wickedly the Epeians behaved.
But my old sire selected for himself
A herd of cattle, and three hundred sheep,
The shepherds too; for Elis owed to him
A large amount. Four horses had he sent
Them, and their cars, to win the Tripod prize
At the great races of the Elean games;
But king Augius seized them, and sent home
Their drivers grieving for their stolen steeds.
'Twas for this theft the old man took so much:
The balance to his people he assigned,
That each his just proportion might receive.
These things we did, and next within the town
To the immortals offered sacrifice.
On the third day the enemy appeared
With all their force, both cavalry and foot;
With them the Molions, twins they were, took part,

Striplings as yet, nor skilled in warlike arts.
There is a city, near a lofty hill
Upon the Alphæus, Thryoëssa called—
Upon the Pylian boundary it stood;
This they invested, eager to destroy.
But when they crossed the plain that very night,
Minerva from the Olympian mansion flew,
And brought us word, commanding all to arm;
But Neleus would not suffer me to fight:
He hid my horses, thinking that I was
Too inexperienced to go to war;
Yet still I went among the cavalry,
Although on foot—Minerva aided me.
  A certain stream there is, Myneius called,
Which, near Arenè, empties in the sea;
There our horse waited till the approach of day,
Whilst swarms of infantry kept marching up.
Thence proceeding we at mid-day reached
Alphæus' sacred stream. Victims then we slew,
And to Alphæus offered up a bull—
To Neptune also, and to Pallas too,
A heifer that had never yet been yoked.
Our supper then we took, and with our arms
Lay on the river's bank and sought repose.
Meanwhile the warlike Epeians stood round,
Eager to take the city and destroy.
But now the mighty hand of Mars appeared,
For at the break of day the fight began:
We rushed to battle, praying to great Jove
And to Minerva. Then Molion I slew,
A famous chief, and bore away his steeds;
He son-in-law to king Augius was,
His eldest fair-haired daughter having wed
Wise Agamedè, who all the virtues knew
Of every herb that grows in field or wood,—
Him to the ground I hurled, leaped in his car,
And stood among the foremost combatants.
In all directions then the Epeians fled

When they beheld their famous champion slain.
Like a black whirlwind o'er the field I rushed,
Took fifty cars, slaying two men in each.
And now the Molion youths I would have slain,
Actor's reputed sons, had not their sire,
The mighty Neptune, saved them from my hands,
In a dark misty cloud concealing them.
Then Jove great vigor in our limbs infused:
O'er the wide plain we followed up the foe,
Slaying and gathering their scattered arms,
Till to Buprasian's fertile lands we came,
And to Olenia and Alisium's mound;
There the last man I slew, and Pallas then
Bade us return; so we to Pylus came,
And of the gods most glory Jove received;
But of the men Nestor most honor gained.
Thus was I once, as sure as I'm alive;
But to himself Achilles keeps his strength;
Yet will he mourn, I think, when he beholds
The Grecian army totally destroyed.
Thus did Menœtius bid thee on the day
That from thy father's house thou went to war,
For wise Ulysses and myself were there,
And heard the orders that thy father gave,
For we at Peleus' palace had arrived
To muster troops. Menœtius then we saw,
And the great chief Achilles, and thou too;
But aged Peleus was in the yard,
Burning fat oxen's thighs to mighty Jove:
A golden cup he held within his hands,
And poured dark wine upon the blazing fire;
But ye were busy round the slaughtered ox.
Then at the threshold of the house we stood,—
Achilles, wondering, from his seat sprang up
And took us by the hand and led us in;
Then on a handsome couch he sat us down
And a collation ordered to be brought.
When we had eat and drunk enough, I then

Exhorted you to come and follow us.
Ye both consented, and your aged sires,
Before ye went, imparted much advice.
Old Peleus his son Achilles urged,
In deeds of valor, always to be first,
And, above all, to be pre-eminent;
Whilst thus thy sire Menœtius thee advised:
My son, Achilles younger is than thou,
But of superior rank and valor too,
Do thou, as eldest, give him oft advice,
And to thy words he doubtless will give heed.
Thus spake thy sire, but thou hast not obeyed;—
But, put Achilles now in mind of this.
Who knows but thou, with Heaven's assistance, may
Bend his stern heart, for friends have oft such power?
But if some sacred prophecy he fears,
And from his goddess mother he has heard
Some message sent him by almighty Jove,
Let him send thee to mingle in the fight—
Thee and the Myrmidons—who much may aid;
And let him give thee too his beauteous arms,
That so the Trojans, taking thee for him,
May fear to fight, and we some respite have.
But ye, as being fresh, can surely drive
Our tired foes back to the town of Troy.
Thus spake the sage, and stirred Patroclus' heart.
Back to Achilles' camp the hero went;
But when to wise Ulysses' ships he came,
Where was the forum, and where stood the shrine
Erected to the honor of the gods,
There, limping as he came, Patroclus met
Noble Eurypylus, Evæmon's son,
With a sharp arrow sticking in his thigh.
The perspiration from his body rolled,
And from the grievous wound trickled dark blood;
But the chief's mind undaunted was and firm.
Patroclus, on beholding, pitied him,
And thus the suffering warrior addressed:

Alas, unhappy men! chiefs of the Greeks,
Is it your cruel fate to perish thus,
Far from your native land? Shall dogs devour
Your tender flesh upon the plains of Troy?
Yet let mê know, divine Eurypylus,
Whether the Greeks can Hector still restrain,
Or must they fall beneath his conquering spear.
He said; and thus Eurypylus replied:
No help there is, Patroclus, for the Greeks;
But to their vessels they must all fall back.
All our best chiefs lie wounded in their ships,
Struck down by Trojans who more daring grow.
But save me now and lead me to my ship,
And from my thigh cut out this deadly shaft,
And with warm water wash away the blood;
Then to the wound some soothing drugs apply,
As by Achilles thou wast taught to use,
Who by great Chiron had himself been taught—
Chiron the justest of the Centaur race,
For Podalirius and Machaon, both
Our good physicians, are not to be had;
One in his tent lies wounded, as I think,
And a physician's succor needs himself,
The other on the battle-field still fights.
He said; and thus Patroclus answered him:
In Heaven's name, oh, how will all this end?
What's to be done, oh, brave Eurypylus?
I to Achilles go to speak the words
That Nestor bade me carry to the chief;
Yet thee I will not leave in this thy need.
He said, and, with his arms supporting him,
Led the afflicted hero to his tent.
The servants spread some bulls'-hides on the ground;
Then, having laid him down, with a sharp knife
Patroclus cut the bitter arrow out,
And with warm water washed the blood away;
A healing root next in his hands he crushed—
It checked the pain, and soon the bleeding ceased.

BOOK XII.

THE RAMPART STORMED.

ARGUMENT.

The Trojans, divided into five bodies, assault the ramparts.—Sarpedon makes the first breach in the wall; then Hector, with a large stone, forces one of the gates, and, followed by his men, drives the Greeks even to their ships.

Thus in his tent Patroclus healed the wound
Of the heroic chief Eurypylus;
But still the Greeks and Trojans fiercely fought.
Nor did the ditch, made to secure their ships,
Nor the high wall, protection longer give;
They built it that their booty might be safe.
  But to the gods no hecatombs they slew,
And the whole structure hateful was to Heaven,
And therefore was not destined to endure.
Whilst Hector and Achilles were alive,
And royal Priam's lofty city stood,
So long remained this rampart of the Greeks;
But when the noblest men of Troy were slain,
And likewise of the Greeks, when some were dead,
And all the others had embarked for home;
When in the tenth year they the town destroyed,
Then Neptune and Apollo counsel took,
How they might sap the wall; turning the streams
That had their sources in Mount Ida's springs;
Rhesus, Caresus, and Heptaporus,
Granicus, and Æsepus, Rhodius,
Scamander's stream divine, and Simois,

Where shields and helmets, buried in the earth,
Showed that a race of demi-gods had fought:
These rivers all were by Apollo turned
Nine days against the wall; and Jove meanwhile
Poured an incessant rain to soften it;
Whilst Neptune, with his trident in his hand,
Gave too his aid; and with his billows washed
The strong foundations, built of beams and stones,
In raising which the Greeks had spent such toil;
Thus he made level all the Grecian shore
That fronts upon the rapid Hellespont,
Covering the place again with drifted sand.
This done, he turned the lovely streams again,
And made them in their former channels flow;
Thus Neptune and Apollo were about
In future times the rampart to destroy.
  But now around the wall the battle raged,
And shouts and clamor echoed from the towers;
The Greeks, subdued by Jove. were hemmed within,
Dreading fierce Hector's furious attack,
Who, like a whirlwind, rushed upon his foes.
And as a lion or a savage boar
Stares on the hunters and the packs of hounds
That gather round, thick fly the showers of darts:
He knows no fear, nor is he put to flight,
But his courageous spirit proves his death;
Oft he attacks, tries how his foes will stand,
But when he turns the assailants then give way:
So Hector rushed impetuous through the throng,
Urging his warriors to pass the trench;
But the swift steeds could not be made to cross.
Standing upon the brink they loudly neighed,
For the wide ditch affrighted the poor beasts.
Steep were the sides, and in the bottom stood
A row of palisades, close set and sharp,
To make the citadel still more secure;
No car could easily find entrance there.

But much the footmen wished to make the attempt,
And thus Polydamas to Hector spake:
  Hector, and all ye warriors of Troy!
'Tis folly to attempt to drive our steeds
Across the trench; sharp palisades are there,
And a high wall upon the other side;
Nor could we in the ditch with ease descend,
Nor with our horses fight in such a place.
If Jove indeed intends to give us aid,
I wish the Greeks would perish even now,
On this same spot, far from their native land;
But if our enemies a rally make,
And we become entangled in the trench,
I do not think one man would e'en be left
To carry back the dreadful news to Troy.
But come, and be ye all advised by me:
Let our attendants watch the chariots,
And we will follow Hector all on foot,—
The Greeks, if I mistake not, then will flee.
  He said; and Hector with his words was pleased.
Down from his chariot with his arms he sprang,
Nor did the others in their cars remain,
But followed when great Hector they beheld.
Each to his charioteer directions gave,
To rein his horses up in order due,
And keep them on the margin of the ditch.
Then in five bands their forces they arranged:
Hector the choicest of the warriors led,
And with him, too, the brave Polydamas;
Cebriones with them went, for Hector left
His steeds in charge of an inferior man;
The next band Paris and Alcathoüs led,
Agenor too; o'er the third division
Deïphobus and Helenus were chiefs,
With Asius, who on fiery steeds had come,
From far Arisba, on Selle's stream;
Over the fourth Æneas was the chief,
He and Archilous, and Acamas,

Both skilled in all the various arts of war.
Sarpedon led on the noble allies,
With his friend Glaucus and Asteropæus;
Both were bold chiefs, but Sarpedon excelled,
Bravest was he of all the allied force.
In close array with bucklers interlaced,
Thus they advanced upon the warlike Greeks,
Who they supposed would not withstand the shock,
But flying would fall back upon their ships.
The other Trojans, and the allies, too,
Followed the counsel of Polydamas;
But Asius, the princely warrior,
Wished not to leave his chariot behind;
But foolishly advanced against the fleet,
Fulfilling thus his evil destiny;
Nor was he ever to see Troy again,
For 'twas his lot to fall beneath the spear
Of the illustrious Idomeneus.
He to the left advanced, whither the Greeks,
They and their chariots, from the field returned.
Thither he drove his steeds, nor found the gate
Closed nor secured with the big wooden bar;
But 'twas left open purposely, that so
Those flying from the field might save themselves.
Onward he rushed, and his men followed him.
Loudly they shouted, for they vainly thought
The Greeks would yield, and fall back on their ships.
But in the gate two famous chiefs they found,
Sons of the warlike Lapithæ; the one
The invincible Polypœtes was,
The other, Leonteus, brave as Mars:
These blocked the way; like mountain-oaks they stood,
Which many a year have weathered wind and storm,
And whose big roots run deep into the ground.
Thus trusting in their strength these warriors stood,
Nor feared the onset that bold Asius made;
But they with war-cries and uplifted shields
Followed their chief, and rushed towards the wall;

The son of Asius, Acamas, was there,
And Iämenus, and Æнomas,
And Thoön, and Orestes, all bold chiefs.
At first the Lapithæ remained within;
But when they saw the Trojans coming up,
And how the Greeks were in confusion thrown,
They darted out, and fought before the gates
Like mountain-boars, which meet the hounds and men.
As trampling through the bush, they gnash their teeth,
And ne'er give up the fight till they are slain:
So fighting hand to hand, their armor rang;
Fiercely they battled, trusting to their strength,
And to their comrades, posted on the wall,
Who, from the towers, to repulse the foe,
Hurled showers of stones, which fell like flakes of snow,
Scattered by wintry clouds upon the earth;
Thus thickly flew from Trojans and from Greeks
Stones, darts, and spears, making their armor ring.
 Then Asius groaned, and thus indignant spake:
Oh, father Jove! full of deceit art thou!
I did not think the Greeks would stand their ground;
But they, like slender wasps or swarms of bees,
Which have their dwellings in some rugged path,
Will not desert their hollow nests at all;
But meet the hunters, and defend their young:
So these bold chiefs, though only two there are,
Will not the gate abandon, but remain
Till they are either captured or destroyed.
He said; but Jove regarded not his words,
For 'twas to Hector glory he would give.
 Meanwhile the contest raged around the gate;
But to narrate each deed that was performed
It would require a superhuman tongue,
For by the wall the battle raged like fire:
The Greeks were forced to fight to save their ships:
And all the deities who wished them well,
With pitying eyes their sad condition saw.
 But the bold Lapithæ commenced the fight;

Damasus was by Polypœtes struck
On his brass casque; the glittering spear went through;
The bones were crushed, and all his brains gushed out.
Ormenus next, and Pylon then he slew.
Then Leonteus, of the race of Mars,
Wounded Hippomachus beneath his belt;
Then, from his scabbard, drawing his sharp sword,
Antiphates engaging hand to hand,
He laid the warrior lifeless on his back.
Next, Menon and Orestes he dispatched,
And Iämenes, after them, he slew,
Whilst they the corpses of their armor stripped.
  The best part of the men with Hector went
And with Polydamas; they most desired
To break the wall, and set the ships on fire.
Designing this, they stood upon the trench,
For, on their left, an augury appeared:
A soaring eagle with a spotted snake,
Which, in his talons, still alive he bore;
Nor was the serpent harmless, but still fought;
Writhing and twisting, he attacked the bird,
Inflicting on its neck a painful wound:
Quickly the eagle dropped its dangerous prize,
And his wings flapping, soon was out of sight.
The Trojans feared, seeing the spotted snake
Dropped in their midst, an omen of great Jove;
And thus Polydamas to Hector spake:
  Oft hast thou chid me, Hector, even when
Meeting in council, good advice I gave;
Since 'tis not proper that a citizen
Should speak in opposition to thy will,
But rather strengthen thy authority;
Yet now I must advise what I think best:
Let us not rush upon the Grecian ships,
For if we do, sure as this omen came,
This soaring eagle, flying on the left,
Holding a spotted serpent in his claws,
Which he let fall, nor carried to his young;

So we, if even this strong wall we break,
And cause our routed foes to make retreat,
Yet could we not undamaged, as I think,
Get back to Troy; for many of our men
We there would leave, whom the Greeks, rallying
Around their ships, would soon exterminate;
This is the meaning of the augury,
And any soothsayer would tell us so.
He said; and Hector sternly thus replied:
Thy words, Polydamas, are out of place;
Thou knowest better, and should'st better speak;
But if thou meanest thus and serious art,
Thou of thy senses surely art bereft,
Bidding me Jove's instructions to neglect,
Who gave me solemn promise of success.
Yet thou would'st have me put my faith in birds.
Little care I for them which way they fly,
Whether towards right or left, or east or west,—
I look to Jove, the ruler of the world,
Who governs mortal men and deities.
The best of omens is our country's good.
What need hast thou to fear the fight so much?
Though all should perish, thou wilt save thyself;
Thou stand'st no chance of ever being slain,
Too timorous and unwarlike is thy soul.
But if I find thee skulking from the field,
Or causing panic in the Trojan ranks,
Pierced by my spear, thou diest on the spot.
Thus having said, he led his warriors on;
With shouts and with applause they followed him.
Then Jove from Ida raised a storm of wind,
Which blew the dust upon the Grecian fleet.
The courage of the Greeks began to droop,
But supernatural strength the Trojans had,—
Trusting in auguries and their own power,
They tried to break the mighty Grecian wall—
The lofty battlements they overturned,
The breastworks too, and with huge levers prized

The buttresses projecting from the towers,
Which, to support the wall, the Greeks had built.
  But at their posts the valiant Greeks stood firm ;
With bucklers interlocked, they fenced the breach,
Wounding their foes as fast as they came up ;
Whilst the two Ajaxes upon the wall,
Ranging among their men, exhorted them,
Giving kind words to some, to some reproof:
  Oh, friends and comrades ! ye who are most brave,
Ye who are brave, and ye who courage lack !
Since men are not by nature formed alike ;
But now abundant work there is for all,
As ye yourselves must evidently see.
Be not dismayed at Hector's shouts and threats,
But, cheering one another, make advance,
For, with Jove's help, we may repulse the foe
And drive them even to their city gates.
  Thus crying out, they urged the Greeks to fight.
As when, on wintry days, thick flakes of snow,
Sent by almighty Jove, incessant fall,
The wind is lulled, the mountain tops grow white,
The meadows too, and fruitful fields of men—
The lofty capes and the indented shore
Are with one dazzling mantle overspread ;
But the dark ocean stays its further course,
And in its waves the tempest melts away,
Thus showers of stones and darts incessant flew,
And great the tumult was along the wall.
  Yet neither Hector nor the Trojans would
The gate have broken, with its massy bar,
Had not great Jove urged Sarpedon, his son,
Against the Greeks, as lions herds attack.
His handsome buckler he before him held,
Plated with brass, by a skilled brazier made ;
The inner circle was of ox-hide formed,
Together sewed with threads of purest gold.
With this before him, brandishing two darts,
The hero to the very front advanced

Like a half-famished lion from the hills,
Whose valiant spirit leads him to the folds,
Where, in their wattled pens the sheep repose,
And though the watchful herdsmen stand around,
Guarding their flock with dogs and glittering spears,
Still from his purpose he will not retreat,
But springing in, either bears off a sheep
Or wounded falls, struck by the faithful guards:
So godlike Sarpedon's heroic soul
Urged him to make advance and break the wall,
And thus his comrade Glaucus he addressed:
Why do we, Glaucus, special honors share
At home in Lycia; sitting at our feasts,
The best of food we have, and flowing cups,
And people deem us little less than gods;
Fine farms we also have on Xanthus' shores,
Large vineyards, and extensive fields of grain?
'Tis proper therefore we should be the first
Among the Lycians in the brunt of war;
So that each Lycian truthfully may say,
'Tis by good right our kings in Lycia rule,
Eating fat sheep and quaffing splendid wines;
Since they in courage all the rest excel,
And fight among the foremost in the war.
Oh, my dear friend, could we from battle fly,
And live forever young and free from death,
Then would not I thus mingle in the van,
Nor urge thee either to heroic deeds!
But as ten thousand fates around us press,
Which we by no contrivance can avoid,
Let us advance, and either for ourselves
Glory secure, or fame to others give!
He said; nor did bold Glaucus disobey.
Onward they went, leading the Lycian bands.
Menestheus seeing them was struck with fear,
For they, on mischief bent, approached his men:
He looked along the battlements to see
Which of the leaders was within his reach;

Both of the Ajaxes he soon perceived,
With Teucer near them, from his tent just come;
But to attempt to call them was in vain,
So great the tumult was; the crash of shields,
Of crested helmets, and the thundering sound
Of battered gates in mingled din arose
High in the air, and even reached to heaven;
A grand assault the Trojans now had made,
And were for bursting every barrier.
The prudent chief to Ajax then dispatched
The messenger Thootes, and thus spake:
Noble Thootes, run and Ajax call,
Indeed call both, for in a little while
There will be hereabouts some bloody work,
So furious the Lycian chiefs rush on,
Who always famous were for warlike deeds.
But if the battle rages yonder, too,
Let Ajax Telamon at least come here,
And with him Teucer, famed for archery.
He said; nor did the herald disobey;
But passing through the crowd, along the wall,
Came where the Ajaxes fighting were,
And to the warlike chiefs his message told:
Oh, ye Ajaxes, leaders of the Greeks!
Menestheus begs your presence for awhile,
So sorely is he pressed, and needs relief;
Both he would have, for bloody work is nigh,
So furious the Lycian chiefs rush on,
Who always famous were for warlike deeds.
But if the battle also rages here,
Let him at least have Ajax Telamon,
And with him Teucer, famed for archery.
He said; nor did bold Telamon refuse;
But thus in haste his valiant friend addressed:
Ajax, do thou and brave Lycomedes
Still remain here, encouraging the Greeks,
Whilst I proceed to meet yon fierce assault;
But when my comrades there I have relieved,

I will with speed return to this my post.
So saying, Ajax Telamon went off,
And with him Teucer, sprung from the same sire;
Pandion bore the skillful archer's bow.
Hastening along, the heroes reached the tower,
Where, sorely pressed, the chief Menestheus stood.
  And now the Lycian warriors rushed on
Like a dark whirlwind, climbing o'er the wall;
The Greeks stood firm, and dreadful was the din.
Then Ajax Telamon Epicles slew,
Comrade he was of noble Sarpedon;
Him with a stone he slew, torn from the wall.
So huge it was, that scarcely with both hands
Could a man lift it, such as men are now;
But Ajax threw it easily, and struck
The hero's helmet, shattering his skull.
He from the ramparts like a diver plunged,
And lifeless lay within the ditch below.
  Next, Teucer with an arrow Glaucus struck
On his bare arm, as he came rushing up;
The wounded Trojan quietly slipped down
From the high wall, lest the proud Greeks might see
That he disabled was, and loudly boast.
  The noble Sarpedon was much distressed
When he perceived that Glaucus had to leave;
Yet he fought on, nor was his strength relaxed,
For he Alcmaön with his javelin pierced,
Then drew his weapon out; the warrior fell,
And as he fell his splendid armor rang.
  At the stone buttress Sarpedon now tugged
With his stout hands; the crumbling structure fell,
And with it a large portion of the wall,
Making a gap where many might pass through.
Ajax and Teucer at the Trojan aimed,
The latter striking him upon the belt
With a keen shaft; but Jove his son's life saved.
But Ajax pierced his shield and pushed him back;

Yet he retreated but a little way,
So bent the hero was on glorious deeds.
And turning round, he to his warriors called:
Oh, Lycians! why so sluggish in the fight?
Brave as I am 'tis difficult for me,
Mounting the breach alone, to reach the ships;
But all come on, and make a bold assault,—
The more there are the easier 'tis done.
He said; and they, fearing their king's reproof,
Gathered around him, pressing towards the wall;
The Greeks, on their side, rallied to oppose.
Great was the work, and sharp the contest now,
For neither could the Lycians pass the breach,
Nor could the Greeks their stubborn foes repulse,
Who still maintained their ground close to the wall.
But as two men with measures in their hands,
Dispute and wrangle in a common field,
With equal warmth about their boundaries:
So did these warriors, along the wall,
Fight foot to foot with spears and clashing shields;
Many were wounded in their naked backs,
And, through their bucklers pierced, were struck and slain;
The buttresses and towers ran with blood.
Yet the bold Greeks could not be put to flight,
But they held on; just as a woman holds
Poised in her hands a pair of balances,
And honestly weighs out a fleece of wool,
By which she gains a scanty maintenance:
So balanced on both sides the contest hung
'Till Jove to noble Hector glory gave,
Who first within the wall an entrance gained,
And to his warriors thus loudly cried:
Rush on, ye Trojan knights! break through the wall,
And on the Grecian fleet hurl blazing fire!
He said; and they against the ramparts rushed
With all their might, and scaled the battlement;
But Hector seized a rugged piece of rock,
Which two men on a wagon could not lift,

As men are now. yet he handled the stone
With greatest ease, for Jove assisted him.
As when a shepherd carries in one hand
A large-sized fleece, and thinks its weight is naught:
So Hector, taking up the ponderous mass,
Aimed at the beams which went across the gate;
But inside were two bars, with lock and key.
Advancing nearer, with his feet apart
That he might firmer stand, he hurled the rock,
And in the center struck the ponderous door,
Breaking the hinges; inside fell the stone,
With a loud sound, and crushed the entire gate,
Bursting the bars, which into shivers flew.
In Hector rushed, with visage dark as night;
His brazen coat of mail terrific shone;
Two lances in his hands the warrior held,
And no one but a god could have restrained
Or barred his path. His eyes like fire burned;
Then turning, he upon the Trojans called
To scale the wall; his comrades all obeyed:
They scaled the wall and thronged within the gates.
The Greeks gave way, retreating to their ships,
And dreadful was the tumult that ensued.

BOOK XIII.

THE ATTACK ON THE SHIPS.

ARGUMENT.

Neptune takes part with the Greeks.—The battle proceeds.—He then takes the form of Thoas and exhorts Idomeneus, who slays Othryoneus and Asius.—Deïphobus now assails Idomeneus.—Alcathous is slain, and a fierce contest takes place over his dead body.

THUS having brought the Trojans and their chiefs
Close to the ships, Jove left them there to fight.
Then his bright eyes to other lands he turned—
To Thracè and Mysia, famous for brave men,
And to those distant realms, where, fed on milk,
The just and virtuous Hippomulgi dwell;
But on proud Troy he never looked at all,
Thinking no deity would dare to give
His aid to either of the combatants.
  But Neptune all the while was on the watch;
He on the woody top of Samos sat,
Gazing with wonder at the dreadful fight.
Mount Ida thence he saw, and Priam's town,
And the Greek fleet drawn up along the shore;
There, from the deep emerging, sat the god,
And gazed with pity on the routed Greeks,
But with Olympian Jove was much enraged.
Down from the rugged mount, with hasty steps,
He came on foot; the forests and the hills
Trembled beneath the footsteps of the god,—

Three strides he made, and at the fourth he reached
His place of destination, Ægæ called;
There, beneath ocean's azure depths, he had
Mansions immortal, splendid, built of gold!
  Arriving there, he to the chariot yoked
His horses, brazen hoofed, with golden manes,—
Gold on himself he put; then seized the lash,
His golden lash, and mounted on the car.
Over the waves his chariot he drove;
The monsters of the deep their master knew,
And from the dark recesses of the sea,
In sportive troops, came gamboling around;
With joy the very billows clave in twain—
O'er the green waves the bounding coursers flew,
Nor was the brazen axle even wet.
  Soon to the Grecian camp the sea-god came.
Between rough Imbrus' isle and Tenedos,
Down in the sea, a spacious grot there is:
There Neptune stopped, unyoked his fiery steeds,
And to them gave ambrosial provender;
Next round their feet fetters of gold he threw,
That they might there remain till his return;
Then to the army of the Greeks he went.
  Meanwhile, like blazing fire or like a storm,
The Trojans followed Hector with loud shouts,
Hoping to capture now the Grecian fleet,
And by their ships to slaughter every Greek;
But Neptune, from the sea emerging, came
To aid his friends—assumed the form and voice
Of the good prophet Chalcas, and drew near
To the two Ajaxes and addressed them thus:
  Ye valiant Ajaxes, on you depends
The honor and salvation of the Greeks.
In other places little do I fear
The warlike Trojans, though they scale the wall;
But when great Hector rages like a flame,
Boasting to be the son of mighty Jove,
Then I much dread some mischief may befall;

But may some deity arouse your souls,
Make you stand firm, and animate the rest,
So may we beat this furious chieftain off,
E'en though it is great Jove that urges him.
  Thus Neptune spake, and with his trident touched
Both of the chiefs, imparting magic power.
Their strength increased—their limbs elastic grew.
Then flew the god away, like a swift hawk,
Which, from the summit of a lofty rock,
Darts to pursue some bird across the plain.
  But Ajax, son of Oïleus, was first
The heavenly visitant to recognize,
And to his comrade Telamon thus spake:
  Oh, Ajax! some one from the Olympian mount
Calls us to battle bravely round our fleet,
For 'twas not Chalcas, though it looked like him.
I saw the traces of a deity
E'en in his footsteps as he moved away,
For heavenly beings easily are known,
And now I feel a supernatural power
To fight with greater vigor than before;
Light are my feet and strengthened is my arm.
He said; and Ajax Telamon replied:
My hands are strengthened too, my spirits rise,
And my feet urge me forward to the fight;
I long to meet fierce Hector all alone.
Thus spake the warriors, joyful for the strength
Which in their minds the god had just infused.
  Neptune meanwhile the other Greeks aroused,
Who by their ships were resting from the fight;
Their limbs were weary with incessant toil,
And, as they saw the Trojans on the wall,
O'ercome with grief, their eyes were filled with tears,
Expecting certainly to be destroyed;
But Neptune, coming up, encouraged them,
Speaking to Teucer and Leitus first—
To the brave Thoas and to Penelaus—
To Meriones and Antilochus,

And to Deipyrus, all skilled in war.
These chiefs approaching, thus the sea-god spake:
 Shame on you, Grecian youths! I thought that you
Would surely stand your ground and save the fleet;
But, if you are remiss, the day has come
When by the Trojans you will conquered be.
Oh, gods! that I should ever live to see
A sight so strange and so lamentable!
The Trojans close at hand and near our ships,
Who were in former times like timid stags,
Straying about the woods, to be the prey
Of lynxes, pards, and wolves, so feeble they.
So, formerly, the Trojans could not stand
E'en for a little while against the Greeks;
But now, advancing from their town, they fight
E'en near our hollow ships, through our chiefs' wrath
And the indifference of our warriors,
Who round the fleet are miserably slain.
And though king Agamemnon was in fault,
Dishonoring Achilles as he did,
You should not be remiss on that account;
Courageous minds are easily appeased.
But 'tis not proper men like you should flag,
Whose courage and capacity are known;
I with a coward would no quarrel have,
Should he hang back and show a fearful heart;
But I feel shame at seeing you act thus.
Oh, foolish creatures! soon some greater ill
Will fall upon you for your sluggishness;
Think of the shame, and the reproach incurred!
A dreadful contest has arisen now,
For valiant Hector, having burst the gates,
Is in our midst, fighting around our ships.
 Thus Neptune roused the courage of the Greeks;
Round the Ajaxes rallying they came,
And had Minerva or fierce Mars been there,
No fault could they have found with what they saw.
The choicest of the warriors were there,

And stood the shock of Hector and his men;
Locked were the spears with spears and shields with shields,
Helmets on helmets pressed, and man on man;
Their nodding horse-hair plumes each other touched,
So close arrayed the Grecian warriors fought.
From their stout hands showers of weapons flew,
Eager to drink the life-blood of the foe.
On rushed the Trojans, Hector at their head.
And as a mighty stone, loosed from a rock
By wintry rains, rolls bounding down a hill,
The forest echoes with the thundering sound;
Onward it rushes to the plain below,
And there its rapid course at last is stayed:
So Hector threatened e'en to reach the sea,
Slaughtering the Greeks amid their tents and ships;
But now the stubborn phalanxes he met,—
They stopped him in his furious career,
And thrust him back with sword and glittering spear.
   The chief retired, thus shouting to his men:
Trojans and Lycians, Dardans brave in fight,
Stand firm! the Greeks will not resist me long,
E'en though they are drawn up in close array;
But from my spear I think they will retire,
If mighty Jove assists me as before.
   So saying, he his warriors aroused.
Then Priam's son, Deïphobus, rushed forth
Full of high thoughts, his shield before him placed;
Him Meriones saw, and at him hurled
His glittering lance, nor did he miss his aim,
But struck him on the shield; the weapon broke.
Deïphobus his buckler held in front,
Fearing the onset of the warlike Greek,
Who now drew back within the ranks, chagrined
For his spear broken, and his victory lost;
Back to the camp he ran to fetch a lance,
Which in his tent he left; meanwhile the fight
With clamor and with fury still went on.
   Then Teucer first the hero Imbrius slew,

Owner of steeds, the son of Mentor he ;
Before the Greeks had to the country come
He in Pedæus dwelt, and had to wife
Medesicastè, Priam's bastard child.
But when the Greeks arrived, to Troy he came,
And lived with Priam, who regarded him
With the same favor as he did his sons.
Him warlike Teucer struck beneath the ear
With his long lance, and drew the weapon out;
He like an ash-tree fell, which on a hill
Is visible afar; but now cut down,
It strews its tender foliage on the earth :
So Imbrius fell, and his bright armor rang.
Teucer came up to strip him of his arms,
But Hector hurled at him his glittering spear,
Which, Teucer seeing, managed to avoid;
It struck Amphimachus upon the breast.
Hector rushed up to tear his helmet off,
But Ajax cast at him his shining lance ;
Yet he the hero's body could not touch,
Protected as it was with dazzling brass ;
But on his shield he struck him and repulsed,
So that behind the bodies he withdrew,
Which now the Greeks triumphant bore away ;
Amphimachus was by Menestheus borne
And Ithicius, who carried him away :
But the bold Ajaxes Imbrius seized.
As two fierce lions carry off a goat
Torn from the hounds, and lifting it on high,
In their vast jaws the carcass bear away :
So the Ajaxes lifted Imbrius up,
And stripped his armor off. But Oïleus,
Who at Amphimachus' sad fate was wroth,
Cut off his head and hurled it 'mid the throng,
Where, in the dust, at Hector's feet it fell.
Neptune was angry for his offspring slain,
And to the Grecian fleet and camp set out,
To rouse the Greeks, and bring fresh woes on Troy.

The god was by bold Idomeneus met,
Who had been helping an afflicted friend,
Fresh from the battle, wounded in the thigh.
His comrades bore him off, and he had given
Directions to the surgeons to attend;
But he was eager to resume the fight,
And Neptune thus addressed him in the form
Of Thoas, who was Andræmon's son,
Who over Pleuron reigned, and Calydon,
And whom the Ætolians honored as a god:
Oh, Idomeneus, governor of Crete!
Where are the threats against the men of Troy,
You and the other Greeks so oft have used?
He said; and thus the king of Crete replied:
Oh, Thoas! no one is to blame, I think,
For all of us are skilled in warlike arts,
Nor do we from the dreadful battle shrink;
But 'tis Jove's pleasure to destroy the Greeks
Upon a foreign shore, far from their home;
But Thoas, for a warrior thou art,
And many men hast marshaled to the field,
Now fight thyself, and urge our people on.
He said; and to him Neptune thus replied:
Oh, Idomeneus! may each coward wretch
Ne'er to his home return, but fall a prey
To savage dogs, here on this Trojan soil;
But let us hasten, taking up our arms,
For though we are but two we much may do;
E'en fearful men are useful when combined,
But we are men of courage, used to war.
The god thus spake, then sought the battle-field.
But Idomeneus, when he reached his tent,
Upon his limbs his beauteous armor put,
And seized two darts; then sallied forth the chiefs.
Like dazzling lightning, which almighty Jove
Flashes from high Olympus' glittering top,
A splendid sign for mortals to behold,
So flashed the hero's arms as on he moved.

When near the tent, good Merion he met,
His faithful servant, searching for a spear.
  Beholding him, the Cretan king thus spake:
Oh, Meriones, dearest of my friends!
Fleet son of Molus! what has brought thee here,
Leaving the field? hast thou a wound received?
Or dost thou bring some tidings of the fight?
I, too, must hasten to the battle-field,
Nor will I longer at my tent remain.
  He said; and thus his trusty friend replied:
Oh, Idomeneus, prudent king of Crete!
I come to seek a spear within thy tent,
For mine I broke; broke it against the shield
Of the proud Trojan chief Deïphobus.
  He said; and thus the king of Crete replied:
Twenty good spears within my tent there are,
The spoils of Troy, ranged round the shining walls,—
Go in, and of those weapons take thy choice.
I with my foes fight always hand to hand:
So I have lots of spears and massy shields
And crested helmets, and bright corselets too.
  He said; and prudent Merion replied:
I too have in my tent and in my ship
Much Trojan spoil; but my tent distant is,
For I when battle rages show no sloth,
But in the front ranks always may be found;
And, though the Greeks of this may take no note,
I think my deeds are not unknown to thee.
  Thus Merion spake, and thus the king replied:
I know thy courage—why talk thus to me?
For should we choose the bravest of our men,
An ambuscade preparing, where 'tis seen
Who has true courage and who has it not,
The coward's face then suddenly grows pale,—
Within his bosom palpitates his heart,
Restless he is, as fearing instant death,
And chattering teeth his inward anguish show;
But the brave man his usual color has,

Nor fears his dangerous duty to assume,
But wishes that the fight may soon come on.
And so wouldst thou appear in such case;
And if thou wounded wert, not in the back,
But on thy breast the enemy would strike
As thou wast rushing foremost in the fray.
But come, not thus like children let us talk,
Lest some may chide us for our sluggishness,
But enter thou the tent and choose thy spear.
He said; and Meriones, like to Mars,
Entered the tent and seized a glittering spear.
With Idomeneus then he went along,—
Great warriors both, and eager for the fight.
As when ferocious Mars to battle goes,
Followed by Terror, his undaunted son,
At sight of whom e'en heroes will grow pale:
From Thrace these armed immortals sally forth
With the bold Phlegyians and the Ephyri,
Siding with either party as they please:
So Meriones and Idomeneus
Rushed to the conflict, clad in glittering brass,
And thus the former his good friend addressed:
Son of Deucalion, where wilt thou take thy post—
Upon the right, the center, or the left?
For on the left the Greeks must need support.
He said; and thus the Cretan chief replied:
Brave men there are to guard the central ships.
The two Ajaxes and bold Teucer, who
In archery is foremost of the Greeks,
They will give Hector quite enough to do,
Fierce as he is; and he will find it hard,
Breaking through them, to set the fleet on fire,
Unless great Jove a firebrand should hurl,
For Ajax Telamon to no man yields
Who mortal is and lives on mortal food
And can be wounded by a mortal hand;
Nor is he to Achilles, in close fight,
A whit inferior, but less agile he.

Then come and let us to the left hand go,
And either glory for ourselves receive
Or by our death to others glory give.
  He said; and Merion, equal to swift Mars,
Rushed forth, and soon the battle-field they reached.
But when the Trojans saw the Cretan king
Flaming around, and with him Merion,
They raised a shout, and all upon him rushed.
Then at the ships a mighty contest rose.
As when, on stormy days, the whistling winds
Sweep o'er the highways, raising clouds of dust:
So the two armies mingled in the fight,
And foe encountered foe, intent to slay;
Spears bristled thick, and eyes were dazzled then
With glittering helmets and with burnished shields:
So fierce the fight that e'en a looker-on
Could not unmoved have gazed upon the scene.
  But the two sons of Saturn, taking part
With different sides, caused lamentable woe.
Jove wished to see Achilles magnified,
And to the Trojans would give victory,
Yet he would not entirely destroy
The Grecian host, but only wished to show
Honor to Thetis and her noble son.
But Neptune, rising from the hoary deep,
Came secretly to aid the struggling Greeks,
Grieving to see them conquered by their foes;
But towards Jove his anger was intense.
Of the same race and lineage were they,
But Jove the first-born was, and knew the most.
So Neptune durst not openly take part,
But, putting on the likeness of a man,
Mingled among the Greeks, assisting them.
Thus the two gods alternate turned the scale
And kept the battle raging dreadfully.
  Then Idomeneus, though no longer young,
Cheered on the Greeks and put the foe to flight,
For Othryoneus first the hero slew;

He from Cabesus came to Priam's house,
On rumor that the war had broken out.
Cassandra he without a dower would wed,
The fairest daughter she that Priam had;
For her he promised wonders to perform,
Even to drive the Greeks away from Troy.
The king agreed and promised him the maid.
So, trusting to these promises, he fought;
But, as the boaster proudly stalked in front,
King Idomeneus struck him with his spear,
Nor did his brazen corselet him protect—
The glittering weapon through his stomach went,
And as he fell, the victor thus cried out:
  Oh, Othryoneus! I will praise thee now
If thou for Priam wilt make good thy word,
And he his daughter promised thee, I believe;
But we in promises can likewise deal,
For we will Atreus' fairest daughter give,
Give thee to wed, and thou mayest lead her home
If thou for us will capture lofty Troy.
But come, and follow us to yonder fleet,
That we about the marriage may confer,
And thou in us wilt good relations find.
  Thus joking, he the corpse dragged by the foot.
Then Asius, to avenge his death, came up—
Came up on foot; behind him were his steeds,
His chariot, and faithful charioteer,—
Eager was he to slay the Cretan king;
But Idomeneus was too quick for him,
And pierced him in the neck beneath his chin.
Lifeless he fell—fell like some sturdy oak
Or towering pine cut on a mountain top
By skillful hands as timber for a ship:
So he, stretched out, before his chariot lay
Gnashing his teeth, grasping the bloody dust.
With panic struck, his trembling charioteer
Turned not to flee, but in his car stood still.
By fierce Antilochus he then was struck,

Who pierced him in the navel with his spear,
Nor did his brazen corselet him protect,
But lifeless from the beauteous car he fell.
The victor seized the steeds and from the field
Drove them away triumphant to his friends.
Grieved at the death of Asius, his friend,
Deïphobus at Idomeneus aimed
And hurled his spear; but Idomeneus stooped,
And o'er his head held his protecting shield—
His shield two-handled, made of hides and brass.
This saved him; but the weapon grazed the shield,
Causing a grating sound, as swift it flew.
But not in vain the deadly lance was hurled;
It struck Hypsener, son of Hippasus,
And pierced his liver, causing instant death;
Then loudly boasted proud Deïphobus,
And in sarcastic language thus exclaimed:
 Not unavenged the noble Asius lies,
Though to dark Pluto's mansions he has gone;
He now can thither go in merry mood,
Since I a Greek have sent him for a guide.
Thus he cried out; his boast the Greeks annoyed,
But most of all Antilochus was grieved;
Yet did he not his comrade overlook,
But coming up, protected with his shield;
Two dear companions then approached the corpse,—
Noble Alastor and Mecistheus,—
And, groaning deeply, bore it to the ships.
 But Idomeneus still untired fought;
His object was the Trojans to destroy,
Or for his country fall a sacrifice.
Then fell Alcathoüs, Æsyetes' son;
He to Anchises, too, was son-in-law,
For he had Hippodamia espoused,
His eldest daughter, and the most beloved,
For she excelled all others of her age
In beauty, goodness, and accomplishments.
And so the most illustrious man in Troy,

Noble Alcathoüs, had wedded her.
Neptune o'er him threw a pernicious spell,
Dimmed his bright eyes, and fettered his fair limbs :
Fixed on the spot immovable he stood,
Nor could he flee, nor could he turn aside ;
Thus standing like a pillar or a tree,
King Idomeneus smote him in the breast ;
His brazen corselet by the spear was split,
Which gave a grating sound as through it went.
Down with a crash the Trojan warrior fell,
The spear-head piercing to his very heart,
Which throbbed, and shook the handle of the lance ;
There the impetuous weapon spent itself.
  Then with a boast the Cretan king exclaimed :
Now are we even, proud Deïphobus,
And more than even ; three we slay for one.
Wretch ! stand thy ground, and come and fight with me,
That thou mayest know that I from Jove am sprung :
He Minos first begat, guardian of Crete ;
The good Deucalion was Minos' son ;
Deucalion was my sire ; succeeding him,
I now am king of that extensive isle ;
Hence in my fleet I came, a curse to thee—
To thee, and to thy father, and to Troy.
  He said ; and doubtful stood Deïphobus,
Whether he should fall back within the ranks,
Or fight the Cretan monarch all alone.
Thus meditating, he made up his mind
To seek Æneas ; he the warrior found
In the rear lines ; with Priam he was wroth,
Because the king showed him not due respect,
Although a valiant hero known to be.
Approaching him the warrior thus spake :
  Æneas, chief of Troy, 'tis now thy part,
If for thy relative thou hast regard,
To save his corpse ; then come and follow me,
And let us go and aid Alcathoüs,

Who in his palace nourished thee when young,
And whom just now the Cretan king has slain.
He said; and roused the courage of the chief,
Who straightway went to meet the valiant Greek;
But Idomeneus feared not his approach,
But stood his ground, like a fierce mountain boar,
Which in a thicket boldly meets his foes;
He bristles up his back, his eyes dart fire,
And gnashing his white teeth, he keeps at bay
The assaulting hunters and the furious hounds:
So the famed spearman Idomeneus
Retreated not before the Trojan chief;
But to his valiant comrades cried aloud,—
To Ascalaphus and Aphareus,
To Meriones, and Deïpyrus,
And to Antilochus, renowned in fight:
Come hither, friends, and aid me; all alone,
I dread Æneas, who an onset makes;
Most brave is he, and multitudes has slain.
He, too, rejoices in the bloom of youth,
Which gives him much advantage over me;
For with my spirit, were we of like age,
Soon either he or I would bite the dust.
He said; and with one heart they all came up,
Each on his shoulder bearing his good shield.
Æneas too on his companions called,—
Called on Agenor, and Deïphobus,
On Paris too, all leaders of the host;
The people followed. As a flock of sheep
Leave their green pastures, following the ram,
Who leads them to a watering-place to drink,
The shepherd sees them follow with delight:
So with delight Æneas saw his men
Following his footsteps as he rushed in front.
Around Alcathoüs the warriors thronged,
Aiming at one another with their spears;
Their brazen armor rattled horribly.
Two warlike men were most conspicuous,—

The bold Æneas and Idomeneus,—
Who sought each other, eager to destroy.
Æneas first at Idomeneus aimed,
Who moved aside and so preserved his life;
From his strong hand the weapon sped in vain,
And quivering, stuck deep in the solid ground.
The Cretan king then smote Œnomaus,
Bursting his corselet; to his stomach went
The cruel spear, piercing his bowels through;
Down to the earth the hapless warrior fell,
His dying hand grasping the bloody dust.
  Then Idomeneus his long spear plucked out
From his dead foe; but of his splendid arms
He was unable to despoil the chief,
Such showers of deadly darts around him fell
For now his feet were not as swift as once,
To move about upon the battle-field;
But as he slowly from the spot retired,
Deïphobus his glittering weapon hurled—
For at the king he ever had a grudge.
He missed his mark, but struck Ascalaphus,—
Ascalaphus, the son of dreadful Mars,—
Piercing his shoulder with his javelin;
He fell, and falling grasped the bloody dust.
  But furious Mars had not perceived at first
That his brave son had fallen in the fight;
He on the summit of Olympus sat,
'Mid golden clouds, excluded from the war,
He and the other gods by Jove's decree.
Now round the dead Ascalaphus they thronged:
Deïphobus his helmet from him tore;
But as he seized it, valiant Merion
With his sharp weapon pierced him through the arm,
And from his hand the crested helmet fell.
The victor then pounced on the wounded man,
Swift as a vulture, and plucked out the spear,
But soon retreated, mingling with his friends.
Polites then his brother led away,

His arm encircling the hero's waist,
And from the field of battle bore him off
To where his steeds and beauteous chariot stood;
So to the city they transported him,
Groaning and bleeding copiously.
  Meanwhile the fight went on with dreadful din;
Æneas next on Aphareus rushed,
And struck him with his spear upon the throat;
With drooping head and casque, and burnished shield,
Down to the earth the warrior fell and died.
Then, as he turned, Antilochus took aim
At Thoas, striking him upon the back,
Severing the vein which from the spine runs up
E'en to the neck; down in the dust he fell,
To his dear friends outstretching both his hands.
On his slain foe the joyful victor sprang
And of his arms despoiled him, gazing round.
The Trojans now from all sides thronging came,
Hurling their darts upon his beauteous shield,
Yet they his tender flesh could never touch,
For Neptune shielded him from all their darts.
The impetuous chief was ever in the van;
His glittering spear was never seen at rest,
But he was ever on the watch to slay
Some Trojan close at hand, or one far off.
Thus full of fight Adamas, Asius' son,
Perceived him, and drew near to make attack,
But Neptune saved him, weakening the blow,
And the sharp brazen spear was broke in twain.
In his round buckler part of it stuck fast,
The other portion falling to the ground.
Backward the warrior stepped among his friends,
But Merion followed him and hurled his spear,
Striking the chief above his private parts,
Where to poor mortals wounds cause dreadful pain.
Around the cruel spear the hero writhed,
As when a struggling ox by sturdy swains,
With twisted cords, unwillingly is led.

So wounded, he for a few moments throbbed,
Till Merion, coming up, drew out the spear,
And death's dark shades forever closed his eyes.
  Then with his Thracian sword bold Helenus
Upon the temple struck Deïpyrus,
Knocking his helmet off, which on the ground
Fell rolling, till some warrior of the Greeks
Lifted it up as it approached his feet.
The hero fell, and darkness veiled his eyes;
Much was the worthy Menelaus grieved,
And with his lance towards Helenus drew near,
Who on his part drew out his polished bow:
Together then they rushed, eager to slay.
The Trojan on the breastplate struck his foe—
Quick from the brass the arrow bounded back.
As when black-coated beans or peas fly off
From the broad fan upon a threshing-floor
By the wind driven and the winnower:
So from the breastplate of the bold Menelaus
The Trojan's deadly shaft rebounding flew;
But the Greek pierced the other in the hand,
Striking the bow; the spear went through and through.
Behind his ranks he hastily drew back,
His wounded member dragging at his side,
Trailing the glittering spear upon the ground,
Which from his hand his friend Agenor drew,
And in a woolen sling bound up his arm,
Which his attendants bore in case of need.
Then upon Menelaus Pisander rushed;
His evil genius drew him to his doom,
To be dispatched by thee, oh, Menelaus!
Nearer they came, but the Greek missed his mark,
And on his shield was by Pisander struck,
Who much rejoiced and hoped for victory.
Vain was his hope, the weapon broke in twain!
The other drew his silver-hilted sword,
And on Pisander rushed; he again raised
His handsome olive-handled battle-axe,

Cutting from off the helmet of the Greek
His horse-hair plume; but noble Menelaus
Smote his opponent just above the nose,
Smashing the bone; his bloody eyes fell out—
Fell at his feet upon the dusty ground.
The dying hero, falling, writhed in pain;
But the Greek placed his foot upon his breast,
And stripped him of his arms, and, boasting, spake:
  Thus shall ye quit the vessels of the Greeks,
Perfidious Trojans! ever fond of strife—
Who basely injured me—accursed hounds!
Regarding not the anger of high Jove
For outraged rights of hospitality:
For this he will destroy your lofty town.
Though kindly entertained, ye stole away
My youthful wife and robbed me of my goods;
And now our fleet ye threaten to attack
And burn it up, and put us all to death;
But ye shall be restrained, bold as ye are.
Oh, Jove! thou ever hast been thought to be,
Above all gods and men, supremely wise,
And yet such things allowest to take place,
Favoring these haughty Trojans in their crimes,
Who never cease from deeds of violence—
Contentious always, ever fond of strife.
There is satiety in everything—
In sleep, in love, in dancing, and in song,
And these are pleasanter by far than war,
Of which the Trojans ne'er can have enough.
  So saying, from the body he stripped off
His bloody arms, and gave them to his friends;
But he at once proceeded to the front.
Then Pylemenes' son upon him rushed,
Harpalion called, who with his father came—
Came to the Trojan war, but ne'er returned.
He Menelaus struck upon the shield,
But could not penetrate the solid brass:
So, shunning death, the warrior stepped back,

Looking around for fear he might be struck;
But Merion aimed at him as he withdrew,
And with an arrow pierced him on the hip;
The deadly weapon through his bladder went,
Passing along e'en to the other side.
Down to the earth the dying hero fell,
Surrounded by his friends, and, like a worm,
Lay stretched upon the dusty blood-stained ground.
The Paphlagonians helped him to his car,
And, grieving, drove him back to sacred Troy;
His father followed, shedding many tears,
But for his son no vengeance he obtained.
Paris was much excited at his death—
In Paphlagonia he his guest had been—
So, full of wrath, an arrow he let fly.
There was a certain chief, Euchenor called,—
Polydus was his sire, a wealthy seer
And worthy man, whose home at Corinth was,—
He, knowing well his fate, embarked for Troy,
For oft the good old Polydus foretold
That his dear son should in his palace die,
Smit with a painful, terrible disease,
Or else should perish by the Trojans slain.
He, to escape his fine and the disease,
Sailed for the war, leaving his friends and home;
Him Paris smote below the jaw and ear—
Down fell the chief, and, falling, soon expired.
Thus, like a flame, the dreadful battle blazed.
But Hector, dear to Jove, knew not, as yet,
How, on the left hand of the fleet, his men
Were slaughtered by the Greeks, who seemed indeed
To be upon the point of victory,
Such great assistance they from Neptune had.
But he still fought upon the very spot
Where first he burst the gate and scaled the wall,
Forcing his way through the strong Grecian ranks.
There, on the margin of the hoary sea,
Protesilaus' and Ajax's vessels were.

Just at that spot the wall was not so high,
And there both horse and foot most fiercely strove;
There the long-robed Ionians fought;
There the Bœotians and the Locrians,
The Phthians and the valiant Epeians.
All these restrained the Trojan from the ships,
But could not drive him off, so daring he.
The choice Athenians battled in the van;
O'er them Menestheus held the chief command;
With him were Phidas, Stichius, and Bias;
The Epeians Dracius and Meges led,
And Amphion too; whilst o'er the Phthians
Bold Medon and Podarces were the chiefs.
Medon was bastard son of Oïleus,
And Ajax's brother; he, far from his home,
Had to Phylachus been compelled to flee,
His uncle having slain. The other chief
Was in Phylachus born, Iphiclus' son.
These warriors all, with the bold Phthians
And the Bœotians, fought around the ships.
But Ajax the swift son of Oïleus,
And Ajax Telamon together kept.
Like two black bullocks drawing a stout plow,
Down from their foreheads rolls the copious sweat,
As o'er the field, bending beneath the yoke,
With equal steps they turn the crumbling soil;
Thus, side by side, these mighty warriors fought.
Round Telamon his valiant comrades thronged,
Ready to aid their champion when fatigued,
And to relieve him of his heavy shield;
But to the other Ajax, not so close
The Locrians stood; they fought not hand to hand,
For they had neither shields nor ashen spears
Nor crested helmets; with their bows alone
They followed their bold chiefs to distant Troy;
Shooting their arrows, they would often break
The Trojan ranks; and as the Ajaxes,
In splendid armor, battled in the front,

Keeping fierce Hector and his men at bay,
They, in the rear concealed, let fly their shafts,
And in confusion threw their enemies.
Then had the Trojans from the ships and tents
Been driven off, and chased to lofty Troy,
Had not Polydamas to Hector spoke:
Oh, Hector! wilt thou never take advice?
Because such valor on thee was bestowed,
Think'st thou in wisdom also to excel?
Thou must not hope to be all things at once.
To one 'tis given to excel in war;
Some shine in dancing, some in harp and song;
To others Jove sagacity imparts,
A precious gift, by which whole states are saved;
But hearken to me, and take my advice,
For now a flame of war encircles thee,
And our brave men, since they have crossed the wall,
Are part for holding back, whilst others fight,
Few against many, scattered round the ships.
But pause awhile, assembling the chiefs,
And let us then consult what plan is best:
Whether to board the fleet, if Jove permits,
Or to retreat whilst we in safety may;
For much I fear lest yesterday's exploits
May by the Greeks be paid us back to-day;
For in that fleet a champion there is
Who will no longer from the war abstain.
Thus spake Polydamas; his good advice
Pleased Hector much; down from his car he leaped,
With sword in hand, and thus, in hasty words,
His friend addressed: Stay here, Polydamas,
And of the bravest troops retain command;
I will give orders to the other chiefs,
Which done, I will immediately return.
He said; and hurried off, moving along
Like a vast snowy mountain through the throng.
Then round Polydamas the warriors flocked,
Soon as they heard the noble Hector's words;

But he meanwhile sought out Deïphobus,
And royal Helenus, and Adamas,
And Asius also, son of Hyrtacus;
Forward he went, and sought them in the van;
Some he found wounded, others lying dead
Around the vessels' sterns, slain by the Greeks;
Many there were struck down within the walls.
Upon the left, Paris he soon beheld,
Cheering his men, and urging them to fight.
Near him he drew, and thus the chief reviled:
  Oh, cursed Paris! beautiful in form!
Fond of the fair sex, and seducer too!
Where is Deïphobus and Helenus?
And where is Adamas, and Asius where?
Where Othryoneus? Now must Troy fall;
Her doom is certain, and is close at hand.
  He said; and thus the handsome youth replied:
Hector, thy blame is causeless; true, indeed,
I have, at times, been negligent in fight,
But Paris never was a coward born;
For since around the fleet the battle raged,
I and my friends have fought incessantly;
But of the comrades whom thou dost inquire,
They all are dead, except Deïphobus
And royal Helenus, who both went off,
Each wounded in the hand with a long spear;
But Jove, in pity, has preserved their lives.
But now lead on, fulfill thy heart's desire,
And we will follow with determined minds,
Taxing our valor to the utmost bound;
And more than that no mortal can perform.
  So saying, he his brother's wrath appeased.
Then in the thickest of the fight they plunged,
Round Cebriones and Polydamas,
Round godlike Polypætes, and Ortheus,
Phalces, and Palmus, and Ascanius
And Morys, brothers, who the day before,
As a reserve, from rich Ascania came;

Jove nerved them for the fight, and on they rushed,
Like boist'rous winds which, sweeping o'er the plain,
Extend far out into the heaving sea,
Stirring it up, and causing it to roll
In loud-resounding billows, white with foam;
So with their chiefs, arrayed in glittering brass,
The Trojans rushed upon their enemies.
  Hector, with godlike valor, led them on,
Holding before him his round ox-hide shield,
Studded with brass; his crested helmet shook,
Nodding with plumes, and gleaming terribly;
He tried the phalanxes on every side,
Advancing toward them, if perchance he might
Break through their ranks, and cause them to give way;
Yet he shook not the courage of the Greeks;
But Ajax, stepping forth, thus challenged him:
  Come hither, noble sir: why fright us thus?
We Greeks are not such novices in war,
But Jove has thought it fit to punish us;
Thou hopest, I suppose, to seize our ships,
But we have force enough to keep thee back,
And before that occurs, thy town is ours;
And not far distant, either, is the day,
When, in thy car retreating from the field,
Thou to great Jove, and all the gods, shalt pray
That thy good steeds may fly as swift as hawks,
And bear thee back within Troy's sheltering walls.
  Whilst he thus spake, an eagle o'er him flew,
On his right hand; the Greeks the omen saw,
And, much encouraged, raised a mighty shout.
Meanwhile illustrious Hector thus replied:
  What hast thou said, vainglorious Ajax?
Would that I only were as sure to be
The son of Jove, or to possess the fame
That wise Minerva and Apollo have,
As that this day brings ruin on the Greeks;
And thou amongst them, too, shalt surely fall,
If thou wilt stand thy ground, and meet my spear,

Which shall thy dainty person lacerate,
And leave thy corpse a prey to dogs and birds.
Thus having spoke, the hero led the way;
The troops all followed, shouting lustily.
The Greeks, on their side, to the shouts replied,
And bravely met the onset of their foes;
The mingled cries of the contending hosts
Rose to the sky, and echoed far and wide.

BOOK XIV.

JOVE CAJOLED.

ARGUMENT.

Agamemnon, with Nestor and the wounded chiefs, proceed to view the fight.—Juno, procuring the girdle of Venus, excites the amorous desires of Jove, and puts him to sleep.—Neptune, taking advantage of this, assists the Greeks.

NESTOR the clamor heard, he and his friend,
As in the tent they sat quaffing their wine;
And thus the old man to his comrade spake:
  Say, good Machaon! how is this to end?
The battle-cry each instant louder grows.
Then stay thou here, drinking the ruby wine,
Till Hecamedè a warm bath prepares,
In which to wash away thy bloody stains;
Meanwhile I sally forth and take a look.
  He said; and seized the handsome brazen shield
Of his dear son, the bold Thrasymedes,
Who used just then the buckler of his sire;
His mighty spear the warrior also grasped.
Thus armed, the venerable chief stepped forth,
And with sad heart a sorry sight beheld:
There were his friends all in confusion thrown,
And their foes chasing them in dreadful rout;
The rampart of the Greeks had fallen too.
As when the heaving ocean darker grows,
A storm foreboding; every wind is hushed,
The swelling waves, as yet, roll neither way,

Until the tempest bursts and drives them on:
So in suspense the aged warrior stood,
Whether at once to mingle in the fight
Or first to go and Agamemnon seek;
Thus pondering, he resolved to seek the king.
  Meanwhile the slaughter raged; loud rang the arms
As brass met brass, and spears and bucklers clashed;
And now the wounded chiefs old Nestor met,
They from their vessels came to see the fight,—
Ulysses, Diomed, and Agamemnon;
Their ships were farthest from the battle-field,
Drawn up upon the margin of the sea;
The first tier of the fleet was near the plain,
Along their sterns the rampart had been built;
For though the shore was large 'twas still too small
To hold the ships; the army crowded was,
Therefore the fleet had been arranged in rows,
And filled the entire margin of the bay,
Which by two jutting headlands was inclosed;
There walked the warriors leaning on their spears,
They came to see the turmoil and the fight,
And greatly were they grieved at what they saw.
Them Nestor met, and thus the Grecian king
Addressed his aged comrade, and his friend:
  Oh, Nelian Nestor, glory of the Greeks!
Why art thou here, leaving the battle-field?
I fear lest Hector's threat may be fulfilled,—
That he would ne'er return to lofty Troy
'Till he had burnt our fleet and slaughtered us:
Such was his threat, nor was his threat in vain.
Ye gods! it seems that all the other Greeks
Are wroth with me, e'en as Achilles is;
Nor will they fight to save our threatened fleet.
  Thus spake the king, and Nestor thus replied:
'Tis true, disasters compass us around,—
Such is our fate, and such is Jove's decree;
For now the wall has fallen, which we thought
Would be a safeguard to our ships and us.

Yet still our warriors nobly stand their ground;
And scarcely could one tell by looking on,
On which side 'tis the Greeks are battling,
So mingled are they with their furious foes,
And the loud turmoil reaches e'en to heaven;
But let us now consult what's best to do.
Yet would I not advise that ye should fight,
For such is not the part of wounded men.
Thus Nestor spake, and thus the king replied:
Since to our very ships the fight has come,
And neither wall nor ditch are of avail,
The works at which we labored hard, and thought
That they would be a barrier to our foes;
For now it is the pleasure of great Jove
That far from home we Greeks should be destroyed.
I knew when formerly it was Jove's will
That victory should perch on our side;
But now I see it is to Troy he gives
The upper hand, and means to humble us.
But come, and as I counsel, ye obey:
The vessels that are nearest to the sea
Let us draw down, and launch them in the deep,—
There we will anchor them 'till night arrives,
When, should our enemies a respite give,
We with the other ships will sail away.
To fly from evil no dishonor is,
E'en in the night; far better so to do,
Than that our army should all captured be.
He said; and sternly eyeing him, replied
The wise Ulysses: Oh, Agamemnon!
What words are these that have escaped thy lips?
Lost to all sense of honor, would thou wast
Chief o'er some coward race, and not o'er us,
Who from our youth, e'en up to hoary age,
By Heaven's decree were always warriors,
And count it glorious to die in war!
Be silent, lest some other of the Greeks
May hear thy speech, which no right-minded king,

So powerful as thou, should e'er have made;
Thy counsel is injurious and unsound,—
Thou bidd'st us stop the war and launch our ships,
So that our foes, elated with success,
May thus become more daring than before,
And ruin and destruction be our lot;
For when the Greeks behold their vessels launched,
They will lose heart at once and fight no more;
Thus thy advice will most pernicious be.
He said; and Agamemnon thus replied:
Thy chiding, oh, Ulysses, gives me pain;
Yet 'twas not my design to force the Greeks
Against their wish to re-embark for home;
But if another man, though young or old,
Can better counsel give, I would rejoice.
That man behold, brave Diomed replied,
Ready to speak if ye will only hear;
And blame me not if I thy junior be,
For I from Tydeus my lineage boast,
Whose bones lie buried under Theban soil.
Three goodly sons to Portheus were born,
Who dwelt in Pleuron and high Calydon;
Melas and Agrius were the names of two,
The third was Œneus; my grandsire he,
A famous knight, and boldest of them all;
He in his native country lived and died.
My father wandering off, to Argos came,
Such was the will of Jove and all the gods;
The daughter of Adrastus he espoused,
Dwelt in a palace, and owned many farms,
Orchards, and vineyards, and vast flocks and herds;
No Greek could equal him in hurling spears.
These things ye ought to know, since they are true.
Reject not then my words, as though I were
A base-born person and of no account:
Though wounded, let us to the field repair;
Beyond the weapons' range we safe may stand,
And thus encourage and urge on the men,

Who have advantage taken of our wounds,
And not performed their duty as they ought.
Thus Diomed spake, and to him all gave heed;
And, the king leading, to the fight they went.
But glorious Neptune still was on the watch,
And in an old man's form the warriors met;
He the right hand of Agamemnon seized,
And thus in hasty words the chief addressed:
Oh, son of Atreus! now is Achilles pleased,
Seeing the rout and slaughter of the Greeks,
For in his breast no spark of pity burns:
So let him perish by some god disgraced;
But the blest gods still have regard for thee,
And thou shalt still thy haughty foes behold
In clouds of dust retreating o'er the plain,
Glad to escape within the walls of Troy.
He said, and shouted, rushing o'er the field:
Loud as the war-cry of ten thousand men
King Neptune shouted, mingling in the throng,
And with fresh courage all the Greeks inspired.
Meanwhile the queen of heaven, golden throned,
Gazed from the summit of the Olympian mount;
With joy her brother Neptune she beheld
Aiding her friends and stirring up the fight.
Jove, too, she saw on Ida's loftiest top,
And to her eyes a hateful sight it was.
Then she considered how she might cajole
Her husband and inflame him with desire,
And, whilst in her embraces he reclined,
Seal up his eyes in soft and genial sleep.
Straight to her chamber then the goddess went,
Which Vulcan, heavenly architect, had built,
And furnished for the doors a secret bolt,
Which none of the celestials could unlock.
There, entering, she closed the splendid doors.
Her lovely person then the goddess washed,
Her skin anointing with ambrosial oil,
So sweet that, when the golden vase she shook,

The fragrant perfume spread through earth and heaven.
With this her body scenting, next she combed
Her beauteous flowing locks of glossy hair—
On her immortal forehead parting them;
Then o'er her an ambrosial robe she drew,
Wrought by Minerva with rich needle-work—
It fastened on her breast with golden clasps;
Next round her waist the goddess bound her zone,
From which a hundred handsome fringes hung.
In her bored ears her ear-rings then she placed,
Each of three drops, with splendid jewels set;
Then over all a new rich veil she threw,
So bright it was it dazzled like the sun;
Her sandals to her shining feet she bound,
And, thus adorned, forth from her chamber went.
Venus she called aside, and in low tones
The laughter-loving goddess thus addressed:
  Dear child, wilt thou comply with my request?
Or does some anger in thy bosom burn
Because I help the Greeks and thou help'st Troy?
  She said; and lovely Venus thus replied:
Speak out and tell thy wish. I will comply
If 'tis a thing that's not impossible
And lies within my power to perform.
  She said; and wily Juno answered her:
Give me that power of love and fond desire
With which thou rulest over gods and men;
For I am on an urgent visit bound,
E'en to the utmost confines of the earth,
Where Oceanus, parent of the gods,
And mother Tethys, have their distant home.
They once from Rhea kindly me received,
And in their mansions kept and nurtured me,
When Jove in wrath cast Saturn out of heaven.
I go to visit them and make them friends,
For in sad quarrels they have long indulged,
Shunning each other's company and bed.
If I these deities can reconcile

And cause them fondly to embrace again,
They will forever love me and revere.
She said; and Venus, smiling, thus replied:
Thy wishes must not, cannot be denied,
For thine it is to share the couch of Jove.
So saying, from her bosom she unbound
Her magic girdle, beautifully wrought:
In it were all the blandishments of earth,—
Caresses sweet, soft love, and fond desire,
And honeyed words, beguiling wisest hearts.
Take it, she said, and in thy bosom bear—
Wondrous its power! all things it contains,
And will perform whate'er thou canst desire.
Thus spake she; venerable Juno smiled,
And, smiling, in her bosom placed the zone.
Then Venus to her heavenly home returned.
But Juno, hastening, left the Olympian mount,
Pieria crossed and rich Emathia,
Flew o'er the snowy mountain-tops of Thrace,
Nor touched she once the surface of the earth.
From lofty Athos then the goddess plunged
And skimmed the foaming billows of the deep—
Lemnos she reached, where godlike Thoas dwelt;
There she met Sleep, twin brother he to Death—
She seized his hand and thus the god addressed:
Oh, Sleep! thou conqueror of gods and men,
Hearken to what I say and grant my wish,
And I from this day forth will be thy friend:
Seal up the sparkling eyes of mighty Jove
When he with me reclines in love's embrace,
And I on thee a present will bestow—
A splendid couch, immortal, made of gold.
Vulcan shall make it—Vulcan, my limping son—
In his best style; to it a footstool too
Shall be attached, on which thy polished feet
May find support when thou art banqueting.
Thus Juno spake, and thus sweet Sleep replied:
Juno, dread Saturn's daughter, true it is

That I all other gods can put to sleep,
And e'en can lull the ocean's roaring waves—
Ocean, the parent of the deities;
But I could not approach Saturnian Jove,
Nor close his eyes unless with his consent,
For once already has he frightened me.
'Twas on that day when Hercules, his son,
From Troy sailed home, when he had sacked the town;
Then, gently stealing over heaven's king,
I closed his eyes, whilst thou meanwhile stirred up
A dreadful tempest, and the hero drove
To distant Cos, far from his friends and home.
At length the almighty Thunderer awoke,
Hustling the deities about in wrath.
But me he chiefly sought, and would have hurled
Like a lost spirit far below the deep,
Had not dread Night, ruler of gods and men,
To whom I flying came, espoused my cause:
So Jove, though angry, did his wrath restrain,
Fearing to make a foe of dangerous Night;
Yet, after this experience, 'tis thy wish
To have me venture on such deeds again?
He spake; and dark-eyed Juno thus replied:
Why talk'st thou thus, oh Sleep? Dost thou suppose
That mighty Jove does for the Trojans care,
Or will on their account be wroth as he
Was formerly for Hercules, his son?
Come, then, deny me not, but grant my wish,
And I will give thee Pasithaë to wife,
The youngest, loveliest of the Graces she,
Whom thou hast been in love with many a day.
She said; and Sleep, delighted, thus replied:
Swear to me, then, by the dread river Styx:
Placing one hand upon the fruitful earth,
The other on the sparkling marble sea,
So that with Saturn all the infernal gods
May of thy promise be the witnesses,

That thou wilt give me Pasithaë to wife,
Whom I have been in love with many a day.
He said; and Junò did as he desired,
Calling to witness the Tartarean gods,
Titans their name. This done, they both set out
From Lemnos, and from Imbro's hazy shore;
With rapid flight their journey they performed.
Ida they reached, famed for wild beasts and springs;
There they first left the sea; flew o'er the land,—
O'er the wide forests flew, and with their feet
Rustled the topmost branches of the trees;
There Sleep remained ere Jove should him observe:
On a majestic fir he took his seat;
Highest it was of all the trees around.
Amid the boughs concealed, quiet he sat,
Taking the form of a shrill mountain-bird,
By gods called Chalcis, whiporwill by men.
But Juno to the highest peak of Ida flew,
The peak called Gargarus; there sat great Jove,
And as his wife approached, his heart with love
Was all inflamed, e'en as at first it was
When to their marriage-bed they slyly stole,
Their parents unaware of their design.
Near her he drew, and thus addressing, spake:
Why from Olympus, Juno, in such haste?
Where hast thou left thy chariot and steeds?
The wily goddess answering, replied:
I go upon an urgent visit, bound
E'en to the utmost confines of the earth,
Where Oceanus, parent of the gods,
And mother Tethys, have their distant home.
They once from Rhea kindly me received,
And in their mansions kept and nurtured me;
I go to visit them, and make them friends,
For in sad quarrels they have long indulged,
Shunning each other's bed and company.
My steeds, which bear me over land and sea,
Stand waiting for me at the mountain's base;

And for their sake it is I hither come,
Lest thou hereafter might be wroth with me,
Should I, unknown to thee, this journey take
To the deep-heaving Ocean's palaces.
She said; and thus cloud-mantled Jove replied:
'Tis well; but let this visit be deferred,
And let us now enjoy the sweets of love;
For ne'er by goddess nor by woman yet,
Have I by love been so inflamed as now;
Not when I loved the wife of Ixion,
Who bore Perithous, for wisdom famed;
Nor when with handsome-ankled Danaë
My heart was smit; Acrisis' daughter she,
Who Perseus bore, of all men most renowned;
Nor when with noble Phœnix' beauteous child,
Mother of Minos, and Rhadamanthus;
Nor when the lovely Semelè I wooed,
Nor fair Alcmenè who in Thebès was born;
Mother of valiant Hercules was she,
But Semelè the joyous Bacchus bore;
Nor when I Ceres loved, the fair-haired queen,
Nor bright Latona, nor indeed thyself;
With none of these was I so much subdued
As I am with thy beauty ravished now.
But wily Juno answering, thus spake:
Oh, son of Saturn! art thou not ashamed,
If we on Ida's open top embrace?
How would it be if any of the gods
Should spy us out and publish it in heaven?
I could not face them then for very shame,
Nor to Olympus venture to return.
But if by love thou art so much o'ercome,
There is a certain chamber Vulcan made,—
Vulcan my son, that skillful architect;
Close are its doors, and well secured its bolts,
There let us go and lie, if such thy wish.
Thus spake she, and cloud-mantled Jove replied:
Juno, fear not that this will be revealed

Either to mortals or to deities;
For I will veil thee in a golden cloud
So dense, that e'en the Sun's all-piercing eyes
Will gaze in vain, and fail to penetrate.
So saying, in his arms he clasped his wife;
Fresh verdure underneath them started forth,
The dewy lotus, and the daffodil,
And the soft hyacinth, which raised them up;
Thus on a flowery couch embraced they lay,
Whilst round them hung a beauteous golden cloud,
And from it sparkling dew-drops trickled down;
Thus Jove, upon the top of Gargarus,
In amorous slumber with his wife reclined.
Meanwhile sweet Sleep to the Greek ships repaired,
That he to Neptune might the message bring;
Near him he drew, and thus the god addressed:
Now, Neptune! aid the Greeks with all thy heart,
And glorify them while the Thunderer sleeps,
For in soft slumber I have veiled his eyes,
And Juno has deceived him with her love.
So saying, Sleep departed from the field.
His word incited Neptune to assist
The Greeks still more; and, rushing to the van,
With a loud voice he thus exhorted them:
Greeks! shall we let proud Hector have his way,
And boast that he has captured our fleet?
He thinks he can, because Achilles sits
By his own vessels, cherishing his wrath;
But little would we miss this sullen chief
If we would aid each other as we ought;
But come, and as I counsel ye obey:
Let us, who are the best and bravest men,
With shields, and glittering helmets, and long spears,
Boldly advance, and I will lead the way;
Nor do I think that furious Hector e'en
Will meet the shock or dare to stand his ground.
And if some skillful warrior should bear

A small-sized shield, let him bestow it on
A weaker man, and he a larger take.
Thus Neptune spake, and to him all gave heed;
The wounded leaders, too, rallied the troops,—
Ulysses, Diomed, and Agamemnon;
Moving about, the warriors' arms they changed—
To the best men the best of weapons gave,
And on inferiors the worst bestowed.
Thus clad in brass they to the conflict rushed;
Great Neptune led them on; he in his hand
Wielded an awful tapering sword, which looked
Like a dread thunderbolt; from that bright sword
Men shrink aghast, and none would dare confront.
The illustrious Hector, on the other hand,
The Trojans led; then was a struggle seen,
The most severe the war had yet beheld:
The roaring sea dashed o'er the ships and tents,
And mighty were the shouts the warriors raised;
The ocean driven by a northern blast
Against a rocky shore, roars not so loud;
Nor the fierce crackling of devouring flames,
When woody mountains chance to be on fire;
Nor winds tempestuous, bending mighty oaks,
Were not so loud as was the battle-cry,
When Greeks and Trojans on each other rushed.
At Ajax then illustrious Hector aimed,—
Aimed with his spear; nor did he miss the chief,
But struck him on the breast, where crossed the belts
Of his round shield and silver-hilted sword;
These to his tender flesh protection gave.
But Hector was enraged when he beheld
His weapon hurled from his stout hand in vain;
To save his life he 'mid the throng withdrew.
As he retreated, Ajax Telamon
Picked up a mighty stone, of which there were
Numbers upon the ground, to prop the ships;
This like a top he threw, whirling it round,

And struck him on the neck, above his shield.
As when beneath the thunderbolt of Jove
An oak uprooted falls, a horrid smell
Of sulphur then arises from the spot;
The terrified beholder starts amazed,
So dreadful is it where the lightning strikes:
Thus, prostrate in the dust, bold Hector fell;
His glittering spear dropped from his nerveless hand;
Down went his helmet too, and burnished shield,
And loudly rang his armor on the ground.
With cheers and shouts the Greeks ran up to seize
Their fallen foe; thickly their weapons flew,
But flew in vain, for none the warriors struck.
His brave companions now surrounded him,—
Polydamas, Æneas, and Agenor,
And royal Sarpedon, and Glaucus too:
Nor was there one that toward him showed neglect;
All gathered round, with their protecting shields.
Then from the field they bore him to his car,
Which, with its driver and its coursers fleet,
Stood in the rear; on it the chief they placed,
Then drove him, groaning deeply, toward the town.
But when to Xanthus' flowing stream they came,
Xanthus the offspring of almighty Jove,
They lift him to the ground, and o'er his face
Sprinkled cool water; then the hero breathed,
Opened his eyes, and sat upon his knees;
Dark blood he then threw up, and, falling back,
Fainted again, still by the blow o'ercome.
But when the Greeks saw Hector carried off,
They, with fresh vigor, on the Trojans rushed.
Then Ajax Oïleus Satnius dispatched
With his sharp spear, whom a fair Naiad bore—
Bore to the shepherd Enops as he fed
His flocks upon the banks of Satnio.
Him Ajax struck, and wounded in the flank:
Down to the earth supine the warrior fell,
And now a dreadful conflict round him raged.

To avenge his death, Polydamas drew near,
And on the shoulder struck Prothœnor:
His massy brazen spear went through and through,
And to the ground he fell, grasping the dust.
Then shouted mightily Polydamas,
And, with an air of triumph, thus cried out:
From my stout hand, my spear flew not in vain;
'Tis planted in the body of some Greek,
And leaning on it, he will now descend
To the infernal realms where Pluto reigns.
He said; and much his boast annoyed the Greeks,
But chiefly Ajax Telamon was moved,
For at his feet it was the warrior fell:
He at the Trojan then his weapen hurled,
But, stooping down, Polydamas escaped,
And brave Archilochus, Antenor's son,
Doomed by the gods, the deadly blow received:
For the spear struck him full upon the neck,
Cutting the tendons; down the warrior fell,
And bending forward, sooner than his legs,
His drooping visage touched the dusty ground.
Then Ajax to Polydamas cried out:
Tell me, Polydamas, and speak the truth,
Have we not made an excellent exchange
For Prothœnor? this man seems to me
Neither a coward, nor from cowards sprung,
But is most like the brother or the son
Of great Antenor, famed for horsemanship:
Thus Ajax spake, well knowing who he was.
But at his death the Trojans were much grieved.
Near his dead brother Acamas then slew
The warrior Promachus, whilst in the act
Of dragging by its heels the corpse away;
And o'er his victim boastingly cried out:
Ye Grecian archers, always full of threats,
Bad luck and sorrow are not all for us;
Ye have your turn, and feel the stroke of death:

See now how I have Promachus dispatched,
And for my brother slain an offset made!
Well is it when a family is blessed
With brothers to avenge a brother's loss.
He said; and at his boasts the Greeks were grieved,
But most the heart of Peneleus was moved:
And on the Trojan chief the monarch rushed.
Quick he drew back, and the destructive spear
Struck Ilioneus, rich Phorbas' son,
His only son, who, most of all in Troy,
Was loved by Mercury, and with wealth endowed.
The weapon pierced him just below the brow,
Forced out the pupil, passing through his skull:
The warrior fell, outstretching both his hands;
His glittering sword king Peneleus then drew,
And, with the spear still sticking in his eyes,
Lopped off his head, just like a poppy flower,
And raised it on his weapon's point on high;
Then loudly boasting, thus the monarch cried:
Go now, ye Trojans, and report the news
Of Ilioneus' death, that his fond sire,
And his dear mother too, may weep and wail,
Just as the wife of Promachus shall grieve,
When we to Greece return, without her spouse.
He said; and terror seized upon them all,—
Each seeking how he might escape from death.
Tell me, ye muses of the Olympian mount!
Who of the Greeks most gloriously fought,
When mighty Neptune turned the scale of war?
First of them all was Ajax Telamon;
Hyrtius he slew, the famous Mysian chief;
Next Mermereus and Phalces were o'ercome
By bold Antilochus; then Merion slew
Morus, and, after him, Hippotion;
Then Periphætes was by Teucer slain,
And Prothoon also; next bold Atreus' son
Struck in the flank the chief Hyperenor:

The deadly weapon through his entrails passed,
And drank his blood; his soul, expelled in haste,
Fled through the wound, and darkness veiled his eyes.
But Ajax Oïleus slew the most,
For he was swiftest of them all on foot,
And so could follow up the flying foe.

BOOK XV.

JOVE AWAKES FROM SLEEP.

ARGUMENT.

Jove chides Juno for her deceit, and sends Iris to bid Neptune cease from the fight.—Apollo arouses Hector, and puts the Greeks to flight. —Ajax Telamon slays many Trojans, as they attempt to fire the ships.

But when the fugitives had crossed the ditch,
And by the Greeks vast numbers had been slain,
Pallid with fright, the remnant made a halt,
And by their chariots and horses stood.
  Meanwhile the Thunderer on Ida's top
Rose from his couch, and looking down beheld
Both Greeks and Trojans, these in dreadful rout
And those pursuing and destroying them,—
So potent was the aid king Neptune gave.
Hector he saw stretched on the dusty plain;
His comrades, in a group, around him sat:
Senseless the hero was, and scarce could breathe,
And now and then dark blood was vomiting,
For by no puny hand he had been struck.
With pity Jove beheld the wounded chief,
And, sternly gazing, thus addressed his queen:
  Oh, Juno! author thou of wicked arts!
By thy contrivance Hector is withdrawn
And his defeated army put to flight;
But thou may'st be the first to reap the fruits
Of this thy fraud and be by me chastised.
Hast thou forgot how once in middle air

I swung thee by the wrists in golden chains,
Fastening two heavy anvils to thy feet?
There in the clouds suspended wast thou seen,
Nor could the pitying gods afford thee aid,
For whom of them I caught approaching thee
I seized and hurled him headlong to the earth.
Such was my wrath on Hercules' account,
Whom thou with storms and winds, harassing, sent
Out of his course, 'till he to Cos was driven.
I took his part indeed and brought him back
To his own Argos, after suffering much.
Think of these things, and cease from thy deceits,
For little will love's intercourse avail,
Or save thee harmless in thy trickery.
He said; and venerable Juno feared,
And to her husband promptly thus replied:
I swear by earth and by the outstretched heavens,
And by the waters of infernal Styx,
An oath most dreadful to the happy gods,
And by thy sacred head, and also by
Our nuptial couch and holy marriage vows,
That 'twas not I that mighty Neptune urged
To aid the Greeks and slay the men of Troy;
For, seeing how the Greeks were driven back,
He for them pity felt and took their part.
But if thou wilt, I am prepared to go
And tell him truly what thy pleasure is.
She said; and with a smile great Jove replied:
If, then, fair Juno, thou wilt think as I
And dwell in heaven. furthering my designs,
Vainly would Neptune strive to counteract
Or thwart us both; but if thou art sincere,
Go quick, and Iris and Apollo call,
And let the first repairing to the Greeks
Bid Neptune from the battle-field retire
And to his palaces at once return,
And let Apollo wounded Hector aid
And give him strength and heal his injuries;

Then let him put the Greeks again to flight
And make them to Achilles' ships fall back.
He then his comrade Patroclus will rouse,
Who in the fight by Hector shall be slain
In front of Troy, and many more besides—
Among them Sarpedon, my son, will fall,
A noble youth. Achilles, then enraged,
Shall Hector slay. The Trojans then will flee,
And with Minerva's aid the conquering Greeks
Shall rout their foes and capture lofty Troy.
Till then I will not lay aside my wrath,
Nor suffer any god to aid the Greeks,
For I Achilles' wishes must fulfill,
As first to him I nodded my assent,
Upon that day when Thetis touched my knees
And begged me to avenge her valiant son.
He said, nor did fair Juno disobey,
But flew from Ida's lofty mountain-top
To the blest mansions of the happy gods.
As when a traveler, who has journeyed much
O'er distant lands, in memory recalls
The various places he has visited,
And in a single flash of thought can say
Once I was here, and once again was there :
So swift the venerable Juno flew,
And high Olympus reached, and entered in
To the assembly of the deities,
Who rose and welcomed her with flowing cups.
She passed the others by and took the bowl
Which Themis, lovely nymph, presented her ;
For she it was who, running to her, came
And thus, in words of inquiry, addressed :
What brings thee hither, Juno, in this state
Of agitation ? Has thy husband Jove
Done ought to ruffle thee or terrify?
To whom the beauteous Juno thus replied :
Why dost thou thus, oh, Themis, question me?
Thou knowest how proud he is and how severe.

Enjoy thy banquet now and pour out wine;
But thou and all the deities shall hear
Distasteful things anon that Jove designs,
Nor do I think that gods or men will have
Much joy hereafter in their pleasant feasts.
She said, and took her seat; the gods all grieved;
She smiled—smiled with her lips alone,
For indignation sat upon her brow,
And thus again the deities addressed:
Bereft of sense we are to strive with Jove,
And yet we fondly hope to govern him,
Whilst he meanwhile sits quietly apart,
Neither regarding us nor our vain schemes,
So mighty and so powerful is he.
Wherefore endure such ills as he inflicts
And make the best of your calamities,
For now, if I mistake not, upon Mars
A sad misfortune he already sends,
For his dear son Ascalaphus is slain,
His favorite son, of mortals most beloved.
Thus Juno spake; then fiery Mars arose
And clapped his hand upon his brawny thigh,
And thus in words of lamentation spake:
Blame me not now, inhabiters of heaven,
If I, repairing to the Grecian fleet,
The murder of my noble son avenge,
E'en though I fall, struck by a thunderbolt
From Jove's right hand, and lie inglorious
Midst bloody corpses stretched upon the ground.
He said, and ordered Terror and pale Fear
To yoke his horses and prepare his car,
Whilst he in shining armor clad himself.
Then on the gods more grievous wrath had fallen
From mighty Jove had not Minerva sprung
Forth from the vestibule and left her throne.
Quickly her angry brother she approached
And snatched the brazen helmet from his head,

And from him took his shield and glittering spear;
Then the impetuous Mars she thus addressed:
  Madman! bereft of sense, thou art undone!
Are thine ears stopped? and hast thou lost thy mind?
Hast thou not heard what beauteous Juno says,
Who from Olympian Jove hast just now come?
Hast thou not woes enough, but would'st be driven
Back to Olympus with fresh grief and shame
And bring more trouble on us deities?
For he would leave Trojans and Greeks at once
And hither come, disturbing heaven's peace.
Us he would punish, seizing one by one
The guilty and the innocent alike.
Then lay aside thy anger for thy son,
For better men than he have oft been slain,
And death's the common lot of all mankind.
  She said, and forced her brother to sit down.
Juno Apollo then and Iris called—
Iris, fair nymph, swift messenger of heaven—
And thus in haste the deities addressed:
Jove calls ye both to Ida's shady mount;
Fly thither then, and what he bids ye, do.
  So saying, venerable Juno went
And took her seat among the deities;
But they flew off and soon to Ida came—
Ida for game renowned and gushing springs.
Jove they found seated on a lofty peak,
A lovely fragrant cloud surrounding him;
They stood before him—he, no longer wroth,
Was pleased that they so quickly had obeyed,
And thus the rainbow goddess first addressed:
  Fly, swift-winged Iris, to king Neptune fly,
And tell him truly what I bid thee tell:
That from the battle-field he must retire,
And either to Olympus' heights repair
Or to the ocean go, his own domain;
But if he should my orders disobey,
Let him think who I am and what my power,

For I outrank him both in strength and age;
Yet he, unlike the other deities,
Vainly imagines he can cope with me.
He said; nor did swift Iris disobey,
But flew from Ida down to sacred Troy.
As when the drifting snow or icy hail
Comes driving on, urged by the northern blasts:
So rapid Iris swiftly flew along,
Drew near to Neptune, and addressed him thus:
Oh, azure Neptune! I have hither come
Bearing a message from almighty Jove;
He bids thee from the battle-field retire,
And either to Olympus' heights repair
Or to the ocean go, thine own domain;
But if thou wilt his orders disobey
He threatens that against thee he will come,
And would advise thee to avoid his wrath,
For he outranks thee both in strength and age;
Yet in thy pride, unlike the other gods,
Thou fondly would'st presume to rival him.
She said; and Neptune, sighing, thus replied:
Good heavens! though powerful he truly is,
Yet he forgets himself, if he intends
To conquer me, his equal every way,
For we three brothers are from Saturn sprung,
Jove and myself, and Pluto, king of hell.
Into three parts the world divided was,
And each his proper dignity received—
The ocean fell to me, Pluto got hell,
And Jove became the monarch of the skies;
The earth was left in common to us all.
Therefore I will not be controlled by Jove—
Let him in quietness his third part rule,
Nor seek with threatening words to frighten me.
When he his haughty temper would indulge,
Let him his sons and daughters terrify,
For they are bound to listen and obey.
He said; and swift-winged Iris thus replied:

And shall I, Neptune, this proud answer bear?
Or wilt thou, as the proudest, change thy mind?
For with the elder born the Furies side.
Thus Iris spake, and Neptune answered her:
Iris, thy counsel is discreet and good,
And well it is when messengers are wise;
Yet it goes hard with me to bear abuse
From one who only equals me in rank;
But angry though I be, I yet will yield.
But this I say, should he spare lofty Troy,
And harm the Greeks in disregard to me,
And wise Minerva, and the queen of heaven,
And skillful Vulcan too, and Mercury,
An endless quarrel shall between us rise.
So saying, he the Grecian army left,
And into ocean plunged, his own domain.
The struggling Greeks their champion soon missed.
And to Apollo, then, the Thunderer spake:
Go, my dear son, to brass-clad Hector go;
For Neptune has departed to the sea,
Wisely withdrawing, to escape my wrath,
Which, had it broken forth, would have been heard
E'en to deepest boundaries of hell;
But he now yields, acknowledging his wrong,
And this is best both for himself and me,
For otherwise much mischief had been done;
But take thy gold-fringed ægis in thy hands,
And shake it terribly, and scare the Greeks,
And of illustrious Hector take good care;
Give him great strength, that he may drive the Greeks
E'en to the borders of the Hellespont;
Whilst I, meanwhile, will meditate and plan
How they, in their turn, may have victory.
He said; nor did Apollo disobey,
But from mount Ida flew, like a keen hawk,
Swiftest of birds that preys on gentle doves.
Illustrious Hector, Priam's son, he found
Now sitting up, and knowing now his friends,

For Jove his strength and senses had restored;
Near him Apollo drew, and thus addressed:
 Why art thou here, oh Hector, Priam's son,
Drooping and sad, nor fighting like the rest?
Has some great grief thy spirits overcome?
 He said; and Hector languidly replied:
Who art thou, best of gods, that face to face
Comes to inquire about my misery?
Hast thou not heard how, in the thickest fight,
Slaying the routed Greeks amid their ships,
Brave Ajax struck me with a ponderous stone,
Bringing my bloody exploits to an end?
And truly I believed this very day
That I to Pluto's mansions would descend,
And mingle with the myriads of the dead,
So near I came to yielding up the ghost.
 He said; and thus the other answered him:
Be of good cheer, for Jove from Ida sends
A great assistant to protect and aid,—
Phœbus Apollo of the golden sword,
Guardian of thee, and of thy lofty town.
Up, then! and head thy numerous cavalry;
Drive thy swift steeds upon the hollow ships;
I will before thee go, and make a path,
And put to flight whoever may oppose.
As when a high-fed horse his halter breaks,
And, rushing o'er the plain, the meadows seeks
Of a wide river where he oft has bathed;
Proud of his beauty, galloping he goes,
Tossing his mane, and mingles with the mares:
So Hector, when he heard Apollo's voice,
Sprang to his feet, and cheered his warriors on
His foes. As dogs and countrymen who chase
An antlered stag or mountain-goat in vain,
Amid the dark recesses of a wood,
For now a lion comes across their path,
And, in their fright, they all turn back and flee:
So the proud Greeks pursued with sword and spear;

But when they saw bold Hector coming up,
They were much troubled, and their courage fled.
Then Thoas, son of Andræmon, spake,—
Bravest of all the Ætolians was he,
And could fight hand to hand or hurl the spear,
And few in oratory the youth could match,—
He raised his voice, and thus his men addressed:
Good heavens! what miracle is this I see?
Hector is up again, escaping death;
Truly we hoped that he had met his fate
By the stout hand of Ajax Telamon;
But some one of the gods has intervened,
And he is at his bloody work again:
For Jove is with him, and has nerved his arm.
But come, and do ye all as I advise:
Let the main body of our force retire,
Whilst we who are the bravest make a stand;
Nor do I think this raging warrior
Will break our ranks, or reach the Grecian camp.
He said; and to his words they all gave heed.
The men of Ajax, and of Merion,
Of Meges, Idomeneus, and Teucer,—
All these stood firm, and, marshaling their ranks,
Were ready for their foes as they advanced,
Whilst to the rear the multitude fell back.
In close array, the Trojans forward marched;
Hector marched first, stalking with lofty strides—
Before him, in a cloud, Apollo walked,
Holding his gold-fringed ægis in his hands,
Dreadful and dazzling, which lame Vulcan made
For routing men, and gave to mighty Jove.
With this the deity led on his friends.
The Greeks stood firm, and from both sides arose
Shrill cries and tumult and the clash of arms;
From gallant hands showers of arrows flew,
And glittering spears; some hit the mark well aimed,
And many youthful warriors were pierced—
Others fell short and stuck into the ground.

Whilst the bright god his ægis held unmoved,
The dreadful fight was equally maintained;
But when he shook it and his piercing eyes
Looked full into the faces of the Greeks,
He at the same time shouting dreadfully,
Then they gave way, and then their courage fell.
As when two savage beasts in a dark night,
The shepherd being absent, rout the flock :
So the enfeebled Greeks were put to rout,
For terror in their hearts Apollo struck,
But glory gave to Hector and to Troy.
Then man slew man, the battle giving way:
Hector slew Stichius and Arcesilaus—
One of the mailed Bœotians was the chief,
The other, comrade of Menestheus;
Medon and Iäsus, Æneas slew;
Medon was bastard son of Oileus
And Ajax's brother; he in Phylacè dwelt,
Far from his native land, for he had killed
His uncle on his mother's side, and fled;
Iäsus of the Athenians was chief,
And from Bucolus and from Sphilus sprung;
Polydamas laid brave Mecistus low;
Clonius by noble Agenor was slain,
And Echius fell by bold Polites' hand;
Paris Deiochus in the shoulder struck,
Flying among the foremost combatants—
Out at his breast the brazen javelin came:—
These of their arms the victor Trojans spoiled.
  The Greeks meanwhile were crowded to the ditch,
And, put to rout, in all directions fled.
Hector then loudly shouted to his men
To follow him and let the spoils alone.
And whom I see lagging behind, he cried,
Him will I put to death upon the spot,
Nor shall his friends for him a funeral make,
But dogs shall prey on his dishonored corpse :
So saying, lash in hand, he urged his car

Onward against the foe, cheering meanwhile;
His warriors shouted too, and drove their steeds
With mighty clamor, following their chief.
Apollo kept before, o'erturned the banks
And threw them easily within the ditch;
O'er the deep trench a causeway thus he bridged—
Broad was the road and a stone's-throw in length.
Onward the Trojans passed, troops upon troops,
Apollo with his ægis leading them.
The wall he leveled easily, as when
Children upon the sea-shore level sand,
Who, in their playfulness, sand-houses build,
And then destroy them with their feet and hands:
Thus Phœbus, archer god, did'st thou destroy
The toil and labor of the routed Greeks,
Who now were chased and driven to their ships.
Then in despair they raised their hands on high
And made their vows and begged for heavenly aid;
But chiefly Nestor, guardian of the host,
Lifting his venerable arms, thus prayed:
  Oh, father Jove! if e'er in fruitful Greece,
Burning the fat of oxen or of sheep,
We begged thee to return us safely home,
And thou did'st promise to fulfill our prayer,
Think of these things and show us mercy now,
That by our foes we be not all destroyed.
  Thus Nestor spake; then loudly thundered Jove,
And heard the prayer of the Geranian sage;
The Trojans heard the thunder too, yet rushed
With increased fury on the yielding Greeks.
And as a wave driven by mighty winds
Comes dashing o'er the bulwarks of a ship,
So with a shout the Trojans crossed the wall,
And, driving in their chariots to the sterns
Of the black ships, they struggled hand to hand
With their sharp spears—one party on the cars,
The other mounted on their lofty decks,
To which with hands and feet they nimbly climbed
By the long poles that propped the vessels up.

Meanwhile Patroclus, as the fight went on
Outside the rampart wall, sat with his friend—
Sat with his friend Eurypylus in the tent,
Healing his wound, and holding sweet discourse;
But when he saw the Trojans burst the walls
And all his countrymen in dreadful rout,
He smote his thigh, and thus lamenting, spake:
I cannot, oh, Eurypylus, remain,
Though needed much, whilst such a fight goes on;
But I must leave thee in some other charge
And to Achilles in all haste will go,
And try to stir him up to give us aid.
Who knows but with Jove's help I may succeed?
For a friend's words are not without effect.
Thus spake the warrior, and hurried off.
Meanwhile the Greeks withstood their Trojan foes,
But though they fewer were could not repel;
Nor could the Trojans penetrate their ranks,
Nor reach the ships, nor mingle with their tents.
But as a plumb-line in a shipwright's hands
Divides in equal parts a piece of plank,
So was the battle equally maintained.
Some fought round one, some round another ship,
But against noble Ajax Hector went;
They at one vessel obstinately strove,
One tried to burn it and one tried to save.
Then Ajax smote Caletor, Clytius' son,
As he approached with fire in his hand;
The blazing torch he dropped upon the ground,
And with a crash the expiring warrior fell.
Hector beheld his valiant cousin fall,
And to his followers thus loudly cried:
Stand fast, my men, nor think of a retreat,
But save Caletor's corpse, nor let the foe
Come up and strip him of his beauteous arms.
He said; and at bold Ajax hurled his spear,
But smote Lycophron, Ajax' serving-man,
Who for a homicide had fled from home,

And with the Grecian champion abode;
He slew him as he by his master stood,
Who shuddered at the sight, and thus addressed
His brother Teucer, skilled in archery:
  Dear Teucer, yonder good Lycophron lies,
Who with us lived and was so much esteemed;
Illustrious Hector sent him to his doom.
But where's thy bow, and where thy deadly shafts,
With which the archer god presented thee?
  Thus spake the chief, and Teucer understood;
And running up with bended bow in hand,
And quiver full of arrows, sent his shafts,
In quick succession, 'mid the Trojan ranks.
Clytus he struck, Pisenor's noble son,
Friend of Polydamas, whose car he drove
Into the very thickest of the fight.
But now his doom he met; for through his neck
The arrow went; he from the chariot fell,
And his scared horses thereupon ran off,
Rattling the empty car across the plain.
Polydamas his friend's mishap perceived,
And swiftly running, caught the frightened steeds;
He gave them to Astynous, begging him
To guide them carefully, and keep in sight;
Then with the foremost combatants he mixed.
  But Teucer at mailed Hector now took aim,
Hoping to slay him; but almighty Jove
Would grant him no such glory; for he snapped
His bow string, and the arrow turned aside.
The archer, shuddering, dropped his faithless bow,
And his bold brother Ajax thus addressed:
Good heavens! some deity against us fights,
Who from my hands has made me drop my bow,
And snapped the newly-twisted string, which I
This very morning made, and thought so strong.
  He said; and Ajax Telamon replied:
Good friend! since then some envious god confounds
Thy bow and arrows, lay them both aside,

And take a good long javelin in thy hands,
And on thy shoulders hang a massy shield;
Then with a gathered band attack the foe,
And if their luck it is to seize the fleet,
Let them not do it without toil and blood.
He said; nor did his brother disobey,
But took his bow and laid it in the tent;
Upon his arm his massy shield he hung,
And on his valiant head a helmet placed,
Crested with horse-hair plumes, which, as he moved,
Waved in the wind, and nodded dreadfully;
Then his huge spear he seized, mounted with brass,
And running up, was soon at Ajax' side.
But Hector seeing Teucer's arrows vain,
His friends encouraged, loudly crying out:
Trojans and Dardans, quit ye now like men!
Rush on the ships, for Teucer's shafts are vain!
In this the hand of Jove is plainly seen,
Who aids us Trojans, frustrating the Greeks;
Fight, then, in close array around the ships,
And should it be the fate of some to fall,
So be it; sure a noble lot it is
To die in the defense of one's dear home;
And when the Greeks depart, his family
Shall be well cared for, and his fortune too.
So saying, he his men with strength inspired,
Whilst Ajax, too, his comrades thus addressed:
Shame on ye, Greeks! the crisis has arrived,
And now 'tis ours to conquer or to die.
Should Hector, the plumed chief, our ships destroy,
Think ye to reach your native land on foot?
Do ye not hear the raging warrior
Urging his men to set our fleet on fire?
Not to a dance his comrades he invites,
But to a battle, and a fierce one, too.
Then let us up and join both heart and hand:
Far better 'tis to conquer or to die
Than thus spin out our lives in bootless fight.
So saying, he their drooping spirits cheered.

Then Hector Schedius slew, a Phocian chief;
And Ajax Laodamas, chief was he
Of the brave infantry, Antenor's son;
But Otus by Polydamas was slain,
Chief of the noble Epeians was he;
Meges beheld, and at the rider aimed,
But, stooping down, Polydamas escaped,
And Crœsmus, by the erring spear was struck—
Struck in the breast; flat on the earth he fell,
And Meges came and stripped him of his arms;
Then Dolops, Lampus' son, on Meges rushed,
And struck him in the middle of his shield,
But his thick corselet saved the hero's life.
This corselet by Phyleus had been brought
From distant Ephyre, on Selle's stream;
Euphetes as a present gave it him,
And so the father's gift preserved the son.
But Meges on the helmet smote his foe,
Cutting sheer off his purple horse-hair crest;
The beauteous plumes fell to the dusty earth.
In single combat thus the warriors fought;
But now to Meges' aid came Menelaus,
Who pierced the luckless Trojan in the back,
The cruel javelin passing through his breast;
Down on his face he fell, and both rushed up
Eager to strip the hero of his arms;
But Hector to his relatives cried out,
And most rebuked the brave Melanippus.
He, ere the war began, had fed his herd
At Percotè; but when the Greeks arrived
He to Troy came, and was respected much.
His house was near to Priam's; and the king
Honored him even as he did his sons.
To him, then, Hector thus reproving spake:
Shall we, oh, Melanippus, thus hold back?
Art thou not moved, seeing thy kinsman slain?
See how they struggle for poor Dolops' arms!
Come on! we must not at a distance fight,

But forward rush; no half-way course there is,
For we our foes must conquer now or die!
So saying, he led on, and following him
The godlike hero, Melanippus, went.
But noble Ajax thus aroused the Greeks:
My friends and comrades, quit yourselves like men!
Think of your honor; with each other vie;
Safety with valor usually is found,
But cowards lose their glory and their lives.
Thus spoke the warrior, and all stood their ground,
Their fleet surrounding with a brazen fence
Of glittering spears; but Jove the Trojans fired.
Then noble Menelaus, valiant in the fight,
Thus to Antilochus his comrade spake:
None of the Greeks, Antilochus, can boast
That he is younger, or more swift on foot,
Or is a stronger, braver man than thou.
Oh, that some Trojan hero thou might'st slay!
He said; and set the young man's heart on fire:
Out from the very foremost ranks he sprang,
And gazing boldly round, his javelin threw;
The Trojans, when they saw him, all drew back;
Nor was his glittering weapon hurled in vain,—
Bold Melanippus on the breast he struck,—
Down, with a crash, the expiring warrior fell.
The victor rushed upon him as a hound
Springs on a fawn slain by a hunter's dart,
As from its shady covert it leaps forth:
Thus, oh, Melanippus, upon thy corpse
Rushed bold Antilochus; but Hector saw,
And running, to the valiant Greek drew near;
Antilochus, though brave, drew back and fled
Like a wild beast that has some mischief done,
Having destroyed some herdsman or some dog,
Then flies before the neighbors can collect:
So fled Antilochus, old Nestor's son.
But Hector and the Trojans rushed ahead,
Like savage lions rushed upon the fleet,

Fulfilling the decrees of mighty Jove,
Who gave them strength, enfeebling the Greeks:
For he would Hector glorify, and wished
To see him set on fire the Grecian fleet,
And thus accomplish Thetis' luckless prayer;
For this Jove waited, till with his eyes he saw
A ship on fire; then would he turn the scale;
Drive back the Trojans, and assist the Greeks.
So he urged Hector, eager enough himself,
For he raged terribly, even as Mars,
Or as an awful fire among the hills,
Destroying forests, wrapping them in flames.
Foam from his mouth came out,
And his eyes flashed beneath his eyebrows grim;
His dreadful plumes shook as the hero fought,
For Jove assistance sent him from on high,
And gave him glory above other men,
For short-lived was he, and his end was near:
Minerva drove him toward the fatal day,
When by Achilles' hand he was to fall.
He rushed into the thickest of the fight
Where'er he saw the bravest, noblest men;
Yet furious as he was, he failed to break
The opposing ranks, for they, compact in squares,
Met his attack like a huge lofty cliff
Which stands the ocean's dashing winds and waves:
So stood the Greeks their ground, nor thought of flight,
But he, like flaming fire, upon them rushed,
And on them fell like an impetuous wave,
Which, by fierce winds impelled, falls on a ship,
Flooding the bark and filling it with spray,—
The trembling sailors are aghast with fear
And think their fatal hour is near at hand.
   But now the wavering Greeks began to yield;
Hector sprang on them as a lion springs
Into a herd of cattle on a marsh.
The timorous herdsman at a distance keeps,
And the fierce beast devours a helpless ox,

Scattering the rest and putting them to flight.
Thus were the Greeks by Hector put to flight
And father Jove ; then slew the Trojan chief
Mycenian Periphetes, Copreus' son,
Who bore a message once to Hercules.
From this inferior father sprang a son
Superior to all his coutrymen,
Accomplished, fleet on foot, prudent and bold.
Hector the glory had of slaying him,
For, turning backward, on the rim he trod
Of his long shield, which reached unto his feet.
This tripped him up, and down the hero fell—
Fell on his back, and loud his helmet rang.
Hector perceived his fall, and, coming up,
Plunged his sharp spear into the warrior's breast.
His friends, though not far off, could give no aid,
So terribly they feared the Trojan chief.
  And now within their foremost tier of ships
They made retreat ; there they came pouring in,
Yet did not through the camp disperse, for shame
And fear restrained. Once more they, rallying, stood,
Exhorting one another with loud cries.
  But most old Nestor, guardian of the Greeks,
Adjured them by their parents, and thus spake,
In earnest tones beseeching every one :
My friends and comrades, quit yourselves like men,
And the respect of others thus secure ;
Think of your wives, your parents, and your homes ;
By all your absent relatives, I beg
That ye fly not, but bravely stand your ground.
  So saying, he their drooping spirits raised.
Minerva from their eyes removed the cloud
Of darkness which before enveloped them,
And light sprang forth, both o'er the hollow ships
And o'er the dusty bloody battle-field.
Then they saw Hector raging in the fight,
He and his men, the front ranks and the rear ;
But lion-hearted Ajax would not stand

Where his brave friends, the other warriors, stood;
He moved about upon the vessels' decks,
Stalking from ship to ship and brandishing
A boarding pike twenty-two cubits long.
And as a horseman skilled in vaulting, drives
Four chosen steeds o'er a broad public road
To a great town, admiring throngs look on
Whilst he from horse to horse alternate leaps
Boldly and safely as they fly along:
So Ajax nimbly sprang from deck to deck,
His shouts terrific reaching to the sky,
Bidding the Greeks defend their ships and tents.
Nor did the valiant Hector either stay
Among his men; but, as the eagle darts
Into a flock of geese or cranes or swans,
Feeding upon some river's verdant bank,
So Hector at a blue-prowed vessel rushed,
Jove with a mighty force impelling him.
Fiercely the battle raged about the ships.
You would have thought they soon had weary grown,
So desperately hard both parties fought.
The Greeks indeed believed their doom was nigh;
The Trojans thought they now would burn the fleet,
The victory gain, and the invaders slay.
Then Hector seized the stern of a fine ship,
Which brought Protesilaus to fatal Troy,
But was not destined to transport him back.
Around this bark the battle fiercely raged,
Nor did they at a distance fight with spears and darts,
But hand to hand with axes, hatchets, swords,
And from their owners' hands many rich swords
Fell to the earth, which ran with purple gore.
But Hector, when he seized the vessel's stern,
Would not let go, but to his comrades cried:
Bring fire, my men! fight on, and stand your ground;
With Jove's kind aid the day has now arrived—
The glorious day—to seize this wicked fleet,
Which has such injuries on us entailed

Through our own ruler's tim'ròus policy,
Who would not suffer me to make assault
Upon the ships, but always kept me back;
But if such counsel was the will of Jove,
He now has changed his mind and urges us.
  Thus spake the chief, and with his comrades rushed;
E'en Ajax now could not sustain their darts,
But from the vessel's quarter deck stepped down
Upon a bench; there with his spear he watched,
Repelling every Trojan whom he saw
Attempting to draw near to fire the ships;
And shouting dreadfully he cheered the Greeks:
  My comrades, heroes, followers of Mars!
Be men! and all your faculties arouse.
Think ye we have assistants in the rear,
Or any rampart whither we may flee?
No tower we have with strong and lofty wall,
From which we may a reinforcement draw;
But on the borders of the sea we sit,
Far from our native land, with foes in front;
So, straining every nerve, we must fight on.
  He said; and charging furious with his spear,
Struck at a Trojan who approached with fire,
Slaying twelve warriors alongside the ship.

BOOK XVI.

DEATH OF PATROCLUS.

ARGUMENT.

Patroclus persuades Achilles to lend him his armor; clad in which, he leads the Myrmidons to battle.—He slays Sarpedon, the son of Jove, and is at last slain himself by Hector.

Thus round the ship the dreadful fight went on;
But to Achilles Patroclus drew near,
His face disturbed, streaming with scalding tears:
Just as a gloomy fountain from a rock
Pours its dark waters forth incessantly.
  Achilles was disturbed beholding him,
And of his dear companion thus inquired:
Why weepest thou, comrade, like a silly girl,
Crying and clinging to her mother's gown,
And wanting to be taken in her lap?
  Dost thou bring tidings to the Myrmidons,
From distant Phthia, or to me myself?
Hast thou heard news that others have not heard?
Thy sire and mine we know are both alive:
Indeed, if they were dead we well might weep;
Or is it for the Greeks that thou dost grieve,
Who for their faults are justly perishing?
Speak out, and tell the secret of thy woe.
  He said; and groaning, thus his friend replied:
Achilles, noblest thou of all the Greeks!
Be not indignant; oh, such dreadful woe
Afflicts the Greeks; all their best warriors,

Struck down and wounded, lie within their ships.
Bold Diomed is wounded, and Ulysses,
And Agamemnon, and Eurypylus,
Who with an arrow in his thigh is pierced.
Skillful physicians, with their healing drugs,
Have gathered round attending on these chiefs;
But thou, Achilles, art inexorable.
May no such anger ever fill my breast
As thou, oh cruel chief, art nourishing;
Who wilt thou ever after this defend,
If thou assistest not thy countrymen.
Hard-hearted man! Peleus was not thy sire,
Nor did the gentle Thetis bring thee forth,—
The stormy ocean bore thee and the rocks,
So savage and so merciless thy heart.
But if some oracle detains thee here,
Spoken by Jove, and by thy mother told,
Send me at least, me and the Myrmidons,
That to the Greeks some succor we may bring;
And give me, too, thy armor to put on,
That so the Trojans, taking me for thee,
May from the field fall back, and thus our friends,
O'ercome with toil, may have a little rest;
For we are fresh, and can with ease repulse
Our worn-out foes, and drive them to the town.
Thus begged the chief unwisely; for he now
Begged his own evil fate, which fast drew nigh.
Then answering with a groan, Achilles spake:
Alas, my noble friend, what hast thou said!
'Tis not an oracle from mighty Jove,
Told by my mother, that detains me here;
This bitter grief I feel, because a man,
A man of power, has done his equal wrong,
And has deprived me of my just reward;
This is the cause that I such sorrows feel.
The maid my countrymen apportioned me,
And whom I won with my good trusty spear,
When I a strong-fenced city had o'erthrown,

Her from my hands has Agamemnon snatched,
As if I were some worthless vagabond.
But let it pass; anger must end at last.
Surely I said I would not be appeased
Until the fight had reached the Grecian fleet;
Then in my famous armor clothe thyself,
And to the battle lead my Myrmidons,
Since throngs of Trojans gather round the ships,
And the retreating Greeks are driven in,
And occupy a small space on the shore.
Troy has poured forth her entire populace,
For they see not my helmet gleaming there;
Soon would they all have fled and been destroyed
Had Agamemnon served me as he should.
Bold Diomed's spear is nowhere to be seen,
Nor can your monarch's odious voice be heard;
Instead of that, Hector's loud voice I hear,
In tones triumphant cheering on his men.
Yet still, Patroclus, on them boldly rush,—
Let them not set our noble fleet on fire,
And from our fatherland cut off return:
Then follow my advice, that thou for me
Mayest honor gain from the applauding Greeks,
So that my beauteous maid they may restore,
And send me many splendid gifts besides.
But when our foes are driven from the ships,
Take heed; I charge thee quickly to return;
And should thou glory gain with Juno's aid,
Be not too anxious to keep up the fight
Apart from me; this would dishonor me;
Nor do thou in the fight exulting lead
Thy men triumphant to the walls of Troy,
Lest some malignant god may meet thee there,
For Troy is by Apollo much beloved;
But come thou back when thou hast saved the ships,
And let the others stay and fight it out.
Oh! would that Greeks and Trojans both were slain,
And that we two alone might capture Troy!
Thus in their tent the warriors discoursed.

Meanwhile bold Ajax, by his foes hard pressed,
Began to yield ; such was the will of Jove.
A dreadful clang his glittering helmet made,
Such showers of blows upon the hero fell ;
His heavy buckler too the chief fatigued,
Yet neither could the Trojans drive him off:
Panting for breath, sweat from his limbs ran down,—
Sad was his plight, and worse and worse it grew.
Tell me now, Muses of the Olympian mount,
How first the fire fell upon the ships ?
Hector came up and struck the glittering spear
Of noble Ajax, cutting it in two;
Vainly his broken spear he brandished then—
Its head cut off, fell ringing to the ground.
The hero shuddered, for he now perceived
That to his foes Jove willed the victory.
So he withdrew; and now the Trojans hurled
Their fire on the fleet, which quickly spread—
The vessel's stern was wrapped in flame and smoke.
Achilles then smote on his thigh, and thus
His friend and comrade, Patroclus, addressed :
Haste thee, oh, Patroclus, most noble knight!
I see the foe, at length, has fired the fleet;
Soon will the ships be burnt, and we, cut off,
Shall ne'er return to our dear fatherland.
Put on thy armor quick, and I, meanwhile,
Will go and put the forces in array.
He said; and Patroclus in shining brass
Arrayed himself; first on his thighs he placed
His handsome greaves; then on his breast he put
The beauteous corselet, glittering with stars;
The silver-hilted sword hung at his side,
And the vast ponderous shield; on his brave head
The helmet next he set, nodding with plumes;
Two javelins he took, for he could not
Manage Achilles' spear; none of the Greeks,
But the great chief himself, that lance could wield—
Of ash it was, cut on Mount Pelion,

And to his sire was by Chiron given ;
Fatal to many heroes had it been.
Then to Automedon he gave command
To yoke the steeds; a trusty servant he,
Next to Achilles, honored most by him.
So the good charioteer the horses yoked—
Xanthus and Balius—rapid as the winds;
Podargè bore them, sired by Zephyrus,
Whilst she upon the sea-side meadows grazed.
Outside of these he harnessed Pedasus,
Who by Achilles, when he Aëtion sacked,
Was led away, among the other spoils—
A mortal courser with immortals yoked.
Meanwhile Achilles armed the Myrmidons;
But they resembled most carnivorous wolves,
Which, in the mountains, having slain a stag,
The carcass tear to pieces and devour,
The savage monsters' jaws are red with blood ;
Then to some fountain, in a pack, they rush,
Lapping the water with their lolling tongues,
Whilst in the stream they vomit clots of blood,
And the fierce beasts are swelled with food and drink:
So round Patroclus rushed the Myrmidons;
Whilst, in their midst, warlike Achilles stood,
Encouraging the warriors and the steeds.
Fifty swift ships the hero brought to Troy,
And in each ship were fifty gallant men;
O'er them five trusty leaders he had set,
But he with iron will controlled them all.
Over one troop Menestheus had command,
The son of Spirchius, a heavenly stream.
Fair Polydora brought the warrior forth,
A woman by a deity embraced;
But Borus was reputed as her spouse,
Who splendid presents giving, married her.
The bold Eudorus led another troop;
Him Polymelè, graceful dancer, bore.
By Mercury this lady was beloved,

Who spied her 'mid the choir of dancing nymphs,
That followed chaste Diana, huntress maid.
Her the fond god led to an upper room,
And there embraced; she this Eudorus bore,
A valiant chief, and very swift on foot;
Then by Echecleüs she was espoused,
Who gave her splendid presents; but the child
Was by the lady's father, Phylas, loved,
Who brought him up as if he were his son.
Warlike Pisander, son of Menelaus,
Was o'er the third; a famous spearman he;
None except Patroclus with him compared.
The fourth division was by Phœnix led,
And o'er the fifth Alcimoden was chief.
Achilles thus the warriors arrayed,
And standing near the men addressed them thus:
Ye Myrmidons! forget not now your threats
Which to the Trojans ye so often made,
And blamed me also for my foolish wrath,
Keeping ye back, who longed so much to fight,
Nor yet would homeward suffer ye to go;
Oft ye reproached me in this bitter strain.
Now what ye longed for has arrived at last;
Go, then, with valiant hearts, and fight the foe.
So saying, he their warlike spirit stirred;
Hearing their king their ranks they firmly closed.
As when a mason, building a high house,
Piles stone on stone, with nicely fitting joints:
So closely they their brazen helmets linked,
And their stout shields; for shield was pressed on shield,
Helmet to helmet joined, and man to man;
Their nodding horse-hair plumes each other touched,
So thick together were the serried ranks;
In front stood Patroclus to lead them on,
He and his comrade, bold Automedon.
Achilles then proceeded to his tent
And opened a rich coffer, given him
By silver-footed Thetis when he sailed,

To hold her son's warm cloaks and tapestries;
In it there was besides a precious cup,
From which no mortal ever yet had drunk,
Nor were libations made except to Jove;
This he took out, with sulphur purified,
And rinsed it next in a pure crystal stream;
Then having washed his hands, filled it with wine,
And praying thus, libation made to Jove:
Oh, Jove! Dodonæan Jove! dwelling far off,
Ruling o'er cold Dodona's wintry heights,
Around thee dwell the Selli, austere priests,
With unwashed feet, and sleeping on the ground,
Thou once did'st hear me, and espoused my cause,
Sending calamities upon the Greeks;
So likewise now, grant this my second prayer,
For I myself will stay beside the ships,
But to the battle I dispatch my friend,
Him and the Myrmidons: grant him, oh mighty Jove!
Success and glory; strengthen and aid him,
So that great Hector may himself find out
That my companion e'en alone can fight,
Without my presence and companionship;
But when he has the Trojans driven back,
Let him, unharmed and safe, return to me
With all his armor, and his comrades too.
Thus prayed the chief, his prayer the Thunderer heard,
One part he granted, and one part denied:
He was allowed to drive the Trojans back,
But he himself should ne'er return alive.
Thus having poured the wine and prayed to Jove,
He the rich goblet to the chest returned;
And stood outside the tent, desiring much
With his own eyes the battle to behold.
Then noble Patroclus, he and his men,
With valiant hearts sprang forth against the foe;
Onward they poured, like wasps that have their cells
Close by the roadside, and which silly boys,
By meddling with them, love to irritate,

Causing a nuisance thus to travelers;
For should one happen to pass near their nests,
In swarms the furious insects all fly out,
Eager to fight and save their young from harm:
Thus from their ships the Myrmidons poured forth,
And dreadful was the clamor that arose;
But Patroclus thus cried, cheering his troops:
Friends of Achilles, valiant Myrmidons!
Quit ye like men, and onward towards the foe,
That we may not our noble chief disgrace,
The noblest warrior he that came to Troy;
And let us show great Agamemnon, too,
How much he erred in slighting such a man.
So saying, he inspired every heart;
With one accord upon the foe they fell,
And awful was the tumult that arose.
But when the Trojans Patroclus beheld,
He and his comrades, clad in glittering arms,
Their hearts were troubled and their ranks disturbed;
They thought Achilles' wrath was now appeased,
And each man looked around with anxious gaze
To see how he might fly and save himself.
Patroclus then first hurled his glittering spear
Right in the midst, where most the Trojans thronged
Around the bark of bold Protesilaus,
And struck Pyræchmes, who from Amydon led
Pæonia's cavalry—led from the banks
Of the wide-flowing river Axius.
Him the warrior smote on the right shoulder;
He, loudly groaning, fell upon his back.
His awe struck comrades fled, o'ercome with fear,
When they beheld their valiant leader slain.
The victor drove them, routed, from the fleet,
And hastily put out the blazing fire.
The ship was left half burnt whilst the foe fled,
And dreadful was the tumult that arose.
As when, upon a lofty mountain-top,
Jove with his lightning bursts through a thick cloud,

The sudden flash illuminates the sky,
The darksome ridge appears as in a blaze,
And all its rocks and hidden glens are seen:
So the Greeks brightened up, routing the foe;
But yet the contest fearfully went on;
The Trojans, though retreating, battled still;
Then chief slew chief, each fighting hand to hand.
First in his thigh, by Patroclus, was struck
Brave Areïlycus as he turned about.
The cruel spear went through, breaking the bone,
And to the earth the dying hero fell;
But Thoas was by Menelaus smote—
Smote in the breast—expiring he fell.
Phylides saw Amphïclus rushing on,
And nimbly pierced the warrior in his calf;
His tendons were all cut, and he was slain.
Then Nestor's son, Antilochus, stepped forth,
And struck Antymnius upon the flank.
He fell, and Maris, who was close at hand
To avenge his brother, rushed upon the Greek;
But he was by Thrasymedes observed,
Who struck him on the arm and cut it off—
Falling, his armor crashed, and he expired.
Thus to dark Pluto's realms two heroes went—
Bold comrades they of noble Sarpedon—
Skilled at the spear—Amisodarus' sons,
Who nourished the destructive Chimæra;
But Ajax, rushing on Cleobulus,
Took him alive and smote him in the neck.
The victor's sword was bathed in purple blood,
And to the earth the dying Trojan fell;
Then Lycon and Peneleus drew near,
For they had hurled their javelins in vain.
Therefore the warriors hand to hand engaged;
Lycon his foe upon the helmet struck
And broke his sword; but Peneleus smote
The other on the neck below the ear;
His severed head hung merely by the skin,

And the unhappy chief expiring fell.
Then Merion, hurrying up, Neamas struck
On the right arm, just as the Trojan chief
Into his car was going to ascend;
Down to the earth he fell and breathed his last.
Next Idomeneus, with his ruthless spear,
Smote Erymas in the mouth--through it went
Into the brain, cleaving the warrior's skull;
His teeth were all dashed out and his bright eyes
Were filled with gore, which, as he fell,
Gushed from his nostrils and his gaping mouth.
Thus one by one these leaders of the Greeks
Slew each his man, and, as destructive wolves
Rush upon timorous kids and gentle lambs,
Snatching the helpless creatures from the flocks,
Which by the shepherd's negligence are left
Upon the mountains, soon as they spy them
They tear in pieces the poor innocents:
So rushed the Greeks upon the men of Troy;
But these thought only how they might escape,
Their former courage quite forsaking them.
Then Ajax with bold Hector longed to fight;
But he, in battle skilled, with his broad shield
Preserved himself, watching the flying darts
And whizzing spears; he knew indeed which way
The victory inclined, still he remained,
And many of his comrades saved from death.
As when o'er heaven, after a clear sky,
Jove spreads swift whirlwinds and tempestuous clouds:
So was the clamor of the fugitives
And the dread rout; nor did they cross the trench
In seemly plight. Hector's swift-footed steeds
Bore him away, deserting now his men,
Whom much against their will the ditch detained.
And many horses, breaking from their poles,
Their masters' chariots left within the fosse.
But Patroclus pursued, cheering the Greeks,
Bent on the utter ruin of the foe,

Who, with loud cries, in all directions fled.
Whirlwinds of dust arose; and the fleet steeds,
With terror struck, rushed onward towards the town;
But Patroclus, where'er he saw the rout
Was greatest, thither drove his thundering car;
Beneath his axle warriors were crushed
And cars upset; so swift Achilles' steeds,
Immortal coursers, bore him o'er the trench.
He longed to strike at Hector, but that chief,
By his fleet horses carried, fled away.
And as when Jove an autumnal freshet sends,
Angry with mortals for some flagrant sin,
Some unjust sentence by their judges given,
Regardless of the vengeance of the gods;
Then all their swelling rivers are o'erflown,
And mighty torrents, cutting through the hills,
With awful roar, flow headlong to the sea;
The fields are flooded, and the toilsome works
Of the laborious husbandman destroyed:
So moaning and distressed, the Trojan steeds
Swept with affright across the battle-field.
  But Patroclus the foe now headed off,
And drove them back again towards the ships:
There, in the midst, between the town and fleet,
Vast throngs he slew, and glutted his revenge.
Then Pronöus, with his spear, he first attacked;
Struck in the breast, the Trojan warrior fell;
Next Thestor, Ænop's son, he rushed upon,—
He in his chariot was huddled up,
And, panic-struck, had dropped the horses' reins,—
Him with his spear the furious Greek attacked;
Through his right cheek the cruel weapon went,
Which in his hands the victor still retained,
And o'er the chariot's rim his victim dragged.
As when a fisherman upon a rock
Draws, with his line and rod, a monstrous fish
Out of the sea, so he the Trojan drew
Out of his car, and dashed him to the ground:

Down on his mouth he fell, and gaping died;
Then, with a stone, Eryalus he smote,
Cleaving his skull; Amphotus next he struck,—
Epaltes, Echius, and Erymas,
Pyres, Tlepolemus, and Icheus,
Ipheas, Polymelus, and Evippus,—
All these, in quick succession, slew the chief,
Heaping their corpses on the fertile earth.
But when the noble Sarpedon perceived
His comrades by bold Patroclus dispatched,
Thus, to the godlike Lycians, he cried:
Shame on ye, Lycians! whither do ye fly?
Cheer up! for I will go against this man,
And, by myself, discover who he is;
Truly much evil has he done to us,
Slaughtering so many of our bravest men.
He said; and from his car sprung to the ground;
Patroclus, when he saw him, did the same.
Then, as when on some high and beetling crag
Two sharp-clawed vultures, loudly screaming, fight
So, loudly shouting, they together rushed.
Jove saw, and felt compassion for them both,
And thus addressed his sister and his wife:
Ah, me! that Sarpedon, noblest of men,
Should by the hand of Patroclus be slain.
Misgivings in my mind begin to rise—
Whether I should withdraw him from the field,
And in rich Lycia safely set him down,
Or by this Greek allow him to be slain.
He said; and Juno to him thus replied:
Oh, mighty Jove! how wildly dost thou talk!
Is it thy wish to rescue from his fate
A mortal man long since decreed to die?
Do so! and all the other gods affront.
But this I say, and on it thou reflect:
If thou this Sarpedon send'st safely home,
Know that the other gods will likewise save
Each some dear son that in the war takes part,

For many of celestial race there are
Around this town of Priam battling,
And great heart-burnings will among them rise;
But if thy Sarpedon be dear to thee,
And thy heart pities his untimely fate,
Let him by Patroclus be now subdued;
But when his life and spirit are extinct,
Send Death and balmy Sleep to bear him off
To the wide, fruitful plains of Lycia:
There will his friends and brethren raise a tomb,
And in his honor funeral rites perform.
  She said; nor did the Thunderer disobey;
But rained some bloody dew-drops on the ground,
In honor of his noble, favorite son,
Whom Patroclus was now about to slay,
In fertile Troy, far from his native land.
  Meanwhile the warriors to the conflict rushed;
Then Patroclus bold Thrasymedus struck—
Comrade and friend of noble Sarpedon;
He smote him on his groin, and he expired.
Next Sarpedon attacked, but missed his aim,
Wounding his horse, Pedasus, with his spear,—
The poor beast moaning fell, and breathed his last;
The other frighted steeds asunder leaped,
The reins entangling, as the side horse lay
Dead in the dust; Automedon sprang out,
And, drawing his sharp sword, the harness cut.
The other horses now were quieted,
And the two chiefs the bloody fight renewed;
Then Sarpedon again took aim, but missed,
O'er Patroclus' left shoulder flew the spear;
Whereon the other hurled his javelin,
And in the midriff smote the Lycian,
Who fell as falls some oak or lofty pine
Which in the mountains wood-cutters hew down:
So fell the hero, stretched beneath his car,
Gnashing his teeth, grasping the bloody dust.
And as a lion slays a noble bull,

Bellowing with fury at his hapless doom,
So Sarpedon, indignant at his fate,
Addressed his dear companion thus, by name:
Glaucus, dear friend! hero 'mid heroes thou!
A glorious chance thou hast to show thyself:
First bid the Lycian chiefs to rally quick,
And come and fight for fallen Sarpedon;
And with thy utmost valor fight thou too,
For it will ever be a shame to thee
Should the Greeks come, and strip me of my arms;
Then stir thyself, and rally all my men.
Thus spake the chief, but death now sealed his lips,
And closed his eyes, and took away his breath.
  But Patroclus his heel placed on the breast
Of the brave warrior, and his spear drew out;
The midriff too came out on the spear's point,
And with it the expiring hero's life.
The Myrmidons held back his panting steeds,
Eager to fly, and from the car break loose;
But bitter grief arose in Glaucus' heart,
Hearing his comrade's voice; aid he could not,
Such pain severe he felt in his own arm
From Teucer's arrow from the rampart shot;
His helpless limb he with his hand compressed,
And to the archer god, Apollo, prayed:
  Hear me, oh mighty king! who somewhere art,
Either in Lycia or fruitful Troy,
For thou canst everywhere a mortal hear
Who grief experiences, as I do now.
A grievous wound I have, and bitter pain;
Nor can I staunch the blood, nor use my arm,
Nor hold my spear, nor go against the foe.
A noble hero too has met his doom,—
Illustrious Sarpedon, the son of Jove,
Who to his offspring no assistance gave.
Heal for me, king, this serious painful wound,
And give me strength to head the Lycian band,
So that this warrior's corpse I may defend.

He said; nor did the god his prayer refuse,
But soothed at once his pain, and healed the wound,
Staunched the dark blood, and strength and vigor gave;
Glaucus perceived the cure, and much rejoiced
That the great deity his prayer had heard.
First on the Lycian warriors he called
To come and fight round fallen Sarpedon;
Then to the Trojans hastening, he advanced
To bold Polydamas and Agenor;
After Æneas, too, the chieftan went,
And noble Hector, whom he thus addressed:
Oh, Hector! thou thy allies dost neglect,
Who, for thy sake, have such a distance come,
Far from their friends, their kindred, and their homes.
Thou wilt not aid them. Sarpedon lies low—
Chief of the bucklered men of Lycia—
Whose wide domain he with such justice ruled;
Him with a spear has Patroclus just slain,
Aided by Mars; but draw ye near, my friends,
Lest the fierce Myrmidons maltreat his corpse,
Enraged that we so many Greeks have killed.
He said; and deeply all the Trojans grieved,
For he a tower of strength had been to them,
Although a foreigner; strong was his force,
And he most valiant was among them all.
They, therefore, on the Greeks an onset made,
Headed by Hector, who was much enraged
At the untimely fate of Sarpedon.
But Patroclus the Grecian chiefs aroused,
And the two valiant Ajaxes addressed:
Ye valiant Ajaxes! 'tis now your time
To repel the foe, and show what men ye are.
He who first scaled our wall, brave Sarpedon,
Lies low; oh, that we might his corpse despoil,
And slay his comrades now defending him!
He said; and eagerly the chiefs rushed on.
Both parties now closed up their serried ranks.
Trojans and Lycians, Myrmidons and Greeks,

Round the dead body gathered with loud cries,
And rattling arms ; but Jove a darkness spread
Over the field, making an awful fight.
  The Trojans first the sharp-eyed Greeks drove back,
Slaying a Myrmidon of great renown,—
Noble Epigeus, Agacleus' son,
Who over Budium formerly held sway;
But he a kinsman of some note had slain,
And fled to Peleus, and his goddess wife;
They sent him with Achilles to the war.
Him as he seized the corpse bold Hector struck,
Struck with a heavy stone, and split his skull.
On the dead body fell the dying chief;
For his dear friend Patroclus deeply grieved.
Right through the foremost warriors he rushed,
Like a swift hawk, that puts to speedy flight
Jackdaws and starlings; so Patroclus, bold knight,
Didst thou upon the Trojan warriors rush,
Greatly excited for thy comrade slain.
Then Sthenelus on the neck he struck,
And Hector and his followers fell back,
Far as a javelin's cast they made retreat;
But Glaucus, leader of the Lycians,
First rallied, slaying wealthy Bathycles,
Who dwelt in Hellas, Chalcas' dear son was he,
And highly honored by the Myrmidons;
Him Glaucus turning, slew as he pursued,
Piercing him in the breast with his sharp spear;
With a loud crash the dying warrior fell.
The Greeks grieved deeply for their fallen chief,
The others much rejoiced and made advance,
And with fresh spirit still the fight went on;
Then Merion a Trojan hero slew,
Laogonus, Onetus' valiant son;
A priest of Jove he was, and like a god
Was held in honor by the men of Troy.
The weapon struck him underneath his ear,
And straight to Pluto's realms his spirit fled;

But now Æneas aimed at Merion,
Advancing, and protected by his shield,
The warrior stooped, and so preserved his life;
The erring weapon stuck into the ground,
And the vexed Trojan thus cried out and said:
Quickly, oh, Merion! though a dancer thou,
My weapon would have slain thee had it struck.
But the brave chieftain thus in turn replied:
Æneas, though a valiant warrior thou,
'Tis not for thee to conquer every one;
Thou too art mortal, and if I should strike,
I would not strike in vain, but send thy soul
With quick dispatch to Pluto's dark domain.
He said; but Patroclus him thus rebuked:
Oh, Merion! wherefore dost thou pattle thus?
The Trojans, my good friend, will not be chased
From yonder corpse by using bitter words;
Ere they do that their life-blood they will spill.
Words are of use in counsel, not in war,
And 'tis our part to fight and not to talk.
So saying, he led on, and close behind
Followed the godlike hero Merion.
And as the crash of wood-cutters is heard
'Mid mountain-dells, and far the echoes spread:
So o'er the plain was heard the clashing sound
Of swords, and two-edged spears, and brazen shields;
Nor could a man, however sharp his sight,
Have recognized the fallen Sarpedon,
So much was he involved, from head to foot,
In showers of darts, in spears, in blood and dust.
Thick round the corpse they crowded. As when flies,
In spring-time, hum around the pails of milk:
So round the body did the warriors throng.
Meanwhile Jove's eyes ne'er from the conflict turned;
He still looked on with mischief in his mind,
Thinking about the death of Patroclus,—
Uncertain whether now, upon the corpse,
The chief by noble Hector should be slain,

And of his splendid armor be despoiled,
Or whether he his doom should still defer,
And the laborious contest still prolong.
Thus pondering, he thought it best to let
The conquering chief still drive the Trojans back,
And yet a multitude of lives destroy;
Wherefore on Hector he a panic sent.
Into his car the affrighted Trojan sprang,
Advising all his comrades, too, to fly,
For he perceived that Jove the scale had turned.
Then the brave Lycians even made retreat,
Seeing their king stretched amid heaps of dead.
His splendid armor now the Greeks stripped off,
And Patroclus, triumphant, sent it back
To the swift ships; then mighty Jove addressed
The archer god Apollo, and thus spake:
Up, dear Apollo, go, cleanse Sarpedon,
Lying 'mid heaps of weapons and dark blood,
Bear him away and lave him in the stream,
And with ambrosia then anointing him,
Clothe him in heavenly robes, give him then
In charge to the twin brothers Sleep and Death,
Those swift conductors, who will carry him
To the broad fertile plains of Lycia;
There will his friends and brethren raise a tomb,
And in his honor funeral rites perform.
He said; nor did Apollo disobey,
But flew from Ida, to the battle-field,
And bearing noble Sarpedon away,
Far from the reach of weapons, carried him
To the clear river stream and washed him there,
Next with ambrosial oil anointing him,
He clothed in heavenly robes, and gave him then
In charge to the twin brothers Sleep and Death,
Those swift conductors, who soon set him down
In the broad fertile land of Lycia.
Meanwhile with fury Patroclus pursued.
Cheering his horses and Automedon.

Close at the Trojans the warrior kept
And came to grief. Infatuated man!
For had he but obeyed Achilles' words
His fatal doom he surely had escaped;
But the Almighty wiser is than men—
E'en the courageous he can put to flight,
And from him grasp the expected victory,
First giving strength, and weakness afterwards.
 Whom first, whom last did Patroclus now slay,
As the gods called him to his hapless doom?
Adrestus first, the impetuous warrior slew,
Antenor, Epistor and Perinnè;
Next Melanippus and Elasus too;
Then Mulion, and Pylartes last of all.
These he dispatched; the others took to flight.
Then would the Greeks have captured lofty Troy,
Led madly on by furious Patroclus,
Had not Apollo stood upon a tower
Devising ills to him, but help to Troy.
Thrice did the chief a frowning buttress mount;
Thrice from the wall Apollo pushed him back,
Striking his shield with his immortal hands;
But when a fourth time like a god he rushed,
The threatening deity addressed him thus:
 Hold, noble Patroclus! stand back, retire,
'Tis not decreed that Troy shall fall by thee,
Nor by Achilles e'en, thy better far.
He said, and, fearing much Apollo's wrath,
The affrighted chief far from the wall retired.
 Hector meanwhile stood with his panting steeds
Close to the Scæan gate, in doubt if he
Should a fresh onset on the crowd attempt,
Or draw his men within the sheltering wall.
Whilst thus he thought Apollo near him drew—
The form of Asius the god assumed,
Hector's maternal uncle, young and brave,
And son of Dymas, who in Phrygia dwelt

Upon the banks of the Sangarius.
Such form assuming, thus Apollo spake:
  Why, Hector, from the fight hast thou withdrawn?
Such conduct ill becomes a man like thee.
Oh that I only thy superior wert
As I inferior am--then from the war
In welcome, if thou chose, thou might'st abstain;
But up and drive at noble Patroclus,
Thou with Apollo's aid may'st conquer him
And reap immortal glory by the deed.
Thus having said, the deity went off,
Mingling again among the combatants.
  Then Hector ordered Cebrion to lash
His horses on into the thickest fight.
Apollo too entered the bloody throng;
He sent an evil tumult on the Greeks,
But glory gave to Hector and to Troy.
Hector the other Greeks passed by, but drove
His furious steeds towards noble Patroclus,
Who from his chariot leaped upon the ground;
In his left hand his glittering spear he held,
And with the other seized a rugged stone.
With all his might he hurled it, nor in vain,
But Hector's driver struck, bold Cebrion,
A bastard son of royal Priam he--
Him, as he held the reins, the missile struck
Full in the forehead, crushing all the bone
And dashing out his eyes, which in the dust
Fell at his feet; he, like a diver, plunged
From his high chariot, yielding up the ghost.
  Then thou, oh, Patroclus, reviling, spake:
Oh, what a nimble man! how well he dives!
Were he but in a ship upon the sea
Groping for oysters, many he might catch,
So well he dives e'en on the dusty plain.
Surely these Trojans first-rate divers are.
So saying, upon Cebrion he rushed
Like a fierce lion, ravaging the folds,

Which now at length is wounded in the breast,
Whose very courage proves his death at last:
So did this ardent chief on Cebrion spring,
Whilst Hector also leaped upon the ground.
They o'er the corpse like two bold lions fought,
Which famished are, and which on mountain-tops
Fight for the carcass of a famished stag:
So over Cebrion, in mortal strife,
These mighty warriors battled lustily;
Hector the body seizing by the head,
Held on; whilst Patroclus the feet retained;
And round them furiously the others fought.
And as the east and south wind meeting strive,
In a deep mountain-valley, in a wood
Of rugged cornel, beech, and bending ash,
Whose long extended limbs each other strike,
Breaking each other's boughs with thundering crash:
Thus Greeks and Trojans on each other rushed,
Nor for a moment feared or thought of flight.
Many sharp spears round Cebrion were fixed,
And swift-winged arrows bounding from the string,
And ponderous stones rang against brazen shields,
Whilst the dead chief, forgetful now of war,
Lay on the ground, hid amid clouds of dust.
As the sun climbed up towards the mid-day sky,
The fight went on, and many people fell;
But when the noon was past the Greeks prevailed,—
Cebrion they drew out of the bloody fray,
And from his corpse his brazen armor stripped.
   But Patroclus upon his foes still rushed,
Intent on utterly destroying them;
Thrice like fierce Mars he charged with horrid cries,
And thrice nine warriors the hero slew;
But when a fourth time he an onset made,
Then Patroclus, 'twas plain, thy end drew nigh,
For terrible Apollo met thee there.
He did not see him coming through the throng,
For in a cloudy mist the god was hid;

And drawing near, with his immortal hand
Smote the impetuous hero on the back ;
Straightway his eyes with giddiness were seized,
And from his head the rattling helmet fell—
Fell to the ground beneath the horses' feet ;
The splendid plumes were soiled with dust and blood ;
Ne'er had that helmet been so soiled before,
For to a mighty warrior it belonged,
Protecting great Achilles' godlike head ;
But now to Hector 'twas about to go,
For Patroclus' destruction fast approached ;
His shattered spear dropped from his nerveless hands,
His big broad shield, which to his ankles reached,
Fell to the earth ; his corselet came unbound,
A stupor seized his brain, his limbs relaxed,
And the illustrious chief astounded stood.
But now a Trojan chief, Euphorbus named,
Superior to any of his age
In hurling spears, in speed, in horsemanship,
Pierced him between the shoulders with his lance ;
Already twenty warriors had he hurled
From their swift steeds, in this his first campaign ;
He it was, Patroclus, that struck thee now,
Nor striking even did he vanquish thee ;
But to the ranks immediately withdrew,
Plucking his bloody weapon from the wound,
Nor dared to meet the hero though unarmed.
But Patroclus, subdued by the god's blow,
And by the brazen spear, fell back somewhat,
Retreating towards his comrades ; Hector saw,
And drawing near him pierced him in the groin ;
Down fell the chief, the Greeks lamenting much.
As when a lion and wild boar contend
Upon a mountain-top, for a small rill,
At which they both desire to take a drink ;
But the wild boar exerting all his strength,
By the fierce lion is subdued at last :
So Hector, Priam's son, with his sharp spear,

Slew the great chief who had so many slain,
And o'er him thus exultingly exclaimed :
  Oh, Patroclus ! thou doubtless didst expect
Our city to destroy, and lead away
Our wives and children to thy fatherland ;
Such was thy hope, thou miserable fool !
But Hector's chariot meets thee in the field,—
Hector conspicuous in warlike deeds,
And ever prompt his people to defend ;
Now hungry vultures shall thy corpse devour.
Unhappy man ! Achilles helped thee not,
Brave as he is, but still remained behind,
And charged thee, doubtless, at thy setting out
To accomplish much : oh, Patroclus, bold knight !
Show not thy face nor to the fleet return
Till thou courageous Hector has destroyed ;
Thus, without doubt, thy friend Achilles spake.
  He said ; and faintly breathing, Patroclus
Then to the boasting warrior thus replied :
  Oh, Hector ! greatly vaunt, for it was Jove—
Jove and the archer god who mastered me ;
They struck me and despoiled me of my arms :
Twenty such men as thou I could have slain ;
Apollo and inevitable fate
Have caused my death ; its mortal author was
Euphorbus, with his well-directed spear ;
Thou the third party and the last art here,
To insult a dying chief, and strip his corpse.
One other word I also have to say,
Ponder it well : thy life will not last long,
Soon in the dust thou prostrate, too, wilt lie,
By the illustrious Achilles slain.
  He said ; and death his lips forever closed ;
His soul, lamenting its untimely fate,
Fled from his manly form and youthful bloom.
  Then Hector the dead hero thus addressed :
Why dost thou, Patroclus, foretell my death ?

Who knows but great Achilles may himself
Die before me, and by my spear be slain?
He said; and drew his weapon from the wound,
Pressing his heel upon the warrior's breast,
Then dashed him prostrate on the dusty ground;
Next at Automedon, Achilles' friend,
Who drove his car, immediately he rushed;
But his swift-footed and immortal steeds,
Gift of the gods, in safety bore him off.

BOOK XVII.

THE FIGHT ROUND THE BODY OF PATROCLUS.

ARGUMENT

Menelaus, defending the body of Patroclus, kills Euphorbus. — Hector puts on the armor of Patroclus and renews the fight.—The Greeks giving way, Ajax rallies them.—The horses of Achilles deplore the death of Patroclus.—The Greeks at length bear off the body.

But Menelaus knew that Patroclus
Had by the Trojans in the fight been slain.
In glittering brass he to the front repaired,
And round the corpse like a young heifer moved,
Which looks with wonder on her first-born calf,
So around Patroclus the warrior stalked,
With spear in hand and buckler on his arm,
Ready to slay whoever might oppose.
But young Euphorbus followed up his prey,
And, drawing near, the Grecian chief addressed :
Stand back, oh, Menelaus ! give up the corpse,
And let me take the bloody spoils I earned.
'Twas I, of all the Trojans, who first struck
With my good spear the valiant Patroclus :
Let me my rightful glory now receive,
Lest I slay thee as I thy friend have slain.
To him the indignant warrior thus replied :
Oh, Jove, what folly 'tis to boast too much !
Neither the savage lion, nor the pard,
Nor the wild boars, those formidable beasts,

Are so exultant as are Panthus' sons.
One I have slain, the young Hyperenor;
He came against me with reproachful words,
Saying I was the meanest of the Greeks.
He saw his wife and family no more.
And such thy doom will be, if thou oppose:
Then be advised in time; approach me not.
Wise men foresee, but fools find out too late.
  Thus spake the chief; but he advised in vain,
For thus the Trojan haughtily replied:
Then for my brother slain thou shalt atone,
Proud Greek, who widowed his young blooming bride,
And to his aged parent caused such woe.
Some comfort to the mourners would it be
Should I thy head and bloody spoils display.
Come on, we'll see whose valor stands the test,
For either one must fall or one must fly.
  He said, and struck the warrior on his shield;
But his spear's point was bent against the brass.
Then Menelaus, having prayed to Jove,
Attacked him with his lance and pierced his throat,
Passing the cruel weapon through and through.
He fell, and loud his brazen armor rang.
His locks, as handsome as the Graces wear,
Were stained with blood, and his luxuriant curls,
With bands of gold and silver intertwined.
  As when a man rears up an olive plant
In an inclosure, nigh some gushing spring,
Soft gentle breezes fan the beauteous tree,
And with white flowers its waving branches bloom,
But by a sudden blast 'tis overturned
And is uprooted, withering on the ground:
So fell Euphorbus, Panthus' youthful son,
By Menelaus smitten and despoiled.
As when a lion, trusting in his strength,
Pounces upon an ox, the best he finds
In the whole herd; its neck he quickly breaks,
Laps up its entrails and its purple blood,

Whilst round him at a distance dogs and men
Shout loudly, though they dread to venture near:
Thus no one dared against the Greeks to go.
  Then had the chief in triumph carried off
Euphorbus' arms, had not Apollo seen
And envied him the exploit; he aroused
Courageous Hector, putting on the form
Of Mentes, leader of the Cicones,
And, drawing near him, thus the chief addressed:
  Hector, thou runnest in a vain pursuit,
Chasing what thou wilt never overtake—
Achilles' steeds; hard 'tis to manage them
And hard to drive, except for he himself,
Whom Thetis, an immortal mother, bore.
Meanwhile by Patroclus stands Menelaus,
And has just slain Euphorbus, Panthus' son,
Bravest of all the warriors of Troy.
  He said, and left him; much was Hector grieved,
And, looking round upon the embattled ranks,
Saw the bold Greek the armor bearing off
And his dead comrade stretched upon the ground.
Then to the front he with shrill shouts advanced,
Like a terrific and devouring flame;
But Menelaus saw him drawing near,
And with a sigh thus with himself communed:
  Ah, me! if I should Patroclus desert
And his invaluable arms resign,
I fear the Greeks would look on me with scorn;
But if I fight with Hector, I'm undone:
He with his friends attack me all alone.
But why on such things should I meditate?
Destruction is the lot of him who fights
Against a man whom heaven decrees shall win,
And I no censure justly can receive
Should I from Hector prudently withdraw.
But could I only valiant Ajax find,
With him I would return and battle e'en
Against a god; so that we might secure

Yon bloody corpse, for great Achilles' sake.
Of evils this would surely be the least.
  Thus while he thought, his Trojan foes advanced,
Headed by Hector; then he drew back
And left unwillingly his comrade's corpse.
Just as a shaggy-bearded lion quits
A sheep-cote, driven off by dogs and men
With spears and clamor, for his courage sinks
And from the fold he's forced to make retreat:
So he dead Patroclus was forced to leave.
And standing once again amid his friends,
He sought for Ajax, son of Telamon.
Quickly he saw him fighting on his left,
And cheering up his men, who had been struck
With a dread panic by the archer god.
Hastening he ran, and thus addressed the chief:
  Come on, my friend, hasten to Patroclus,
So that we may at least his body bear
To great Achilles, his beloved friend:
His splendid arms plumed Hector has secured.
  He said; and stirred the warlike hero's heart,
And to the front with Menelaus he went.
Hector meanwhile the warrior had despoiled
Of his rich armor, and the body dragged
That from its shoulders he the head might cut
And throw the carcass to the Trojan dogs,
When Ajax, with his towering shield, came up.
Then Hector, stepping back, sprang to his car
And to his men the splendid armor gave,
To bear it (glorious prize) to sacred Troy.
  But Ajax, covering with his shield the corpse,
Stood like a lion that defends its young,
On which the hunters rush, in a thick wood:
Dreadful it looks, and draws its eyebrows down,
Hiding its eyes: so the Greek warrior strode
Round Patroclus extended on the ground.
Close by him valiant Menelaus stood,

Whilst heavy grief upon his bosom weighed.
But Glaucus, leader of the Lycian bands,
Sternly on Hector gazed, and thus reproved:
Truly thou, Hector, hast a warlike look,
And yet art wanting when a fight takes place!
Great fame thou hast, and yet a fugitive!
Contrive as best thou may to save thy town,
For we, the Lycians, will not assist,
Since we no thanks receive for all our toil.
How hast thou shamefully preserved a man
Of no repute, and suffered Sarpedon,
Thy guest and comrade, to become a prey
To the proud Greeks! He to thy city was
A bulwark and a champion indeed;
And yet thou didst not from him drive the dogs.
Go home, ye Lycians! such is my advice;
And utter ruin soon on Troy will fall,
For had the Trojans strength and spirit such
As men should have who for their country fight,
Soon into Troy would Patroclus be dragged
And we might ransom from the humbled Greeks
The splendid armor of bold Sarpedon
And gain his body, now a prey to dogs,
For the companion of a man is slain
Who most illustrious is among the Greeks;
But thou durst not the valiant Ajax face,
Who it appears is braver far than thou
He said; and sternly Hector thus replied:
How durst thou, Glaucus, to insult me thus?
I thought o'er all who in rich Lycia dwelt
Thou for good judgment stood pre-eminent;
But now I plainly see thy lack of sense,
Saying that I of Ajax am afraid.
I fear not battled hosts nor fiery steeds,
But Jove's dread counsel ever is supreme:
One time the valiant man he puts to flight,
And at another gives him victory.
But come, my friend, and see me how I fight,—

Truly I am a coward, as thou sayest,
If some of these proud Greeks I fail to rout.
So saying, to his comrades he exclaimed:
Trojans and Lycians! quit ye now like men,
Whilst I Achilles' beauteous arms put on,
Which from illustrious Patroclus I stripped
After I slew him with my brazen spear.
Thus having said, plumed Hector went his way,
And, running fast, his comrades overtook;
They to the town in haste were carrying
Achilles' splendid arms; he stood apart
And clad himself in the immortal suit
Which on Achilles' sire the gods bestowed.
Peleus the armor wore e'en to old age,
But so 'twas not decreed the son should do.
As Jove beheld the Trojan thus arrayed
With great Achilles' arms, he shook his head:
Alas, poor wretch! thou think'st not of thy death,
Which fast draws near, but the immortal arms
Thou hast put on of an illustrious chief,
Whom all men fear; thou too his friend hast slain,
The noble Patroclus, gentle and brave,
And stripped his armor off indecently.
But this day thou at least shalt glory gain,
For never shalt thy wife Andromache
Receive thee with thy spoils in lofty Troy.
So spake great Jove, bending his sacred head.
But the rich armor fitted Hector well,
And Mars' undaunted spirit entered him.
His limbs with strength and vigor were infused;
With lusty cheers his noble friends he sought;
All glittering like Achilles' self he looked;
Inspiring the allied chiefs, he spake,—
To Glaucus, Medon, and Thessilocus,
To Asteropeus, Chromius, and Disenor,
To Hippotheus, Phoreys, and Eunomus,
Eunomus skilled in augury,—
Hear me, ye countless allies dwelling round!

I did not bring ye here wanting a crowd,
But that ye might with a good will defend
Our wives and children from the warlike Greeks;
For this my people furnish you supplies
And presents make; then let us now decide
And be prepared to conquer or to die,
For one or other is the chance of war,
And he who Patroclus shall drag away,
In spite of Ajax, half his spoils shall have,
And share the glory that belongs to me.
He said; and they with lifted spears advanced,
In serried ranks, direct upon the Greeks;
They thought from Ajax to draw off the corpse.
Fools! they were slain as fast as they came up.
Then Ajax called to Menelaus and spake:
Oh, my good friend! I tremble for ourselves;
All care for Patroclus we must resign,
And his poor corpse must fall a prey to dogs.
Hector, that cloud of war, is rushing on,
And utter ruin must o'erwhelm us all.
But come, cry out and call the bravest Greeks,
If haply they may be disposed to hear.
He said; and Menelaus cried aloud:
Oh, comrades, chieftains, leaders of the Greeks,
Who with the king and Menelaus drink
The public wine and exercise command,
But fame and honor come from Jove alone!
So great the strife, I cannot reach ye all,
But, oh, let some advance, and feel ashamed
That Patroclus should be devoured by dogs.
He said; and soon Oïlean Ajax heard,
And first came up advancing through the crowd;
With him came Idomeneus and his friend,
Bold Merion, courageous e'en as Mars.
But who can all the other names recount
That came in throngs and rallied round the corpse?
The Trojans too rushed on, by Hector led.
As when an ocean wave rolls at the mouth

Of some great river, roaring furiously,
And the white surf breaks on the sandy shore,
With such a clamor did the Trojans rush.
But around Patroclus the Greeks stood firm,
Protected by their shields; o'er them great Jove
A hazy vapor settled, for he loved
Patroclus during life, and wished him well,
Nor could he bear to see his corpse become
A prey to vultures and devouring dogs;
So he aroused his comrades to defend.
But first the Trojans drove away the Greeks,
Who the dead body left and made retreat;
Yet none were slain, but the foe seized the corpse,
But only for a moment could retain,
For Ajax, who in beauty and in deeds
Next to Achilles was, rallied his men,
And like a savage boar, which puts to flight
Among the mountains blooming youths and dogs,
So through the Trojan ranks the warrior broke,
Scattering the phalanxes who fondly hoped
That they dead Patroclus would take to Troy.
Meanwhile Hippothous was dragging him
With a stout strap around his ankle bound,
Much to the joy of Hector and his friends;
But soon he came to grief, for Ajax now
Rushed through the crowd and smote him on the head;
His helmet by the blow was cleft in twain,
And from the wound the bloody brains gushed out.
Then he let fall the foot of Patroclus,
And o'er the warrior's body dying fell,
A corpse himself, far from his native land.
Nor did he live his parents to requite
For their kind nurture; slain by the ruthless spear
Of noble Ajax. Hector now took aim
At Ajax, but his weapon hurled in vain;
The hero stepped aside and the lance struck
Schedius, a valiant leader, who ruled o'er
The Phocians, a numerous race of men.

He in the middle of the breast was pierced,
The weapon at his shoulder coming out.
He fell; and falling, loud his armor rang.
Then warlike Phorcys was by Ajax slain;
Him while defending Hippothous he slew;
His cruel spear straight through his entrails went,
Breaking his corselet; down the hero fell,
Grasping the bloody dust with outstretched hands.
Then Hector and his men began to yield;
But the Greeks, shouting, drew the bodies off
Of valiant Phorcys and Hippothous,
And their rich armor from the bodies stripped.
Then had the Trojans into Troy been driven,
Against the wishes of almighty Jove,
Had not the archer god Æneas roused,
Taking the form of aged Periphus.
Likening himself to him, he thus began:
How couldst thou, oh, Æneas, Troy defend
If Heaven had sided with thy enemies,
Who on their strength and valor only lean?
Yet Jove decrees the victory to us,
And still ye tremble, and refuse to fight.
He said; .the warrior recognized the god,
And, loudly shouting, Hector thus addressed:
Oh, Hector, and ye other allied chiefs!
A great disgrace on us would surely fall
If we should be compelled to make retreat.
Just now a god stood by me, and declared
That Jove is with us; let us onward then,
Nor let the foe dead Patroclus remove.
He said; and springing forth, rushed to the van.
The Trojans rallied now and stood their ground.
Then bold Æneas wounded with his spear
Leocritus, Lycomedis' good friend,
Who pitied much the warrior as he fell,
And drawing near, bold Apisaon struck—
Struck in the liver and deprived of life.
From fertile Pæonia he had come,

And next to Asteropeus foremost ranked.
His comrade's death this chief took much to heart,
And forward rushed to mingle in the fight;
Yet could he not to Patroclus draw nigh,
Whose corpse on every side was fenced with shields
And glittering spears; Ajax was in the midst,
Cheering his men, and battling furiously.
The earth was red with blood; in heaps they fell,
Trojans and Greeks upon each other piled;
Yet fewer perished, as they fought with skill,
And every warrior was on his guard.
  Thus blazed the fight like a devouring fire;
Nor would you say that sun or moon were safe:
They too like that fierce throng were wrapped in haze.
But all the others in full daylight fought,
Beneath the splendor of the dazzling sun,
Without a cloud or vapor over them,—
They battled at their ease, and chose their ground;
Whilst those around the fallen chief were plagued
With preternatural darkness as they fought.
  But two brave heroes—Thrasymedes one,
Antilochus the other—had not heard
That Patroclus was dead, but thought he was
Still living, fighting 'mid the foremost ranks.
These warriors had by Nestor been advised
To fight apart, and were some distance off,
Whilst to the others all day long there was
Terrific contest. Sweat in torrents rolled;
With eyes and hands incessantly employed,
They tugged and strained, with legs and knees and feet,
Around the body of Achilles' friend.
And as men work the hide of a huge ox
Moistened with grease, each standing at his post
Seizes the skin, and pulls with all his might
Till to its proper size 'tis stretched at last:
So they on both sides dragged the corpse about—
The Greeks endeavoring to draw it off
And carry it in safety to their fleet;

The Trojans, to transport it to the town.
Awful the combat was. Had Mars been there,
Mars or Minerva, neither had found fault,
Such brilliant feats of valor were displayed.
So terrible a struggle Jove decreed
Should for the corpse of Patroclus take place.
Meanwhile Achilles knew not of his death,
For the dread fight was distant from the fleet,
Even beneath the towering walls of Troy;
He dreamed not therefore of his hapless fate,
But thought that he perhaps would reach the gates
And then return; for he knew well enough
That without him the town would ne'er be sacked.
This from his mother he had often heard,
For so by mighty Jove it was decreed;
Yet she had not informed him of the news
That his dear comrade was already dead.
Meanwhile around the corpse the fight went on:
Sharp spears were crossed, and many heroes fell;
And thus some Greek would to his comrade say:
Friends, we must never think of a retreat!
Rather be swallowed by the yawning earth
Than let the Trojans bear the body off.
Thus spake the Greeks, and thus would Trojans speak:
Comrades, though all of us should perish here,
Let us not yield, but still maintain our ground!
Thus cheering one another, they fought on;
The clash of arms reached even to the sky.
Achilles' horses wept when they perceived
Their charioteer had fallen in the dust
Beneath illustrious Hector's fatal spear.
Automedon tried hard to urge them on
With his sharp lash, with threats, with soothing words;
But they would neither to the fleet retire
Nor onward move and mingle in the fight,
But like a monumental column stood
Stock still; detaining motionless the car,
Their drooping heads hung to the very ground;

Their splendid flowing manes were all defiled,
And from their eyes warm tears in torrents flowed,
So much at Patroclus' sad fate they grieved.
Almighty Jove the spectacle beheld,
And felt compassion for the sorrowing beasts.
Shaking his head, thus to himself he spake:
Ah, luckless pair! Why did we ever give
To royal Peleus horses such as ye?
For ye immortal are, and free from age.
Was it that ye might share in mortals' griefs,
Associating with unhappy men?
For of all creatures moving on the earth,
Man the most miserable and wretched is.
Yet Hector, Priam's son, shall never be
Borne in his car by horses such as ye.
Enough it is that he the armor has,
And as a joyful victor vainly boasts;
But in your limbs fresh vigor I will throw,
That ye Automedon may safely bear
Back to the camp; for to the Trojans I
Must victory give e'en 'till they reach the fleet,
Until the sun shall set and night draw on.
So saying, in the steeds fresh strength he threw.
Shaking the dust from off their flowing manes,
They swiftly bore the chariot off the field;
On rushed Automedon, though deeply grieved
For his lost friend; on in the car he rushed
Like a fierce vulture 'mid a flock of geese,
For from the Trojans easily he fled,
Or easily pursued them through the throng,
Yet he unable was to stay his foes.
Alone he rode, and 'twas impossible
To hurl a spear and drive the fiery steeds.
At length a comrade, bold Alcimedon,
Beheld him, and drew near and thus addressed:
What god, Automedon, has thee bereft
Of thy good sense! so foolishly to act
Fighting alone amid the foremost ranks?

For thy good friend is slain, and Hector vaunts,
With great Achilles' armor on his back.
He said; and thus Automedon replied:
Who of the Greeks, Alcimedon's, like thee
To drive immortal steeds and hold them in,
Unless wise Patroclus were such a man
Whilst he still lived? but he, alas! is dead.
Take then the lash and seize the handsome reins,
Whilst I, descending from the car, will fight.
So saying, from the chariot he leaped;
The other springing in, assumed his place.
Hector perceived; and to Æneas spake:
Æneas, I Achilles' steeds behold
In feeble hands; if thou wilt only aid,
I think we easily may capture them.
He said; nor did Æneas disobey.
Onward they went, in shining armor clad;
With them went Chromius and Aretus, too;
Great hopes they had the warriors to slay,
And get possession of the long-necked steeds.
Foolish! they would not without harm return,
For to great Jove Automedon had prayed;
New strength he felt, and thus his friend addressed:
Drive not far off thy steeds, Alcimedon,
But keep them closely breathing on my back;
For Hector, Priam's son, will surely fight
'Till he slays us and on our chariot mounts,
Or until he among the first is slain.
So saying, to his other friends he called:
Ye Ajaxes, and prince Menelaus,
Chief of the Greeks! yonder dead body leave,
Leave to the bravest warriors to defend,
And come and succor us who still survive,
For hither Hector and Æneas rush,
The boldest leaders of the Trojan host;
But how 'tis all to end the gods know best,
Yet I my spear will hurl and trust to Jove.
He said, and, aiming, hurled his glittering spear,

Which struck Aretus' shield and pierced it through,
Cutting his belt and entering his groin.
As when a strong man striking a wild bull
Behind its head and horns, severs the spine,
Forward it leaps and falls upon the ground,
So he sprang forward, falling to the earth;
The quivering lance into his entrails went,
And his strong limbs were now relaxed in death.
  Then Hector at Automedon took aim
With his sharp spear, but he its point escaped
By bending forward, and the weapon stuck
In the soft ground and spent its mighty force.
Now hand to hand the warriors had fought
Had not the valiant Ajaxes approached;
Then Hector and Æneas made retreat,
And godlike Chromius; fearing the bold chiefs.
They left Aretus then a bloody corpse,
Whom of his arms Automedon despoiled,
And of his exploit boasting thus cried out:
Surely the grief for Patroclus I felt
Seems lighter now, since I have slain this man,
Although inferior he to my dear friend.
  So saying, in his chariot he placed
The bloody spoils; then into it he leaped,
His brawny hands and feet besmeared with blood,
And looking like a lion that has just
Devoured an ox. Meanwhile round Patroclus
The battle raged, tearful and bloody.
Minerva, sent from heaven by mighty Jove,
Urged on the dreadful conflict with good will;
And as when Jove a purple rainbow sends,
A sign of battle or of coming storms,
Afflicting herds and flocks, and causing men
To stop their work, so she, obscured in cloud,
Mingled among the Greeks and stirred them up.
  But first the gallant Menelaus she roused,
Taking the form of Phœnix, and thus spake:
Oh, Menelaus! what a burning shame

Will on ye fall if dear Achilles' friend
Should be abandoned as a prey to dogs!
Then stir thyself and all thy warriors rouse.
She said; and thus the other made reply:
Phœnix, my father, venerable man!
Oh that Minerva would afford me strength,
And shield me from the weapons of the foe!
Then I would willingly defend the corpse,
For much was Patroclus beloved by me;
But Hector rages like a flaming fire;
Jove is his friend, and on him glory sheds.
He said; the goddess heard and much rejoiced,
Because to her his prayer he first had made.
Into his limbs great vigor she infused;
Put in his heart the boldness of a fly,
Which, though oft driven from the body, still
Persists in biting—blood is sweet to it:
So obstinate the hero now became,
And to the corpse with rapid steps advanced,
Hurling his spear. Among the Trojans was
One Podes, Etion's son, wealthy and good,
By Hector chiefly honored, for he was
His boon companion when he banqueted;
Him the Greek smote, striking him on the belt,
And drove his brazen weapon through him quite.
Apollo stirred up Hector in the form
Of Phenops, son of Asius, who was
His friend beloved, and at Abydos dwelt;
Taking such form, the archer god thus spake:
Hector, who other of the Greeks will now
Fear thee who fearest feeble Menelaus?
Yet he triumphantly is bearing off
Yonder dead body, and has slain besides
Thy trusty comrade Podes, Etion's son.
He said; and heavy grief did Hector feel,—
In glittering brass he strode to the front ranks.
Then Jove his ægis took, splendid and fringed;
Ida he wrapped in clouds, lightnings he flashed,

And loudly thundered, shaking the whole mount.
To the glad Trojans victory he gave,
And put their enemies, the Greeks, to flight.
Peneleus, the Bœotian, foremost fled;
He on his shoulders, facing still the foe,
By brave Polydamas was slightly struck;
Then Hector Leitus pierced, Alectryon's son—
Pierced in the wrist—and so disabled him;
Trembling, he looked around holding his spear,
For he no longer now could hope to fight.
Then royal Idomeneus Hector struck—
Struck on the breast—as he at Leitus rushed,
But in his corselet the long weapon broke.
The Trojans shouted, and their mighty chief
Aimed at the Cretan monarch in his car,
But failed to hit; and Cœranus pierced
Merion's attendant and charioteer,
Who followed him from Lyctus' famous town.
The chief himself had battled first on foot,
And would have perished if his faithful friend
Had not come up and helped him with his steeds;
And now he fell himself by Hector's hand,
Who smote him by his jaw-bone and his ear.
The cruel lance forced out his pearly teeth,
And cut him through the middle of his tongue;
Down from his chariot the warrior fell,
Dropping the reins, which Merion took up,
And thus to royal Idomeneus spake:
  Lash on, till thou hast reached the hollow ships,
For we are surely destined to defeat.
He said; and Idomeneus lashed the steeds—
The steeds with handsome manes; he also feared
Ajax and Menelaus too perceived
That Jove to Troy decreed the victory,—
And thus great Telamon his friend addressed:
  Alas! a fool might see that father Jove
Is to our enemies affording aid;
Their weapons take effect whoever throws,

Whether he skillful or unskillful is.
'Tis Jove directs them; ours are hurled in vain,
And all fall harmlessly upon the ground.
But come and let us plan how best we may
Bear off our friend's poor body to the fleet,
And please our comrades with our safe return:
They finding that we stay are doubtless grieved,
And think we victims are of Hector's rage.
But would that I could some companion see
Who to Achilles might a message bear,
For he I think has not as yet received
The mournful tidings of his comrade's death;
But nowhere such a person I perceive,
In such a gloomy cloud we are obscured.
Oh, father Jove! this darkness take away;
Let this thick, murky vapor be dispersed;
And, if thou wilt destroy us, grant at least
That in the light of day we be destroyed.
He said; and Jove took pity on his tears—
Scattered the mist, and lifted off the cloud.
The sun shone forth, and all the fight was seen.
Then to brave Menelaus Ajax spake:
Look round, oh, Menelaus, and try to find
Antilochus; if living, send him quick
To great Achilles with the mournful news
That his beloved companion has been slain.
He said; nor did the other disobey,
But as a lion from some fold goes off,
Round which he prowled during the tedious night,
Eager a fatted bullock to devour,
But dogs and men are there to watch the herd:
He on them rushes, but is driven back,
For blazing brands and darts are at him hurled,
And early in the morning he departs
With saddened mind, baffled in his attempt:
So from dead Patroclus went Menelaus,
Fearing the Trojans would secure the corpse.
And as he went, the Ajaxes addressed

And valiant Merion: Ye Ajaxes
And Merion! brave leaders of the Greeks,
Think of the gentleness of our poor friend!
For, while he lived, courteous he was to all,
But now he's gone, victim of death and fate!
  Thus having said, the hero started off,
Gazing on all sides, like an eagle which
Of all the birds 'tis said can farthest see;
Soaring amid the clouds, e'en the swift hare
Escapes it not, hid in its leafy nest;
On it he pounces and deprives of life:
So gazed thou, Menelaus, with searching glance,
Seeking out Nestor's son if still he lived.
Soon on the left hand of the battle-field
The gallant chief he saw cheering his men;
Near him he drew, and thus his friend addressed:
  Come here, Antilochus, and hear the news—
Would that I had not such sad news to tell!
Thou must perceive thyself that 'tis some god
Afflicts the Greeks, and victory gives to Troy,
For Patroclus, our bravest chief, is slain.
Run quickly, then, and let Achilles know;
Perchance he may assist us to secure
The bloody corpse; the armor Hector has.
  He said; his comrade shuddered as he heard,—
Speechless he was, and his eyes filled with tears,
Yet Menelaus' bidding he fulfilled.
His armor to Laodacus he gave,
His faithful friend, who with his car was near;
Then, weeping, quickly to the fleet he ran
To bear the dreadful news to Peleus' son.
Nor didst thou, Menelaus, desire to go
And aid the men Antilochus had left,
But thither sentest bold Thrasymedes.
  He to dead Patroclus again went back,
Stood by the Ajaxes and thus addressed:
Him I have now to great Achilles sent,

And yet I scarce believe that he will come,
Though at illustrious Hector so enraged ;
For he without his armor could not fight.
But come, and let us plan how best we may
Draw off the corpse, and we ourselves escape
The fatal doom that seems to threaten us.
Thus spake the chief, and Ajax thus replied :
Wisely thou speakest, noble Menelaus;
Then thou and Merion stooping, quickly lift
The body, and remove it from the field,
Whilst we with Hector and his men will fight,—
We who so oft have fought with them before.
He said ; and they with great exertion raised
The bloody corpse, and bore it in their arms ;
Which, when the Trojans saw, they raised a shout.
Rushing like dogs upon a wounded boar,
One while indeed thy rush, eager to tear,
But when he turns they all are put to flight :
So steadily the Trojans now pursued
And now held back, trembling and pale with fright
When the two Ajaxes turned and made a stand.
Thus towards the fleet the corpse they quickly bore ;
Behind them swept the battle like a flame,
When an extensive city is on fire ;
Down go the houses in the mighty blaze,
And with the conflagration roars the wind :
So a terrific din of men and steeds
Followed close on them as they left the field.
But as when mules exerting all their strength,
Drag from a mountain, o'er a rugged path,
A piece of timber for the shipwrights cut,
Wearied with labor and with sweat they move :
So they with labor bore the corpse away,
Whilst the two Ajaxes held the foe in check.
Like a strong dam across a river stretched,
Which checks the rapid waters of the stream,
Nor can they through it burst, though swelled with floods :
So in the rear the Ajaxes repelled

The Trojan foe, who still pursuing kept;
But two among them most conspicuous were—
The illustrious Hector, and Anchises' son.
And as a flock of starlings, with shrill cries,
Fly from a hawk they see pursuing them:
So from bold Hector and Æneas fled
The clamoring Greeks, forgetful of the fight,
Their handsome armor dropping as they ran,
So hot was the pursuit, so sad the rout.

BOOK XVIII.

THE SHIELD OF ACHILLES.

ARGUMENT.

The news of Patroclus' death is brought to Achilles, who is overwhelmed with grief, and seeks to destroy himself.—His mother, Thetis, hears his lamentations, and greatly distressed thereat, leaves her home and visits her son to know the cause of his trouble.—He informs her of the death of his friend, and the loss of his armor, whereupon she goes to Vulcan, and persuades him to fabricate a new suit; the book closes with a description of the shield.

Thus like a blazing fire the fight went on.
Meanwhile Antilochus, the messenger,
Came to the fleet, and there Achilles found,—
Found him foreboding what had just transpired.
 Groaning, the chief thus with himself communed:
Alas! alas! why are the long-haired Greeks
Thus driven in confusion to their ships?
I fear the gods more woes have on me piled,
As was foretold me by my mother once,
That the most noble of the Myrmidons,
While yet I lived, should fall by Trojan hands.
Ah, yes! dear Patroclus is surely dead!
Obstinate man, I to him warning gave,
That when he had the enemy repulsed,
Quick to return, and not with Hector fight.
 Thus while the hero with himself communed,
Antilochus, great Nestor's son, drew nigh,
Shedding hot tears, and thus his message told:

Alas, Achilles! mournful news I bear;
Would it were not so! Patroclus is dead;
E'en now around his corpse the fight goes on,
And Hector, the plumed chief, his armor has.
He said; the hero was overwhelmed with grief;
Handfuls of ashes on his head he poured,
Marring the beauty of his countenance;
The cinders covered all his splendid robe.
Then in the dust he threw himself, and tore
With both his hands his handsome auburn hair.
The captive maidens taken in the war
All shrieked aloud, and from the doors rushed out;
Around their lord they thronged, beating their breasts,
And fainted when the piteous sight they saw;
Antilochus shed tears, and deeply groaned.
Holding Achilles' hands—for much he feared
Lest with his sword his friend would cut his throat—
Loudly and fearfully the hero moaned.
His venerable mother heard his moans.
In ocean's depths, close to her sire, she sat.
She likewise into lamentations burst;
The Nereids, sea-goddesses, flocked around,
All rising from the bottom of the sea—
Cymodè, Thalia, and Glaucè,
Nesæa, Spio, Thoa, and Halia,
A bright-eyed nymph; and Cymothoë too,
And Lymnoria, who in marshes dwelt.
The swift Amphithoë and Irea came:
Doto, Agavè, and Melita,
Proto, Dynamenè, and Doris,
Dexamenè, and Amphinomè the fair,
And Callianira, and Pherusa,
And famous Galatea, and Nemertes,
Apseudes too, and Callianassa;
There too was Clymenè, and Janira,
And fair-haired Amatheïa, and Mæra,
And Janessa, and Orythia,
And many other Nereids were there;

The splendid glittering cave was filled with them.
With one accord they beat their heaving breasts,
Whilst Thetis, weeping, thus her grief revealed:
  Hear me, ye sister Nereids, and know
What sorrows wretched Thetis must endure!
Ah, woe is me! Alas, unhappy me!
Who, in an evil hour, brought forth a son
Noble and brave—a prince of heroes he.
Like a fair tree my blooming boy shot up—
Like a fair tree reared in a fruitful field.
Then to the Trojan war I sent the youth,
And ne'er expect to see him home again;
Through all his life he grieves, and still complains,
Nor if I visit him can I relieve;
Yet I will go and see my darling son,
And learn what now it is that troubles him.
  Thus having said, the azure cave she left,
The sea-nymphs all in tears accompanying her.
They cleft a passage through the ocean wave;
But when to Troy they came, they to the shore
Ascended, where Achilles' vessels lay.
  His venerable mother, wailing loud,
Went to her son, folded him in her arms,
And thus in lamentable tones began:
Why weepest thou, oh my son? what grief invades?
Speak out! nor from thy mother hide thy woes.
The things for which to Jove thou badest me pray
Are all accomplished: that the proud Greeks,
For insults heaped on thee, should routed be
And driven in confusion to their fleet.
  She said; and groaning, thus Achilles spake:
True, mother dear, Jove's promise is fulfilled;
But what of that—since Patroclus is dead!
The man I honored most of all my friends,
And loved as dearly as I love myself,
Has perished! and his armor Hector has.
Those splendid, wondrous arms which the gods gave,
As a great gift, to Peleus, my sire,

When he a goddess to his bosom took.
Oh, that thou had'st with thine own race remained
In ocean's depths, with deities marine,
And that my sire a mortal had espoused;
But now thou hast been wedded that great grief
May be thy lot, for thy son's early doom,
Whom thou shalt ne'er receive returning home:
Since I'm resolved to live no longer, nor
Consort with men, till Hector first is slain,
And pays the penalty for slaughtering
The noble Patroclus, Menœtius' son.
He said; and Thetis, weeping, thus replied:
Short-lived thou wilt be, as thou sayest, my son,
For, soon as Hector dies, thy turn will come.
With a deep sigh, Achilles answering, spake:
Let me die now, since I could not prevent
My comrade's death, nor help him with my spear;
Far from his native land he met his doom,
Thinking that I would aid him and protect.
Oh, that contention ne'er with men had place!
For 'tis through them that I shall ne'er see home,
And failed to save the life of Patroclus,
And many others of the Greeks who fell,—
Whilst thus I sit sullen beside my ships,
A burden on the earth, useless to all,
And yet the foremost of them all in war,
Though others may in counsel me excel.
Oh, that fierce wrath were banished from the earth,
And anger, which the wisest oft invades!
Like smoke it rises in the breasts of men,
Sweeter than honey—bitter in the end;
And thus with Agamemnon I was wroth;
But what is past cannot be now recalled.
'Tis time our angry passions were subdued.
I against Hector, slayer of my friend,
Will now do battle, and accept my doom
Whene'er it pleases Jove that doom to send,
For e'en great Hercules escaped not death,

Dear as that hero was to mighty Jove;
Yet fate subdued him and dread Juno's wrath:
So also shall I fall when it is decreed,
And yet illustrious glory shall be mine,
And Trojan widows frequently shall sigh,
Wiping their tears away with both their hands.
Soon will they know when I am in the field;
Therefore, though loving me, persuade me not,
Nor try to keep me from the bloody fight.
He said; and thus his mother answered him:
Truly, my son, thy words are just and wise,
For 'tis commendable to serve our friends;
But thy bright handsome arms the Trojans have—
Plumed Hector seized them, and in triumph wears;
Yet short his triumph, since his death draws near.
But go not thou upon the battle-field
Before thou hither see'st me returned,
For by to-morrow's dawn I will be back,
And fetch thee splendid arms by Vulcan made.
So saying, from her son she turned away,
And thus her sister Nereids addressed:
Descend ye now beneath the ocean's waves;
Go to my father's mansions and relate
To the marine old man what ye have heard.
Meanwhile to high Olympus I repair,
To Vulcan, heavenly artisan, and try
To get resplendent armor for my son.
She said; and they into the ocean plunged;
But silver-footed Thetis started off,
And quickly the Olympian mansions reached,
In quest of splendid armor for her son.
Meanwhile the Greeks, with fearful uproar fled—
Fled from fierce Hector, and their navy reached,
Upon the borders of the Hellespont;
Nor could they get the corpse of Patroclus
Drawn from the reach of darts that showering fell,
For horse and infantry again rushed on,
And Hector like a blazing flame of fire.

Thrice Hector seized the body by the foot,
And thrice Ajax drove the Trojan back;
He trusting to his strength, would now advance
And now stop short, shouting tremendously;
Yet the pursuit he never quite gave up.
But as the shepherds cannot drive away
A hungry lion from his carcass-prey,
So neither could the Ajaxes repulse
The indomitable Hector from the corpse;
And now he would indeed have gained his point,
And with immortal honor crowned himself,
Had not the swift wing-footed Iris come—
Come to Achilles, from Olympus sent
By Juno secretly. She standing near,
Thus to the chief her hasty message gave:
Rise, son of Peleus—terriblest of men!
Aid thy friend Patroclus, on whose account
A dreadful conflict rages near the ships,
And fearful slaughtering is going on.
Some are there fighting to defend the corpse,
Which to proud Troy the Trojans seek to drag,
But chiefly noble Hector—most of all
He would the body seize, cut off the head
And stand it up, transfixed upon a stake.
Up, then, at once—no longer tarry here;
Let reverence touch thy soul, lest thy dear friend
May a sweet morsel be to Trojan dogs.
Should his dead body be at all defiled,
It would a sad dishonor be to thee.
She said; and thus the warrior replied:
Pray, tell me, Iris, goddess, which of the gods
Has sent thee thus a messenger to me.
He spake, and Iris to him made reply:
'Twas Juno sent me, noble wife of Jove;
Jove knows not of it, nor the other gods,
Who on Olympus' snowy summit dwell.
Then answering, Achilles quickly said:
How can I fight when they my armor have?

My mother also charged me not to arm
Ere she returned; she promised to bring here
A splendid suit of arms by Vulcan made.
None other know I of that I could wear,
Save the great shield of Ajax Telamon;
But he, I trust, is in the foremost ranks,
Fighting around the corpse of Patroclus.
Right well I know, the rainbow goddess said,
Thy handsome armor others now possess;
But go e'en thus, upon the ramparts stand,
And to the haughty Trojans show thyself.
Perchance with terror struck at sight of thee
They may fall back, and so the tired Greeks
May have a little respite from the war.
Thus having spoke, swift Iris flew away.
Then rose Achilles, dear to mighty Jove;
Her ægis o'er his shoulders Pallas threw,
And on his head settled a golden cloud,
Upon it lighting up a brilliant flame.
As when a cloud of smoke is seen to rise,
Far in the distance, from some island town
Which foes invest; and all day long they fight;
But when the sun goes down torches are lit,
Whose dazzling flames are visible afar,
So that their friends in ships may bring relief:
Thus from Achilles' head a fire blazed.
Then by the trench he stood, nor fought at all,
Minding the counsel that his mother gave;
But there he stood and shouted; and there, too,
Minerva stood, shouting tremendously,
Raising a dreadful uproar 'mid the foe.
Clear and distinct the warrior's voice arose,
As when a trumpet's pealing tones resound,
Startling the dwellers in a town besieged.
But when Achilles' brazen voice was heard,
All hearts were troubled, and the long-maned steeds
Reeled back, foreboding evils were ahead;
The charioteers were panic-struck when they

Saw on the hero's head terrific flames;
Thrice o'er the trench shouted the mighty chief,
Thrice in confusion were the Trojans thrown;
Twelve of their bravest warriors there fell,
Hurled from their cars and stretched upon the ground.
Then joyfully the Greeks drew Patroclus,—
Drew from the darts, and placed upon a bier;
His friends and comrades, weeping, gathered round.
Achilles followed, shedding scalding tears
When he beheld his dear companion laid
Upon a bier, his body torn with wounds;
'Twas he indeed that sent him to the fight,
But ne'er was destined to receive alive.
But venerable Juno bade the sun
Back to the ocean go against his will;
Then set the sun; and then the noble Greeks
Poured from the terrible destructive fight.
The Trojans also from the field withdrew,
And from the chariots unyoked their steeds;
Before they supped they to the council rushed.
In the assembly they all stood up,
None took a seat, so terror-stricken they,
Because Achilles had appeared again.
Then rose Polydamas, wise counselor,
Comrade of Hector, born on the same night;
One great in counsel was, and one in war,
He soundly arguing, thus harangued, and said:
Be well advised, my friends! on both sides look;
I counsel that we to the town return,
Nor wait to-morrow's dawn upon the plain;
Our lofty walls will a protection be.
Whilst this man with his monarch was enraged
'Twas easier to combat with the Greeks;
And I myself with pleasure spent the night
By our foes' ships, in hopes to capture them;
But now Achilles greatly do I fear,
So violent and proud; he will not stay
Upon the plain where hitherto we fought;

But on our city and our wives will rush.
Then hear me, let us to the city go
Whilst it is night, and we have time to go;
For if this man to-morrow rushes forth,
Many will rue it; happy will they be,
Who, safe in Troy, escape devouring dogs,—
Oh, dreadful thought! may such things never be!
But if ye hearken to my words, though sad,
We may within our walls protection find;
But on the morrow, for the fight arrayed,
We on our lofty towers will take our stand,
And he will vainly battle with us there;
Around the city he his steeds may drive,
Then disappointed to his fleet return,
Our sacred town uncaptured and secure.
He said; and sternly gazing at his friend,
Thus the plumed Hector haughtily replied:
Thou speakest things, Polydamas, to me
Distasteful, counseling a base retreat,
That we within our city should be cooped.
Have ye not been imprisoned there enough?
Once noble Troy a wealthy place was thought,
But now our substance strangers have devoured,
Since we have known the wrath of mighty Jove;
But at this time when we have gained so much,
Triumphing o'er the Greeks e'en at their ships,
Give not such counsel, foolish man, as this;
For thy advice the Trojans will not take,
Nor would I let them do so; but come on,
At present let us sup, and mind the watch;
But if there any be who fear to lose
Their treasure, let them distribution make:
Better allow their comrades to enjoy
Than fall into the proud invaders' hands;
But on the morrow, with the early dawn,
We will the fight renew; Achilles, then,
Will find it worse for him, if he comes forth:

I will not shun him, but will gladly meet
And take the chance of war, whate'er it be.
He said; and shouting, all applauded him.
Foolish they were; for of their senses them
Minerva had bereft; the good advice
Of wise Polydamas was not obeyed.
Then, from the council, they to supper went.
Meanwhile the Greeks, lamenting all night long,
Wept o'er Patroclus; but Achilles most,
Who took the lead, upon his comrade's breast
Placing his hands, and weeping all the while.
As a fierce lion that has lost his whelps,
Stolen by a hunter in a shady wood,
His loss he soon discovers, and laments;
Then up and down the valleys he goes forth,
Tracking the hunter's steps, in hopes to find;
For rage terrific in his bosom burns:
So sighing, he the Myrmidons addressed:
Oh, heavens! how vain a promise did I give!
Encouraging Menœtius in our halls,
Saying that I to Opus would bring back
His noble son, laden with Trojan spoils;
But Jove men's expectations crosses oft,
For we in Trojan soil shall both be laid.
Neither old Peleus, the knight, my sire,
Nor Thetis, shall receive me in their halls,
But the same earth shall be our sepulcher;
Yet since I thee survive, oh, Patroclus!
I will not have thee buried till I bring
Hither thy murderer Hector's bloody head
And his bright arms; and also shall behead
Twelve of the noblest warriors of Troy,
Before thy tomb, in reverence of thee;
And round thee night and day shall Trojan dames,
Captured by us, their lamentations make.
Thus having said, Achilles bade his friends
To set the brazen tripod on the fire,
To bathe the corpse, and wash away the blood.

They filled with water, and piled on the wood;
The rising flames encircled the bright brass;
Then, when the hissing water fairly boiled,
They washed the corpse, anointing it with oil;
A precious ointment in the wounds they poured.
Then on a couch they laid him, and o'erspread
A linen covering from head to foot,
And over that a splendid mantle laid.
Around Achilles wept the Myrmidons,
Lamenting all night long for Patroclus.
  Then Jove his consort Juno thus addressed:
And so, oh, Juno, thou hast gained thy point—
Rousing Achilles from his sullenness;
Surely these Greeks descended are from thee.
  Then answered him his venerable spouse:
Imperious son of Saturn, what a speech!
Surely a mortal might effect as much.
And shall not I, of goddesses the first,
Both by my birth and also as thy wife,
Bring evils on the Trojans, if enraged?
Thus they with one another converse held.
  Meanwhile the silver-footed Thetis reached
Vulcan's great brazen palace—starry domes—
A wonder even to the deities;
Built by the heavenly architect himself.
Him she found sweating, working at his forge;
Full twenty tripods he was finishing,
Which were to stand around his palace walls;
Beneath the base of each were golden wheels,
Which, of their own accord, moved forward to
The heavenly council, and then back again—
A wondrous work; so far he had progressed,
And now the handles he was putting on
And rivets forging. Whilst thus he toiled,
Thetis, the silver-footed nymph, approached.
  The beauteous fair-veiled Charis, Vulcan's spouse,
Saw her, and, going to her, took her hand;
And thus, in words of kindly greeting, spake:

Why, long-robed Thetis, venerable, beloved,
Dost thou this visit make to our abode?
'Twas not thy custom to do so before.
Then enter, and of friendly fare partake.
She said; and led her noble guest within,
And set her on a silver-studded throne,
Placing a footstool underneath her feet;
Then to her lord she went, and thus addressed:
Come hither, Vulcan, Thetis asks for thee.
To whom the illustrious artisan replied:
An awful, much-loved goddess then we have
Beneath our roof; she saved me in distress,
When, by my shameless mother, because lame,
I from my heavenly birthplace was cast down;
And dreadful would my case indeed have been
Had not good Thetis and Eurynomè
Within their bosoms kindly nurtured me,—
Eurynomè, the daughter of the sea.
Nine years I dwelt with them, and in their cave
Wrought many curious works of art in brass,
Buckles and twisted bracelets, clasps and bands,
Whilst all around us, murmuring with foam,
The dark immeasurable ocean rolled;
Nor was my hiding-place to any known
Except to Thetis and Eurynomè,—
And now she comes and visits my abode;
Therefore to Thetis some reward is due.
Set thou before her, then, the best we have,
Whilst I meanwhile my work will lay aside,
And put away my bellows and my tools.
He said; and, limping from his anvil, rose,
A wondrous bulk, with weak and tottering legs—
His bellows from the furnace he withdrew,
And placed his tools within a silver chest.
With a soft sponge he wiped his face and hands,
His brawny neck and broad and shaggy breast;
Then he put on his robe, his scepter seized,
And, limping as he went, his workshop left.

Handmaidens, formed of gold, accompanied him—
The work of his own hands the figures were.
Briskly they moved about their artist king;
Voices they had, strength and intelligence,
And were instructed by the immortal gods.
Thus hobbling, on a splendid throne he sat
Alongside Thetis, seized her hand and spake:
  Why, long-robed Thetis, venerable, beloved,
Dost thou a visit make to our abode?
'Twas not thy custom to do so before.
Tell me thy wish and it shall be performed,
If in my power it is and fate decrees.
  Him Thetis answered, bursting into tears:
Who of the goddesses, oh, Vulcan, has
Endured such woes as have afflicted me?
Me from the other dwellers in the sea
Jove took, and made me marry Peleus,
Sharing a mortal couch, against my will;
Within his palace, bending with old age,
My husband lies; and other woes I have:
I bore a son, a prince of heroes he;
Like a fair tree my blooming boy shot up—
Like a fair tree nursed in a fruitful field.
Then to the Trojan war I sent the youth,
And ne'er expect to see him home again.
Through all his life he grieves, full of complaints;
Nor, should I visit him, can I relieve.
The maid that was selected as his prize
King Agamemnon basely robbed him of.
Grieving for loss of her he pined away,
Whilst the Greeks, routed by the men of Troy,
Were driven back e'en to their very fleet.
The chiefs and elders supplicated him,
And costly presents promised he should have,
But he refused; yet in his armor Patroclus he clad,
And sent him to the battle with his men.
All day around the Scæan gate they fought,
And would upon that day have taken Troy,

But by Apollo Patroclus was slain,
And he great glory to plumed Hector gave.
But now I come and beg thee on my knees
To give my short-lived and unhappy son
A shield and handsome greaves, fitted with clasps--
A helmet and a burnished corselet too,
For his own arms his faithful comrade lost
When in the field he fell by Trojans slain,
And he meanwhile lies stretched upon the ground,
Sad groans and lamentations uttering.
  She said; and noble Vulcan thus replied:
Cheer up and leave the matter all to me.
Would that I could thy son preserve from death
When fate decrees and his sad doom draws near,
As I for him a suit of arms will make
Which shall to mortal men a wonder be!
  He said; and to his bellows straightway went,
Turned them towards the fire and bade them work.
Full twenty bellows then the furnace blew
With equal and well-regulated blast,
And stopped and moved just as the king desired.
Then precious gold, silver, and brass and tin,
He in the red-hot blazing fire threw,
And placed his mighty anvil on the block;
Then took his tongs and hammer in his hands
And with good will and spirit went to work.
  And first a shield,* massy and large, he made--
All over it was full of ornament;
Around it was a triple glittering rim,
From which there hung a splendid silver belt.
Five-folded was the shield, on which he formed,
With cunning art, a mass of curious work.
  On it he carved the earth, the sky, the sea,

---

* This description of the shield of Achilles has been greatly admired by all writers, ancient and modern. It is most beautiful and graphic,—abounds with charming rural imagery, and gives us an authentic and valuable insight into the manners and customs of those remote times.

The unwearied sun, and full-orbed silvery moon;
There might be seen the constellations, too,
The Pleiads, and the Hyads, and Orion;
Also the Bear, by some the Wagon called,
Which circling moves and seems to watch Orion;
Of all the constellations, it alone
Ne'er dips itself beneath the ocean wave.
Two handsome cities then the artist made:
In one were marriages and festivals;
The brides they were conducting from their homes,
With brilliant torches, and with bridal songs;
The youthful dancers followed, wheeling round,
And merry pipes, and sweet-toned lyres were there;
And as the gay procession passed along,
The women, thronging to their doors, admired.
Next on the shield a crowded court he carved;
And there a suit at law was going on,
About a ransom for a homicide;
The slayer of the man stoutly affirmed
The fine was paid; the other this denied,
And the two parties to the judge appealed;
Each his supporters had, and each was cheered,
Whilst heralds posted there kept back the crowd.
The elders sat around on polished stones,
Holding their staves of office in their hands,
And one by one arose and plead the cause;
Two golden talents in the midst were placed,
To be by him received who gained his suit.
The other city was beset with foes;
Two glittering armies had beleaguered it,
Offering their terms, either to burn the town,
Or have it given up with half the spoil;
The citizens as yet had not complied,
But secretly prepared an ambuscade;
Meanwhile upon the wall the old men watched,
They and their tender children, and their wives.
The warriors from the city sallied forth,
Mars was their leader, and Minerva, too,

Both made of gold, both clad in golden robes;
Splendid their weapons and their armor was,
And beautiful in shape, and large were they,
Radiant all o'er—resembling gods indeed;
The people were all formed of humbler size.
But when they at the proper place arrived,
Upon the margin of a flowing stream
Where flocks were watered, there they hid themselves;
Two spies walked on in front, watching to see
When the horned oxen and the sheep drew near.
Soon they advanced, two shepherds tending them,
Not knowing that an ambuscade was there,
But playing on their flutes as they approached.
Up sprang the men, and in upon them ran,
Slaughtering the oxen and the snow-white sheep,
And slew the unsuspecting shepherds, too.
The other army soon the tumult heard,
And springing on their steeds rushed to the fight;
A furious battle by the stream was fought.
There Discord and dread Tumult might be seen,
And Fate inexorable, saving some
And some destroying; terrible she raged,
A crimson garment o'er her shoulders thrown,—
A garment crimsoned with the blood of men;
Like living beings they appeared to move,
To fight, and drag away wounded and slain.
Upon the shield the artist pictured next
A thrice-plowed fallow field, fertile and large;
There with their teams were many plowmen seen,
Some driving up and down, some turning round;
But when the border of the field they reached,
A man stood ready with a cup of wine,
And gave to each; in order due they moved,
And all were glad as they the place approached;
Behind, the land looked black, as plowed land does;
A marvelous piece of work it was indeed.
A corn-field next he made; reapers were there
With sickles in their hands, cutting the grain,

Which as they mowed fell down; binders were seen
Who picked it up and bound it into sheaves;
Three workmen at the binding were employed,
And boys supplied them, handfuls gathering.
In silence in their midst the master stood,
With staff in hand, delighted in his heart;
Servants were in the distance busy seen,
Slaying a fatted ox, beneath an oak;
Whilst women were at work with barley flour,
Preparing for the men their evening meal.
A vineyard then he made, laden with grapes;
Golden and beautiful the vineyard was:
From silver poles the purple clusters hung.
Round the inclosure was an azure trench,
And hedge of tin: one path there only was,
By which the gatherers went in and out;
Virgins and youths carried the luscious fruit
In woven baskets; in the midst a boy
Played sweetly on a harp, and sweetly sang,
Whilst they, with shouts and dances, followed him.
On it a herd of cattle, too, he wrought;
Of gold and tin the speckled kine were made.
With lowings, from their stalls they sallied forth
And sought the pastures, near a murmuring stream
Whose verdant shores rustled with flags and reeds;
Four golden herdsmen with the cattle went,
And nine swift dogs; but two great lions rushed
Upon the herd, and fastened on the bull.
He, loudly bellowing, was dragged away;
The young men followed after with their dogs
To attempt a rescue; but the savage beasts
Tore off the creature's skin, and lapped his blood.
Vainly the men, urging their dogs, pressed on;
But they the lion shunned, and would not bite.
Near them they only stood, and looked and barked.
A lovely grove the artist sculptured next;
Within it was a pasture filled with sheep—
With snow-white sheep, and folds, and cottages.

Then on the shield a labyrinthian dance
Great Vulcan made, like that in Gnossus formed
By Dædalus for fair-haired Ariadnè.
There danced alluring virgins and young men,
Holding each other by their wrists and hands;
The girls in finest linen robes were dressed,
With garlands of sweet flowers; the youths were clad
In woven tunics, glittering all o'er,
With golden swords hanging from silver belts.
Nimbly and easy as a potter's wheel
The youthful dancers gracefully spun round;
Then intermingling through each other ran
Back to the places they had started from.
A large assembly had collected there,
And gazed delighted on the lovely scene,
Whilst in their midst two clowns, with comic songs,
Spinning around, their jokes and antics played.
As a last border round it all he formed
The rolling billows of the ocean stream.
When thus the shield he finished, next he made
A splendid coat of mail that shone like fire,
And a strong helmet fitted for his head;
Beauteous it was, and variously carved,
And mounted with a splendid golden crest.
Lastly he made him greaves of ductile tin.
When Vulcan thus had finished all his work
He took it up, and before Thetis placed.
She from Olympus' snowy top flew off—
Flew like a hawk, and, darting through the air,
Carried the shining armor to her son.

BOOK XIX.

THE RECONCILIATION.

ARGUMENT.

Thetis carries the armor to Achilles, who is greatly delighted at receiving it.—Achilles and Agamemnon are reconciled, and the whole army is assembled; presents are bestowed on the pacified chief, and the lady Briseis returned to him.—He arms for the battle, and reproaches his horses for allowing his friend Patroclus to be slain, whereupon one of them is endowed with the gift of speech and prophesies his master's coming doom.

The saffron morn rose o'er the ocean waves,
Bringing to mortals and immortals light,
As Thetis at the Grecian camp arrived,
Bearing the splendid present of the god.
She found her son stretched upon Patroclus,
Deeply lamenting; whilst around him were
His numerous dear companions all in tears.
Near him the goddess drew, and seized his hand,
And thus the afflicted warrior addressed:
  Grieved as we are for Patroclus, my son,
Yet let him lie; he fell by Jove's decree.
But take these noble arms by Vulcan made—
Such armor mortal shoulders never bore.
  She said; and laid them at Achilles' feet;
Loudly they clashed. Fear seized the Myrmidons;
Nor could they bear to look on them, but fled.
But at their sight Achilles raged still more;
His eyes shot fire; with fierce delight he took

And held the immortal present in his hands,
And, as he gazed, thus to his mother spake:
Mother, the god indeed has furnished arms
Worthy a god; no man such arms could make.
Now I will put them on. Meanwhile I fear
These insects gathering round my comrade's corpse
Will maggots breed, and make it putrefy.
He said; and Thetis to him thus replied:
Be not concerned, my child, I'll see to that,
And find a means to drive away these swarms
Which eat the flesh of heroes slain in war;
And though he here should lie for a whole year
His corpse shall be as now, or fresher still.
But go, and to a council call the Greeks,
And, making peace again with Agamemnon,
Arm for the field and put on all thy might.
She said, inspiring in her warrior son
Most daring courage. Then ambrosia she,
And ruby nectar, in the nostrils poured,
Making the body incorruptible.
Meanwhile Achilles went along the shore,
Shouting most dreadfully, and roused the Greeks,
And those who used to stay aboard the ships—
The pilots and the pursers and the stewards—
These all came forth and to the council thronged,
Soon as they saw Achilles show himself,
For, for a long time he had not been seen.
There also went two famous sons of Mars,
Ulysses and the noble Diomed,
With limping gait, and leaning on their spears,
For still they suffered from their painful wounds.
Advancing, on the front seats they sat down;
Last came the king, great Agamemnon,
Wounded by Coön, brave Antenor's son.
When all assembled were, Achilles rose,
And, standing in their midst, harangued them thus:
Oh, son of Atreus! better had it been
For me and thee had we continued friends

And for a girl's sake not have fallen out!
Would that by Dian's shaft she had been slain
Upon the day that I Lyrnessa took!
So many Greeks would not have bit the ground
Had it been so, nor Hector thus prevailed.
Long will this feud of ours remembered be;
But let it pass—we must our wrath subdue,
Anger must not forever be indulged.
But come, and to the battle urge the Greeks,
That I may forward move and try the foe,
If near our ships they wish to spend the night.
But many will, I think, be glad to flee
And save themselves from my devouring spear.
Thus spake the chief; the well-armed Greeks rejoiced
Seeing Achilles had renounced his wrath.
Then from his seat, not moving, spake the king,
And thus his chiefs and trusty men addresed:
Friends, heroes, sons of Mars! hearken to me—
Hearken to me, and let none interrupt:
Hard 'tis to speak even for one who's skilled;
But in an uproar who can hear or speak?
I to Achilles will address myself;
But listen, that ye may my meaning learn:
Much blame has by the Greeks been thrown on me;
Yet I am not to blame, but Jove and fate,
And dreadful Erinnys roaming about—
Roaming about among the gloomy shades,
Who on that day sad evil did to me
When in the council I Achilles robbed.
What could I do against the deity—
Against pernicious Até, child of Jove,
Who injures all? She walks not on the ground,
But steps with tender feet o'er mortals' heads,
Injuring us all, and one she binds in chains.
Once e'en on Jove an injury she put,
When Juno by her cunning him deceived—
Upon that day when Alcmenè was near,
Being delivered of great Hercules

In high-walled Thèbes. He, boasting, thus had spoke:
Hear me, ye gods and all ye goddesses!
This day Ilithia, who rules o'er births,
Shall bring into the world a certain man,
Who over all his neighbors shall hold sway,
For from my blood the illustrious hero springs.
He said; and Juno, full of guile, replied:
Thou liest, and wilt not to thy purpose stick.
Come then, Olympian, seal it with an oath
That he indeed shall o'er his neighbors rule,
Who from a woman's womb shall this day fall,
And who is of thy lineage and blood.
She said; but Jove perceived not her design,
But swore the mighty oath, and was befooled,
For Juno, springing forth, from heaven flew,
And to Achaiac Argos came in haste,
Where the fair spouse of Sthenelus she knew
Was pregnant of a son for seven months.
By her own power the babe she brought to light,
But kept back Alcmenè's delivery,
And then, returning, bore to Jove the news.
Great Jove, who hurlest the red lightning bolts,
I will remind thee of the words thou spake:
A noble man, Eurystheus, is born,
Son of great Perseus, who sprang from thee,
He o'er the Argives shall and ought to rule.
She said; but Jove was grievously enraged,
And Até seized by her long shining curls,
Swearing a mighty oath that she should ne'er
Enter Olympus, nor the starry skies,
Wretch as she was, who lives to injure all.
So saying, he from heaven cast her down,
Whirling her round. And now this deity,
Busy at mischief ever, dwells with men;
And Jove beheld with grief his favorite son
Great woes enduring by Eurystheus' hands:
So I, when devastating Hector raged,
Thought of the wrong I foolishly had done.

But since bereft of sense I suffered harm,
I will appease thee now with splendid gifts;
But go thou to the fight, urge on our men,
And I the promised presents will prepare,
Such as Ulysses spoke of yesterday.
Yet if thou wilt, tarry a little while,
Until my servants hither fetch the gifts,
That thou mayest see thyself what gifts they are.
He said; and great Achilles answering, spake:
Most glorious son of Atreus, king of men!
Whether thou furnish gifts or furnish not
Is naught to me; now let us rise and fight,
And not in idle talk consume the time;
A mighty work there is for us to do.
And when ye see Achilles in the van,
The Trojan ranks destroying with his spear,
Let each one look on him and bravely fight.
He said; and thus Ulysses, rising, spake:
Brave as thou art, Achilles, urge not thus
The fasting Greeks to rush on lofty Troy,
For when the fight begins it will last long;
But give command to feed our army first,
For he who hungers cannot fight all day;
Though full of spirit, yet his strength will fail,
And weak and languid will his limbs become.
But he who is with wine and food supplied,
Will battle all day long without fatigue.
Come, then, at once, and order a repast,
And let our king his promised presents bring,
And set them in our midst that all may see,
And thou too mayest behold them with delight;
And let him, too, upon his honor swear
That he Briseis never has embraced.
Then let thy heart be kindly, too, to him,
And let him a rich banquet for thee make,
That naught be wanting to conciliate;
And for the future, son of Atreus, thou
Wilt be more just towards thy associates;

Nor does a king degrade himself the least,
When he a man appeases whom he wronged.
  He said; and Agamemnon thus replied:
Thy words, Ulysses, cause me to rejoice,
For thou hast spoken with propriety,
And I will take the oath thou hast proposed.
But let Achilles yet stay here awhile,
And all ye others, 'till the gifts are brought
And leagues are struck; and thou, Ulysses, take
Some of our choicest youths that they may fetch
The presents that I promised from the ships,
And women too; and let Talthybius
Prepare a boar, that we may offer it
To mighty Jove, and the bright archer god.
  He said; and thus Achilles answer made:
Most glorious son of Atreus, king of men!
These matters may hereafter be arranged
When we have time and when my ardor cools,
But now our friends lie mangled on the field;
And as for food, I would excite the Greeks
To hurry to the fight e'en while they fast;
And at the setting sun prepare a feast,
When we have put away our late disgrace;
'Till then no food nor drink shall pass my lips.
My dear companion lying in my tent,
Mangled and dead, his comrades mourning round:
These make me think of bloodshed and revenge,
Of conflict, and of slaughter, and of groans.
  He said; and wise Ulysses thus replied:
Oh, son of Peleus! renowned Achilles!
Bravest by far of the heroic Greeks,
Thou art in war superior to me,
But not in prudence, for I older am.
Wherefore be thou persuaded by my words:
Soon is the contest ended when men fall
Beneath a hero's devastating spear;
But often mighty Jove decides the day.
Nor should our stomachs suffer for the men

Who fall by thousands; we have need of rest,
And our dead comrades must be buried, too;
But they who live must think of food and drink,
That we may stronger be to meet the foe.
Now we will not exhort our men again;
And woe to him who lingers at the ships,
For in a body we will rush on Troy.
He said; and for his comrades chose the sons
Of glorious Nestor; and Meges, too,
And Melanippus, and Lycomedes,
And Thoas also, and brave Merion;
These to the tent of Agamemnon went.
Seven tripods thence they brought, the promised gifts,
And twenty splendid goblets, and twelve steeds;
Seven accomplished ladies then they led,—
Briseis, lovely maiden, was the eighth.
Ten talents then of gold Ulysses weighed,
And thus they bore the presents in the midst.
The king rose up, he and Talthybius,
A herald with a voice like to a god—
A boar he held, and with his knife the king
Cut off its forelock, praying to great Jove:
Be witness, Jove supreme and best of gods,
And earth and sun, and furies who chastise
False swearers, here by ye all I swear
That I the maid Briseis ne'er embraced,
But she is still inviolate and pure;
And if I falsely speak, may I receive
Such woes as always fall on perjurers.
He said; and slew the boar, cutting its throat.
Talthybius cast it whirling in the sea.
And now Achilles, rising, thus began:
Oh, Jove, 'tis thou that sendest woes on men,
For Agamemnon could not have aroused
My wrath so much, nor robbed me of my girl,
If Jove had not designed that death should be
The portion of so many of the Greeks.

But now partake of food, and after that
We will march forth and battle with the foe.
He said; and hastily dispersed the throng,
Each going to his ship. The Myrmidons
The presents of Achilles bore away,
To his tent taking them—them and the maids;
The horses to the stables next they led.
But when Briseis Patroclus beheld
Stretched dead and mangled with the cruel spear,
Weeping, she threw herself upon the corpse
And tore her lovely face and wept aloud.
Oh, Patroclus, she said, most dear to me!
I left thee, noble chief, alive and well;
But now, on my return, I find thee dead.
To wretched me, how woe succeeds to woe!
The hero whom my parents chose for me
I saw before the city pierced with wounds,
And three dear brothers too I saw dispatched
Upon that dreadful and unhappy day.
But thou my flowing tears didst wipe away
When my betrothed was by Achilles slain
And Myro's sacred city was destroyed.
Thou saidst I should become the victor's wife,
And that thou wouldst escort me to my home,
And there prepare for me a nuptial feast;
Therefore I greatly sorrow at thy death,
So gentle wert thou ever and so kind.
Thus spake she; and the other women too
Joined in her grief and wept for Patroclus:
Yet 'twas for their own woes they really mourned.
Around Achilles gathered all the chiefs,
Begging the hero to partake of food;
But he refused, and, moaning deeply, said:
I beg you, my beloved comrades, not
To ask me to partake of food or drink,
Since such a load of grief oppresses me;
But till the setting sun I will refrain.
So saying, he the other chiefs dismissed;

But the two sons of Atreus remained,
And Nestor and Ulysses the renowned,
And Phœnix, the old knight, and Idomeneus:
Their sorrowing comrade they all tried to soothe;
But he would not be soothed until he rushed
Into the dreadful scenes of bloody war;
But his dead friend remembering, thus he spake:
Surely, unhappy one, thou too wouldst once
A plenteous banquet have prepared for me
When we against the Trojans sallied forth.
Now thou liest mangled, and I take no food
Out of regret for thee, though pressed to take.
No greater woe than this could be my lot,
Not e'en should I hear of Peleus' death,
My aged sire, who perhaps now weeps
In Phthia at the absence of his son,
Whilst I, far off, against the Trojans fight
For cursed Helen, cause of all our woes,
And godlike Neoptolemus, my son,
May too be dead. I hoped that I alone
Should die at Troy, expecting thou, my friend,
Would lead my darling boy back to his home,
Show him my wealth, my high-domed palaces,
And throngs of slaves. But Peleus, I suppose,
Is either dead or barely is alive,
Worn out with sorrow and extreme old age,
Expecting of my death each day to hear.
Thus he spake, weeping; and the chiefs all groaned,
Remembering, too, their absent families.
Jove saw and felt compassion at the sight,
And his dear child Minerva thus addressed:
My daughter, thou thy chief deserted hast—
Dost thou no longer for Achilles care?
Mourning his friend, he sits beside his ships,
Whilst all the others to a feast repair,
But he alone is unrefreshed and fasts.
Go, then, and nectar in his breast instill
And exquisite ambrosia, lest he faint.

So saying, he the willing goddess urged.
She, like a broad-winged harpy, darted down
From lofty heaven, flying through the air;
And, whilst the Greeks were arming for the fight,
She luscious nectar to the hero gave
And food ambrosial, that he might not faint;
And to her sire's mansions then returned,
As the vast host was marching to the field.
And as when snow-flakes in the winter-time
Fall drifting thick before the northern blast,
So from the vessels crowded helmets poured,
And shields, and massy corselets, and stout spears;
Their dazzling light reached to the very sky,
And the earth smiled beneath the splendid brass,
As the loud tramping of their feet was heard.
Noble Achilles in the midst was seen.
He gnashed his teeth, and from his eyes flashed fire;
Anger and grief within his bosom burned
As he with Vulcan's presents armed himself.
First on his legs his handsome greaves he placed;
His corselet then upon his breast he clasped,
And from his shoulders slung his glittering sword.
Then his great shield he seized, the light of which
Darted afar, bright as the full-orbed moon.
And as to mariners a blazing fire
Shines on a rock-bound coast, whilst they are driven
By adverse winds far out into the sea,
So from Achilles' splendid shield the light
Reached to the sky. Then on his head he set
His massy helmet, crested with horse-hair;
It glittered like a star, with golden tufts
Which nodded ever as the hero moved.
Thus did he try his arms if they would fit,—
Like wings they proved, and almost bore him up.
Last from its case his father's spear he drew,
Mighty and stout; no Greek could brandish it
Save he alone. A Pelion ash it was,
Which Chiron cut upon Mount Pelion,

And to his sire gave; it had been the death
Of many heroes, and was yet to be.
 Then by Automedon and Alcimus
The steeds were yoked; and rich the collars were;
The bridles were arranged, and quickly then
Seizing the shining lash, Automedon
Leaped on the car; Achilles mounted too—
Mounted behind him, like the dazzling sun;
And his fleet steeds thus terribly addressed:
 Xanthus and Balius, of illustrious race,
Podargè's offspring! mind and carry back
Your driver in a different plight from what
Ye did before, when ye left Patroclus,
Mangled and dead, upon the battle-field.
 But Xanthus, his swift steed, thus made reply—
Hanging his head and mane down to the ground—
For fair-armed Juno gave him power to speak:
 Impetuous Achilles, we this day
At least will bear thee safe; but thy career
Is nearly finished. Nor are we to blame,
But Destiny and some Immortal power.
For 'twas not by our carelessness or sloth
That Patroclus lay stretched upon the field;
But 'twas Apollo's hand that laid him low,
And to Troy's champion the glory gave.
And though we can as swift as Zephyrus run,
Yet 'tis thy fate shortly to be subdued –
Struck down by Heaven and some mortal hand.
 He ceased; the Furies cutting short his voice.
And thus the chief indignantly replied:
 How durst thou, Xanthus, thus predict my death?
Thy words uncalled for are, and out of place!
I know myself I'm doomed to perish here,
Far from my kindred, and my native land;
Yet still I will not cease until I give
Our haughty foes more than they want of war.
 He said; and shouting, 'mid the foremost ranks
Drove his swift steeds into the thickest fight.

BOOK XX.

THE BATTLE OF THE GODS.

ARGUMENT.

Jupiter calls a council of the gods, and allows them to mingle in the fight and assist either party.—The battle of the gods described; Æneas encounters Achilles, and is by Neptune's assistance preserved; Achilles next meets Hector, and is on the point of killing him, but he is protected by Apollo, who conveys him away in a cloud.

Thus around thee, Achilles, near the ships,
The Greeks were marshaled, eager for the fight,
Whilst their foes gathered on the sloping plain.
Then Jove bade Themis summon all the gods
To an assembly. Round the goddess went,
And to Jove's palace told them to repair;
Nor of the rivers was there absent one
Save Oceanus; and the nymphs were there,
Inhabiters of pleasant groves and springs,
And flowery meads; all took their seats upon
The polished benches by lame Vulcan made;
Neptune came too, emerging from the sea,
And thus of Jove inquired his design:
  Why, lightning-flasher, hast thou bade the gods
To meet in council? dost thou meditate
Something about the Trojans and the Greeks?
For now to arms both parties rush again.
  He said; and thus cloud-driving Jove replied:

Thou knowest thyself, oh, Neptune, my design:
These men, though mortal, are a care to me;
Yet on Olympus' top I will remain,
And gaze delighted on the scene below.
But go ye all and aid which side ye please,
For if Achilles fights the men of Troy,
Short will the contest be; the sight of him
Has terrified before and made them flee;
But now enraged at his dear comrade's death,
I fear, lest contrary to fate, he may
Capture proud Troy before her time has come.
  Thus spake the Thunderer, stirring up the strife,
And the discordant gods to battle rushed.
Juno and Pallas to the fleet repaired,
And Neptune, and ingenious Mercury,
And Vulcan, savage-looking, limped along;
But to the Trojan side went fiery Mars,
Beardless Apollo, and Diana, famed
For skill in archery; Latona, too,
And Xanthus, and the smiling Queen of love.
  Whilst the gods kept aloof the Greeks rejoiced,
Because Achilles on the field was seen,
And fear and trembling on the Trojans fell.
But when the immortals entered on the field,
Then horrid Strife began; Minerva then
Shouted aloud, now standing by the trench,
And stalking now along the echoing shore;
Mars like a whirlwind yelled from lofty Troy,
Running at times along the Simois' banks,
Or o'er the top of Callicolon's hill:
Thus the gods urged the dreadful battle on.
Terribly thundered mighty Jove on high,
Neptune beneath shook the entire earth,
The mountains quaked, Ida, and lofty Troy,
And the Greek fleet. Pluto, the king of hell,
Leaped from his throne, and, terror-struck, cried out,
Fearing the earth would open and disclose
The horrid secrets of his dark domain,

Revolting scenes e'en dreadful to the gods :—
Such was the din when the celestials fought.
  Apollo to king Neptune was opposed,
Mars to Minerva, and queen Juno went
Against Diana, famed for archery;
Latona Mercury met, and Vulcan
To the deep river Xanthus was opposed ;
Thus battled gods with gods. But Achilles
Longed to meet Hector and to spill his blood.
  Meanwhile the archer-god Æneas roused
Against Achilles, and endued with might;
Lycaon's form he took, old Priam's son,
And thus the Trojan warrior addressed:
Where are the threats, Æneas, which thou mad'st
'Mid thy carousings, promising that thou
Wouldst fight alone with Greece's champion?
  He said; and thus the Trojan chief replied :
Why dost thou, son of Priam, bid me go
Against my will, and with Achilles fight?
To him I have already been opposed
When he attacked our flocks, and with his spear
Chased me from Ida, laying waste the towns
Lyrnessa and Pedasus; but great Jove
Preserved me, strengthening my nimble limbs;
If not for that I surely had been slain,
For Pallas helped and gave him victory;
Therefore no man against this chief can stand,
Since by his side a goddess always goes;
Besides, his aim is sure and never fails.
Yet should some deity give aid to me,
He would not quite so easily prevail.
  Thus spake the chief, and thus the god replied:
But do thou too, oh, hero, boldly pray
To the immortals, for 'tis said that thou
Art son to Venus, daughter of great Jove,
But he to some inferior deity.
From mighty Jove thy mother sprang, and his

From an old sea-god. Rush then upon him,
Nor by his haughty language be deterred.
Thus saying, to the chief great strength he gave;
Clad in bright brass he to the front advanced.
Juno perceived him and the gods addressed:
Think, Neptune and Minerva, how things stand,
Æneas has advanced against our chief;
Apollo aids him, let us drive him back,
Or let one of us assist Achilles,
And let him know the mightiest of the gods
Are on his side, whilst for the Trojan cause
The weakest and the vainest are employed
'Twas for this purpose we this day came down
From high Olympus,—what his end may be
The future will reveal, as fate decrees.
But now when he perceives that we befriend
He will not fear, else an opposing god
Will surely terrify Achilles e'en.
She said; and thus earth-shaking Neptune spake
Juno, no need there is to be enraged;
Let us sit down and watch the coming fight.
But should Apollo or impetuous Mars
Oppose Achilles, then may we take part;
Nor will the issue long remain in doubt,
For back to heaven these baffled deities
Will be right glad to speedily return.
Thus having said, king Neptune led the way
To Hercules' high wall, which Pallas made,
She and the Trojans, for that demi-god
When the sea-monster he escaped by flight,
Which chased him from the ocean to the plain.
In a dark cloud involved, there they sat down,
Whilst around thee, Apollo, and fierce Mars,
The others sat on Callicolon's hill.
Thus quiet they remained, yet scheming much,
And each unwilling to commence the fight.
Jove sat aloft meanwhile and cheered them on.
But the whole plain was filled with steeds and men,

Their brazen armor glittering in the sun—
The solid earth echoed beneath their tramp;
Two men conspicuous were and rushed in front,
God-like Achilles and Anchises' son;
And first Æneas, threatening, advanced,
His helmet nodding as he proudly moved—
His shield he grasped and shook his brazen spear.
  Achilles on the other side rushed on
Like a fierce lion against whom a throng,
E'en a whole village, go, eager to kill,
Yet he stalks on regardless of his foes.
But when he has been wounded by a dart,
With mouth wide open he prepares to spring;
He growls and foams with rage, lashing his tail,
Rousing himself to fight; grimly he glares,
And leaping recklessly among the crowd,
Slays his opponents or himself is slain.
  Thus the invincible Achilles rushed
Upon the illustrious warrior Æneas.
When they had nigh to one another come,
He first the Trojan hero thus addressed:
  Why steppest thou forth, Æneas, to the front?
Wilt thou contend with me in the vain hope
That thou wilt make thyself the king of Troy?
Yet shouldst thou slay me, Priam still will reign,
For he is firm and steady, and has sons
Or have the Trojans promised thee rich lands,
For vineyards suitable and golden grain?
Thy task thou wilt not easily effect.
Methinks I chased thee from the field before.
Hast thou forgotten how I drove thee once
From thine own oxen, causing thee to flee
With rapid steps down the Idean mount?
Nor didst thou once look back 'till thou escaped
Into Lyrnessa, which I captured too,
Assisted by Minerva and great Jove.
Many fair dames I also captive led;
Nor will the gods, I think, protect thee now.

Then take my warning words and draw thee back,
Else thou mayest perish ere thou art aware,
For fools the truth discover when too late.
He said; and thus the Trojan answered him:
Think not, Achilles, to affright me thus
With empty words, as if I were a boy.
I, if I chose, could utter threats myself.
We know each other's race—our parents know—
Know them of old, as common rumor speaks,
Though thine I never saw, nor thou sawest mine.
They say thou art from famous Peleus sprung,
Thy mother Thetis, a fair sea-nymph she;
But I my birth from great Anchises boast—
Venus my mother is; of these the one
Or other shall this day have cause to mourn,
For not in childish words this thing shall end.
But of my lineage, if thou wish to learn,
Know that Dardanus was by Jove begot,—
Dardania he built, for sacred Troy
Existed not; round Ida's base they dwelt;
Rich Erichthonius from Dardanus sprang,
The wealthiest mortal he that lived on earth.
Three thousand mares, each with a foal, he owned;
With some of these Boreas, as they fed
Upon the verdant marsh, enamored was,
And covered them in likeness of a steed.
These being pregnant brought forth twelve she-foals:
So swift of foot they were that they could run
Over the top of a ripe field of grain,
Nor break the stalks, and skim the crested waves
Of the blue sea. From Erichthonius
Tros descended, monarch of lofty Troy.
Tros was the sire of three illustrious sons—
Ilus, Assaracus, and Ganymede,
Who was the handsomest of mortal men;
He for his beauty was snatched up to heaven,
And made Jove's cupbearer; Ilus begat
Renowned Laomedon, who was the sire

Of Priam, Tithonus, and Lampus,—
Of Clytius, and bold Hicetaon.
Capys was offspring of Assaracus,
And he the father of Anchises was;
His son I am: but noble Hector
Was old Priam's son. Such is my race and blood.
But Jove gives valor as he wills to men,
For he almighty is, and rules o'er all.
But come, no more of these things let us talk
Like little boys; for we could both revile
And utter e'en a ship-load of abuse,
For mortal language very copious is;
Vast choice of words men have at their command,
Yet what we speak that we are apt to hear.
Then why should you and I dispute and rail,
Like angry women in a public street,
Who truth and falsehood utter as they please?
No words of thine will turn me from my course;
Come quickly, then, and let the fight begin.
He said; and hurled his brazen spear and struck
His dreadful shield, which echoed with the blow;
Achilles, fearful, held his buckler off,
That the sharp weapon might not penetrate.
Foolish! he never once reflected that
Heaven's glorious gifts may be relied upon.
The Trojan's glittering lance went through two folds,
But the gold stopped it; for king Vulcan made
Five coverings to the shield: two were of brass,
Two tin, and one of gold, which stopped the spear.
Achilles then his weapon hurled, and struck
Æneas' shield upon the outside rim,
Where it was thinnest; through and through it went—
Æneas crouched; the lance passed o'er his back,
Striking the earth, still eager to fly on.
The chief stood still—with terror struck, because
The dreadful weapon had so near him come:
But the bold Greek sprang on him with his sword,
Shouting aloud; Æneas seized a stone,

Which two men could not lift, as men are now.
Then had he forward rushed and lost his life
In the close fight, had not king Neptune seen,
And thus in haste addressed the immortal gods:
Ye gods, I pity for Æneas feel,
Who by Achilles quickly will be slain;
Nor can Apollo save him from his doom.
Why should this guiltless man thus suffer woes
Brought on by others? He has ever been
Pious, and offers costly gifts to Heaven.
Come, let us save him, then, lest Jove be wroth
Should such an unoffending man be slain.
He from Dardanus sprung, and that loved race,
It is decreed, shall ne'er become extinct;
For Priam's race is hateful to great Jove,
And this Æneas must o'er Trojans rule.
Thus spake he; and the queen of heaven replied:
Do with Æneas as thou wilt, but I
And Pallas have declared with solemn oath
That we the Trojans never will assist;
Not e'en when Troy in hostile flames is wrapped,
Fired by the warlike and victorious Greeks.
Hearing these words, king Neptune started forth,
Traversed the field of battle, and drew near
To where Æneas and Achilles were.
Over Achilles' eyes darkness he threw;
Took up his spear, and laid it at his feet.
Æneas then he pushed, lifting him up,
And brought him to the rear, where stood arrayed
The Caucans; then the chief he thus addressed:
Which of the gods, Æneas, bade thee thus
To fight Achilles? mad was such attempt!
For he is dearer to the gods than thou,
And braver too; confront him not, lest thou,
E'en contrary to fate, may'st meet thy doom.
But when he falls, then boldly fight in front,
For by no other Greek shalt thou be slain.
He said; and left him. Then from Achilles

Lifted the cloud; clearly the hero saw,
And, deeply grieving, with himself communed:
Ye gods, a mighty marvel I behold!
Here is my spear now lying at my feet;
Nor do I see the man I hurled it at.
Surely Æneas, too, is dear to Heaven,
Though I supposed his words were idle boasts.
But let him go; he will not like again
To cope with me; too glad already he
To have escaped from my relentless spear.
But come, my warriors I will first cheer on,
And then against some other Trojans go.
He said; and, springing forward, cheered his men:
Ye noble Greeks, rush on, and hang not back!
But let each warrior single out his man;
Brave as I am, 'tis hard for me to fight
With a whole host; not even Mars himself
Could such tremendous odds as this sustain.
Yet I nor strength, nor hands, nor feet will spare,
But will rush on into the thickest ranks,
And woe to him who near my weapon comes!
Thus spake the chief; and on the other side,
Illustrious Hector thus his men addressed:
Ye Trojans, of Achilles have no fear,
I, too, could fight with words, e'en with the gods;
But to contend with deeds is harder far.
Nor shall Achilles' words be all fulfilled;
Against him I will go, although his hands
Were like to fire, and his strength as brass.
Thus he encouraged. On his warriors rushed:
Great was the conflict, loud the clamor was.
Then to bold Hector thus Apollo spake:
Hector, keep thou away from this great chief,
And let him mingle in the thickest throng,
Lest with his sword or spear he take thy life.
He said; and Hector, startled at his voice,
Drew back, nor ventured further to the front.
Achilles then among the Trojans leaped

With dreadful shouts; and first the hero slew
Gallant Iphytion, Otrynteus' son,
Ruler o'er many people, whom the nymph
Naïs brought forth, by snowy Tmolus' mount;
Sacker of cities Otrynteus was.
Him with his javelin in the head he struck
And split in two; crashing, the warrior fell,
And thus Achilles boasted over him:
   Gallant Iphytion, terriblest of men,
Now thou hast fallen, death is on thee here;
Thy birth and home was by the Gygaen lake,
By Hermus' eddying waves, and Hyllius' stream.
Thus he spake boasting, as the hero died.
The chariots and horses of the Greeks
Tore his dead body as in front it lay.
   Antenor's son Achilles next dispatched,
Demoleon called; a famous warrior he;
Him in his temples through his casque he pierced,
Breaking the bone, and smashing all his brains.
   Next Hippodamas in the back he struck,
As from his chariot he leaped to flee;
He breathed his last, groaning, as when a bull
To Neptune's altar by stout youths is dragged.
   Then with his spear at Polydore he went,
The youngest son of Priam, whom his sire
Did not permit to fight, being too young;
His father's favorite he, and famed for speed;
Through youthful folly, and to show himself,
He ran along the front and lost his life.
Him in the back valiant Achilles smote,
Where his belt's golden clasp and corselet met;
Out at his navel came the pointed spear.
Uttering a groan, he fell upon his knees,
Holding his gushing bowels in his hands.
   When Hector saw his brother Polydore
Thus rolling on the earth in agony,
He was no longer master of himself,
But like a flame upon Achilles rushed;

Who, when he saw him, boastingly cried out:
Here is the man who most has stung my soul,
Taking the life of my most valued friend;
Let us draw near and battle hand to hand.
  But not dismayed, plumed Hector thus replied:
Oh, son of Peleus! think not me to fright
With threatening words, as if I were a boy;
I could rail too, if such my pleasure was.
I know, indeed, thou braver art than I,
Yet the immortal deities have power
To give the victory to whom they please.
  He spake; and, aiming, hurled his glittering spear;
Minerva, gently breathing, tossed it back,
And before Hector's feet the weapon fell.
  Achilles, shouting dreadfully, advanced,
But he was by Apollo borne away
In a thick cloud; thrice rushed the warrior on,
And with his spear thrice smote the hazy cloud;
But when with superhuman power he made
A fourth attempt, he fiercely thus cried out:
  Vile dog! thou hast escaped thy death again;
Apollo saved thee, whom thou prayest to
Whene'er thou steppest forth to meet the foe.
Yet with the help of some one of the gods,
I will hereafter meet and finish thee.
At present after others I will go.
  So saying, Dryops on the neck he struck;
The warrior fell and at his feet expired.
  Him then he left, and smote Philetor's son,
Demuchus, whom he struck upon the knee.
And then dispatched him with his mighty sword.
  Laogonus and Dardanus next he pushed
Out of their chariot, and slew them both.
  Then Tros, Alastor's son, he also smote,
Who towards him came, and took him by the knees,
Begging for Heaven's sake to spare his life;
For they were both of equal age, he said.
Fool that he was, to think he could persuade!

For his stern heart for pity was not made.
Swift through his liver went his glittering sword;
A flood of gore poured from the ghastly wound,
And death's dark shades forever closed his eyes.
  Next Mulius in the ear Achilles smote,
Piercing him even to the other ear.
  Then Echeclus with his mighty sword he struck,
And cleft his skull, bathing his sword in blood.
  Deucalion also through the hand he pierced:
With arm dropped down he saw his end draw near;
Then through his neck he smote him with his sword,
Knocking his head and helmet far away:
His marrow from the severed spine sprang forth.
  Then towards Rhigmus, Pireus' famous son,
Who came from fertile Thrace, the hero rushed.
Him in the stomach with his spear he pierced,
Which in his bowels stuck; down to the earth
The dying Trojan fell; whilst in his back
Areithous, his charioteer, he struck,
Just as he was about to turn his steeds.
The faithful man was from his chariot hurled,
And his scared horses in confusion thrown.
  As when a blazing fire burns through the dells
Of a dry mountain, forests are consumed;
And driven by fierce winds the whirling flames,
Leaping about, in all directions turn:
So he on all sides like some deity
Swiftly pursued, destroying as he went.
And as when oxen on a threshing-floor
Trample white barley underneath their feet,
So, by Achilles driven, the fiery steeds
Trod over corpses, over spears and shields.
The axle-tree beneath was red with blood,
And the whole chariot's rim spattered about
By the swift wheels and by the horses' hoofs,
So eager after glory was the chief,
His hands invincible all stained with gore.

BOOK XXI.

THE RIVER FIGHT.

ARGUMENT.

The Trojans fly before Achilles, some to the town and others to the river Scamander.—He takes twelve captives, and slays Lycaon.—Neptune and Minerva assist the hero; the rivers Scamander and Simois fight against him; Vulcan opposes the rivers, almost drying them up with his flames.—The gods then battle with each other; by Apollo's contrivance, the Trojans escape within the walls of Troy.

But when at length they reached the lovely shores
Of eddying Xanthus, stream by Jove begat,
Dividing there, the fugitives he chased,
One portion to the city o'er the plain
Where on the day before the Greeks had fled
From Hector and his devastating spear,
With a dense cloud Juno their progress checked.
The other portion in the river plunged:
Great was the splash, loud rang the echoing banks
With noise and clamor; there the Trojans swam,
The silvery eddies whirling them around,
As swarms of locusts driven by the fire
Fly in the air to reach some friendly stream
And terror-stricken in the water fall.
Thus by Achilles Xanthus was filled up
With a promiscuous heap of steeds and men:
The hero left his spear upon the bank
Leaning against a tamarisk; then leaped,

Leaped like a god, with nothing but his sword,
Into the stream, bent on atrocious deeds,
Destroying right and left. Sad groans arose,
And the pure crystal tide grew red with blood.
As from a dolphin frightened fishes fly
Into a harbor for a safe retreat,
Yet he pursues them, slaughtering all he takes:
So in the caves along the river shore
The Trojans hid, and sought to save themselves.
But as he weary of the carnage grew,
Twelve youths he took alive, a penalty
For his dead friend and comrade Patroclus;
These, stupefied, he seized, and led them out
Like timid fawns, their hands behind them bound
With their own straps, and sent them to the fleet.
But he rushed on again, eager to slay.
Then Priam's son, Lycaon, he espied
Escaping from the stream, whom he had once
A captive taken from his father's farm
Whilst he was busy at a chariot wheel,
Which from a fig-tree he was cutting out;
Then 'twas he seized him and to Lemnos sent,
Selling to Jason, who resided there.
His guest, Ætion, ransomed him again,
To great Arisbè sending, whence he fled
And safely reached his father's home at last.
Eleven days he there enjoyed himself,
But on the twelfth the deity again
Placed in Achilles' hands the unhappy youth
Whose fate it was, though most unwillingly,
To take his journey now to Pluto's realms.
When the Greek chief beheld his helpless foe
Flying, and overcome with toil and heat,
His helmet and his weapons cast away,
Thus to himself indignantly he spake:
Good heavens! what wondrous sight do I behold!
Truly the Trojan warriors I have slain
May come to life, as this man now returns,

Who as a slave to Lemnos' isle was sent,
Nor could the boundless sea confine him there.
But come, he now shall taste my ruthless spear,
And I will see if he gets back again
When to his mother earth he is consigned.
Thus spake the chief, still standing where he was.
  Meanwhile Lycaon, terror-struck, drew near,
Anxious to clasp his knees, for much he wished
To shun his doom and save his precious life.
His spear Achilles raised, prepared to strike,
But he stooped down, ran under it, and seized
The warrior's knees. Over his back it flew,
Thirsting for blood, and stuck into the earth.
The suppliant with one hand the hero held,
And with the other firmly grasped the spear,
And thus in piteous tones addressed the chief:
  Thus on my knees, Achilles, I entreat
Have pity on me and regard my prayer:
With thee, Jove-nurtured one, I have broke bread:
'Twas on the day when, on my father's farm,
Thou took'st me prisoner and to Lemnos sent;
A hundred oxen's price I brought thee then,—
Now for my life that price I thrice will pay.
Twelve days it is since I returned to Troy,
After much suffering, and now sad fate
Has placed me helpless in thy hands again;
Surely great Jove some grudge against me bears.
My mother, Laothoë, was Altè's child,
Who rules the warlike Leleges, and dwells
In lofty Pedasus, on Satnio's stream;
My mother Priam married, and she bore
My brother, godlike Polydore, and me.
Him thou hast slain already, and will now
Slay me, since so it seems that Jove decrees;
Yet I a thing will tell thee—ponder it:
Though Priam was my sire, I was not born
Of the same womb with Hector, he who slew
Thy comrade Patroclus, gentle and brave.

Thus to his conqueror the suppliant spake,
But in return received a stern reply:
Talk not to me of ransom, fool, nor name
The word. Ere Patroclus was slain I oft
Relented towards my foes and saved their lives;
But not a Trojan now I mean to spare,
And Priam's hated sons the least of all;
So die, my friend, thou must;—why dost thou weep?
A better man than thou was Patroclus,
Yet he is dead. Seest thou how tall I am—
How tall and fair; a goddess brought me forth,
And by a noble sire I was begot.
But death, relentless death, awaits us both,
Whether at morn or evening or mid-day.
He said; the other heard and lost all hope,
Let go the spear, and stretched out both his arms.
With his sharp sword Achilles struck his neck—
The blood flowed forth and to the earth he fell;
Then by his foot he seized, and in the stream
Threw the dead Trojan, and thus boasting, spake:
Lie with the fishes there, which, unconcerned,
Will lap the blood that oozes from thy wound;
Nor shall thy weeping mother bury thee,
But on Scamander's waves thou shalt be borne
To the dark bosom of the boundless sea.
Up to the surface hungry fish will leap
To nibble the white fat about thy loins.
So fare ye all till sacred Troy is ours;
Nor shall your eddying river ye avail,
To which ye many bulls have offered up
And noble steeds. Atonement must be made
For slaughtered Greeks and Patroclus' sad death.
He said; and much the river was enraged,
Thinking how best to stop the chief's career
And save the Trojans from their coming doom.
Meanwhile the hero with his mighty spear
On Asteropeus rushed, from Axius sprung,
And son of Pelagon and Peribæa;

He, from the river stepping, held two spears;
Xanthus had strengthened him, enraged because
Achilles in the stream such carnage made.
As they drew near the latter thus began:
Who and whence art thou, daring thus to come
Opposed to me? Unhappy men are they
Who venture to encounter me in fight.
To him the son of Pelagon replied:
Why, son of Peleus, dost thou ask my race?
I come from rich Pæonia's distant lands,
O'er the Pæonian heroes bearing rule;
Eleven days ago I came to Troy.
To flowing Axius my descent I trace,—
Axius the loveliest river on the earth,—
He Pelagon begat, my honored sire:
But now, Achilles, let us battle join.
He said; and great Achilles hurled his spear;
The other hurled both lances at one time,
For he left-handed was, and struck the shield
Of the Greek hero; but his spear was stopped,
For the gold buckler was a heavenly gift;
His other weapon smote him on the arm,
Then stuck into the earth; the blood gushed out.
Next in his turn Achilles hurled his spear,
But missed his aim; it stuck into the bank,
Up to the middle, with such force it flew;
Then on his foe with his drawn sword he rushed.
The Trojan thrice attempted, but thrice failed,
To pluck the weapon out, then tried to snap;
But now Achilles took away his life,
Smiting him in the belly; forthwith gushed
His bowels out, and sinking down he died.
The victor now despoiled him of his arms,
And leaping on his breast, exulting spake:
Lie so! 'tis difficult for thee, I think,
Though from a river sprung, to cope with me,
Whose lineage from a higher source is traced,
For from Saturnian Jove my race I boast.

Peleus, the ruler of the Myrmidons,
My sire was, the son of Æacus,—
Of famous Æacus, who sprang from Jove,
And Jove is mightier than the rivers are.
Besides, a river here is close at hand;
Let it defend thee if it has the power,
But it knows better than to fight with Jove;
Great Achelöus with him could not contend,
Nor Oceanus, with his mighty strength,
From which flow all the rivers, and wide seas,
And fountains, and deep wells; yet even he
Trembles beneath the thunder-bolts of Jove.
He said; and from the bank plucked out his spear,
And left his victim floating on the sand,
With eels and fishes nibbling around.
Meanwhile the victor hastened to pursue
The warriors of Pæonia, who fled
When they perceived their valiant leader slain.
Then he slew Thrasius, and Ænius,
And Ophilestes, and Thersilocus,
Mydon, and Mnesus, and Astypyles;
And many more he would have soon dispatched
Had not the eddying river grew enraged,
And a man's voice assuming, from its depths
Thus in indignant tones the chief addressed:
True, oh, Achilles! thou excellest in strength,
Helped by the gods; yet dost unworthy deeds.
If 'tis thy lot the Trojans to destroy,
Drive them from me and slay them on the plain;
My pleasant stream is with dead bodies filled,
Nor can I pour my waves into the sea;
And yet without remorse thou slayest still.
But cease; a stupor seizes me—oh, cease!
He said; and thus the warrior answer made:
Scamander, with thy wish I will comply;
Yet I must slaughter still these perjured men,
Nor cease 'till, chased within their city walls,
Hector I meet, and trial make of him.

Thus saying, like a god he still rushed on;
And to Apollo thus the river spake:
  Alas! thou archer-god and child of Jove,
Thou with thy sire's wish hast not complied,
Who bade thee to assist the Trojans till
The sun should set, and evening's shades prevail.
  He said; and from the bank Achilles leaped,
Bent on more carnage; but the stream upheaved,
Swelling its turbid and excited waves.
Like a bull, roaring, he the corpses pushed,—
Pushed them along, and cast them on the shore;
The living he preserved, concealing them
Within his channels and his rocky caves.
The angry flood around Achilles raged,
Dashed on his buckler, and oppressed him so
That on his feet the chief could scarcely stand;
Then with his hands a branching elm he seized,
Falling, it tore away the entire bank,
And bridged the whirling stream from shore to shore;
Then from the gulf the warrrior leaped out,
And, struck with terror, hurried o'er the plain.
  Nor did the god desist; but followed him,
Blackening the surface of the ground, that so
He might Achilles thwart, and favor Troy.
The chief sprang backward, far as a spear's throw,
Impetuous as an eagle, king of birds;
And as a ditcher leading down a stream
From a deep spring, through gardens and through fields,
With spade in hand, all obstacles removes,—
The pebbles roll before the swelling tide,
And it descends outstripping e'en the man:
So the dark river overtook the chief,
Swift as he was; so potent are the gods.
Oft as Achilles tried to baffle it,
So often o'er his shoulders came a wave;
Then sad, he forward sprang, and then the stream
Would wash the sand away beneath his feet.
The warrior groaned, and thus to Heaven prayed:

Oh, Jove! will none of all the gods assist?
Send on me any misery but this!
But of the deities I chiefly blame
My mother, who deceived me with false hopes—
Saying, that by Apollo I should fall,
Beneath the lofty walls of sacred Troy.
Would that by Hector I had been dispatched!
Then would a hero have a hero slain.
But now 'tis mine to die a shameful death—
Drowned in a river like a swine-herd boy
During a freshet in the winter-time,
Who as he fords a stream is swept away.
He said; and Neptune and Minerva went,
In shape of men, and seized the hero's hand;
And thus the sea-king, cheering him, addressed:
Oh, son of Peleus, dismiss all fear,
We are thy allies, and have Jove's consent,
Nor by a river shalt thou be o'ercome,
It soon shall cease to plague, as thou shalt see;
But be courageous thou, and battle still,
And drive the Trojan host within the town;
Then, having Hector slain, in triumph come
Back to thy fleet, for so the gods decree.
Thus having spoke, they left and went to heaven.
He, strengthened, now proceeded towards the plain,
Which by the swelling river was o'erwhelmed;
Corpses of warriors slain were floating there,
And handsome armor. But the chief moved on,
Endowed with heavenly fortitude and strength.
Scamander from his purpose ne'er relaxed,
But at the warrior was more enraged;
He swelled his waves, and thus to Simois called—
Simois his brother stream, that near him flowed:
Dear brother, let us both restrain this man,
Who quickly will destroy great Priam's town;
Nor can the Trojans cope with him in fight.
Come, then, fill all thy fountains to the brim
And swell thy rivulets, and raise a wave,

Stirring up stumps of trees and stems and stones,
That we may check this mad, impetuous chief,
Who aims at deeds of supernatural power;
Yet will his strength, nor beauty, nor firm arms
Avail him aught when he shall lie submerged
Within my channel covered up with mud.
Abundant sand I will pour o'er him too,
So that the Greeks shall never find his bones;
There shall this haughty warrior have his tomb,
And tomb enough indeed it sure will be.
He said; and raging with his turbid flood,
Murmuring with foam, with corpses and with blood,
Rushed upon Peleus' son, arresting him.
Then Juno cried aloud, fearing the Greek
Would by the eddying stream be swept away,
And thus to Vulcan, her dear son, began:
Arise, my son! we thought that Xanthus was
Held in due check, and matched enough by thee.
Aid with all haste, and kindle up thy flames:
Meanwhile I will a furious blast of wind
Raise from the sea, and cause so great a fire
That Trojans and their arms shall be consumed.
Do thou burn up the trees upon the shore,
And on the stream itself hurl thy fierce flames;
Nor be restrained by threats, or friendly words;
Nor cease from fight till I the signal give.
She said; and Vulcan darted forth his fire:
First on Scamander's plain he kindled it,
Burning the many corpses o'er it strewed;
The flood was stayed, and the whole surface dried,
As when the north wind a moist garden dries,
Which now the joyful gardener can till.
Then on the stream his dazzling flames he turned.
The elms, the willows, and the shrubs were burned—
The lotus, too, the rushes, and the reeds,
Which on the lovely banks abundant grew;
The slimy eels and fishes were harassed,
And through the whirling flood dived here and there.
The river was exhausted, and thus spake:

Who can withstand thee, Vulcan, and thy fire?
Cease from this contest, and Achilles may
Drive, if he please, these Trojans from their town.
Why should I meddle with the fight at all?
Thus the scorched river spake; his waters boiled
As fat within a pot boils o'er the fire;
The rising steam oppressed him and restrained,
And thus to Juno he addressed his prayer:
Why does thy son, oh, Juno, plague me thus?
I am no more to blame than all the rest,
Who to the Trojans have assistance given.
But now I will desist if 'tis thy will,
And let him cease; I promise solemnly
That I henceforth no aid will give to Troy,
E'en should the Greeks consume the town with fire.
He said; and Juno heard and straightway spake:
Abstain, my noble son; it is not fit
That, for the sake of men, a deity
Should be tormented thus. Vulcan obeyed,
Lowering his flames and putting out his fire,
And the fair stream resumed its former bed.
The river thus subdued, the strife was closed,
And Juno, though enraged, restrained herself;
But with the other gods the fight went on,
As with each party they had taken sides.
Great was the tumult, and the earth and sky
Re-echoed with the clamor that arose;
Jove heard it, sitting on Olympus' heights,
And laughed to see the deities at war.
Then Mars on Pallas rushed, and thus exclaimed:
How durst thou, oh, most impudent! contend
And join in battle with the other gods?
Hast thy great soul impelled thee thus to fight?
Hast thou forgotten how thou urged on me
Illustrious Diomed, Tydeus' son,
Aiming his spear thyself, thou tore my flesh?
Now for thy misdeeds I must punish thee.
He said; and struck her horrible fringed shield,

Which e'en Jove's thunder-bolts will not subdue.
She stooped and seized a rough and heavy stone,
Used from old times as landmark for a field;
With this upon the neck fierce Mars she struck—
Down fell the god, his brazen armor rang;
He covered seven acres as he lay,
And his bright hair was all defiled with dust.
  Minerva laughed, and, boasting o'er him, spake:
Fool, dost thou think thyself a match for me?
Thy mother's furies thou dost expiate,
Who is enraged that thou hast left the Greeks
And to the perjured Trojans givest thy aid.
Thus having spoke, the goddess turned away.
  But Venus took her brother by the hand
And led him, groaning deeply, from the field.
Slowly his spirit and his strength revived.
Juno perceived him and to Pallas spake:
  Oh, child of ægis-bearing Jove, behold!
And see how she, most impudent, again
Leads from the battle-field destructive Mars;
But follow thou. She said; and Pallas rushed,
And, springing on her, smote her on the breast.
She swooned, and both now lay upon the earth,
And, o'er them boasting, thus Minerva spake:
  Would that the allies all of lofty Troy
Would fight like Venus when she succors Mars!
This war had then been o'er, and long ago
Old Priam's city had been overthrown.
She said; and Juno smiled. Then Neptune spake,
And to Apollo thus his challenge gave:
  Why from the contest do we two refrain?
The others have begun, and 'tis a shame
If we without a fight to heaven return.
Commence, for thou art younger far than I;
I as thy elder know far more than thou.
Hast thou forgotten, fool, what we endured
Upon this spot when we in former times
Came to Laomedon and worked for hire

For a whole year? I for the Trojans built
A handsome city and extensive wall,
And thou 'mid Ida's vales their oxen fed.
But when the jocund hours brought round the day
When we our promised pay should have received,
Then were we cheated by that haughty king.
He threatened that he would our ears cut off,
And bind and sell us into distant lands;
Then we came back defrauded and chagrined.
Is it for this that thou dost aid this race?
Why not oppose them, taking sides with us,
And help us to destroy them root and branch?
He said; and thus the archer-god replied:
Neptune, thou wouldst thyself pronounce me mad
If I should enter into strife with thee
For miserable mortals, who, like leaves,
Bloom for a little while and then decay.
Let us be wise and neither party join,
But rather let them fight it out themselves.
He said; and turned away, for much he feared
To have a contest with his relative.
But his bold sister, Dian, huntress queen,
Sharply rebuked him, and addressed him thus:
Fliest thou, Apollo! giving up the field
To Neptune, and afraid to use thy bow!
No longer after this I'll hear thee boast
That with the sea-king thou wouldst dare to fight.
She said; but naught the archer-god replied.
Then Juno to the virgin goddess spake,
In bitter language thus addressing her:
How durst thou, wretch! oppose thyself to me?
Although an archeress thou, I am thy match:
A lioness among women sure thou art.
'Tis better for thee rustic stags to slay,
And hunt wild beasts upon the mountain-top,
Than with thy betters vainly to contend.
But if with thy superior thou wouldst strive,
Come on, and make a trial of my strength.

She said; and with her left hand seized her wrists,
And with her right her bow; then, smiling, beat
About her ears the huntress queen, who writhed:
The arrows from her quiver falling out.
Weeping she fled, as from a hawk the dove,
Who flies for shelter to some hollow rock.
Then Mercury Latona thus addressed:
Latona, I will not contend with thee;
We must not combat with the friends of Jove;—
Boast, if thou wilt, that thou hast conquered me.
He said. Meanwhile Latona gathered up
The bow and arrows that had fallen down.
Following her child, she to Olympus came,
For Dian at Jove's palace had arrived.
Weeping and trembling by her sire she sat,
Who, smiling, drew her towards him and thus replied:
Who of the heavenly deities, my child,
Has served thee thus, as if a criminal?
Juno, thy wife, it was, the maid replied,
Who is continually the cause of strife.
Thus they conversed. Meanwhile to sacred Troy
Apollo came, fearing the Greeks that day
The city should destroy before its time;
The other gods to high Olympus went—
Some boasting, others angry and chagrined;
There by their sire, cloud-driving Jove, they sat.
Meanwhile Achilles still the Trojans slew,
Them and their steeds. And as a fire sent
By Heaven in wrath upon some guilty town,
Sorrow and grief dispensing: so the chief
Sorrow and grief dispensed on helpless Troy.
Upon a lofty tower old Priam stood,
Watching Achilles, who, on the plain below,
Sad rout and havoc on the Trojans made.
Groaning, he quick descended from the wall,
And to the guards and city gates repaired.
Wide open throw the gates, he cried, until
The flying people all are safe within;

Achilles close behind is routing them,
And dreadful deeds of carnage I foresee.
Soon as they all are safe within the wall,
Close them again, lest he may enter too.
Unbarring then the gates, they opened them;
Apollo forward leaped to aid his friends,
Who, parched with thirst, and covered o'er with dust,
Came flying o'er the plain towards the town.
Achilles, furious, followed close behind,—
Madness and thirst of glory filled his soul.
Then had proud Troy been captured by the Greeks
Had not Apollo brave Agenor stirred,
Antenor's son; a blameless hero he;
Into his breast the god fresh courage threw,
And stood beside him, as with heavy heart,
Against a beech-tree, spent with toil, he leaned.
When he beheld the raging chief approach,
In doubt he stood, and to himself thus spake:
Ah, me! if from Achilles I attempt to fly,
By the same way these others all pursue,
I surely will be captured and destroyed;
But if I leave the wall, and take the road
That leads to Ida's shady groves and lawns,
There in the river I may bathe myself,
And in the night return refreshed to Troy;
But why stand here indulging such vain thoughts?
Surely he'll see me making for the plain,
And swiftly following, o'ertake and slay.
But what if I should go and meet this chief,
Though Jove his helper is, and honors him?
Yet still they say he's not invulnerable,
But mortal is, like all the rest of men.
So saying, he his courage plucking up,
Awaited till Achilles should draw near,
For with that hero now he burned to fight.
And as a panther from a thicket comes
Against a hunter, nor is put to flight,
Nor aught disturbed by all the shouts it hears;

And e'en though wounded, still persists to fight
'Till it comes off victorious, or is slain:
So bold Agenor, great Antenor's son,
Would not draw back till he Achilles met;
But with his shield before him, aimed his spear,
And loudly shouting, thus his foe addressed:
  Thou think'st, Achilles, this day to take Troy.
Fool! with much blood and toil it must be done,
For many valiant warriors are there,
Who will defend their wives and little ones.
Although a terrible and daring chief,
Thy fate is sealed, and now thou meet'st thy doom.
  He said; and from his hand his weapon hurled,
Striking the warrior just below the knee;
His greaves of tin resounded horribly;
But the lance bounded back, and did no harm,
The armor gift of Heaven prevented it.
The other, then, the Trojan chief attacked,
But by Apollo's aid he was preserved,
Who in a cloud removed him from the field.
Achilles next he cheated, and drew off,
For he the likeness of Agenor took;
And with swift steps the hero followed him,
Chasing him even to Scamander's stream.
  Meanwhile the Trojans gladly reached the walls,
Filling the town; nor dared to stay without,
Nor stopped to ask about the saved or lost,
So eager was each one himself to save.

BOOK XXII.

THE DEATH OF HECTOR.

ARGUMENT.

Hector remains alone outside the walls.—His father and mother beg him to re-enter the town, but are unable to persuade him.—Achilles chases him three times round the city, after which he makes a stand against him and is slain.—The victor ties his victim to his chariot, and drags him over the field, in the sight of his father and mother and wife; their agony and cries at the spectacle are described.

Thus driven to the town like frightened fawns,
They wiped away their sweat, and quenched their thirst,
Leaning against the splendid battlements.
The Greeks meanwhile came up close to the walls,
Their ponderous shields upon their shoulders hung.
But Hector's fatal destiny impelled
To keep him by the gate, outside the town.
Then to Achilles thus Apollo called:
Why, son of Peleus, dost thou chase me thus?
Me a swift god, and thou a mortal man.
Thou hast left caring for thy routed foes,
Who now within the city are inclosed,
And from thy course hast turned to follow me:
Yet canst thou slay me not, for I'm a god.
He said; and thus the angry chief replied:
Much hast thou wronged me, cunning deity,
Drawing me off far from the city walls.
Many a Trojan could I have destroyed

Ere they had found a refuge in the town;
But thou hast saved thy friends, and me hast robbed
Of my due glory. Oh, had I the power,
How would I punish thee for such a wrong!
  He said; and, bent on mighty deeds, returned
Straight to the town, like a victorious steed
Accustomed in the race to win the prize.
  Old Priam first beheld his near approach:
He saw him coming swiftly o'er the plain,
Splendid and shining, like that noted star
Which blazes brightly on autumnal nights,—
Orion's dog by mortals it is called,—
A baleful sign to miserable men;
The sure precursor of oppressive heat:
So shone the glittering armor of the chief.
  The old man groaned, and raised his hands on high,
Smiting his head, and crying to his son,
Who by the Scæan gate still kept his place,
Eager to fight the champion of the Greeks.
Him his old father piteously besought,
And stretching forth his arms, addressed him thus:
  Hector, dear son, oh stay not thus alone!
Nor meet this man, who soon will seal thy doom—
So much superior is he to thee.
Cruel, hard-hearted! did but the gods dislike
As I dislike him, and he soon would be
Devoured by hungry dogs and birds of prey.
Then would this aching heart find some relief;
For he has me deprived of many sons,
Noble and brave, whom he has sold or slain.
And now within the city, safe from harm,
No longer bold Lycaon I behold,
Nor Polydore, my much beloved sons,
Whom Laothoe, queenly dame, brought forth:
Them, if they live, with gold we can redeem,
For aged Altes gave his daughter much;
But if they should be slain, great grief will be
The portion of their mother and of me;

But less will be the misery of us all
If thou, my noble Hector, art but spared.
Haste then, my son, and come within the wall,
And save thy life, and save thy countrymen;
Nor let Achilles triumph o'er thee dead.
Have pity on me, a distressed old man!
Destined myself shortly to be destroyed,
After enduring such a host of ills.
My sons all slain, my daughters captive led;
Their chambers plundered, and their little ones
Dashed to the earth by fierce, relentless foes.
And I, perhaps, at last prostrate shall lie
Upon my palace floor, slain by the Greeks;
And this poor body shall be torn by dogs,
By my own dogs, whom I brought up and fed,
Who now infuriate will lap my blood,
And then lie down beneath the portico.
To a young man who in the battle falls
'Tis not unseemly to meet such a fate,
For he is dead, and that an honor is,
Whatever after may befall his corpse;
But when the dogs dishonor the white head
And beard and privates of an aged man,
That is a pitiable sight indeed.
  The old man said; and tore his hoary locks.
Yet on his son his words had no effect.
His wailing mother, too, shed many tears,
And, laying bare her breast, addressed him thus:
  Hector, my son, attend to what I say,
And show at least some pity upon me!
'Twas I that, when an infant, suckled thee:
Think of these things! Oh fight within the wall!
Nor stand thou all alone against this man.
Wretched thy fate if he should conquer thee;
For then will neither I nor thy rich wife
Mourn o'er thy body laid upon a bier,
But far away, among the Grecian ships,
By hungry dogs, thy corpse will be devoured.

Thus did the parents, supplicating much,
Call to their son, but called to him in vain;
For he renowned Achilles would await,—
And as a serpent on rank poisons fed,
Coiled in its den awaits a man's approach,
Its eyes glare horribly, it swells with rage:
So Hector, with indomitable soul,
Would not retreat, but leaned his spendid shield
Against the stones of a projecting tower,
And, with a sigh, thus with himself communed:
Ah, me! if I should enter now the city wall
Polydamas would load me with reproach,
Who gave advice that I my men should lead
Within the town, in the disastrous night
When fierce Achilles to the field returned.
To his good counsel I did not attend;
And now, since by my stubbornness, I have
Destroyed the people, my inferiors will
With scorn point at me as the scourge of Troy.
Better it is to meet him boldly now,
And either conquer him, or nobly die.
But what if I lay down my crest and shield,
And lean my spear against the wall, and go
And tell Achilles Helen we'll restore
With all the wealth that Paris brought with her,
And that the chiefs of Troy will take an oath
That they, concealing nothing, will divide
Half of our city's treasure with the Greeks?
But why these vain discussions? doubtless he
Would slay me ere I could come up to him,
E'en without pity, naked and unarmed;
Nor could we with each other converse hold,
As youths and maids converse in rural shades.
No, it is better to contend with him,
That we may know as soon as possible
To whom great Jove the victory will accord.
He said; and near him now Achilles drew
With his terrific spear, like dreadful Mars,

His glittering armor shining bright as fire,
Or like the splendor of the rising sun.
A sudden tremor then on Hector seized,
Nor could he stand his ground, but turned and fled.
The son of Peleus swiftly followed him,
Like as a hawk pursues a gentle dove;
She flies obliquely to avoid her fate,
But he keeps close at hand, screaming aloud,
And pouncing on her, speedily destroys.
So, eagerly, Achilles Hector chased;
Who, struck with terror, fled around the wall.
Then by the Prospect-ground they steered their course,
And by the waving fig-tree, keeping close
To the town wall, along the public road,
Reaching the double springs from which arise
The eddying waters of Scamander's stream.
Two fountains here there are: the one quite warm,
O'er which a steaming vapor ever floats;
The other, e'en in summer, cold as ice.
Here were stone basins, beautiful and large,
And here the lovely maids and dames of Troy
Washed their fair robes before the war began.
By this they passed, one chasing and one chased:
A brave man fled, a braver still pursued;
The prize was not a bullock or a hide,
But the grand stake was noble Hector's life.
And as at funeral games when heroes die,
And chariot steeds run swiftly round the course,—
The prize a tripod or a handsome maid,—
So thrice they made the circuit of the town.
The gods beheld, and thus great Jove began:
Alas! a much-loved hero I behold
Chased round the wall; for Hector I lament,
Who many oxen sacrificed to me
On Ida's lofty top, and in the town
Achilles now pursues him round the wall.
But come, ye gods, a consultation hold:
Whether 'tis best that Hector be preserved,
Or perish now, by brave Achilles slain.

He said; and thus Minerva made reply:
Oh, father, hurler of white thunder-bolts,
Driver of clouds! what sort of speech is this?
Wouldst thou this mortal's destiny postpone,
Whose hour of doom was long ago decreed?
Do it, but we the gods refuse assent.
Thus Pallas spake; and thus great Jove replied:
Courage, my child, I am not serious;
Do as thou wilt, I will not interfere.
He said; and she, encouraged by his words,
Sprang forth, descending the Olympian mount.
But swift Achilles Hector still pursued.
As when a dog pursues a mountain-fawn
Through glens and thickets; struck with panic, it
Will often crouch and hide within a brake;
Yet he holds on, tracking it all the while:
So Hector from his foe could not escape.
Oft as he tried to keep beside the wall,
So that his friends upon the battlements
Might with their missile weapons give him aid,
The other on the watch, would head him off,
And keep him running on the open plain.
As in a dream one chases and one flies;
The one unable seems to make escape,
The other seems unable to pursue:
So neither could Achilles overtake
Nor could the Trojan warrior escape,
Had not Apollo for the last time came
To rouse his courage and renew his strength.
But to his men Achilles shook his head,
Forbidding them at Hector to take aim,
Lest some one wounding him might glory gain,
And he the second honor only share.
But now when at the fountains they arrived
For the fourth time, Jove took his golden scales,
And in them put the fatal weights of death;
Poised in the middle, he the balance held.
Achilles' weight went up and Hector's down;

Apollo then the Trojan hero left,
And to Achilles swift Minerva flew,
And standing by the warrior thus spake:
 Illustrious Achilles, dear to Jove,
I hope we now will gloriously return,
This Hector having slain, so fierce in war;
Escape for him is now impossible,
Nor would Apollo's prayer prevail with Jove.
But stand thòu still, and I will him persuade
Also to stand, and challenge thee to fight.
 She said; and he rejoicing much, obeyed;
Leaning upon his long brass-pointed spear,
She left him then, and to bold Hector went;
The likeness of Deïphobus she took.
And standing by the hero, him addressed:
 Dear brother, swift Achilles on thee gains,
Pursuing thee round Priam's lofty town:
Come, then, and let us stand and beat him off.
 She said; and Hector thus replying spake:
Dearest of brothers, good Deïphobus,
I always loved, but love thee now still more,
Since for my sake thou durst the city leave,
Whilst all the others stay within the walls.
 The goddess then in turn the chief addressed:
My brother dear, our parents begged me much,
And all my comrades too, to stay within,
But with sad grief my bosom was harassed.
But come, and let us fight, nor spare our spears,
That we the contest may decide, and know
Whether Achilles shall prevail, or we.
 Thus with a fraud Minerva led him on;
And when they had approached, thus Hector spake:
No longer, son of Peleus, will I fly:
Thrice have I fled round Priam's lofty town,
Nor dared to stop and meet thee in the fight;
But now I am resolved to make a stand:
I either shall slay thee, or shall be slain.
But come, and let us swear by all the gods,

That I, if victor, will not outrage thee ;
But having spoiled thee of thy armor, will
Send back thy body to thy weeping friends,
And that to me thou wilt like kindness show.
  But sternly answering, thus Achilles spake
Hector, most cursed, talk not to me of oaths;
As men and lions make not faithful leagues,
Nor wolves nor lambs can in agreement live :
So between us no friendship can exist,
Nor leagues be made ; but one of us must fall,
And dreadful Mars behold our dying blood.
Call up thy courage, then, for there is need,
Since with Minerva's aid thou shalt be slain,
And pay for all the mischief thou hast done.
  He spake, and hurled his spear ; the other stooped,
And the sharp weapon stuck into the ground.
But Pallas plucked it out, and gave it back,
Unseen by Hector, to Achilles' hands,
And thus the Trojan chief his foe addressed :
  Thy lance has missed, Achilles, and my fate,
Which thou didst prophesy, still unfulfilled.
Thou art a prater, full of cunning speech,
And thought to terrify me by thy words ;
But now in turn take heed of my sharp spear.
Would that in all thy body it might strike !
Then might we easier finish this long war,
For thou hast ever been our greatest curse.
  He said ; and struck Achilles' mighty shield ;
His spear rebounded, and was hurled in vain.
Hector dejected stood, for he had not
Another with him ; so he loudly called,
Asking Deïphobus to hand him one,
But his dear brother was not to be seen ;
And the truth flashed upon the hero's mind,
As with a sigh, thus to himself he spake :
  Alas ! without doubt, the gods have doomed me now ;
I thought Deïphobus was by my side,
But he is still within the city walls,

And by Minerva I have been deceived.
But now my death is near, and no escape:
Long were Apollo and great Jove my friends,
Who in great perils oft protected me;
But cruel fate o'ertakes me at the last:
Yet I will not ingloriously fall,
But do some deed that future times will praise.
Thus having said, he drew his huge sharp sword,
And forward rushed with all his might and main.
Like a high-soaring eagle, which swoops down
From gloomy clouds upon a lamb or hare,
Filled with fierce rage, Achilles too rushed on;
In front he held his beautiful carved shield;
His splendid helmet nodded on his head,
Waving the golden plumes that shaded it;
His glittering spear shone like the evening star.
Achilles poised the weapon in his hand,
Eyeing fair Hector's person where he might
With the best chance inflict a mortal wound.
But the fine brazen armor he had on,
The spoils of Patroclus, protected him;
Yet there appeared a spot, a mortal spot,
Near to his neck, beside the collar-bone:
There fierce Achilles drove his mighty spear,
So that the point went through his tender neck;
Yet did it not his windpipe cut away,
So that his victim still had power of speech,—
Yet in the dust he fell; and o'er him thus
Achilles boastingly the chief addressed:
Hector, when spoiling Patroclus thou thought
Thou wast quite safe, since I was far away.
Fool! thou hadst then of me but little fear;
But I, though quiet at my vessels then,
Am, as you see, his brave avenger now.
The dogs and birds thy carcass shall devour,
But he will have an honorable tomb.
Then Hector groaning, languid, thus replied:
By thine own soul! and by thy parents dear!

I supplicate and beg thee not to let
My body be devoured by the dogs;
But take abundantly of brass and gold,—
Which my fond parents gladly will bestow,—
And to the Trojans send my body back,
That on a funeral-pile it may be burnt.
But sternly looking, thus Achilles spake:
Dog that thou art! nor beg, nor supplicate,
Nor by my soul, nor by my parents dear!
Such things thou hast done to me that I could
Tear e'en thy flesh to pieces and devour!
Nor is there any one can drive away
From thy cursed carcass the devouring dogs.
Yet even should they hither bring and give
Tenfold such ransoms, yea, or twentyfold!
Not e'en if Priam gave thy weight in gold,
Thy venerable mother never shall
Lament thee, having laid thee on a bier,
But dogs and birds shall into pieces tear!
He said; and Hector, dying, him addressed:
Knowing thee well, I might have this foreseen,
For in thy breast there is an iron soul;
But think that some day Heaven may plead my cause
When, at the Scæan gate, brave as thou art,
By Paris and Apollo thou shalt fall.
Thus as he spake dark death o'ershadowed him.
His wailing soul to Pluto's realms flew down,
Leaving his vigor and his youthful bloom.
And him, though dead, Achilles thus addressed:
Die! and for me, my doom will only come
When Jove and all the deities see fit.
So saying, from the corpse he plucked his spear
And laid it down, and stripped his armor off.
The Greeks now gathered round, admiring much
The noble form and stature of the chief;
Nor was there one who did not strike the corpse,
Thus speaking to his comrade that stood by:

Hector can now be touched, and gentler is
Than when with fire he assailed our ships.
  But having stripped him, thus Achilles spake:
Oh, friends and leaders, princes of the Greeks!
Since with Jove's help we have this man subdued,
Who did us greater harm than all besides,
Come, let us round the city trial make,
And know if they their fortress will desert
Or will remain, their champion being slain.
But why of such things should I cogitate?
The corpse of Patroclus unburied lies;
Him, while I live, I never will forget,
But will remember e'en in Pluto's realms.
Come, Grecian youths, a song of triumph raise,
And to our ships the body let us bear;
Great glory to our camp we carry back,
For we have Hector slain, who like a god
Was worshiped by the citizens of Troy.
  He said; and on great Hector's person planned
Unseemly deeds; for both his feet he bored
From heel to instep, fastening in the holes
A leather strap, which to his car he bound,
Leaving his head to be thus trailed along.
His chariot then he mounted, taking up
The splendid armor; then his steeds he lashed,
Which o'er the plain swift as the lightning flew;
Great clouds of dust arose round Hector's corpse;
His handsome azure locks swept o'er the ground,
And his once graceful head was all defiled;
For Jove had granted to his enemies
Thus to disgrace him on his own dear soil.
  His mother saw her son, and wept aloud,
And tore her hair, and cast away her veil;
And his dear father piteously groaned,
And from the people lamentations rose,
As if the town of Troy were all on fire.
Scarce could the citizens the old man hold,
Eager to rush outside the Scæan gate,

For rolling in the dust, with tearful eyes
Each by his name he supplicated thus:
  Detain me not, my friends, but let me go
And supplicate this stern and reckless man;
Perhaps he may respect my hoary head,
And have compassion on me for my age.
His father Peleus is an old man too,
Who brought him up to be the curse of Troy;
But yet on me the heaviest sorrows fall,
So many of my blooming sons he slew.
And yet I mourn not for the whole of them
As for this one, my noble Hector slain;
My grief for him will sink me to the tomb.
Ah! had he only died within my arms,
Then his unhappy mother and myself
Had o'er him wept, and thus have been consoled!
  Thus he spake, weeping, and the people groaned;
And 'mid the Trojan ladies then began
His mother, Hecuba, to make lament:
  Oh, my poor son! why do I, wretched, live,
Whilst thou art dead? thou who by night and day
I boasted of! my darling and my pride!
The bulwark, too, of all the citizens,
Who honored and revered thee as a god!
And well they might, for thou their glory wast;
But now sad fate and death possesses thee.
Thus weeping, Hecuba bewailed her son.
  But Hector's wife as yet had nothing learned,
For none had told her that her spouse remained
Outside the gates. But in her noble house,
In a retired room, the lady sat,
Weaving a splendid piece of tapestry.
Directions to her maidens she had given
To set the largest tripod on the fire,
That Hector, on returning from the fight,
Might a warm bath enjoy. Ah, foolish she!
Who knew not that her husband, far from baths,
Already by Achilles had been slain.

She heard the shriek and wailing on the tower,
And her limbs shook, and from her trembling hands
The busy shuttle fell upon the ground;
In haste her fair attendants she addressed:
Come hither two of you, accompany me,
That I may know what 'tis that has transpired.
My venerable mother's voice I heard,
And to my mouth my heart in terror leaps,
And my limbs under me are quite benumbed:
Some evil has befallen Priam's sons.
Ah! dreadful thought! I fear Achilles may
Have turned my noble Hector from the gates,
And having driven him towards the plain,
Have wrought some mischief on my valiant spouse,
Who, with the rest, was ne'er content to stay,
But forward leaped, where danger threatened most.
Thus having spoke, she through the palace rushed
With palpitating heart, like one deranged,
And her fair maidens both accompanied her.
But when she reached the tower and throng of men
She o'er the rampart looked, and saw him dragged
By the fleet steeds in front of lofty Troy:
Toward the Greek fleet they drew him ruthlessly.
Then her sight failed her, and she backward fell,
Fainting away. Then from her head fell off
Her beauteous head-gear, her embroidered veil,
Her garland, and her fillet, and her net.
The splendid ornaments that Venus gave—
That Venus gave her on her bridal day—
When Hector led her from her father's halls
And loaded her with costly marriage gifts.
Her sisters and her female relatives
Gathered around her and supported her;
Then she revived, and sobbing, thus began:
Oh, Hector! wretched we! unhappy both!
We both were born to a like dismal fate:
Thou in the palaces of lofty Troy,
And I in Thebè, in Aëtion's halls;

He brought me up, ill-fated too, himself.
Would that he never had begotten me !
And now thou goest to Pluto's gloomy realms,
And I am left a widow in thy house,
With thy unfortunate and tender boy.
Naught canst thou do for him, oh Hector, now !
Nor he for thee ; should he escape the Greeks,
Labor and sorrow will his portion be :
He of his property will be deprived,
His landmarks moved ; the orphan has no friends ;
Dejected and forlorn, he sits alone,
And his pale cheeks are ever wet with tears.
In want he goes to his dead father's friends,
One by his cloak, one by his tunic, plucks,
To gain their notice ; some may pity him,
And of their wine give him a little share,—
Enough to wet his lips, and scarcely more.
His youthful comrades who have parents still,
Shall drive him from their banquets, striking him,
And loading with reproaches : Off ! begone !
Thy father even should not feast with us !
Then weeping, to his mother he returns.
He who, one time sat on his father's knee,
Eating rich marrow and the fattest sheep,
And when inclined to sleep, on couches slept,
In a soft bed, with his kind-hearted nurse :
Thus shall Astyanax, as he was called,
Great ills endure, now that his father's dead.
Soon wilt thou die, and be the prey of dogs
Beside the fleet, and thy fair, tender flesh
By worms and swarms of insects be devoured.
As for thy handsome clothes, them I will burn,
No use to thee will they hereafter be ;
But, in the sight of Troy, of them I'll make
A funeral pile in honor of thy death.

Thus spake Andromachè, bedewed with tears,
And all the other women likewise wept.

BOOK XXIII.

THE FUNERAL GAMES.

ARGUMENT.

The ghost of Patroclus appears to Achilles while asleep, demanding the rites of burial.—A funeral pile is built, and twelve Trojan youths sacrificed upon it.—The fire being slow in burning, Achilles prays to the Winds, who come at his request, and increase the flames.—He then institutes games, and offers various prizes for the successful competitors.

Thus from the town went up a cry of woe;
But when the Greeks reached the broad Hellespont
They scattered, each one going to his ship.
But not as yet Achilles would allow
His men to separate, but thus addressed:
Chivalrous Myrmidons, companions dear!
Let us not yet unharness our swift steeds,
But gathering round the corpse, armed as we are,
Let us lament for Patroclus our friend;
Such is the proper honor to the dead.
Then when we have enough indulged our grief,
We will unyoke, and for the feast prepare.
Thus spake the chief, and the whole band bewailed;
Thrice round the corpse he led the mourning host.
Thetis their hearts had melted, and all wept;
The sand was moistened with their flowing tears,
And their bright armor. Such a friend was lost!
The mourning by Achilles was commenced;

He laid his hands upon his comrade's breast
And thus began : Hail to thee, Patroclus !
Though thou art dead and absent from us now,
I have accomplished all I promised thee ;
Hector is hither dragged, a prey to dogs,
And on thy pile twelve noble Trojan youths
Shall, for thy early death, be offered up.
He said ; and vilely noble Hector served,
Casting him headlong in the dust before
His comrade's bier. Then they unyoked their steeds,
And laid aside their glittering brazen arms,
And sat in throngs beside Achilles' ships.
He furnished them a proper funeral feast,—
White oxen, sheep, and bleating goats were slain,
And many fatted hogs were roasted there :
Blood flowed abundantly around the corpse.
The chiefs then led Achilles to the tent
Of Agamemnon. He unwilling went,
Oppressed with grief, for his dear comrade slain.
Then to the presence of the king they came,
Who bade his heralds place upon the fire
A mighty tripod, that his guest might wash
The blood away, with which he still was stained ;
But he refused, and added, with an oath :
No, by great Jove! who is the best of gods,
It is not right I should ablutions make
Before the corpse of Patroclus is burnt,
And a tomb raised, and I have shorn my hair ;
No sorrow shall I e'er endure like this.
Yet to the loathsome feast I now will yield ;
But on the morrow bid them, king, prepare
Abundant wood, and have it so disposed
That the dead body quickly be consumed,
And to their occupations all return.
He said ; and his directions they obeyed.
Supper was furnished, and they all partook,
Then for the night each to his tent repaired.
But with his Myrmidons Achilles went,

And moaning deeply, lay upon the shore,—
Upon the shore of the resounding sea.
On a clear spot near where the billows dashed,
Sweet sleep soon seized him, for he was fatigued
By chasing Hector round the walls of Troy.
There as he slept a spirit came to him,
The spirit of the wretched Patroclus;
The form, the voice, the handsome eyes were his,
And such the very garments that he wore.
Close to his head the apparition stood,
And thus the sleeping warrior addressed:
Sleep'st thou, Achilles? am I forgotten now,
Now that I'm dead? 'twas not so when I lived.
Oh, haste, and bury my poor corpse, that I
May gain an entrance into Hades' gates!
The images and spirits of the dead
Drive me away, and will not suffer me
To mingle with them, nor to cross the stream;
And thus round Hades I keep wandering.
Give me thy hand, for I will ne'er return
After my funeral rites are once performed:
Never again sweet converse shall we hold,
As was our custom when we were alive;
But a sad fate has snatched me from the earth.
And thou, Achilles, godlike as thou art,
Art fated too, to fall by lofty Troy.
Another thing I bid thee: mind and lay
My gathered bones in the same tomb with thee;
For we as boys together were brought up
Within the palace of thy aged sire,
When I a lad was exiled from my home
For having caused unwittingly the death
Of Amphidamas' son, when we at play
Quarreled unhappily about some dice;
Then Peleus kindly furnished me a home,
And named me as thy comrade and thy friend.
He said; and answering, thus Achilles spake:
Why hast thou come, my venerable friend,

Bearing commandments to me such as these?
All will accomplished be in order due.
But come thou nearer, that we may embrace,
And though it be e'en for a little while,
Our sorrows intermingle and our griefs.
He said, and stretched to clasp him in his arms;
But the pale ghost eluded his warm grasp,
Sank in the earth—and so went gibbering off.
Achilles in amazement then sprang up,
And clapped his hands, and dolefully broke forth:
Surely enough in Hades there exist
Men's images and spirits, but, alas!
No substance and no body they possess;
For all night long the soul of Patroclus
Stood by me, moaning and lamenting much
In piteous tones, telling me what to do;
And wonderfully was he like himself.
Thus spake the chief, causing his men to weep;
And as they wept, the rosy Morn appeared.
But Agamemnon sent his men for wood
With burden mules, and Merion at their head;
Axes they carried and well-twisted ropes,—
O'er winding ways up and down hill they went.
To Ida's shady forests soon they came,
Then fell the towering resounding oaks;
The wood they split and bound upon the mules;
Descending then, they to the plain returned.
The men were ordered to bear trunks of trees;
They laid the loads in order on the shore,
Where for a tomb Achilles marked a spot.
Then having thrown vast quantities of wood,
They rested from their labors and sat down;
Then his brave Myrmidons Achilles bade
To arm themselves, and yoke the fiery steeds;
So a vast throng of cavalry in front
And footmen following, in procession joined;
Amid them was the corpse of Patroclus,
Borne by his friends; o'er it they spread their hair;

Cut as a token of respect and love.
Achilles walked behind, holding his head,
Lamenting much, for he was burying
A blameless man, and a beloved friend;
Then at the place marked out they laid him down.
Achilles now thought of another thing:
Standing apart, his auburn hair he cut—
The hair he had designed for Sperchius—
And, gazing on the sea, thus moaning, spake:
In vain, oh, Sperchius! my father vowed
That I this hair should dedicate to thee,
With sacred hecatombs, on my return,
And fifty sheep should sacrifice besides,
By thy clear fountains, where there stands a grove,
An altar also for thy worshipers:
Thus vowed my sire, but he vowed in vain;
And now, since I return not to my home,
These auburn locks to Patroclus I give.
So saying, in his comrade's hands he placed
The hair he had cut off, causing his men,
Who gazed upon the piteous sight, to weep:
Thus had they mourned e'en till the set of sun
Had not Achilles to the king thus spake:
Oh, son of Atreus, ruler of the host!
Respectful sorrow e'en must have an end;
Therefore dismiss the people from the pile,
And bid them to prepare their evening meal.
We will remain attending to the corpse;
And also let the chiefs remain with us.
He said; and Agamemnon obeyed,
The warriors dismissing to their ships,
Whilst the remainder stayed to build the pile.
A hundred feet each way they measured off,
And raised the woody structure, and on top,
Grieving at heart, their comrade's body laid;
Many choice sheep and oxen then they slew,
The fat of which, with care, Achilles spread
Over the corpse, placing the meat around;

Vases of oil and honey he arranged,
And also threw upon the massy pile
Four noble horses, and two dogs that once
With seven others to his friend belonged;
Twelve Trojan youths in order next he slew,
And to the whole applied a blazing torch;
And thus, with groans, to his dead comrade spake:
  Hail to thee, Patroclus! dead as thou art.
I now fulfill all that I promised thee!
Twelve noble Trojans with thee shall be burned,
But Hector shall no funeral enjoy;
He by the hungry dogs shall be devoured.
  Thus he spake, threatening; but his threats were vain,
For Venus, night and day, drove off the dogs,
And with ambrosial oil anointed him,
So that his bruises speedily were healed;
And o'er him too Apollo drew a cloud,
That the hot sun might not dry up the corpse.
But the huge funeral pile would not ignite.
Achilles then to the two winds made prayer,
To Boreas and Zephyr, offering vows,—
Libations from a golden cup he poured,
And begged that they would speedily approach
And fan the fire that the wood might burn.
Swift Iris heard the godlike hero pray,
And to the winds as messenger repaired.
  They were at home holding a festival
When Iris, hastening, on their threshold stood.
When they beheld her, courteously they rose
And begged her to come in and take a seat;
But she refused, and thus the goddess spake:
No seat for me, for I o'er ocean fly
To Æthiopia's far distant lands,
Where they make splendid offerings to the gods,
Of which I also have a right to share.
But now Achilles supplicates ye two,
Zephyr and Boreas, begging that ye come
And fan the funeral pile of his dear friend.

Thus having spoke, the swift-winged Iris left;
They, in great haste, tumultuously set off,
Driving the clouds before them as they went,
Blowing; they speedily the ocean reached,
And raised the billows with their roaring blast.
Then to the fertile plains of Troy they came,
And fell upon the pile, causing the fire
To mightily resound. Thus all night long,
With their shrill blasts, they tossed the blaze about,
And all night long Achilles poured out wine
From a large golden goblet, calling to
The spirit of his comrade Patroclus;
And as a father mourns a youthful son
Lately espoused, so did Achilles mourn,
Pacing beside the pile continually.
But when the star-herald of day arose
And saffron morn was o'er the ocean spread,
The fire grew languid and the flame decayed;
Then the winds left and crossed the Thracian sea,
Whose rising billows groaned beneath their track.
Achilles then departed from the pile,
And lying down fatigued, soon fell asleep;
Round Agamemnon the others thronged,—
Achilles was awakened by the noise,
And, sitting up, he thus addressed the king.
Oh, son of Atreus, and ye other chiefs!
Extinguish now the fire with ruddy wine,
And let us gather up our comrade's bones,—
Them we may easily discriminate,
For he lay in the center of the pile;
The others were arranged upon the edge,—
And let us place them in a golden vase,
With fat enveloped, until I shall die;
Then build a tomb of moderate extent,
Which at my death must greatly be enlarged.
He said; and they the hero's words obeyed.
With ruddy wine the fire they put out;
The ashes then fell in, and, gathering up

The warrior's bones, they put them in a vase,
With fat inclosed, and laid them in the tent.
Over the whole a linen veil they spread;
Then they marked out the area of the tomb,
And set to work, and raised an earthen mound.
  Achilles bade the people to remain,
And caused the vast assembly to sit down;
Then prizes from his vessels he brought forth—
Goblets and tripods, oxen, steeds, and mules,
And iron too, and women of fair form.
First for the chariot-race he staked, as prize,
A handsome woman, skilled in various works,
With her a tripod also, of large size;
Then an unbroken mare, just six years old,
And big with foal, he for the next put up;
A smaller tripod for the third he staked,
And for the fourth two talents of pure gold;
A double cup he promised for the fifth.
And, standing up, he thus addressed the Greeks:
  Ye sons of Atreus, and and all ye Greeks,
Behold the prizes for the charioteers!
If for some other man these games were held
I the first prize would surely bear away.
No horses, as ye know, can cope with mine,
For they indeed are of immortal birth;
By Neptune were they given to my sire,
And he in turn presented them to me;
But I and my good steeds will stand apart,
For they have lost their driver and their friend,
Who often washed and oiled their flowing manes;
With drooping heads they stand grieving at heart,
And their long manes reach even to the ground.
Prepare ye others then who have a mind,
And think your steeds are fitted for a race.
  He said; and up the charioteers arose.
Eumelus was the first, a royal chief,
Who in equestrian skill surpassed them all;
Next valiant Diomed, with steeds of Tros,

Which from Æneas as his spoil he took ;
In the hard fight Apollo saved his life.
Good Menelaus after him stepped forth,
He Agamemnon's mare, Æthè, drove,
And swift Podarge, a stallion of his own.
The mare a gift to Agamemnon was
From rich Echepolus, of Sicyon famed ;
He gave her as an equivalent that he
Might not to battle go, but stop at home.
Antilochus came next, old Nestor's son,
Swift Pelion-born steeds his chariot drew ;
And from his sire this good advice he got :
  Antilochus, my son ! Neptune and Jove
Have loved thee, although young, and taught thee how
To manage horses ; so there is small need
Of my advice ; but slow thy horses are,
And though thou skillful art, thou still may'st fail ;
The others have good steeds, but not thy skill.
Come, then, and let us plan how thou may'st win.
More skill than strength the wood-cutter employs,—
'Tis by his skill the pilot steers his bark,
And thus it is that charioteers excel.
One who relies too much upon his steeds,
Wanders about the course and loses ground ;
But he who prudent is, with horses worse,
Keeps his eye fixed intently on the goal ;
Watches the car before him, eager that
He may outstrip him as they reach the turn.
Now look, and I will point thee out the goal ;
'Tis yonder post of wood, a cubit high,
Of oak or larch, with stones on either side ;
It was the tomb of some one long since dead,
Or may have been a goal in former times.
To it drive close thy chariot and steeds,
Incline thy body somewhat to the left,
And whip thy right-hand horse, and urge him on ;
But keep thy left-hand steed close to the mark,
So that thy wheel may almost graze the post ;

Yet touch it not, lest thou thy chariot break
And to thy rivals be a laughing-stock.
But if the goal, my son, thou canst but pass,
All will be well, and none can overtake;
Not even if Arion he should drive,
Adrastes' noble steed, of race divine;
Or the famed horses of Laomedon,
Which in these regions were brought forth and reared.
Thus having spoke, old Nestor took his seat,
And Merion as fifth his horses yoked;
Then on their cars they mounted and cast lots.
Achilles shook the vase, and forth there leaped
The lot of Nestor's son, Antilochus;
Next Eumelus, and Menelaus after him,
And Merion next, and last bold Diomed.
The distant goal Achilles pointed out,
And as the umpire godlike Phœnix chose,
The armor-bearer of his aged sire.
With one accord their lashes then they raised,
And jerked their reins, and cheered the noble steeds.
Swift o'er the plain the rapid coursers flew;
Their manes were tossed on high, and from beneath
Rose clouds of dust; sometimes, indeed, the cars
Ran o'er the ground, and then would bound aloft.
Erect the drivers stood, with beating hearts,
Eager for victory, as they cheered their steeds;
But when they were completing their last round,
And to the shore returned, then might be seen
The excellence of each. Then Eumelus
Foremost came, and valiant Diomed next,
Nor was he distant either, but quite near;
His horses hung upon his rival's car,
Leaning their heads o'er Eumelus; he felt
Upon his neck and shoulders their warm breath.
And now had Diomed the other passed
Had not Apollo, in a fit of rage,
Shaken his hands, and made him drop his lash;
The indignant hero wept at his mishap.

But to his aid Minerva quickly came,
Restored his whip, and cheered his coursers on;
But the car-yoke of Eumelus she broke,
So that his mares got loose, and the stout pole
Dashed on the ground, whilst he himself, thrown out,
Was injured in his arms, his nose, and mouth;
Tears filled his eyes, and his strong voice was choked.
Then, with Minerva's aid, bold Diomed
Bounded ahead, leaving the rest behind.
 Next after him came fair-haired Menelaus.
And then Antilochus cheered on his steeds:
Push on, exert yourselves with all your might;
I do not hope to pass brave Diomed,
To whom Minerva gives celestial aid,
But haste, and Menelaus overtake,
Lest by his mare Æthè ye be shamed;
Why should such steeds as ye be left behind?
And mind what now I say for your own good:
My father, Nestor, if ye chance to fail,
Will slay ye both; so put on all your speed;
As for the rest, I will look out myself,
And see to pass him in the narrow turn.
 He said; and they, dreading their master's threat,
Now faster ran. Antilochus perceived
The narrow passage that before him lay—
It was a gully washed by wintry storms.
Toward it the eager rivals quickly drove;
But Menelaus feared, and thus cried out:
 What dost thou mean, oh rash Antilochus,
Driving so close to me, in such a spot?
Then check thy steeds, lest running foul of me
Both of our chariots be in pieces dashed.
 He said; the other did not seem to hear,
But faster urged his steeds and lashed them on;
Far as a vigorous youth can hurl a quoit
So far they ran abreast; but Menelaus,
Fearing an accident, now checked his car,
And to his rival spake in chiding words:

Oh, what a plague, Antilochus, thou art!
Avaunt!—we thought thee once a prudent man;
Yet not e'en thus shalt thou the prize obtain
Without an oath. He said, and cheered his steeds.
Be not kept back, nor sorrow in your hearts;
Yonder poor beasts cannot compare with you.
Urged by their master's exhortation, they
Now fleetly ran, and their lost time regained.
Meanwhile the assembled Greeks beheld the cars,
As amid clouds of dust they scoured the plain.
Then first Idomeneus, king of Crete,
The horses recognized; on a high seat he sat,
Outside the circus; he the voices knew,
And now perceived a steed remarkable
Coming in first: chestnut its color was,
And on its forehead was a round white spot.
He stood erect, and thus the throng addressed:
Comrades and leaders, chieftains of the Greeks!
Do I alone the horses recognize?
Or do ye too? new steeds are foremost now,
And I perceive a different charioteer;
Those mares which were the first must injured be;
I surely saw them as they turned the goal,
But now I see them not upon the plain.
Their driver must have turned unskillfully,
And without doubt has fallen from his seat;
His mares have bolted, and his car is broke.
I cannot well distinguish; stand and look!
Yon driver who in triumph leads the race
Is an Ætolian warrior, I think,
The son of Tydeus, bold Diomed.
He said; then Ajax, son of Oïleus, spake,
And thus in bitter words reproved the king:
Wilt thou, oh, Idomeneus, babble still?
Those noble, prancing mares are still ahead.
Thou art not very young, nor do thine eyes
See with such sharpness as in other days;
Nor shouldst thou prate whilst better men stand by.

I say Eumelus' mares are still ahead,
As first they were, and he is with them too.
He said; the king indignantly replied:
  Ajax, thou art inferior to all;
Good at abuse indeed, cross and morose.
But come, we will a cup or tripod stake,
And Agamemnon shall umpire be—
He shall decide whose horses foremost are:
Thus for thy vain presumption thou shalt pay.
  Thus spake the king; and Ajax, full of wrath,
In a harsh strain, was ready to reply.
And now to strife the warriors would have come
Had not Achilles interposed, and spake:
  Ajax and Idomeneus, 'tis not fit
To have this altercation; ye, yourselves,
Would blame another who should do the like.
Then sit ye down, and look upon the steeds;
Soon will they all arrive, and ye will know
Who takes the foremost prize, and who does not.
  He said; meanwhile bold Diomed approached
With upraised lash; his steeds like lightning flew
'Mid clouds of dust, dragging the car along,
Whose rapid wheels scarce left a track behind;
Torrents of sweat down from the horses rolled.
  Then from his shining car the hero leaped,
Resting his whip against the chariot-yoke;
His comrade, Sthenelus, was not remiss,
But seized the prize, the tripod and the dame,
And gave them to his men to bear away,
Whilst the triumphant chief unyoked the steeds.
  Next after him Antilochus drove up,
Outstripping Menelaus by fraud alone;
Yet even thus, the other came quite near,—
Distant as is a horse from his car-wheel:
Although at first such distance intervened
As when a skillful player hurls a quoit;
Yet his lost space the warrior soon regained,
So swift and strong was Agamemnon's mare,

Renowned Æthè, beautifully maned;
And had the course a little longer been
Without a doubt he would have come in first.
  Merion came next, a spear's throw in the rear;
His lagging steeds the slowest were of all,
And he himself unskillful with the whip.
Last came Eumelus, he his horses drove
Before him, and his beauteous chariot dragged.
Achilles saw, and pity for him felt;
And rising, thus addressed the assembled Greeks:
  The best man of them all comes in the last.
Come, then, and let him have the second prize,
For Diomed indeed has won the first.
  He said; and all consented to his words.
And now the mare he surely had received
Had not Antilochus rose up and spake—
Spake to Achilles on the score of right:
  Achilles, I shall very angry be
If to Eumelus thou shalt give this mare;
For doing so, thou robbest me of my prize,
Because so skillful he and by mishap
Injured his steeds and broke his chariot car,
For doing so thou robbest me of my prize.
Why did he not to the immortals pray?
Then he would not have failed, nor come in last;
But if thou pitiest him, and wilt consent,
Thou hast much gold and brass within thy tent,
Oxen and maidens, and swift-footed steeds;
Give him of these, and great will be thy praise,
But I the mare will not consent to yield,
And he who takes her must first vanquish me.
He said; and at his words Achilles smiled.
He loved Antilochus, and thus replied:
  Since 'tis thy wish, Antilochus, that I
Should to Eumelus give another prize,
I am content; and will the corselet give
Which I from Asteropeus fighting took;
Brazen it is, entwined with shining tin—

A costly piece of work by all allowed.
He said; and told Automedon to fetch
The valuable present from his tent,
Which by Eumelus was received with joy.
Then arose Menelaus, grieving much,
For with Antilochus he was enraged.
A herald placed the scepter in his hands,
Bidding the people silence to observe;
And thus the royal, godlike hero spake:
What hast done, oh rash Antilochus?
Once thou wast thought to be a prudent man.
My skill thou hast disgraced, and wronged my steeds,
Driving ahead with thy inferior ones.
Come, then, ye chiefs and leaders of the Greeks,
And judge impartially between us both,
Lest some one of the brass-mailed Greeks may say
That Menelaus by falsehood gained the prize
With horses known to be inferior,
Whilst he superior was in skill and strength.
Then let the matter thus decided be,
For in no way more just can it be done.
Hither I pray thee come, Antilochus,
And, with the pliant lash touching thy steeds,
Swear by earth-shaking Neptune thou didst not
By any stratagem impede my car.
He said; the other prudently replied:
Have patience, royal Menelaus, since I
Am thy inferior far in age and rank.
Thou knowest what errors are the part of youth;
His mind is volatile, his counsel weak.
Bear with me, therefore, and I'll give thee up
The mare that has been just adjudged to me;
And should'st thou still a greater favor ask
I with thy wish will willingly comply,
Rather than from thy good opinion fall
And sin besides against the immortal gods.
He said; and led the mare to Menelaus,
Whose mind was cheered and brightened up like dew

Spread o'er a glittering field of waving corn—
So was the soul of Menelaus cheered;
And thus, in answer, he the youth addressed:
I from my wrath, Antilochŭs, will cease,
For thou hast hitherto most prudent been,
Though now to youthful rashness thou didst yield;
Avoid a second time to overreach
All who above thee are in age and rank,
For none but thou could have appeased me thus;
But thou and thy good brother and thy sire
Have suffered much for me, and much performed.
Then take the mare; I give her back again,
That all may see how quickly I forgive.
He said; and to Nœman gave the steed,
To lead away for young Antilochus.
Merion, the fourth aspirant, took the gold;
The fifth prize, which was left, Achilles gave
To royal Nestor, and addressed him thus:
Receive this as a keepsake for the dead,
Whom we shall never look upon again.
I give it thee because thou ne'er shalt fight,
Nor wrestle, nor in any game engage,
For sad old age has robbed thee of thy strength.
He said; the other joyfully received,
And to the godlike warrior thus spake:
Surely, my son, all that thou sayest is true;
My limbs are weak, my feet no longer swift;
Would I were young, and had my strength as when
The Epeians Amarynceus interred—
A king he was, and at his funeral
His sons in honor of him prizes staked;
No one was equal to me in those games,
Neither among the Pylians nor Epeians,
Nor the magnanimous Ætolians.
In boxing I Clytomedon excelled,
And in a wrestling-match Auceus threw.
In running I swift Iphicles outstripped;

And when we came to hurling the sharp spear,
Phyleus I overcame and Polydore.
Actor's two sons drove past me with their steeds;
But there were two of them. They envied me
My skill, and the best premium they knew
Was to the victor in the chariot-race;
But they were two; one held the shining reins,
The other with the lash the horses urged.
Thus was I once; but now let younger men
Perform such deeds, for I must yield to age,
Though at that time 'mid heroes I excelled;
But thou go on, and with thy funeral games
Do honor to the memory of thy friend.
This gift indeed I willingly accept,
Pleased that thou ever bearest me in mind,
And that among the Greeks thou honorest me,
And may the gods requite thee for it all!
Thus spake the sage. Then through the throng of Greeks
Achilles went when he had heard his praise.
And now a boxing-match the chief proposed,
Leading a mule unbroken, six years old.
He in the circus placed it as a prize,
And for the vanquished set a goblet up;
Then, rising, he the assembly thus addressed:
Ye sons of Atreus, and ye well-armed Greeks!
We invite whoe'er at boxing will contend.
The victor shall this sturdy mule receive,
And he who vanquished is, this double cup.
He said, and forthwith bold Epeus rose,—
Skillful at boxing he, Panopus' son.
Upon the mule he laid his hands and said:
Let him step out who would the cup receive;
As for the mule, I think it will be mine.
In battle I to many must give place;
But when it comes to fists I yield to none,
For no one can in everything excel;
But this I say, my rival must take heed,
For broken bones will surely be his lot,

And let his friends stand by to bear him off.
He said ; and all in silence on him gazed.
  Then rose Euryalus, a godlike chief,
Son of Mecistus, from Talarian sprung,
Who in old times to attend a funeral came
To Thebès, and vanquished all that met him there.
Him his friend Diomed encouraged much,
Wishing that he the victory might gain.
First with a strap his loins he girded tight,
Then bound the leathern thongs around his hands.
  Then in the circus they both took their stands,
And soon their heavy fists each other met;
Then there was heard a horrid crash of jaws,
And from their limbs the perspiration poured.
Now a hard blow Epeus on the cheek
Gave his antagonist, and made him reel;
And as a fish upon the sea-shore cast
By the dark billows flounders on the sand,
So floundered on the ground Euryalus.
But Epeus stooped down and raised him up,
And his dear comrades gathering around,
Led him away spitting out clotted blood,
With drooping head, and quite insensible,
His tottering limbs dragging upon the earth.
Then they departed and received the cup.
  Next for a wrestling-match Achilles staked
A tripod, of large size, for him that won,—
'Twas valued at the price of twelve good steers.
The vanquished was a female to receive,
Well skilled in various accomplishments,
And at four oxen's value was set down.
Then standing up the chief addressed the Greeks:
Ye who would trial make for these, arise.
  He said; and Ajax Telamon arose,
And wise Ulysses, skilled in stratagems.
These, having girt themselves, arose and stood
Within the circus, grasping each other's arms
With their strong hands like rafters of a dome

Which a judicious architect has raised,
Stable enough to stand the fiercest winds.
Then their backs creaked and copious sweat poured down,
And their stout muscles swelled with purple blood.
Eager was each the victory to win ;
Neither could trip the other nor throw down ;
But when at length the people weary grew,
Thus Ajax his antagonist addressed :
  Noble Ulysses, skilled in stratagems,
Either let me lift thee or thou lift me,
And let us consequences leave to Jove.
So saying, he the other lifted up ;
Yet was Ulysses all prepared for this :
At his thigh aiming, he the hero struck,
Relaxed his limbs, and threw him on his back ;
Ulysses too fell down upon his breast :
The wondering throng with admiration gazed.
Next did the wily warrior lift him up
A little from the ground, on bended knees,
Then they both fell together in the dust.
  And now they rose, and would have tried again
Had not Achilles stopped them, and thus spake :
No longer thus exhaust yourselves for naught,
The palm of victory to each belongs,
And ye shall each receive an equal prize :
Now let the other Greeks their contests have.
  He said ; and they with willing minds obeyed,
And, wiping off the dust, put on their robes.
  Next a rich cup the godlike hero staked,
A prize for him who should the swiftest prove.
The cup six measures held, of silver made ;
In workmanship and beauty it excelled,
And by Sidonian artists had been wrought ;
Phœnician merchants brought it o'er the sea,
Presenting it to Thoas as a gift :
Eunæus to the hero Patroclus
Gave it to ransom one of Priam's sons.
This for the swiftest man the chief proposed ;

And for the second best, a noble ox;
And for the last, of gold a talent half.
Then he stood up, and thus the throng addressed:
Arise, ye who would trial make for these.
Then rose swift Ajax, son of Oïleus,
And wise Ulysses, and Antilochus,
Who of the youths in swiftness all excelled.
Achilles pointed out to them the goal.
Then first sprang forth the son of Oïleus,
And behind him the wise Ulysses rushed:
Close as a shuttle's throw by a dame held,
So near his rival did Ulysses run;
Breathing upon his shoulders and his head,
And on his footsteps trod ere filled with dust:
The Greeks admiring, gazed, and cheered him on.
And as their final course the racers made
Thus the wise hero to Minerva prayed:
Hear me, oh, goddess! and my steps assist.
The goddess heard, and to his limbs gave strength;
Then, as they just were reaching to the goal,
Ajax fell down,—Minerva was the cause,—
Slipping upon the dung of the fat steers,
Which for his friend Achilles just had slain:
So, running in, Ulysses seized the cup,
And Ajax for his prize received the ox.
He held it by the horns, and from his mouth
Spat out the dung, and to the Greeks thus spake:
Alas! it was a goddess tripped me up,
Who, as a mother, ever aids her chief.
He said; and heartily the people laughed.
Antilochus the prize of gold bore off;
And smiling, thus the assembled throng addressed:
Age, my good friends, is honored by the gods,
For Ajax somewhat older is than me,—
Belonging to a former race of men,—
And few in fleetness can compete with him,
Yet swift Achilles can outrun us all.
So spake the youth, praising the godlike chief,

Who with his words was pleased, and answered thus:
Thy praise, Antilochus, shall not be vain,
A talent half of gold I add to thee.
So saying, he the treasure to him gave.
The youth with joy received it from his hands.
  Achilles next within the circus placed
The glittering arms of godlike Sarpedon,
Which from the Trojan Patroclus had won.
Then he stood up, and thus addressed the Greeks:
Let any two who are for courage famed
These arms put on, and a fair trial make.
He who first wounds and draws the purple blood
This silver-studded Thracian sword shall have,
The beauteous blade which in fair fight I took
From Asteropeus; let them share the arms:
And for them, in my tent, I will prepare
A splendid feast, such as the brave deserve.
  He said; and Ajax Telamon arose,
That mighty chief, and valiant Diomed;
Apart they armed, then towards each other drew,
Eager to fight, and looking dreadfully:
Amazement seized the Greeks as they beheld.
Approaching nearer, thrice they onward rushed,
And thrice attacked each other, hand to hand;
Then Ajax pierced his adversary's shield,
But the good corselet saved his flesh from harm;
Then with his spear bold Diomed essayed
To strike the other's neck, above his shield.
The Greeks for Ajax feared, and stopped the fight,
Declaring each an equal prize should take.
However, the great sword Achilles gave,
With its rich belt, to noble Diomed.
A mass of iron then the chief set up,
Which strong Aëtion was wont to hurl;
But when Achilles slew him, he, as prize,
Seized it, and brought it with him in his ship.
Then he stood up, and thus addressed the Greeks:
Ye who would trial make of this, arise;

However wide-extended be his fields,
This would last any man five years at least;
Nor would his plowman, nor his shepherd, need
Into the city go for a supply.
He said; and warlike Polypœtes rose,
Leonteus, and Ajax Telamon,
And Epëus; these all in order stood:
The latter seized the mass, and whirling threw;
But at his throw the Greeks all laughed outright.
Then bold Leonteus threw, and Ajax third;
But when brave Polypœtes seized the mass:
Far as a herdsman throws his bended crook,
Which flying passes o'er the oxen's heads,
So far beyond he through the circus hurled.
At his great feat, the people shouted loud,
And his companions bore the prize away.
Next, for the archers, did Achilles stake
The best of iron, fit for making shafts,
And ten large battle-axes, and ten small:
Also a vessel's lofty mast he raised
On the sea-shore, at a great distance off;
On this a dove, tied by its feet, he placed,
Ordering the candidates to shoot at it.
Whoe'er, said he, shall hit yon timid dove,
Shall have the battle-axes as his prize;
But he who hits the cord, missing the bird,
The smaller axes for his prize shall take.
He said; and Merion and Teucer rose,
And in a brazen helmet shook the lots;
Teucer came first. An arrow then he shot,
But failed Apollo to propitiate,
Nor promised him a hecatomb of lambs.
He missed the bird indeed, but cut the string
Close to his foot, cutting the cord quite through;
The timid dove, set free, mounted on high,
And the admiring Greeks shouted applause.
Then Merion snatched the bow, and aimed his shaft,
Holding it steady; vowing that he would

To the great archer-god an offering make
Of choicest lambs. He saw the dove on high,
Beneath the clouds, and hit it on the wing,
The arrow passing through. Down fell the shaft
E'en at his feet; the bird lit on the mast,
Then drooped his neck, and fell upon the ground.
The people gazed with wonder at the sight.
Then Merion the larger axes took,
And Teucer bore the smaller ones away.
Lastly, Achilles to the circus brought
A glittering spear, and caldron never used,
Worth a fat ox. Then up the spearmen rose,
King Agamemnon and bold Merion;
Then to the monarch thus the hero spake:
Oh, Agamemnon! well we are aware
That thou excellest all in rank and skill,
Therefore thou mayest retire with the prize;
But let us to good Merion give the spears.
He said; nor did the other disobey,
But gave the glittering spear to Merion;
And to Talthybius the herald, gave
The brazen caldron just assigned to him.

BOOK XXIV.

HECTOR'S BURIAL.

ARGUMENT.

The gods, after deliberation, agree that Hector's dead body shall be restored to his friends.—Priam sets out for the tent of Achilles, bearing many presents.—Mercury, in the form of a young man, meets him, and acts as his guide.—The old king falls at the feet of Achilles and begs his son's body.—The chief grants his request, and after detaining a night, sends him home.—The Trojans run out to meet him, and Andromachè, Hecuba, and Helen break forth into lamentations.

The games were thus concluded, and the throngs,
The field deserting, to their ships returned;
The banquet and sweet slumber followed next.
  But still Achilles for his comrade wept,
Nor could he sleep; but, restless all night long,
Did naught but sorrow for his darling friend.
He thought of all he had achieved with him,
Heroic battles, toils by sea and land:
Remembering these, warm tears ran down his cheeks.
At one time on his side the warrior lay,
Then on his face, and then upon his back;
Then, starting up, he wandered to the shore,
And saw the day-break rise across the sea.
Back to his tent he went and yoked his steeds,
And tying Hector to his chariot-car,
Dragged him three times around his comrade's tomb,
Then in the dust he let the body lie.

Apollo, full of pity for the chief,
Preserved with care the uncorrupted corpse;
And with his golden shield encircling him,
Kept him from being torn when rudely dragged.
Thus was brave Hector by the Greek abused;
The gods looked down, and greatly pitied him,
Inciting Mercury to steal the corpse;
But Juno, Neptune, and Minerva gazed
On Hector's insults with complàcency;
Stubborn they were; for from the very first
They hated Troy on Paris' account,
Who had affronted much the goddesses,
When to his cottage they a visit made,
Preferring human beauty to divine.
But on the twelfth day thus Apollo spake:
Oh, cruel and injurious deities!
Has not good Hector often burned for you
The thighs of bulls and choicest of the goats?
And now, when dead, ye will not let his wife,
His kindred, nor his people look on him.
They on a pile his honored corpse would burn,
And every funeral rite perform for him;
But ye Achilles rather would befriend,
In whom no justice dwells nor sense of shame,
But like a lion, skilled in savage deeds,
Feasts on the slaughter of his fellow-men.
Others have lost dear friends and ceased to mourn,—
For time will soften e'en the deepest grief,—
But this fierce man the godlike Hector drags,
Behind his chariot, round his comrade's tomb!
Base and unwise such conduct surely is.
Let him beware lest the indignant gods,
For these his reckless doings, punish him.
He said; and thus offended Juno spake:
Such words as these, god of the silver bow,
Are right if equal honor ye ascribe
To Hector and Achilles; but ye know
Hector, an infant, sucked a woman's breast,

But great Achilles from a goddess sprang :
His mother I brought up, and dearly loved,
And to the hero Peleus wedded her,—
A mortal much respected by the gods.
Ye all were present at the marriage-feast;
Thou too, Apollo, evil, faithless one,
Wast present at the banquet with thy lyre.
She said; and Jove, cloud-driver, thus replied:
Juno, be still, and set thy mind at rest,
These men shall not an equal honor share;
Yet of the people who inhabit Troy
Hector is dearest to the gods and me:
He on my altar banquets oft prepared,
And offered odorous incense, as was just;
Yet let us not steal Hector's corpse away,
Nor could we easily, for on the watch,
By night and day, Achilles ever is,
Like a fond mother. Some one go and call
Thetis to me, that I may counsel her,
So that this chief may gifts from Priam take
As ransom for his noble, warlike son.
He said; and as a whirlwind swiftly rose
The goddess Iris, heaven's messenger.
Between rough Imbrus' coast and Samos' isle
Half way she flew, then plunged into the sea.
The ocean groaned; down to the bottom then
Sudden she sunk, like a big leaden ball
Dropped o'er the gunwale by a fisherman.
Thetis she found within her hollow cave,
And many sea-nymphs too were gathered there;
She in their midst still mourned for her poor son,
Whose doom it was to perish too in Troy,
Far from his kindred and his native land.
Near her swift Iris drew, and thus addressed:
Rise, Thetis, thou by mighty Jove art called.
To whom the goddess of the sea replied:
What business can the Thunderer have with me?
Ashamed I am, thus loaded down with grief,

To mingle with the happy deities.
Yet must I go, if such is Jove's decree,
For words of his are never spoke in vain.
She said; and her dark azure garments then put on—
No darker robe than that was ever seen.
Then swift-winged Iris leading, she set forth,
The waves retiring made a path for them.
At length they reached the shore and rose to heaven.
They found the son of Saturn and the gods,
And near to Jove Thetis assumed a seat,
Minerva rising up and making room.
Into the stranger's hand Juno then placed
A beauteous golden goblet, cheering her;
Thetis returned it after having drunk.
Then to the assembled gods Jove thus began:
Thou, Thetis, well I know, hast sadly come
To high Olympus, grieving in thy heart.
I called thee hither. Heaken to my words:
Nine days the immortals have a contest had
About Achilles and great Hector's corpse;
Some wish to steal it from the victor's hands,
But 'tis my wish to glorify thy son,
And also to show favor unto thee.
Descend, then, with these orders to the chief:
Tell him the deities offended are,
And I especially, because in wrath
Hector's dead body he will not give up:
Perchance he will respect and honor me.
Meanwhile to Priam, Iris I will send,
And bid him ransom Hector with great gifts—
With gifts that will Achilles overpower.
He said; nor did the goddess disobey,
But swiftly rushing, from Olympus flew
To her son's tent; she speedily drew near,
And found him mourning still his comrade's loss.
His friends meanwhile a sumptuous feast prepared,
Slaughtering a goodly sheep within the tent;

His mother took a seat near her dear son,
And, with her hand caressing, thus began:
Oh, my dear son! how long is this to last?
How long wilt thou bewail and grieve thy heart,
Mindless of food and the delights of love?
For love of women healthful is for man.
Thy doom is near, and death is close at hand;
But hearken, for Jove's messenger I am:
He says the gods are angry at thy course,
And he the most of all, because in wrath
Hector's dead body thou wilt not release.
But come, release, and ransoms shall be thine.
She said; and thus Achilles answering spake:
Let him who ransoms brings approach and take,
If such indeed is mighty Jove's command.
Thus, at the ships, mother and son discoursed.
Iris, meanwhile, was sent by Jove to Troy.
Go quickly, thus he said, swift Iris, fly
Down from the Olympian mount to sacred Troy;
Tell Priam he must ransom his dear son,
Going alone unto Achilles' tent,
And pacify his wrath with precious gifts;
But let some aged herald go along,
To guide the mules, and the dead body bring;
Nor let him fear that any harm will come,
For Argus-killer Mercury I'll send,
Who quickly will conduct him to the tent;
And the great chief will screen him from all ill,
For he is neither impious nor profane,
But will humanely treat a suppliant.
He said; and Iris with her message flew
Swift as the wind, and soon reached sacred Troy.
She came to Priam's palace, and found there
Wailing and lamentation. Priam's sons
Their sire surrounded in the splendid hall,
Drenching their robes with tears. The old man sat,
Sat in their midst, in a long mantle wrapped;
His head and neck were covered o'er with dust,

Which with his hands abundantly he spread
Whilst rolling on the ground. His daughters too,
And his sons' wives, were weeping through the house,
Lamenting the sad loss of noble men
Who lay upon the field, slain by the Greeks.
Then Iris quietly her message told,
And thus the agitated king addressed:
Courage, Dardanian Priam, and fear not;
I come not for thy harm, but for thy good.
Jove's messenger I am, who, though far off,
Highly regards and greatly pities thee;
He bids thee ransom Hector with great gifts,
With gifts that will Achilles overpower;
But let some aged herald go along,
To guide the mules, and bring the body back;
Nor need thou fear that any harm will come,
For Argus-killer Mercury he'll send,
Who quickly will conduct thee to the tent;
And the great chief will screen thee from all ill,
For he is neither impious nor profane,
But will humanely treat a suppliant.
Thus having spoke, swift Iris flew away.
The king then bade his sons prepare his car,
And to tie on it a capacious chest;
Then to a lofty, perfumed room he went,—
A room wherein his rarities he kept,—
And calling Hecuba, his wife, thus said:
Unhappy me! a messenger has come
From high Olympus, with commands from Jove,
Bidding me ransom my beloved son—
Going with costly presents to the Greeks,
With gifts that will Achilles overpower.
Thus spake the king; but his spouse wept and said:
Ah, me! and whither has thy prudence fled,
For which thou wast distinguished far and near?
Why wilt thou to the Grecian camp repair
To see the slayer of thy noble son?
Truly, thy heart is bold to venture thus;

For should'st thou in the power of this man fall,
But little pity may'st thou expect,
So cruel and perfidious he is.
Then let us, sitting in our halls, lament
Our wretched son, nor crave his mangled corpse ;
Fated he was to meet a cruel death,
And to become the prey of ravenous dogs,
Far from his parents' sight. Oh! had I but
That fierce man's heart, I would
Tear it in pieces, and devour it too;
Thus for my son's ill treatment he should pay.
For my dear son ne'er played a coward's part,
But fell contending for his countrymen.
She said; and godlike Priam thus replied:
Do not detain me, eager to depart,
Nor as a bird of evil omen croak;
For had some prophet, soothsayer, or priest
Urged me to this, we might have thought him false;
But I was ordered by a deity,
And saw her face to face; and go I shall.
And if I'm doomed to die, when I arrive
Within the Grecian camp, then be it so.
I by Achilles' hand will be dispatched,
Holding my noble Hector in my arms.
He said; and opening the handsome chests,
A dozen beauteous mantles thence drew out;
Twelve rugs of tapestry, and twelve fine cloaks ;
Of tunics likewise he a dozen took,
And then weighed out ten talents of pure gold;
Two glittering tripods and two goblets then
He also took, and with them then a cup,—
A cup that from the Thracians he received
When on a certain embassy he went;
A rare possession was that splendid cup.
Yet this he spared not, such was his desire,
At any cost, to ransom his dear son.
Then from the porch the gazing throng he drove,
Chiding them thus, with sharp reproachful words:

Depart, you wretched creatures! why come here?
Have ye not griefs enough at your own homes
That ye come here in crowds annoying me?
Think ye a little thing it is that Jove
Afflicts me with the loss of my brave son?
Ye will experience his loss yourselves,
By the Greeks routed, your defender slain.
He said; and with his staff chased them away.
Likewise he chid his sons who stood around,—
Pammon, Antiphon, and Polites,
Paris, and Helenus, and Agathon,
Brave Dius, Hippothoüs, Deïphobus;
To these their angry sire his orders gave:
Make haste, ye lazy, and disgraceful set!
Would that instead of Hector ye were slain!
Ah, me! unhappy, that I should beget
The bravest boys of any born in Troy,
And none of them, I think, is left to me.
Mestor, and Troilus, the charioteer,
And Hector, who was more a god than man;
These noble sons have perished in the war,
And worthless, good-for-nothing ones remain,—
Liars and dancers, choristers and thieves.
Hasten, I say! and bring my chariot here,
And load it up, that I may quick be off.
He said; and they, dreading their angry sire,
Brought out his new and handsome chariot:
Mule-drawn it was; on it they tied the chest.
Then they took down the yoke, of box-wood made:
Embossed it was, with rings and all complete.
Next came the band, nine cubits long it was;
This to the pole they fixed, lapping it twice;
Then from the hall the costly gifts they brought,
And on the polished chariot piled them up.
The splendid mules next to the car they yoked,
A present from the Mysians to the king;
Priam's good trusty steeds, fed by himself,
They then led forth and harnessed to the car.

Then came his mourning wife, bearing sweet wine
In her right hand, a brimming goblet full,
That ere they went they might libations make.
Near to her spouse she drew, and thus began:
Pour out this wine, and offer up to Jove
A fervent prayer that thou mayest safe return,
Venturing, against my wish, among thy foes;
Pray then to Jove, who now looks down on Troy.
Look for his bird, his favorite messenger,
Look on thy right hand; if thou seest him there,
In perfect confidence thou may'st depart;
But if this omen Heaven refuse to give,
I by all means advise thee not to go.
She said; and godlike Priam thus replied:
Truly, my wife, thou givest good advice;
For right it is to offer prayer to Jove,
That he will pity me in my distress.
He said; and bid the handmaid water pour
Upon his hands; for near him stood the maid,
Holding an ewer and basin in her hands;
Thus having washed, the goblet he received.
Then standing in the yard the monarch prayed,
Looking on high, and pouring out the wine:
Oh, father Jove, ruling from Ida's mount,
Glorious and great! grant that Achilles may
Show favor, and have pity on my woes;
And send thy favorite bird, thy messenger,
That on my right hand I may him behold;
Then to the Greeks with confidence I'll go.
He said; and to his prayer Jove, hearkening, sent
An eagle, most indubitable sign,
Percnos its name,—Black Hunter also called,—
Its wings were of the size of a wide door;
And on their right hand did the bird appear,
Rushing with lightning speed above the town.
Seeing this omen, greatly they rejoiced.
Then quickly on his car the old man stepped,
And through the vestibule and porch drove out.

First went the burden-car, Idæus drove,
Then came the king, lashing his noble steeds,
And passing through the city rapidly;
His friends accompanied, weeping as they gazed,
As for one going to most certain death.
But when they reached the plain his relatives,
From the king parting, to the town returned;
Nor did the bold adventurers escape
The eyes of Jove, who thus his son addressed:
Oh, Mercury! dear son, who lovest much
To be the associate and friend of men!
Go now conduct old Priam to the ships,
And so conduct that none may him perceive
Till he gets safely to Achilles' tent.
He said; nor did the messenger delay.
Quick to his feet his sandals he attached—
Beauteous they were, ambrosial, made of gold;
Swift as the wind they carry him o'er sea
And o'er the earth. He took his rod also,
With which he soothes men's eyes and puts to sleep,
And at his pleasure wakens them again.
Thus holding in his hands his potent wand,
The Argus-slayer swiftly flew away;
He reached the Troad and the Hellespont,
Having the shape and look of a young man,
A blooming, graceful youth of princely birth.
Meanwhile old Priam and Idæus reached
The tomb of Ilus; there their cars they stopped,
That at the fount their steeds and mules might drink,
For now twas twilight; but the herald spied
The approach of Mercury, and the king addressed:
Beware, oh, son of Dardanus, beware!—
Yonder's a warrior who will slay us sure;
Come, let us fly while we have power to fly,
Or let us kneel and beg him spare our lives.
He said; and greatly did the old man fear;
His hair stood upright,—stupefied, he gazed;
But Mercury drew near and took his hand,

And thus with words of kindness questioned him :
Whither, my father, through the ambrosial night,
Dost thou direct thy course whilst others sleep ?
Dost thou not fear thy foes, the valiant Greeks,
So close at hand ? Should they observe thee thus
Bearing these valuables in the night,
What think you they would do ? for thou art old,
And this thy comrade is an old man too,
Unfitted to repulse an enemy ;
Yet I approach thee not to do thee harm,
But, if attacked, would rather take thy part,
For thou resemblest much my own dear sire.
He said ; and godlike Priam thus replied :
Surely, my son, thou speakest but the truth ;
Yet by some god I must protected be,
Who sends a stranger thus to pilot me,
So beautiful in form and so discreet,—
Blest are thy parents having such a son.
Old man, the other said, thy words are wise ;
But come, speak out and frankly tell me this :
Where art thou going with these costly things ?
Would'st thou in some safe place conceal thy wealth
Are ye all now deserting sacred Troy ?
In thy son's death a champion you lose ;
In fight he equaled any of the Greeks.
But who art thou, kind friend, the old man said,
Who of my son so honorably dost speak ?
To him the stranger courteously replied :
Ah, thou would'st know my thoughts about thy son,
Whom often in the glorious fight I saw
Slaying the valiant Greeks, and driving them
With dreadful slaughter even to their ships.
We stood and gazed and marveled at the sight,
For our great chief, Achilles, kept us back
Out of the fight, enraged at Agamemnon.
One of his Myrmidons I am ; my sire
Polyctor is, a wealthy man, about as old as thou.
Six sons he has, and I his seventh am ;

On casting lots, the duty fell to me
To follow to the war; and now I come
Strolling across the plain, for on the morn
The Greeks intend to battle round your walls;
Nor by their leader can they be restrained,
So eager are they to renew the fight.
He said; and godlike Priam answering, spake:
If thou a follower of Achilles art,
Come, tell me, is my son still at the ships?
Or has his conqueror torn him limb by limb
And cast him forth to be devoured by dogs?
He said; and thus the deity replied:
Neither have dogs nor birds devoured thy son,
But he still lies before Achilles' tent;
And though twelve days have passed, the corpse is fresh,
Untouched by worms nor putrid in the least.
Doubtless he'll drag him round his comrade's tomb
At early morn; but he will not defile.
If thou should'st see him thou would'st wonder much
To see how fresh he is, how free from blood;
His wounds all closed, for many wounds he had.
Thus do the happy gods respect thy son,
Even when dead, for he was dear to them.
He said, and filled the old man's heart with joy,
Who to the stranger answering, thus replied:
Surely, my son, this shows how good it is
To give due gifts to the immortal gods;
For while he lived, my Hector ne'er forgot
The beings who on high Olympus dwell—
Therefore, in death, they still remember him.
But come, accept from me this splendid cup;
Take me in charge, and, with the help of Jove,
Conduct me safely to thy master's tent.
Old man, thou temptest me, the god replied,
Thinking to take advantage of my youth;
Nor would I dare without my chief's consent
To take a gift that ought to go to him,
For of Achilles much I stand in awe

Yet I to thee would be a trusty guide
To distant Argos e'en, by land or sea.
He said; and leaping on the chariot-car,
Took quickly in his hands the reins and lash,
Breathing fresh strength into the steeds and mules.
But when they reached the ramparts and the trench
The sentinels were busy at their feast;
But the god put them with his wand to sleep.
The gates he opened, then pushed back the bars,
And led in Priam, and his splendid gifts;
Then to Achilles' lofty tent they came,
Built by the Myrmidons. Of fir it was,
With rushes thatched, with a strong fence around;
One mighty bar of fir the door secured;
It took three men to fasten and remove,
But by Achilles it was moved with ease.
The god for Priam opened the stout gate,
And led him in, him and his costly gifts;
Then from the chariot he leaped, and said:
Old man, 'tis Mercury escorts thee here;
Sent by great Jove. Now I return indeed,
Not wishing by Achilles to be seen;
For 'tis not proper that the immortal gods
Should give to men so openly their aid.
But enter now, and supplicate the chief
By his old sire, his mother, and his son,
That he will favor show, and grant thy wish.
He said; and to Olympus straightway flew.
And Priam from his car leaped to the ground,
Leaving his friend to guard the steeds and mules;
Into the tent the old man quickly passed.
He found the chief, Jove's favorite, within;
All of his comrades absent were save two,
Automedon and Alcimus, heroes both.
They to him ministering, stood close at hand,
For he had just partaken of his meal,
The table still remaining. He saw not
When Priam entered; but the king ran up and clasped

The mighty warrior's knees, and kissed his hands—
Those dreadful hands that had in battle slain
So many of his noble, valiant sons.
And as when one for murder forced to flee
From his own country, to the palace comes
Of a rich man, and stupor seizes all,
Gazing upon the trembling refugee :
Just so Achilles wondered at the sight
Of godlike Priam—the other wondered too,
Looking at one another; but the king,
In supplicating language, thus began :
  Think, oh, Achilles ! of thy noble sire.
He is an old man too, about my age ;
His neighbors are perhaps wishing him dead,
And no true friends he has to succor him ;
But 'tis his joy to know thou art alive ;
And every day his dear son he awaits,
Expecting his return from distant Troy.
But I most wretched am in every way,
For I begot the bravest sons in Troy ;
Yet all of them I now may say are dead.
Fifty I had when this sad war broke out :
One mother bore nineteen ; the others were
Children of other women that I had.
Most of them died upon the battle-field.
But Hector was my favorite ; 'twas he
That was the chief defender of our town.
Him, fighting for his country, thou hast slain ;
And now I come e'en to the Grecian camp,
To ransom him from thee, with countless gifts.
But, oh, Achilles ! reverence the gods !
Have pity on me ! think of thy aged sire,
Whose miseries will not compare with mine ;
For I have had a wretched lot indeed—
One that no other mortal has endured—
To kiss the hands of him who slew my son.
  He said ; and stirred the warrior's inmost soul,
Making him think of his old absent sire.

He took the aged suppliant by the hand,
Pushing him gently from him; and both wept:
Priam for Hector, rolling on the ground,
The other for his sire, and Patroclus.
Their lamentations sounded through the house.
But when Achilles' tears had ceased to flow,
He rose, and lifted up the aged king,
Pitying his snow-white head, and hoary beard;
And then addressing him, he thus began:
  Alas! thy woes are many, wretched man!
How couldst thou dare to venture thus alone
Into the camp, into the sight of him
Who slew so many of thy noble sons?
Surely thou must possess an iron heart.
Come, sit thee down, and put away thy grief,—
Grief an unprofitable passion is.
By Heaven's decree mortals were born to woe,
The gods alone from trouble are exempt.
In front of mighty Jove two vases stand.
One full of good, and one with evils filled;
Their mingled contents he on some bestows,
And such experience happiness and woe.
On others he the evil vase inflicts,
And they to life-long sorrows are exposed;
Hungry calamity is their sad lot,
They wander o'er the beauteous earth despised,
Both by the gods and by their fellow-men.
On Peleus, my sire, great gifts were showered,
For riches most conspicuous he was;
Over the valiant Myrmidons he ruled.
On him, a mortal too, the gods bestowed
A goddess wife. But evils, too, were his:
No mortal offspring filled his palace halls,
But he begot only one short-lived son;
Nor am I with him now in his old age,
But here in Troy remain, far from my home,
A source of grief to thee, and to thy sons.
Of thy great riches too, in former times,

Old man, I've heard, within the country wide,
Bounded by Lesbos north, and Phrygia south,
And westward by the rolling Hellespont;
Among these people, 'tis reported thou
Wast for wealth and family renowned;
But since the gods have brought this curse on thee,
Tumult and carnage round thy city rage.
Arise, indulge not this incessant grief,
Be not too much afflicted for thy son,
It will not bring him back to life again;
And other and fresh ills may still be thine.
He said; and godlike Priam thus replied:
Make me not take a seat, Jove-nurtured man,
While Hector in thy tent unburied lies;
But take my gifts and let me see my son.
And the great ransom may'st thou long enjoy,
And reach in safety thy dear fatherland,
Since thou hast saved my life and favored me.
But swift Achilles sternly answered him:
Press me not thus, old man, for I myself
Thy son will ransom of my own free will;
For my own mother, daughter of the sea,
Came hither lately, messenger from Jove;
And well I know, oh, Priam! that some god
Has to the Grecian fleet conducted thee;
For none, though blessed with youth and strength, would dare
Into this camp to come, guarded so well;
Nor could have opened thus its massy gates.
Therefore, old man, beware, and fret me not,
Lest I may harm thee, though a suppliant,
And so do violence to Jove's command.
He said; the old man feared him and obeyed.
Then, like a lion, from the door leaped forth
The son of Peleus; with him went
The heroes Alcimus, and Automedon,
Whom, next to Patroclus, he honored most;
They loosened from the yoke the steeds and mules,

And brought the herald in, and sat him down;
And from the car the precious ransom took,
Leaving a well-made tunic, and two cloaks,
To cover Hector's corpse, when home it went.
The warrior then his female servants called,
Bidding them take the body and anoint,
And wash it secretly; lest Priam might,
Seeing his son, in sudden grief break forth;
And he, to anger roused, might slay the king,
And so do violence to Jove's command.
But when the servants had the body washed,
With oil anointing, they threw o'er it then
A well-made tunic, and a handsome cloak;
Achilles on a litter lifted it,
And with his comrades set it on the car.
But the chief moaned, and thus his friend addressed:
Oh, be not angry with me, Patroclus!
If thou shouldst hear, e'en in the other world,
That I have ransomed Hector to his sire;
For he to me has given worthy gifts,
A share of which I will bestow on thee.
So spake the chief, and to the tent returned,
Taking his seat; and thus the king addressed:
Thy son is ransomed, as thou didst desire.
Stretched on a bier he lies; at early dawn
Thou shalt behold, and carry him away.
But for a banquet let us now prepare;
For fair-haired Niobè of food partook
E'en when she lost six daughters and six sons:
Apollo with his shafts the lads destroyed,
And Dian slew the girls, because she had
Dared with Latona to compare herself;
She said Latona brought forth only two,
Whilst she a numerous family had borne.
In their own blood nine days the children lay,—
For into stones her people had been turned,—
But on the tenth the immortals buried them;
Yet, when fatigued with grief, she tasted food.

Now in the desert mountains, amid rocks,
In Sipylus, where they say the nymphs repose—
The nymphs who lead the dance round Acheloüs—
There, though transformed she is into a stone,
She stands a statue, brooding o'er her griefs.
Come, then, renowned old man, and let us too
Partake of food; then, to thy heart's content,
Thou may'st shed tears for thy beloved son,
And carry off his corpse to sacred Troy.
He said; and springing up, slew a white sheep;
His comrades quickly dressed, and roasted it.
In handsome baskets then Automedon
Brought loaves of bread, and handed to the guests.
Achilles carved the meat, and all partook;
But when they had all eaten, and were filled,
Priam with wonder on Achilles gazed—
So large he was, so beautiful in form,
And though a man resembled more a god;
Achilles also marveled at his guest,
Looking upon his amiable face,
And listening to his speech, discreet and wise.
So when they had each other much admired,
Old Priam thus the warrior addressed:
Let me retire now, Jove-nurtured man,
That we may take our fill of balmy sleep;
For never have these weary eyes been closed
Since by thy hands my Hector lost his life;
But ever moaning my unhappy lot,
I rolled in dust within my palace walls;
But now I've tasted food, and drunk sweet wine,
For the first time in company with thee.
He said; and then Achilles bade the maid
Couches to place beneath the portico,
And o'er them handsome purple mats to spread;
Embroidered carpets too, and cloaks besides.
The servants went with torches in their hands,
Performing all their lord had ordered them.
And thus the warrior jocularly spake:

Thou must, old man, an outside chamber take,
Lest some one of the leaders might step in
To counsel with me on affairs of state;
Seeing thee here at night, he would return,
Reporting what he saw to Agamemnon,
And so thou might'st encounter some delay.
But come and let me know how many days
Thou dost require for Hector's funeral,
That so I may keep quiet, and restrain
The warlike Greeks, nor suffer them to fight.
He said; and thus old Priam answered him:
If 'tis thy wish to let me celebrate
With proper rites great Hector's funeral,
Thou wilt indeed a mighty favor grant;
For well thou knowest how we are hemmed in,
And what a risk the Trojans have to run
In fetching wood from Ida's distant mount.
Nine days within our halls we would lament
Our champion's death, and bury on the tenth;
The people with a feast should be supplied
On the next day; a tomb we would erect;
And on the twelfth, if need be, we would fight.
These things, the warrior answered, all shall be
As thou desirest; I will the fight defer.
He said; and, to assure him, grasped his hand.
Then Priam and his friend slept on the porch,
Whilst in his tent the warrior reposed,
And by his side the fair Briseis lay.
Meanwhile the gods and all the fighting men
Slumbered the night away. But Mercury
Still kept awake, revolving in his mind
How he might guide old Priam back again
Without the notice of the sentinels.
To him he straightway went, and thus addressed:
Old man, thou actest rashly, sleeping thus
Amid thy foes, within Achilles' tent;
Thou thy dear son hast ransomed, giving much,
But thrice that price thy other sons would pay

To ransom thee, should Agamemnon find
That thou art slumbering in the Grecian camp.
He said; the old man feared and woke his friend.
The god then yoked the horses and the mules,
And drove them unperceived beyond the camp;
But when they came to Xanthus' eddying stream,
Then Mercury to high Olympus went.
And now the morn, in saffron garments clad,
Diffused her rosy light o'er all the earth.
With lamentation then the Trojans drove
The car and chariot towards the gates of Troy.
Nor was their coming by the people known,
Save by Cassandra. Fair as Venus, she
Had mounted to the citadel, and saw
Her sire and the herald drawing near;
The corpse she also saw upon the car.
The sight o'ercame her, and she shrieked aloud,
And her loud cries were heard throughout the town.
Ye Trojans, men and women, all come forth!
See Hector coming, stretched upon his bier!
Oft have ye joyed at seeing him return
Alive and safe from many a battle-field,
For to us all he was indeed a joy.
She said; and to the gates they swarming came;
Nor was there any in the city left,
Such grief possessed them; there they met the corpse.
Then Hector's wife and aged mother rushed
Up to the chariot, plucking out their hair,
And touched his head; the crowd stood weeping round;
And so they would have wept for the whole day,
Had not old Priam thus the throng addressed:
Give way, and let me pass, me and the mules;
When I have borne him to his home ye may
Weep and lament till ye are satisfied.
He said; and they stood off and let him pass.
But when they had him to the palace borne,
They laid him gently on a handsome bed,
And placed around him singers, who set up
A funeral dirge; and all the women too

Broke forth responsive, in loud sobs and groans;
Whilst fair Andromachè, the hero's wife,
Holding her husband's head within her arms,
The mournful lamentation thus began:
  Oh, my dear youthful husband! thou hast died,
And in thy palace left me desolate,
A widow, with thy infant, orphan son;
Nor will he reach to years of puberty.
Long before that this town will be o'erthrown,—
Since thou who didst protect it art no more,—
And we shall be led captive far away.
And then my son will be a captive too,
Performing menial work for some stern lord:
Or in his wrath some warrior of the Greeks
Will seize and hurl thee from the battlements,
Enraged because thy sire his kin hath slain;
For he indeed slew many in his time,
So fierce and valiant was he in the fight.
  Thus wailing, spake she. All the women wailed.
Then in her turn, his mother, Hecuba,
Vehement lamentation also made:
  Oh, Hector! dearest thou of all my sons!
Alive, thou wast the favorite of the gods,
And e'en in death they showed a care for thee;
My other sons Achilles seized and sold,
Selling and sending them to distant lands,—
To Samos, Imbros, and to Lemnos isle;
But when he slew thee with his glittering spear
He dragged thy corpse around his comrade's tomb;
Yet this did not avail to raise him up.
But now thou liest in the palace, fresh
As if by silver-bowed Apollo slain,—
Slain by his gentle darts, and free from wounds.
Thus spake she weeping; and the others wept.
  Then Helen also her lament began:
Oh, Hector! dearest thou by far of all
My husband's brothers! Paris my husband is,
Who brought me from my home to distant Troy;
Would I had perished ere that fatal day!

And now the twentieth year has rolled away
Since I came thence, quitting my native land,
Yet ne'er from thee heard I an angry word.
But when my husband's relatives reproached,
Or Hecuba, his mother,—for his sire
Was gentle to me as I were his child,—
Then thou didst to them admonition give,
And by thy kind example check them all.
With reason therefore may I grieve for thee,
Whilst grieving at my own unhappiness;
For I have not a friend in all wide Troy,
But all abhor me Thus fair Helen spake;
The countless multitude around her groaned.
Then Priam thus addressed the listening crowd:
Oh, Trojans! now prepare to gather wood,
And in your minds no apprehension have,
That by the Greeks an ambush may be laid;
For from Achilles I a promise had,
That for twelve days a truce should be maintained.
He said; and they their mules and oxen yoked,
And with their wagons set themselves to work.
Nine days they were employed, and gathered wood
In quantities immense; on the tenth morn
Hector they carried forth, and, all in tears,
Placed his dead body on the funeral pile;
Then to the heap combustible set fire.
But when the rosy-fingered morn appeared,
The thronging people gathered round the pile,
Extinguishing the embers with dark wine.
His weeping brothers, and his comrades, then
The white bones gathered up, and placed them in
A golden urn, which with soft purple robes
They covered up, and laid it in a grave;
On top of it they raised a pile of stones.
The tomb thus finished, to the city then
They all returned, and of a feast partook,—
A splendid feast in Priam's palaces.
Such were the rites the citizens performed,—
Such Hector's death—and such his burial.

www.ingramcontent.com/pod-product-compliance
Lightning Source LLC
LaVergne TN
LVHW021135110826
845150LV00005B/1037

* 9 7 8 1 4 2 5 5 4 9 7 0 1 *